Alternative Decision-Making Models for Financial Portfolio Management:

Emerging Research and Opportunities

Narela Spaseski
International University of Sarajevo, Bosnia and Herzegovina

A volume in the Advances in Finance, Accounting, and Economics (AFAE) Book Series

IGI Global
DISSEMINATOR OF KNOWLEDGE

Published in the United States of America by
IGI Global
Business Science Reference (an imprint of IGI Global)
701 E. Chocolate Avenue
Hershey PA, USA 17033
Tel: 717-533-8845
Fax: 717-533-8661
E-mail: cust@igi-global.com
Web site: http://www.igi-global.com

Library of Congress Cataloging-in-Publication Data

Names: Spaseski, Narela, 1982- author.
Title: Alternative decision-making models for financial portfolio management : emerging research and opportunities / by Narela Spaseski.
Description: Hershey : Business Science Reference, [2017]
Identifiers: LCCN 2017014596| ISBN 9781522532590 (hardcover) | ISBN 9781522532606 (ebook)
Subjects: LCSH: Portfolio management. | Finance--Management. | Risk management.
Classification: LCC HG4529.5 .S683 2017 | DDC 332.601/9--dc23 LC record available at https://lccn.loc.gov/2017014596

This book is published in the IGI Global book series Advances in Finance, Accounting, and Economics (AFAE) (ISSN: 2327-5677; eISSN: 2327-5685)

British Cataloguing in Publication Data
A Cataloguing in Publication record for this book is available from the British Library.

All work contributed to this book is new, previously-unpublished material.
The views expressed in this book are those of the authors, but not necessarily of the publisher.

For electronic access to this publication, please contact: eresources@igi-global.com.

Advances in Finance, Accounting, and Economics (AFAE) Book Series

ISSN:2327-5677
EISSN:2327-5685

Editor-in-Chief: Ahmed Driouchi, Al Akhawayn University, Morocco

MISSION

In our changing economic and business environment, it is important to consider the financial changes occurring internationally as well as within individual organizations and business environments. Understanding these changes as well as the factors that influence them is crucial in preparing for our financial future and ensuring economic sustainability and growth.

The **Advances in Finance, Accounting, and Economics (AFAE)** book series aims to publish comprehensive and informative titles in all areas of economics and economic theory, finance, and accounting to assist in advancing the available knowledge and providing for further research development in these dynamic fields.

COVERAGE

- Macroeconomics
- Applied Accounting
- Labor Economics
- E-finance
- Microeconomics
- Environmental and Social Accounting
- Economics of Agriculture and Biotechnology
- Ethics in Accounting and Finance
- Economics Geography
- Economics of Risks, Uncertainty, Ambiguity, and Insurance

IGI Global is currently accepting manuscripts for publication within this series. To submit a proposal for a volume in this series, please contact our Acquisition Editors at Acquisitions@igi-global.com or visit: http://www.igi-global.com/publish/.

The Advances in Finance, Accounting, and Economics (AFAE) Book Series (ISSN 2327-5677) is published by IGI Global, 701 E. Chocolate Avenue, Hershey, PA 17033-1240, USA, www.igi-global.com. This series is composed of titles available for purchase individually; each title is edited to be contextually exclusive from any other title within the series. For pricing and ordering information please visit http://www.igi-global.com/book-series/advances-finance-accounting-economics/73685. Postmaster: Send all address changes to above address.

Titles in this Series

For a list of additional titles in this series, please visit:
http://www.igi-global.com/book-series/advances-finance-accounting-economics/73685

Technological Integration as a Catalyst for Industrial Development and Economic Growth
Bryan Christiansen (PryMarke, LLC, USA) and Ülkü Yüksel (The University of Sydney Business School, Australia)
Business Science Reference • ©2017 • 272pp • H/C (ISBN: 9781522523192) • US $185.00

Handbook of Research on Economic, Financial, and Industrial Impacts on Infrastructure ...
Ramesh Chandra Das (Katwa College, India)
Business Science Reference • ©2017 • 466pp • H/C (ISBN: 9781522523611) • US $230.00

Handbook of Research on Policies and Practices for Sustainable Economic Growth ...
George M. Korres (University of Aegean, Greece) Elias Kourliouros (University of Aegean, Greece) and Maria P. Michailidis (University of Nicosia, Cyprus)
Business Science Reference • ©2017 • 440pp • H/C (ISBN: 9781522524588) • US $255.00

NFC Payment Systems and the New Era of Transaction Processing
Vibha Kaw Raina (Birla Institute of Technology, India)
Business Science Reference • ©2017 • 193pp • H/C (ISBN: 9781522523062) • US $155.00

Social, Health, and Environmental Infrastructures for Economic Growth
Ramesh Chandra Das (Katwa College, India)
Business Science Reference • ©2017 • 355pp • H/C (ISBN: 9781522523642) • US $200.00

Method of Systems Potential (MSP) Applications in Economics...
Grigorii Pushnoi (Independent Researcher, Russia)
Business Science Reference • ©2017 • 162pp • H/C (ISBN: 9781522521709) • US $135.00

Outward Foreign Direct Investment (FDI) in Emerging Market Economies
Tomasz Dorożyński (University of Lodz, Poland) and Anetta Kuna-Marszałek (University of Lodz, Poland)
Business Science Reference • ©2017 • 377pp • H/C (ISBN: 9781522523451) • US $210.00

For an enitre list of titles in this series, please visit:
http://www.igi-global.com/book-series/advances-finance-accounting-economics/73685

IGI Global
DISSEMINATOR OF KNOWLEDGE

701 East Chocolate Avenue, Hershey, PA 17033, USA
Tel: 717-533-8845 x100 • Fax: 717-533-8661
E-Mail: cust@igi-global.com • www.igi-global.com

Table of Contents

Preface

As an economist, I find myself caught in the nineteenth century metaphor of methodological individualism. Despite the fact that 1991-2016 are the decades that invent the future, neoclassical theory has not only been able to survive but also dominate the academic intellectual world. Why and how would be open for discussions ranging from social to political explanations and yet might be the beginning of a rather complex solution that is a game changer for our economic world as we know it.

I am not a physician neither a mathematician that is criticizing economics as a scientific discipline. I am a PhD economic student, passionately in love in every branch of the economics, who is disappointed by the masses who are keeping economics disconnected and out of forward motion. We should realize that an overly formal and dogmatic education is a serious part of the problem. If we look closely at finance and economics scholars, we will realize that they were indoctrinated and forced to squeeze explanations out of subject topics. Gaussian methods have been simply drilled into their minds.

In support, I will share few classroom examples:

Ask economic students to explain what will happen to the country's GDP if the export increases. The answer will be given to you in a second, and will be the following: if the country's export increases then the GDP will also increase. Now ask them how they come to that end. Silence.

As a second instance, ask the students to maximize profit function. They should get the first derivative with respect to quantity, setting the derivative equal to zero, and solving for the quantity. This frequently used operation in economics will not be puzzled out by most of the pupils in the course of study. Do you know why that happens?

Or my favorite example is to ask an economics student to explain what the indifference curve represents? As always you will get a perfect answer: an indifference curve is a curve that shows all combinations of goods that provides the same level of utility.

If you give them more time, they would draw fancy graphs and explain to you how people should choose different combination of goods. Then they will tell you that the consumer theory uses indifference curves and budget constraints to generate consumer demand curves. Stop. Do our students know that different people may choose different combinations of goods, even though they have the same budget? Different people prefer different things, therefore a combination that offers maximum utility for one consumer will be different than the combination that offers maximum utility for another consumer. But what fascinates me the most is how then economist knows how peoples' indifference curves look like? How the economists get knowledge of these preferences as all analysis is based on them?

Proper understanding of the situation in the market is essential. For that reason, this book's main aim is to provide an explanation of what's wrong with the perception of economics, and why it's important to concentrate our effort in developing alternative decision making models.

The focus point is on the application of the methods organized in statistical physics, combinatorial stochastic processes, fractals and wavelet-based multifractal analysis which have been proven useful in analyzing complex evolving systems, including financial markets. Many finance books focus on the theory of investment and mathematical formulation of the problems, leaving the details of the implementation to the reader. On the contrary, this is a book with real data cases that provides upper level students and investment professionals with the concepts and tools they need to make the intelligent decision under risk. As Taleb (2007), noted: "you cannot go from books to problems, but the reverse, from problems to books."

I also believe that this book will assist many young brains to understand why the tangible world is not always Gaussian, and that the possibility that an extreme/rare event will occur is more frequent than would be expected.

In Chapter 1, I discuss the dominance of the neoclassical theory. The effort here is to highlight the importance of studying economics as an adaptive complex system where the fractal structure and interaction play a fundamental explanatory role and individual details are largely relevant.

In the first section, we refer to the established histories of economic thought and modelling; explaining how the economist borrowed from Physics and build up models which disconnect the economics from the reality. In the second section a brief explanation of the neoclassical financial theory is given, with a stress on the theories of investment. And in the final section I conclude with a summary of the main findings, putting the accent on the importance of studying? The history of economic thought and its role in modern economics.

In continuation of this book I will demonstrate how to implement standard financial models based on general equilibrium theory (GET) and Gaussian distribution using a real market data. I will also point out the advantages and disadvantages of their implementation and offer fundamentally different approaches following the methods of statistical physics, bio-statistics, wavelet analysis and combinatorial stochastic processes. You may notice that the list of alternative models is quite long.

But along this way, I understand that this book is not just a search for a better model, or a proof that we did it wrong. Instead, it is a desperate scream, hoping that will wake the economic and financial scholars from their winter sleep and shake their mechanistic minds.

Maybe your professors are not aware that they are trapped in the rigorous theories, but this should not be the reason for your failure.

In chapter 2, I illustrate the essentials of using a decision tree for making financial decisions, and demonstrate how a decision is made using both criteria: expected monetary value and expected utility. Moreover, the environment in which decision are made can be classified according to the degree of certainty (certainty, uncertainty and risk) and for that reason we apply different techniques of analysis. At the end, I discuss the imperfectability of the traditional techniques and tools and suggest alternative decision tools inspired by some areas of research in signal processing, known as wavelet analysis.

Chapter 3 provides the theoretical underpinning of the two optimization approaches, Mean-Variance and Mean-VaR approach, followed by a section describing how to apply the theories in practice using computer programs and spreadsheets, and finishes with their shortcomings.

The main goal behind the concept of portfolio management is to combine various assets into portfolios and then to manage those portfolios so as to achieve the desired investment objectives. To be more specific, the investors' needs are mostly defined in terms of profit and risk, and the portfolio manager makes a sound decision aimed ether to maximize the return or minimize the risk. But we should be very careful because this classical model is valid only if the return is multi-varieties normally distributed and the investor is averse to risk (prefers lower risk), or if for any given return which is multi-varieties distributed the investor has a quadratic objective function. In short, the probability that the extreme event will occur is very small. The expected losses in real world markets are higher and with catastrophic outcomes. Here it seems that the fact that we could lose a certain amount of money 95% or 99% of the time tells us absolutely nothing about what could happen the other 5 or even 1 percent of the time. For that reason, instead of estimating the certain loss as shown in chapter 3 we introduce in chapter 4 a technique known as a "tail risk protecting strategy" or "the barbell investment strategy".

In the extension of chapter 4, I am going to lay out the ins and outs that made me put together a portfolio that should protect me from the rapidly rising prices-inflation. Analyzing the copper market movements, I understand that the market has been conditioned to believe that the copper demand will exceed its supply. These activities should take the copper price to its highest peak in 2020, which is mathematically well supported. I argue that this falsity application of the theory would lead us to new market crash. Finally, in the last section I find out how the decision is made.

Chapter 5 recognizes the importance of the stochastic programming as an important tool in financial planning. The current practice of portfolio optimization is still limited to the simple formulation of linear programming (LR) or quadratic programming (QR) type. For that reason, relevant literature on asset-liability management (ALM) model has been reviewed and two different ALM approaches are compared: first piecewise linear function; and second a nonlinear utility function.

This chapter shows that the mathematical programming methodology is ready to challenge the huge problem arising from LP portfolio optimization. A special emphasis was put on the shape of the investors' payoff functions in asset price equilibrium. The results underpin our claim that the nonlinear ALM model generated better asset allocation.

Another important model that has evolved in the field of finance, is founded on the hypothesis of random walks and most often refers to a special category of Markov chain or Markov process. In general, this theory throws serious doubt on many other methods for description and prediction of stock prices that occupy the academic world, for example, the statistical and technical analysis. In finance, technical analysis is the forecasting of future financial price movements based on an examination of past price movements and volume, such as the relative strength index, moving averages, regressions, inter-market and intra-market price correlations, cycles or, classically, through recognition of chart pattern.

At the very beginning of the Chapter 6, I constructed a Markov chain model where both time and space are discrete. Such a construction will demonstrate how to use a discrete time Markov chain, which will also be helpful in the continuous time setting of the next section in the chapter. In the extension, I am showing how these analyses could be used on copper market data and in conclusion I try to present the response to the following question: Whether the random walk theory explains the actual stock price moves?

The performed analysis in this chapter certifies the doubted that the discrete and continuous Markov processes as representations of stationary stochastic processes, cannot accurately anticipate the short-term trend of prices and returns. Does this mean that markets are unpredictable because they are random? If this is true, then with a longer time horizon, we can be far more successful. Eventually the market will reach its equilibrium where we can calculate the stationary distribution vector. In fact, applying this method, we expect the process to reach its equilibrium. This is one of the many assumptions we apply in our models to explain the dynamics of financial markets.

At the end of this chapter, I understand that the stock's price/returns movements generally cannot be described using normal (or Gaussian) distribution and Markov processes. So, if a random walk theory can be rejected, then a predictable component in the stock market exists. But, if there is a way to predict future prices from past data it would have immediately been exploited and eliminated. Then I realized that all this time I was looking in a wrong place- the price patterns exist, but we do not need the entire history of returns. Systems does not remember where there were 1 year or 2 years ago. The information in complex systems declines exponentially. Or as Einstein said "God doesn't play dice with the world".

In Chapter 7, I set my focus on complex dynamics, an area that was around for about one hundred years ago and continues to inspire much ongoing research. In the first section I argue that things happen for a reason, returns are not normally distributed and that the prediction is possible.

In the second section, I present the Wavelets. I believe that wavelet-based modelling underlies the process that generates financial market data. It is a method that decomposes a time series into several layers of time series, making it possible to analyze how the local variance, or wavelet power, changes both in the frequency and time domain.

In the third section, I analyze the role of the Hurst exponent in the prediction of market singularities, as well as the effect of the surface. It is evident that the stock market surface is not smooth (flat), therefore, "as the wind is roughening the surface of the river, something is roughening the stock market surface".

And in the final part, I talk about the use of Euclidian axioms in observing the dynamics of the financial securities industries. These axioms in finance unfortunately, or fortunately, depending, on how you look at them, does not resemble reality. Financial markets are non-linear, chaotic, fractal and exhibit self-similar behavior over a finite range of scales. So, in the final section I propose a novel methodological approach that analyzes financial market dynamics via chaos theory and fractal. Here, the local Holder exponent is used to estimate stable and unstable fixed point, or regularity and singularity and based on them, one can adapt its buy-sell strategy timely. In short, fractal geometry can be seen as a universal language by which nature can be explained or at least described and quantified. Financial markets are one of them.

Acknowledgment

First and foremost, I would like to express my deepest gratitude to Dr. Mehmet Can, a professor of mathematics. I feel privileged to have had such a talented supervisor, who not only possesses expert knowledge in his research areas, but who also has sacrificed innumerable hours of his time to patiently answer my questions and provide spontaneous guidance.

Due my master and PhD studies, he urged for particular courses to be incorporated in the economics curriculum and accept to teach them even knowing that I would be the only economic student attending. Then I was too young and inexperienced to understand the importance of these courses, but now, thanks to his persistence I am writing this book. Thank you my professor, I cannot imagine anyone who could have done a better job.

I would also like to thank my husband, Petar Spaseski, for allowing me to follow my ambitions and write this book. He has been my inspiration and motivation for going forward to improve my knowledge.

Finally, I would like to thank my parents who were the very first in showing me the importance of science. As my mother wants to say "every action has its own reaction". If you push on anything, it pushes back on you. That's why, if you lean against the wall, you don't just fall through it. The wall pushes back on you as hard as you push on it, and you and the wall stay in place.

You were all my wall, and this book is the consequence of your chosen actions.

Chapter 1
Theory and Modelling

ABSTRACT

In this chapter, I discuss the dominance of the neoclassical theory. The effort here is to highlight the importance of studying economics as an adaptive complex system where the fractal structure and interaction play a fundamental explanatory role and individual details are largely relevant. To discard equilibrium in the standard sense and to move on to study out of equilibrium dynamics is surely the right way to proceed but is perhaps too big a step for economics at this time. Inspired of the Newton's model of the universe, economists developed an economic model that had the same formal properties. So, once economics and finance made it their goal to develop the concept and the idea of the elegant model form, they go along with the simplified assumptions of that form. Therefore, financial models can leave us unable to see many of the most important aspects of financial markets.

INTRODUCTION

Research is a continuous intellectual process, which is done to find and report new knowledge and understanding of the world around us. In this chapter the task is to make clear how the economists used the scientific research in order to generate the economic and financial theory. Inspired of the Newton's model of the universe, economists developed an economic model that had the same formal properties. The problem is that the model is used too often, at any time and place. In doing so, we keep economics disconnected from

DOI: 10.4018/978-1-5225-3259-0.ch001

reality. It is essential to realize that system's properties are not constant over time; they are changing and constantly adapting to the environment.

People enjoy reading stories, so, I will tell you the story where finance sector damages the economy because it does not function as well as the models content. In 1998 a financial investment company, hedge fund called Long-Term Capital Management (LTCM) faced almost-instant bankruptcy. It used the methods and risk expertise of two "Nobel economists," Myron S. Scholes and Robert C. Merton who were called "geniuses" for developing the "new method to determine the value of derivatives". Using bell curve-style mathematics they convince themselves and major players on Wall Street that it was great science and thus turning the entire financial establishment into big losers, or as Taleb (2007) wants to say suckers.

Now, was an equation to blame for the financial crash? No. The equation was just one ingredient and the main reason is that the entire financial system is poorly understood and highly unstable. The complexity, interaction and extreme event were not taken into consideration at all. But my concern is that we do not see this story as a lesson, or as a reason to implement more rigid financial reforms. A major change didn't happen, except some people had less money.

Today we are still allowing our politicians to derive inappropriate polices without any recognition of their shallow foundations. Our students are still taught How to think, not What to think, and the academicians are either unaware or pretend to be unaware. The neoclassical theory dominates the economics curriculums and there is never time or need to present other viewpoints. It is time to seriously rethink how the economics is taught, because students working only with mainstream economic tools forget to ask broader questions. They do not know as Thompson (1997) stated, that the capital cannot be measured; that utility is metaphysical; that optimisation is non-falsifiable; that capitalism is inherently unstable. Or that, as Ricardo discovered, when we say 'supply and demand' we are explaining nothing (Dobb, 1975).

Today economic students should study applied mathematics and statistics, sociology, history of economic thought, psychology, statistical physics and political science. The paradigm won't give away until there is one to replace it. What we need is not reformed neoclassical economics, but rather a new approach. As you can see it is not easy to be a good economist.

I will close this section with the letter of French graduate students in economics, in a manifesto, criticizing their academic education in economics naming it as "autistic" and "pathologically distant from the problems of real markets and real people":

We wish to escape from imaginary worlds! Most of us have chosen to study economics so as to acquire a deep understanding of the economic phenomena with which the citizens of today are confronted. But the teaching that is offered. .. does not generally answer this expectation... This gap in the teaching, this disregard for concrete realities, poses an enormous problem for those who would like to render themselves useful to economic and social actors (see Bigelow, 2005)

THE HISTORY OF ECONOMIC THEORY AND MODELLING

Modern economics is sick. Economics has increasingly become an intellectual game played for its own sake and not for its practical consequences for understanding the economic world... The consequence is that we now understand less about how markets work than did Smith or even Leon Walras (Blaug, 1997).

Usually I have trouble remembering certain situations, but my first college class of history of economic thought, I can recall it as if it took place yesterday. I remember that in front of me, at the desk there was a massive book. We use to say that you could drown yourself in the lake with that kind of book. When I opened the book, and began leafing through I noticed it was full of some names and years. I never enjoyed learning about history, so I was little disappointed, frequently asking myself why I need this. And then the first lesson started and the very first professor sentences were: “This record is like a phone book, full of relevant data. The difference is that you will have to memorize this book, all the names and years, and preserve this knowledge for the next generations.” Then he made jokes with all this name, saying: “… you will never have a problem with choosing a name for your baby.”

Now I bear a moral obligation to share this knowledge with you and try to answer one of the major questions raised today: If in a very large degree the dominant neoclassical theory was modelled on physics, then one might reasonably ask, why then do we depart from the modern physics?

This story starts like this: once upon a time in 1870s since the economist wanted to be seen as a scientist, consequently, had to not exactly imitate-but rather modelled on Physics.

Three writers from three different countries with three different backgrounds, the Englishman- William Stanley Jevons, Frenchman- Leon Walras and an Austrian- Carl Menger, independently suggested the same modelling methodology for economic systems and eventually displaced all other competing schools of thought in those countries. Details of their work are not mentioned in most textbooks, which is rather kept as a salient fact that raise the doubt that the neoclassical theory was supported and commanded to become a dominant theory.

Stanley Jevons and Leon Walras as founders of the neoclassical theory were not obsessed with economics and politics, but with classical mechanics and Newtonian modelling. Trained as engineers, they developed an economic model that has same formal properties as Newton's model of the universe. See what Jevons wrote:

All branches and divisions of economic science must be pervaded by certain general principles ["the general principles of mechanics"]. It is in the investigation of such principles-to the tracing out of the mechanics of self-interest and utility, that this essay has been devoted. The establishment of such a theory is a necessary preliminary to any definite drafting of the superstructure of the aggregate science. [Emphasis added] (Jevons, 1970, p. 50)

Without detailed empirical research, they, the three writers, defined a set of concepts which identified the fundamental properties of economics just to accommodate them with the analogies of physical relations modelled at that time by classical mechanics. They took the equations from the mid-nineteenth century physical theory and changed the names of the variables. Let us also see the following formulations: "bodies" translates "individuals" or "agents", "motions" translates "exchange of goods", "forces" translates "desires" or "preferences" which, when summed become "supply and demand", "mechanical equilibrium" becomes "market equilibrium" and "physical systems "translates "markets."

Edward Fullbrok point out that this was just the beginning of the neoclassical fabrication and in his essay "Economics and Neoliberalism" he wrote:

To make the model determinate, it was necessary to define the terms "exchange of good", "individuals" and "preferences", and "markets" in bizarre ways. All the exchanges were said to magically take place at the price that equated demand and supply. This elimination of dynamics placed the focus entirely on when the market is in equilibrium ignoring actual market processes. Moreover, the individuals were defined as atomistic, that is, as having no social dimension, and within their isolated selves as being one-dimensional, meaning that they have only one criteria, preference satisfaction, for making decisions. And the preferences of these non-social beings were defined as unchanging, completely independent of life experiences, including consumer ones. (Fullbrok, 2006)

According to Mirowski, understanding economics in the nineteenth century begins with understanding the law of conservation of energy in physics. This law allowed physicists to build models and represent the behavior of total energy in a closed system known as a closed Hamiltonian model. Here, all energy that was given up by one entity in the system had to be absorbed, in one form or another, by the other entities in the system. If we assume a system with only kinetic and potential energies, it would in principle be possible to see the evolution of the system from its current state to any future state.

Most of us, the economists, are not familiar with the established theories in physics and their implementation in practice. Therefore, in what follows, I will shortly describe few prime physical principles. Classical mechanical physics (unlike quantum mechanics) teaches us that the system consisting with bodies, forces and motions, tend toward equilibrium and the equilibrium is reached when the sum of the forces acting on each body of the system is zero, nothing is happening. To model physical system deterministic models are applied, signifying that if a change in one of the system's variables is supposed, then the terminal state of the system can always be anticipated. Could you now see the similarity?

The famous economist Irvin Fisher, who wrote his dissertation with the thermodynamicist Josiah Willard Gibbs, was convinced that economists could learn important lessons from physics. Some central concepts driven from physics and transferred to economics are: utility as a substitute for energy, the sum of utility for potential energy, the expenditure of kinetic energy and the conservation of energy resembled the conservation of utility plus expenditure. The remark given by Gibbs is that only in a closed Hamilton system the energy can be absorbed and in open system it could go anywhere. Unfortunately, this point was not taken in consideration by Fisher.

Despite the criticisms, the economists are not ready to acknowledge the weaknesses of standard teachings. None of these now famous people seemed to realize that the sum of income and utility in neoclassical economics is not conserved and that the conservation principle is quite meaningless in any real economic process. It is, in fact, a mistake that today's economists face the consequences for.

On the one hand, mathematicians have known for some time that some equations simply cannot be solved, or are incredibly difficult. On the other hand, economists are often dedicated to proving the existence of equilibrium, and they have to stick to overly simplistic analysis, where equations can definitely be solved. This makes us to rely excessively on "imaginary world models" which are constructed to explain the empirical realities of capitalistic society. Since equations have to have clearly defined parameters, can simply be considered as serious as their assumptions and the outcome may not have clear implementations, such is the nature of modelling complex systems. But what is interesting, despite all these criticisms, neoclassical theory has not only been able to survive but also dominate the academic intellectual world.

Let us now return to our story. Economics as a distinct academic discipline arose at a time when Europe was undergoing a social transformation, known as a transformation to capitalism. In this period the capitalist class faced social and political barriers and restrictions. Therefore, the economic theory armed them with the idea that a system of government was not needed to maintain social order, instead social order and harmony arise naturally in a market economy where each individual makes "rational" choices and takes "rational decisions" in "self-interest". This idea was also found in Smith's famous "invisible hand" doctrine which played a key role in the transformation process during the 18th century in Europe.

Only an individual does not live in isolation. He or she is a member of a family and society and therefore the individual should be placed in a social context, as observed by the economist, Nobel Prize winner Haavelmo (1989).

Economists, since the 18th century, proposed that the essential feature of a market social order was 'equilibrium'—reflecting a state of social harmony. Keen (2004), has rightly pointed out that 'if, instead of equilibrium, economists had promised that capitalism would deliver chaos; if, instead of meritocracy, economists had said that capitalism could concentrate inequality, then economists could have hindered rather than helped the transition to capitalism'.

Also, Fullbrook (2005) pointed out that 'equilibrium' is more than just a concept in neoclassical economics, it is a sweeping ontological pronouncement on the nature of capitalist social reality and, therefore, it is not open to direct confirmation. By using economics doctrines, economists try to rationalize the belief that capitalism is a rational system—in the sense that maximizing utility (self-interest). Thus, the resistance to stick with economic theory is deeply embedded in ideological reasons. This explains Stiglitz's (1941) assertion that economics has suffered from the 'triumph of ideology over science'.

I am quite sure that by now you've gained opinion that physics is the economics disease. You start to come along with the group of economist that think that we should use less math and natural philosophy in economics and concentrate more on psychological, societal and emotional factors affecting the investor's decisions. I agree, partially. But using physics does not mean to put investor's psychology aside. To bring you closer to this fact, I'll give you an example from our reach economic history.

Maury Osborne as a statistician trained in astronomy, began thinking about the stock market around 1956, after his wife had given birth to a second set of twins- the Osborne's eighth and ninth children. He decided that was time to think about financing the future. His contribution to the theory of market behavior is reviewed and amended Bachelier's thesis. Unlike Bachelier who analyzed the price distribution, Osbornes focus was on the stocks rate of return. He argued that investors don't really care about the absolute movements of stocks, instead they care about the percentage change. Here is his example: "imagine that you have a stock that is worth $10, and it goes up by $1. You've just made 10%. Now imagine that stock is worth $100. If it goes up by $1, you are happy- but not as happy, since you have made only 1%, even though you have made a dollar in both cases. If the stock starts at $100, it has to go all the way up to $110 for an investor to be as pleased as if the $10 stock went up to $11. And logarithms respect this relativized valuation: they have the nice property that the difference between log (10) and log (11) is equal to the difference between log (100) and log (110). In other words, the rate of return is the same for a stock that begins at $10 and goes up to $11 as for a stock that begins at $100 and goes up to $110."

Statisticians would say that the logarithm of price has an "equal interval" property. Osbornes conclusion given in the paper "Brownian Motion in the Stock Market" is that we should be interested in the logarithms of prices because logarithms of prices better reflect how investors feel about their gains and losses. It seems that mathematical modelling of financial markets is not only consistent with thinking about markets in terms of the psychology of investors, but the best mathematical models will be the ones that, like Osborne's and unlike Bachelier's, take psychology into account.

In the end, it turns out that physics is economics and finance remedy, if only we learn how and where to implement it. But my biggest concern is the absence of any grand alternative competing theory. The survey of alternative schools of thought given by Siddique and Ansari (2010), shows that there are several emerging trends against neoclassical economics. Their work is mostly restricted to the critical evaluation of microeconomics and they have largely failed to provide any rigorous alternative framework to analyze capitalist social order.

In the end, we cannot say that this story has a happy ending, not yet. But at least we are aware that economics will continue to celebrate its triumph, thanks to missing alternatives.

FINANCE THEORY WITHIN A NEOCLASSICAL FRAMEWORK

A new scientific truth does not triumph by convincing its opponents and making them see the light, but rather because its opponents eventually die, and a new generation grows up that is familiar with it. (Planck, 1949)

Neoclassical economics is based on the idea that the way of understanding complex economic phenomena is to examine the random walk of a representative agent where the value of any financial instrument is determined such that the present values are the best prediction one can give for future values. To be more specific, in order to maximize utility, the agents buys when they expect the price to give higher than average returns and sell when they expect lower than average returns. The problem that can occur is, in doing this they will change the very patterns they are attempting to exploit: buying increases the price and selling drives the price down. Thus, an endogenous process balances the market out.

But in neoclassical finance the price changes follow a random walk, because the change is explained by an exogenous process (external shock). This idea was firstly introduced by Bachelier in his thesis in 1900. What is interesting is that his work went unnoticed for many years and then became the very foundation of financial market theory, not considering the thesis report given at that time by the famous Henri Poincaré the great French mathematician. He, Henri Poincaré, clearly stated that one should not take this seriously as a way of modelling financial markets, as individuals do not act independently, but are constantly influenced by others and will always be prone to herd behavior.

But while I was reading the book "The Physics of Wall Street" I understood that Bachelier was not the first person to take a mathematical interest in the game of change. The distinction goes to the Italian Renaissance man Gerolamo Cardano. I also learned that Bachelier was not properly appreciated for what he had done and the audience was the problem. When he was studying, and writing his thesis, economics were only barely a professional discipline- and of the few economists, would be able to understand the mathematics Bachelier used.

Cardeno was born in Milan around the16th century and he was the most accomplished physician of his days. But his real passion was gambling. He believed that there was a simpler way to understand betting. So, he wanted to bring modern mathematics to bear on his favorite subject. In 1526, while still in his twenties, Cardavo wrote a book that outlived the first attempts at a systematic theory of probability. He never published this book, but the manuscript was found among his papers when he died and ultimately was published in 1663.

Then how was Bachelier works discovered?

Leonard Savage, was a professor of statistic at the University of Chicago. He had just finished writing a textbook on probability and statistics when he ran into a textbook in the university library in 1914 that he had never seen before. He soon figured out that it was some pioneered work on probability. The book had a few chapters dedicated to what the author called "speculation". Here the probability theory was applied to market speculation. He thought that maybe his colleagues have heard about Bachelier and Savage sent them postcards. Paul Samuelsson was the only recipient of Savage's postcards who bothered to look Bachelier's work. Samuelsson is the first American economist who won the Nobel Memorial Prize in Economic Science.

Samuelsson was impressed enough to spread what he found. Bachelier's writings on speculation became an interesting reading among Samueson's students at MIT. But Bachelier was officially recognized in 1964 when Paul Counter also a professor at MIT, included an English translation of Bachelier's thesis as the first essay in "The Random Character of Stock Market Prices". This was the moment when the full credit was assigned to Bachelier for his discovery of the random walk hypothesis in stock markets.

What is more, to avoid the problem with multiple equilibrium, neoclassical economists use representative agent models where systems always generate a unique equilibrium. If knocked out of the state of equilibrium, the economy will return to a stable state as a result of some adjustment process. However, this approach lies open to familiar criticisms and the key to the problem in the stability of the equilibrium states (see Kirman 1992, Judge, Stoker and Wolman 1995, Aoki and Yoshikawa 2007). Moreover, the basic market model has been shown to use remarkably little information when functioning at equilibrium. But as Saari and Simon (1978) have shown, if there were a mechanism that would take a General Equilibrium, (Arrow–Debreu) economy to an equilibrium, that mechanism would require an infinite amount of information. Thus, the stability problem was basically unsolvable in the context of the general equilibrium model.

Another postulate of the mainstream neoclassical theory is the distribution used in modeling price changes. It is linked to the central limit theorem (CLM), where the stochastic process will be characterized by a Gaussian (normal) distribution. However, the variables that are normally distributed tend to exhibit rather mild fluctuations and the model is not capable to deal with extreme large fluctuations that correspond to stock market crashes. If we plot the price changes against time, we will see that there are far larger changes than the standard model suggests. Contrary, econophysicists believe that the probability distribution is best matched by power-law tails rather than a Gaussian distribution. And the existence of a power-law distribution often points to the underlying complexity in the system that generates it. But one of the McCauley's objections is that "the empirical distribution is not fixed once and for all by any law of nature, but is also subject to change with agent's collective behavior". This means that the market reflects what we are doing economically, and the apparent rules of behavior of the market, can change rapidly with time. This non-stationary is a general feature of adaptive complex system.

These neoclassical principles are encoded in the central tool for pricing financial derivatives: the Black- Scholes-Merton model (BSM) (Black and Scholes, 1973; Merton, 1973). In particular, the BSM model brings the concepts of thermodynamic equilibrium in finance. This is defined in the financial context as a steady state reached when the underlying stock and the stock option are balanced in terms of the payoff they yield compared to the risk they entail.

But the economic system contains multiple agents (producers and consumers, individuals and firms, etc.), all competing for finite resources and interacting in such a way as to generate the properties and dynamics of economic system and subsystems. Therefore, what we observe at the aggregate level will not mimic what we observe at the individual level, nor will it correspond to the behavior of some representative individual. Indeed, the major changes at the aggregate level can be provoked by small events at the micro level. Taking these characteristics in consideration economic systems is an obvious candidate for the complexity treatment. Economic systems can be observed and analyzed as an adaptive complex system, where the individual subunits modify their properties and behavior with respect to a changing environment resulting with generation of new system properties. These properties reflect the change that the environment has undergone.

However, Latora and Marchiori (2004, p. 377) point out that these characteristics miss out the network structure of the subunits. Much recent work in modeling of complex systems and of the "real-world" economic phenomena such as price dynamics, has focused on the structural features of such networks, rather than nonlinear interaction between individual subunits (see Amaral and Ottino, 2004; Kirman, 2009).

In short, financial systems should be treated as a complex system where fractal structure and interaction play a central explanatory role and individual details are largely relevant. If we are to move towards better modelling, we will have to incorporate explicitly the idea that the economy is a system of interacting individuals.

Theory of Investment

According to economists, investment includes mainly the purchase of new real durable assets, which are not consumed today but are used in the future to create wealth. This definition differs from the rest of the world. For example, if you ask a banker about investment, she/he will start talking about financial assets and loans. In both cases, the financial asset of one agent in the economy is counterbalanced by a financial liability of another agent or corporation. Thus, when we aggregate the wealth of all members of the economy, these assets and liabilities cancel and financial assets disappear. Meaning, investment does not rise.

Therefore, economists usually reserve the term investment for transactions that increase the magnitude of real aggregate wealth in the economy. This indicates that investment refers to the creation or purchase of new durable assets such as factories and machines, which are used for production. Here please note that the resale of the assets is not counted in such investments.

The first model of finance is presented by Fisher (1930) in his book "Theory of Interest", known as a Fisher's separation theorem. Here, the primary objective is the maximization of its present value, regardless of the preferences of its shareholders. In the model, we can notice that the stock of capital does not exist. Rather, all capital is, in fact, investment. The first extension of Fisher's theorem was made by Modigliani and Miller (1958), where the market value of a firm depends only of its profit stream and is invariant to its capital structure. This theory has been of outstanding importance in the literature of corporate finance.

Nevertheless, in this segment, we will focus on the neoclassical theory of investment (NTI) as a cornerstone of the micro foundation of neoclassical macroeconomics. The output is a function of employment given the capital stock, and output growth is determined in the capital market by the interest rate that linked the demand for investment with the supply of saving. It is a theory of how markets efficiently coordinate the decisions of agents, creating coherence, harmony and optimality where chaos might otherwise have been. Neoclassical theory adopts the assumption that the agent can assign numerical probabilities to all possible future economic states, as well as the probability distribution of expected returns to every possible choice available to them. In this context, the future is assumed to be certain, therefore, the interest rate is the risk-free rate.

Moreover, according Lensink, Bo and Sterken (2001), in the modern neoclassical theory of finance three pillars are usually mentioned: no arbitrage, optimality, and equilibrium (also known as Arrow-Debreu's world). No arbitrage refers to the notation that the same asset has to have the same price in each period in absence of any restriction, by optimality is meant rational agents strive for optimal returns, and equilibrium refers to the mainstream idea that the markets are cleared by price adjustment at each moment in time. In this case markets are complete, where present value prices of investment projects are well defined. Otherwise, the markets alone will not provide a well-defined signal for the value of investment.

The neoclassical theory of investment was originated by the Jargenson's and Tobin's "q" theory.

Dale Jorgenson developed the concept of the user cost of capital, and explained its fundamental role as a determinant of investment behavior. In Jorgenson's (1963) investment model, fixed asset investment is described as a process of optimal capital stock adjustment. He predicts that profit-maximizing firms will invest in capital stock until the expected marginal return of a unit capital equals its marginal cost. In a long-run a steady-state relationship between the firm's optimal capital stock and the elasticity of substitution is given in Equation 1.

$$K = y + \theta - \sigma r \text{ , } where\ \theta\ is\ a\ constant \tag{1}$$

Here, y is the production level, K is the capital stock, r is the user cost and σ is the elasticity of substitution.

Higher planned production levels, generate a rise in the desired capital. Contrary, a higher user cost, leads to a decrease of a firm's capital; its extent is determined by the elasticity of substitution.

Moreover, Jorgenson in his model presented the real user cost, r, as a function of:

Real user cost= f (the real cost of finance, ρ; depreciation rate, δ; the tax rate on investment, T; output, Pk/Py; and relative price of investment, π.)

Or,

$$r = \frac{P_k}{P_y}\left(\rho + \delta - \pi\right)\frac{1}{\left(1 - T\right)} \tag{2}$$

In short, the real user cost, r, increases:

- With the real cost of finance - which represents the opportunity cost of holding capital.
- When the higher depreciation rate occurs, since the value of fast-depreciating assets falls more rapidly.
- With the tax rate on investment by making investment goods more expensive in comparison to other goods.
- With a rise in the relative price of investment by making the output more expensive in comparison to other goods.

At the end, the real user cost falls with higher expected growth in the relative price of investment, capturing capital gains.

In the neoclassical theory, to arrive at a relationship between investment and its underlying determinants they use the equation 3. This is recognized as a capital accumulation relationship. Here, the capital during any period of time is equal to the depreciated amount from the previous period plus gross investment.

$$K_{t+1} = \left(1 - \delta\right)K_t + I_t \tag{3}$$

Where K_{t+1} is capital stock in period t+1, δ is the depreciation rate, K_t is capital stock in period t and I_t is investment in period t.

A firm brings the current capital stock back to its desired level by adjusting the level of investment, i. In the steady state the level of production, γ, is constant or it is growing by constant rate. Therefore, transformed into logarithms, in the long run, equation 4 holds.

$$i = k + \gamma \tag{4}$$

Where γ is a constant.

By combining equations (1) and (4) we will get the long run relationship between the investment to output ratio and the real user cost of capital. (See equation 5)

$$i - y = \theta + \gamma - \sigma r \tag{5}$$

where i is the investment, y is the production level, σ is the elasticity, r is the user cost and θ is constant.

In this neoclassical approach, policy prescriptions centre is allowing the market to operate freely and efficiently by promoting the flexibility of prices. In other words, collective bargaining is anathema for free markets. The neoclassical theory has proved very useful in understanding only the long- run investment behavior, but it does not explain the large short- run fluctuations in investment that are seen in reality.

In essence, since the neoclassical theory assumes that the capital adjusts immediately and completely to the desired capital stock the investment function is basically wiped out. This implies that investors do not have to look to the future because they can respond so quickly and effectively and their expectations are essentially static. Therefore, what Jargenson delivered was more a theory of optimal capital stock than a theory of optimal investment theory. On the other hand, Tobin's theory of investment explicitly assumes profit/value maximization and explains how firms decide whether to make investment of physical capital or not. Here, the rate of investment is a function of, q, the ratio of the market value of new additional investment capital for their replacement cost. (See Equation 6.)

$$q = \frac{\text{market value of installed capital}}{\text{replacement cost of installed capital}} \tag{6}$$

Tobin reasoned that companies should accumulate more capital when q>1, because capital once installed and producing goods and services is priced more highly than its cost, and should draw down their capital stock when q<1.

For example, a logistic company owns 50 trucks, which replacement cost is $5000 each or in total $250.000. Suppose it has 10.000 outstanding shares of stock valued at $30 per stock. Thus, the market value of the company is $300.000, and the replacement cost is $250.000, so Tobin's q is 1.2.

Since the tracks are worth more in the company than outside, q>1 or 1.2>1, the company should evidently buy more tracks. That is, what it makes a profit on the new investment. The profit will influence the dividend paid out by the company, which will tend to raise the company's stock price. These will lead to new investments. But the problem here as Dixit and Pindyck (1994) discovered, that the companies may delay expansion or contraction for some time and may only do so if q remains significantly above or below unity. Moreover, when a firm expands its capital stock it will face diminishing returns. Thus, the marginal product of capital will fall as the capital stock grows. This will tend to cause q to revert back towards unity. However, the efficient market hypothesis suggests that share prices will provide firms and agents with the correct signals regarding how to allocate capital. If a company is positively viewed by the markets, then q will rise and the company should increase its capital stock, by purchasing capital equipment or by taking over the assets of other firms.

However, Tobin's "q" theory also has a few drawbacks. First, the role of production part has never been clear; second, if a firm can freely change its capital stock, and so it will proceed to increase or diminish its capital stock until q is equal to unity. Meaning, some sort of adjustment cost also lies behind the theory. Also, there might be financial constraints preventing firms from engaging in large and sudden expansions of their capital stock.

CONCLUDING REMARKS

Modeling the madness of people is more difficult than the motion of planets (Sir Isaak Newton, after losing his savings in the South Sea Bubble of 1720).

I believe that a primary reason for studying the history of economic thought is to become a better economist. Studying old ideas will foster new ones. But the mainstream economists have made remarkable efforts to keep this course out of the economic curriculum, with the explanation that there is another more important subject to be studied. Unfortunately, this was the case also in my department, where the history of economic thought is offered as an elective course.

Keeping economic theory disconnected from the reality and an overly formal and dogmatic education in the economic sciences and financial mathematics is a serious part of the problem. Therefore, despite all the critics in the past two decades mainstream economists still insist on their "representative agent" models. We should all together admit that the damage is done and it is no longer acceptable to study relationship between aggregate variables without taking in consideration the individual interaction. The aggregate behavior does not correspond to that of a "rational individual" who takes "rational decisions" in "self-interest". More important, as Kirman (2009) stated, the vast majority of mainstream economists who work in business and government, including those at the International Monetary Fund and the World Bank, are not terribly concerned with the most advanced theoretical work in their discipline. Legions of these economists are engaged on a daily basis in developing analyses and making predictions that guide decision-making of global economic planners. They serve to justify assumptions about economic reality in the neoclassical economic paradigm. After this I can only conclude that the Long-Term Capital Management (LTCM) hedge fund account will be retold sooner than we imagine.

Now let us return to the major questions asked in this chapter: Why then do we depart from the modern physics? Why is neoclassical theory still dominating university textbooks?

The possible answers are given below.

1. Ancient Greek students learned mathematics, physics and philosophy with the idea that it would benefit them in whatever they did, even if they did not become mathematicians, physician or philosophers. But economics and finance did not simply evolve to become mathematical science. This was imposed and set out to make it so by its practitioners. Therefore, elegant formulas that explain complex subjects have great convincing power among their users. So, once economics and finance made it their goal to develop the concept and the idea of the elegant model form, they go along with the simplified assumptions of that form. Therefore, Weatherall (2013) stressed that in practice, financial models can leave us unable to see many of the most important aspects of financial markets; and in that blindness, lie the roots of the catastrophe.

But why we are doing this? Is this simply the easiest way and we do not expand our descriptions because it's difficult?

2. Have us move a little further and assume that economist agree to include financial mathematics and statistical physics in university curriculums. What would be the result of this?

In one example Weatherall (2013) credit science for development. He explained how the "highly secretive Chicago options-trading firm" O'Connor and Associates spotted a flaw in Black-Scholes-Merton and adjusted its models accordingly, giving it a competitive advantage and make the model to fly and not to crash.

So, if we encapsulate this knowledge in the formal education, then the economic and financial students will understand the equations limited application and its shallow foundation in economics. The problem in economics is that it uses equations borrowed from physics and implement them without taking into consideration that economic systems cannot be analyzed in isolation. The result in this case would be as the econometricians want to say bias. At the end, like it or not, this would declare the end of the neoclassical dominance, and define it nothing more than as an ideology serving the interest of economic elites in a capitalist society.

3. Another relevant answer is provided by Krugman (2009) stating that the vested interests are strong and to ask economists to take up a new set of tools is probably asking too much. To discard equilibrium in the standard sense and to move on to study out of equilibrium dynamics is surely the right way to proceed but is perhaps too big a step for economics at the present time.

At the end of the day each of us, no matter in which group we belong academicians or practitioners, we should ask ourselves whether this is what we want finance to look alike. I will close this chapter with the statement from the famous Yale economist, Irving Fisher. He referred directly in the 1940s:

The goal on which my heart has been mostly set, the goal of economics becoming a true science comparable with physics.

This goal is still in the hearts of many financial economists, including me.

REFERENCES

Amaral, L. A., & Ottino, J. M. (2004). Complex networks. *The European Physical Journal B-Condensed Matter and Complex Systems*, *38*(2), 147–162. doi:10.1140/epjb/e2004-00110-5 PMID:15505227

Aoki, M., & Yoshikawa, H. (2007). *Reconstructing Macroeconomics: A Perspective from Statistical Physic and Combinatorial Stochastic Processes*. Cambridge University Press.

Beigelow, G. (2005, May). Let There Be Markets: The Evangelical Roots of Economics. *Harper's*, 310(1860), 33–38. Retrieved from http://harpers.org/archive/2005/05/let-there-be-markets/

Black, F., & Scholes, M. (1973). The pricing of options and corporate liabilities. *Journal of Political Economy*, *81*(3), 637–654. doi:10.1086/260062

Crucitti, P., Latora, V., & Marchiori, M. (2004). Model for cascading failures in complex networks. *Physical Review E: Statistical, Nonlinear, and Soft Matter Physics*, *69*(4), 045104. doi:10.1103/PhysRevE.69.045104 PMID:15169056

Dixit, A. K., & Pindyck, R. S. (1994). *Investment under uncertainty*. Princeton university press.

Dobb, M. (1975). *Theories of Value and Distribution since Adam Smith: Ideology and Economic Theory*. Cambridge: Cambridge University Press.

Fullbrook, E. (2005). *"Are You Rational?", A Guide to What is Wrong with Economics*. Edward Fullbrook London.

Haavelmo, T. (1992). Econometrics and the welfare state. *Economic Sciences, 1981-1990: The Sveriges Riksbank (Bank of Sweden). Prize in Economic Sciences in Memory of Alfred Nobel*, *2*, 261.

Jevons, W. S. (1965). *The theory of Political Economy*. New York: A.M. Kelley John. (Original work published 1871)

Judge, D., Stoker, G., & Wolman, H. (1995). Urban politics and theory: An introduction. In *Theories of urban politics* (pp. 1-12).

Kirman, A. (2009, November 6-7). What's Wrong with Modern Macroeconomics: The Economic Crisis is a Crisis in Economic Theory. *Proceedings of the CESifo Economic Studies Conference*, Munich.

Kirman, A. P. (1992). Whom or what does the representative individual represent? *The Journal of Economic Perspectives*, *6*(2), 117–136. doi:10.1257/jep.6.2.117

Krugman, P. (2009). How did economists get it so wrong? *New York Times*.

Landreth, H., & Colander, D. (1976). *History of economic theory*. Boston: Houghton Mifflin.

Lensink, R., Bo, H., & Sterken, E. (2001). *Investment, capital market imperfections, and uncertainty: Theory and empirical results*. Edward Elgar Publishing.

McCauley, J. L. (2004). *Dynamics of markets: econophysics and finance*. Cambridge University Press. doi:10.1017/CBO9780511606588

Merton, R. C. (1973). An intertemporal capital asset pricing model. *Econometrica*, *41*(5), 867–887. doi:10.2307/1913811

Mirowski, P. (1999). *More Heat than Light: Economics as Social Physics, Physics as Nature's Economics*. Cambridge University Press.

Poincaré, H. (1905). *La valeur de la Science Flammarion*. Paris.

Saari, D. G., & Simon, C. P. (1978). Effective price mechanisms. *Econometrica*, *46*(5), 1097–1125. doi:10.2307/1911438

Siddique, Z., & Javed, A. (2010). *Microeconomics in Pakistan: Theory, Practice and Evaluation*. Pakistan Business Review.

Taleb, N. N. (2007). *The black swan: The impact of the highly improbable*. Random House.

Thompson, H. (1997). Ignorance and Ideological Hegemony: A Critique of Neoclassical Economics. *Journal of Interdisciplinary Economics*, *8*(4), 291–305.

Weatherall, J. O. (2013). *The physics of wall street: a brief history of predicting the unpredictable*. Houghton Mifflin Harcourt.

Chapter 2 Decision Tree Analyses

ABSTRACT

As a branch of statistics that uses probability, decision trees have been widely applied to variety problems from numerous disciplines and serve two primary goals. First, they help us to resolve uncertainties in making investment decisions. Second, using decision trees we can determine which alternatives, at any point in time produces the most favorable, or least painful, consequences. In contrast, classical statistics focus on estimating a parameter, such as the population means, constructing a confidence interval, or conducting a hypothesis test. Classical statistics do not address the possible consequences of a decision. In this chapter I illustrate the essentials of using a decision tree for making financial decisions, and demonstrate how a decision is made using both criteria: expected monetary value and expected utility. At the end, I discuss the imperfectability of the traditional techniques and tools and suggest alternative decision tools inspired by some areas of research in signal processing, known as wavelet analysis. To set up and solve decision tree problems, TreePlan, and add-in for Excel, is used.

The possible solution to a given problem emerges as the leaves of a tree, each node representing a point of deliberation and decision (Niklaus Wirth, 1934, Programming language designer).

INTRODUCTION

The first comprehensive and authoritative book on decision tree analysis is published by Howard Raiffa in 1968. As a branch of statistics that uses

DOI: 10.4018/978-1-5225-3259-0.ch002

probability, decision trees have been widely applied to variety problems from numerous disciplines and serve two primary goals. First, they help us to resolve uncertainties in making investment decisions. Second, using decision trees we can determine which alternatives, at any point in time produces the most favorable, or least painful, consequences. In contrast, classical statistics focus on estimating a parameter, such as the population means, constructing a confidence interval, or conducting a hypothesis test. Classical statistics do not address the possible consequences of a decision.

There are 4 basic elements in decision theory, namely: acts, events, outcomes, and payoffs.

- Acts are the actions being considered by the agent. In the decision tree, it is represented by a square, ■, or a decision node. This node could refer to the decision to invest or not invest, or how much to invest.
- Event occurrences are taking place outside the control of the agent. This uncertain events are represented by a circle, ●, or chance node. Uncertain events may occur before or after decision.
- Outcomes are the result of the occurrence of acts and events. They are represented with a triangle, ◄.
- When a decision process arrives at an outcome, the decision maker knows the payoff he will receive. The payoffs can be positive or negative.

A decision tree extends from a starting point through a series of branches, showing the flow from the question to the answer. It is used to make sequences of decisions. The order in which the shapes are connected is very important. For example: a square that is followed by a circle means that a decision is made before the uncertainty is resolved and vice versa. (See Figure 1)

CONSTRUCTING A DECISION TREE

Giving an Example

To illustrate the essentials of using a decision tree for making financial decisions, consider the following example:

Figure 1. Decision Tree Notation

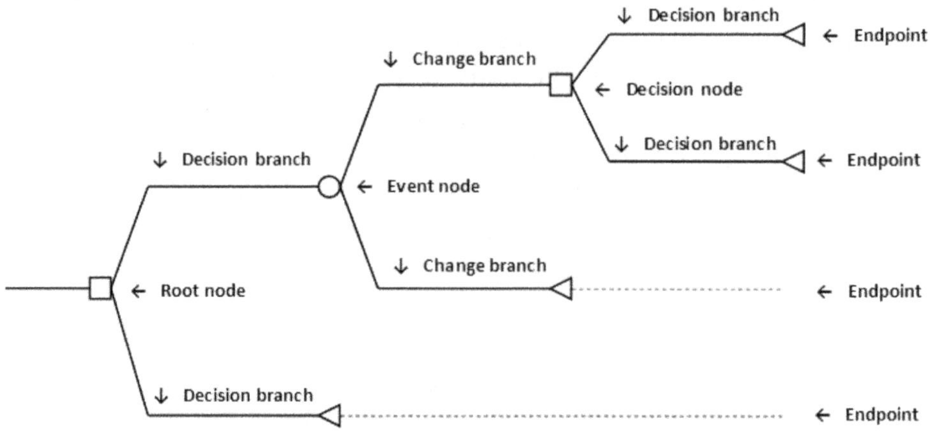

Petar as an owner of a small software company, needs to decide in which securities to invest his savings. There are 3 actions available: to invest in stocks, bonds or mutual funds. The investment will expire within one year. He should decide which of the actions, is the best one under each economic condition. After in-depth analysis of the financial markets, the predicted returns of $100.000 investment under four economic conditions: recession, stability, moderate growth, and boom are shown in the payoff table (Table 1).

Designing the Tree

A decision tree can be used in either a predictive manner or a descriptive manner. In either instance, they are constructed the same way and are always used to visualize all possible outcomes and decision point that occur chronologically.

Table 1. Payoffs by economic conditions

Economic Conditions	Stock A ($)	Bonds ($)	Mutual Funds ($)
Recession	200	300	-300
Stable Economy	600	300	300
Moderate Growth	1100	300	2000
Boom	1400	300	2500

Note: the cost to hire a broker is $20.

Lay Out Alternatives

It is often useful to represent a decision problem by a tree, where the starting point is the first decision. In our case, Petar has two alternatives as a decision: either to hire a broker to do the market research or not (see Figure 2). To build the trees we use the Tree Plan add in, and the details are given in the Appendix.

If Petar decides to hire a broker then we start the analysis with the top branch. Here, the economic conditions in which the investment could occur are: recession, stable economy, moderate growth and boom. Because the results of the market research are out of Petar's control, we represent this uncertain event in the tree with a circle, as shown in Figure 3.

Then we repeat these steps for the case when Petar does not hire a broker. As we can notice in Figure 4, the decision made done before the uncertainty about the economic conditions, which was not the case in the example above. Therefore, the final decision tree is just like a probability tree.

Quantify the Risk

Before we quantify the risk in the problem we should know that the environments in which decisions are made can be classified according to the degree of certainty. There are three basic categories: certainty, risk, and uncertainty, and they require different techniques of analysis.

Category 1: Decision Making Under Certainty.

When the decision maker knows for certain which state of nature will occur, he will choose the alternative that has the highest payoff, or the

Figure 2. Construction of the decision tree

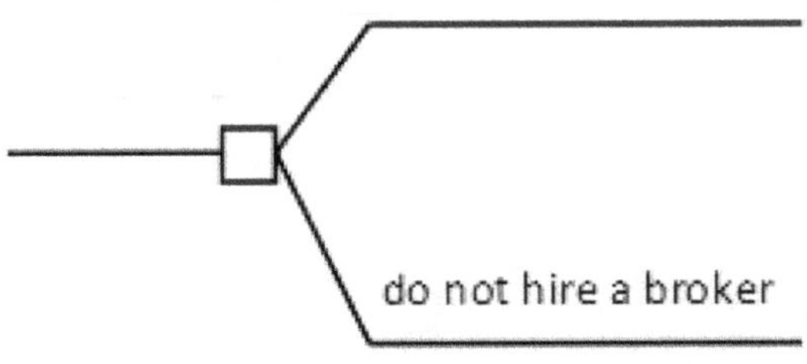

Figure 3. Uncertain event in the decision tree

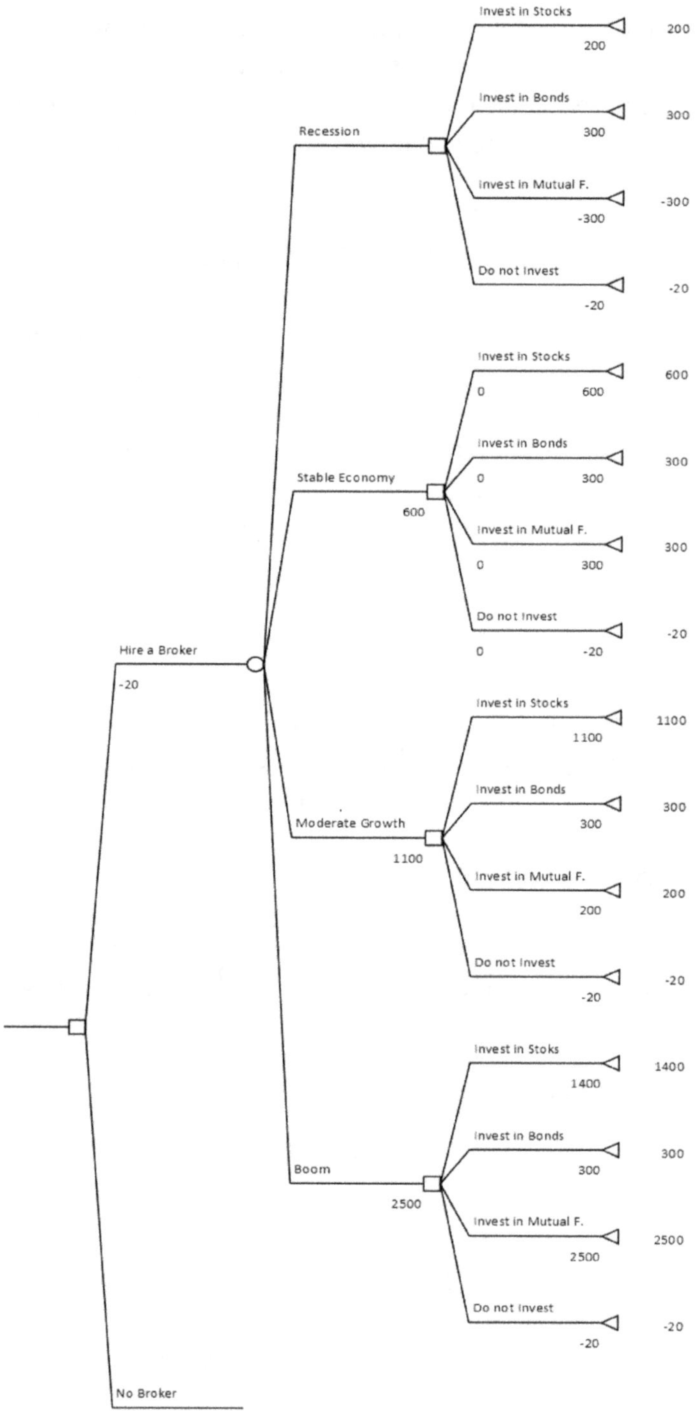

Decision Tree Analyses

Figure 4. Final decision tree

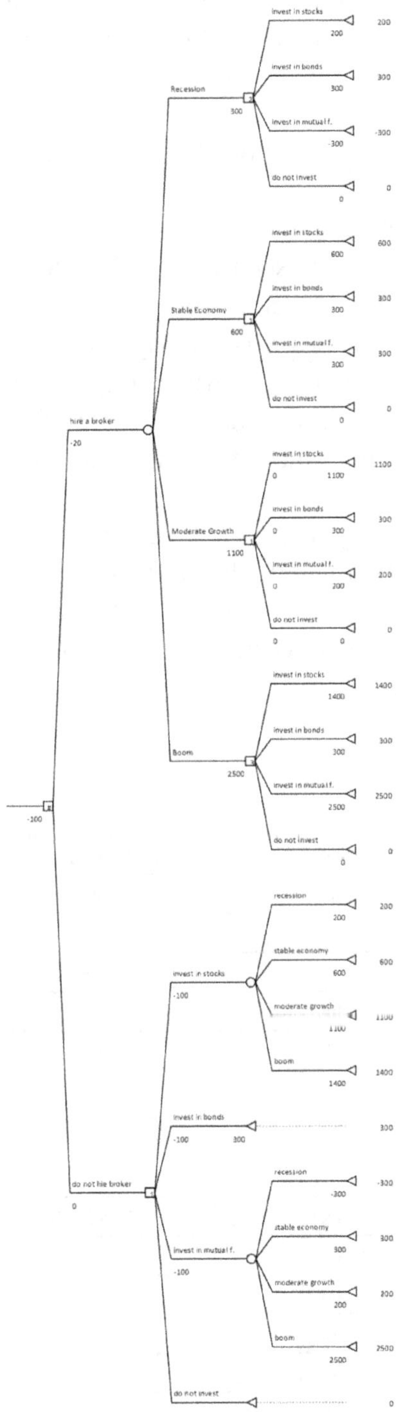

smallest financial loss, under that state of nature. In the above investment decision problem, suppose that it is known with certainty that the economy will be stable. The highest profit in stable economy is $600 and therefore Petar should invest in stocks. (See Figure 4)

Category 2: Decision Making Under Uncertainty.

Under complete uncertainty, probabilities are not used in the choice of the best alternative. Here, the most used rules for the choice of the best alternative are known as maximax and maximin rules.

The maximax payoff criterion is appropriate for extreme optimists that expect the most favorable situation. Meaning, the investor will choose the alternative that could result in the maximum payoff.

Using this criterion, Petar should do the following:

1. Find the maximum payoff for each action.
2. Choose the action that has the highest of these maximum payoffs.

Because maximum of the maximum profit is $2500, Petar should choose to invest in mutual funds.

Table 2. Maximum Payoffs

Economic Conditions	Stocks ($)	Bonds ($)	Mutual Funds ($)
Recession	200	300	-300
Stable Economy	600	300	300
Moderate Growth	1100	300	200
Boom	1400	300	2500
Maximum payoffs	1400	300	2500

Table 3. Maximin Payoff

Economic Conditions	Stocks ($)	Bonds ($)	Mutual Funds ($)
Recession	200	300	-300
Stable Economy	600	300	300
Moderate Growth	1100	300	200
Boom	1400	300	2500
Minimum payoffs	200	300	-300

On the contrary, the *maximin payoff criterion* is a pessimistic payoff criterion. Using this criterion, Petar should do the following:

1. Find the minimum payoff for each action.
2. Choose the action that has the highest of these minimum payoffs.

Because the maximum of the minimum profits is $300, Petar should choose to invest in bonds.

Category 3: Decision Making Under Risk.

In this case, Petar doesn´t know which state of nature will occur, but he can estimate the probability of occurrence for each state. These probabilities may be subjective - estimates from experts in a particular field, or they may reflect historical frequencies. In the discussed investment decision problem, Petar assigned the following probabilities to different economic conditions-events:

P (recession) = 0.2

P (Stable Economy) = 0.4

P (Moderate Growth) = 0.3

P (Boom) = 0.1

Now we have enough information to complete the decision tree. The outcomes are labelled, A, B, C, D, E and F. (See Figure 5).

Specify the Objectives

The Expected Monetary Value (EMV) criterion does not take into account the decision making toward risk. If the amount of money involved in the risky decision problem is small, then the risk is usually not important and expected monetary value is an applicable criterion.

On the other hand, if the amount of money involved in the risky decision problem is large then the expected monetary value is not adequate. In this

Figure 5. Assigning probabilities to different economic conditions-events

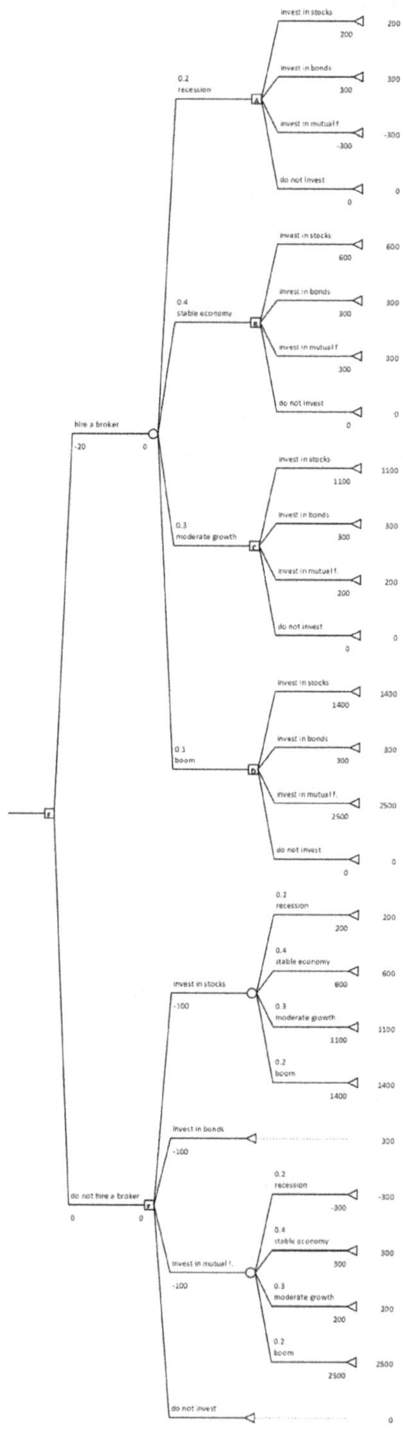

case, in the textbooks utility theory is suggested, which gives a possibility to incorporate risk into decision analysis.

In our case in order to solve the decision tree, we assume that Petar when faced with two or more alternatives, he will always prefer the one with the highest expected monetary value.

SOLVING THE TREE

Here we will demonstrate how a decision is made using both criteria: expected monetary value and expected utility.

Expected Monetary Value Analysis

After the decision tree has been constructed, we do not need to examine every possible strategy. Instead, we will use a single best strategy known as a backward induction or average back and fold back process. This process leads to the selection of the highest payoff value and the corresponding decision for that node. The process is repeated until the starting decision node is reached, as illustrated below.

Step 1:

If Petar is at point A, B, C, or D he should decide either to invest or not. (See Figure 5)

- At point A Petar knows that the economy is in recession, therefore, he decides to invest in bonds as less risky securities where the return is $300.
- At point B and C he should invest in stocks because the return is highest, $600 and $1100 accordingly.
- When the economy is in boom (point D) then he should choose to invest in mutual funds where the return is $2500.

Step 2:

If Petar is at point E in Figure 5, then the decision that he needs to make is more complicated, because he does not know for sure what the consequences of her action will be. Therefore, he should calculate the Expected Monetary

Value (EMV), which is widely used approach to decision making under risk, as shown in Equation 1.

$$EMV_{(j)} = \sum_{i=1}^{N} X_{ij} P_i \tag{1}$$

where, $EMV_{(j)}$ is expected monetary value of action, X_{ij} is the event that occurs when course of action j is selected and event i occurs, P_i is the probability of occurrence of event i and N is the number of events.

As shown in Table 4, the EMV is calculated by multiplying each payoff that the alternative can yield by the probability for the relevant state of nature and summing the products. This value is computed for each alternative, and the one with the highest EMV is selected.

The expected monetary value, or profit, for stock is $750, for the bond is $300 and for mutual funds is $910. Accordingly, Petar should choose to invest in mutual funds because the EMV is the highest. Here the expected rate of return on the $100 investment is 9.1% for Mutual Funds and the net expected cash flow is 910-100=$810.

Step 3:

Finally, we should see what Petar will decide at point F. Here, he needs to compare expected monetary values for top and bottom path.

The simplified tree given in Figure 6, will help Petar easily to calculate the net expected cash flow for the top path. Using Equation 1, minus the cost of hiring a broker, the EMV is:

$$\left[\left(0.2 * 300\right) + \left(0.4 * 600\right) + \left(0.3 * 1100\right) + \left(0.1 * 2500\right)\right] - 20 = \$860$$

For the bottom path the net expected cash flow is calculated above and is $810. According the calculations, Petar's decision should be to pay to a broker, as it increases his expected cash flows by $50, from $810 to $860.

Expected Utility Analysis

The exponential utility function is of the form:

Table 4. Shows the computations of the expected monetary values (EMV)

Probability, Pi	Economic Condition, Event	Stock	XijPi	Bond	XijPi	Mutual Funds	XijPi
0.2	**Recession**	200	200(0.2)=40	300	300(0.2)=60	-300	-300(0.2)=-60
0.4	**Stable Economy**	600	600(0.4)=240	300	300(0.4)=120	300	300(0.4)=120
0.3	**Moderate Growth**	1100	1100(0.3)=330	300	300(0.3)=90	2000	2000(0.3)=600
0.1	**Boom**	1400	1400(0.1)=140	300	300(0.1)=30	2500	2500(0.1)=250
	EMV		**750**		**300**		**910**

Note: the payoff is in thousands

Figure 6. Decision at point F

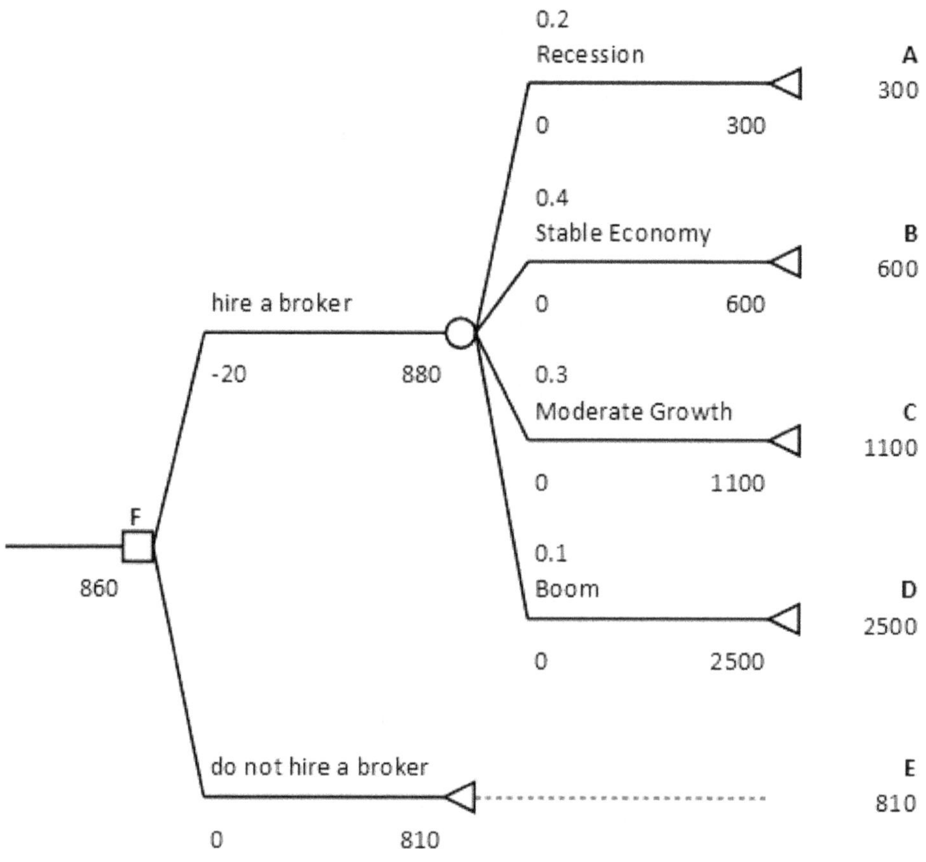

$u(x) = 1 - \exp - x / R$ *where* $R > 0$ is a parameter that controls the curvature of the utility function and x is the payoff. *R* is the so-called Risk Tolerance coefficient, which is needed in the exponential utility function. Larger values of R mean higher risk tolerance, i.e. lower risk aversion.

In our example the risk tolerance coefficient is 50. Using the Tree Plan Add-In for excel we compute expected utilities and select the decisions with maximum expected utility, as shown in Figure 7. Accordingly, Petar's decision should be to pay to a broker, as the expected utility is 260,22.

Figure 7. Decision tree with maximum expected utility

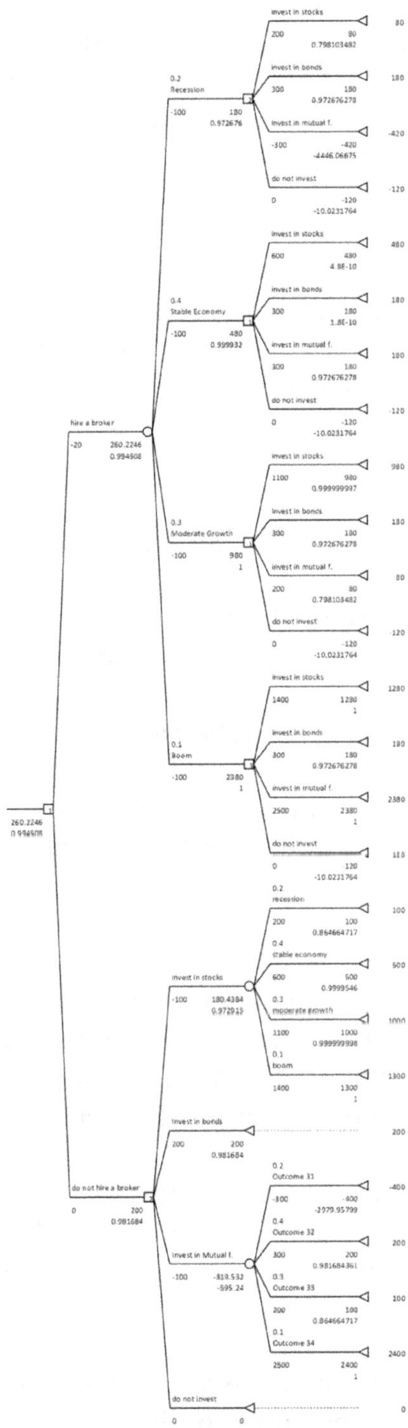

Exercise

Try different possible payoff / probability combinations, as well different values for the risk tolerance coefficient in order to raise the Expected Monetary Value for the "do not hire a broker". What combinations would make this EMV superior to the "hire a broker"?

Note

Expected Monetary Value is not a particular payoff amount that the investor will earn for each event occurred. It represents an average payoff if the trial were repeated many times, but most of the real-world decisions do not have the advantage of being repeatable.

COMMENTS ON DECISION TREES

People with high levels of personal mastery… cannot afford to choose between reason and intuition, or head and heart, any more than they would choose to walk on one leg or see with one eye. A blink, after all, is easier when you use both eyes. (Peter Senge in The Fifth Discipline, 2006).

The decision tree is traditional rational decision making technique that can be very helpful when we are faced with lots of options. Some advantages of decision trees are:

- They are universal.
- They are simple to understand and to interpret. Trees can be visualized.
- They make more accurate the structure of the decision process.
- They facilitate a communication among solvers of the decision problem.
- They force the decision maker to appreciate all consequences of his decisions.
- They use a white box model. If a given situation is observable in a model, the explanation for the condition is easily explained by Boolean logic. By contrast, in a black box model (used in artificial neural network models), the results may be more difficult to interpret.

On the other hand, decision trees have some limitations. One limitation is that only one decision criterion can be considered, otherwise the tree becomes too complicated and the number of the calculations is too large. Like most of the models, the decision tree is an abstraction and simplification of the real problem. Therefore, a small variation in the data might result with a completely different tree.

But the structure of the economy is in constant change and the changes may occur faster than the speed at which people assess the economy. What is more, agents have to make a decision about adaptive complex systems in which rich dynamics exist. Here traditional tools as Expected Monetary Value and Expected Utility will provide unrealistic answers. For that reason, there is a growing acceptance among practitioners of the techniques and tools based or inspired by some areas of research in computer science. The intention is to overcome the limitation of the traditional theory in which many unrealistic assumptions are made (like homogeneous expectations or full rationality).

Faced with imperfectability of decision making, Simon (1955) suggests that people would make rational decisions if only they could gather enough information. He also argues that in practice executives make decisions with only "bounded rationality", because of the cost of acquiring information, limited time, complex circumstances and inadequate mental computational power. Moreover, Tversky and Kahneman (1979), in their Prospect Theory, identify factors that cause people to decide against their economic interest even when they know better. They demonstrate how a rational model of economics fails to describe how people arrive at decisions when facing the uncertainties of real life.

Another decision-making tool offered as an alternative to the traditional ones is the *human intuition*. Decision-making consultant Gary Klein (2002), in his book *Intuition at Work*, expresses the common wisdom when he says that intuition is "at the center of the decision-making process" and that analysis is, at best, "a supporting tool for making intuitive decisions." Isenberg (1987) also explains that executives often combine rigorous planning with intuition when faced with a high degree of uncertainty. While Gladwell (2007) has explored the notion that our instantaneous decisions are sometimes better than those based on lengthy, rational analysis.

What got my attention during my research was the developments in brain-mental imagery techniques. They have made it possible to explore the neural foundations of logical and mathematical cognition. Imaging is beginning to resolve some of the oldest questions about what logic and mathematics are, and how they emerge and evolve through visuo-spatial cognition, speech communication, executive functions and emotion. But the most important finding is given by Damasio, a neurological scientist in 1994. Working with brain-damaged patients demonstrated that in the absence of emotion, it is impossible to make any decision at all. Thus, emotions are a major component in the interactions between environmental conditions and human decision processes. This signifies that people do not always make rational decision.

Alternative Decision Tools

During the last decade, there has been intense discussion among practitioners and academicians about effectiveness of technical trading rules and the Efficient Market Hypothesis (EMH).

If one were to state that "market prices instantaneously and fully reflect all relevant information available," one would be discussing the Efficient Market Hypothesis, popularly known as the Random Walk Theory. In other words, past prices should provide no information about future prices that would allow an investor to earn excess returns. As such EMH categorically negates the possibility of obtaining excess returns from technical analysis.

On the contrary, a great deal of literature dedicated to technical analysis rules, establishes that the technical analysis is able to identify trend (bullish or bearish markets) or reversals in trajectories of prices (Kallberg and Pasquariello, 2008; Manchanda et al., 2007; Laschi et al., 2007).

"Technical analysts do not claim their methods are magical; rather that they take advantage of market psychology" (Neely, 1997). The aim is to uncover the signals given off in a current market by examining past market signals, because traders will tend to react the same way to the same market conditions and therefore, the subsequent price movements are likely to be similar.

Here we will concentrate on the most relevant evolutionary time-domain analysis: wavelet analysis and chaos theory.

Signal processing is a method of extracting information from a signal and the nature of the information it carries. And in the past few decades, chaos is widely studied using signal processing techniques.

Wavelet methods are more novel ways of analyzing time series and can be viewed as a natural extension of the Fourier analysis; the most widely used signal processing tool in science and technology.

The Fourier transform reveals the frequency composition of a time series by transforming it into the frequency domain. The problem here is that the time information is lost completely. The assumption of so called "natural" periods and stationery that are inherent in the Fourier methods are also problematic. The variation in frequencies and "non-natural" periods are an inherent part of a financial time series. Therefore, the Fourier methods do not work here. But the Wavelet methods work naturally in time series where chaos regions are nonlinear. Thus, they provide insight beyond that of standard time series methodology. In particular, wavelet methods can be considered as the lens, which can be used to zoom in on the details and draw an overall picture of a financial time series in the same time.

Some pioneering work has been made, but these papers have not been widely cited and have, in fact, been largely ignored in the finance theory. More or less important works are Gencay et al (2001, 2002), Dalkir (2004), Lee (2004), Fernandez (2005), Gallegati (2008), Ranta (2010), Blackledge (2010), and Vidal (2014).

We should seriously reconsider the application of the chaos theory in analyzing the dynamics of financial time series. In this book a detailed account of wavelet analysis with its application and uses, is given in chapter 7.

REFERENCES

Allen, F., & Karjalainen, R. (1999). Using genetic algorithms to find technical trading rules. *Journal of Financial Economics*, *51*(2), 245–271. doi:10.1016/S0304-405X(98)00052-X

Arifovic, J. (1994). Genetic algorithm learning and the cobweb model. *Journal of Economic Dynamics & Control*, *18*(1), 3–28. doi:10.1016/0165-1889(94)90067-1

Arifovic, J. (1996). The behavior of the exchange rate in the genetic algorithm and experimental economies. *Journal of Political Economy*, *104*(3), 510–541. doi:10.1086/262032

Bauer, R. J. (1994). *Genetic algorithms and investment strategies* (Vol. 19). John Wiley & Sons.

Blackledge, J. (2010). Systemic risk assessment using a non-stationary fractional dynamic stochastic model for the analysis of economic signals.

Bullard, J., & Duffy, J. (1998). A model of learning and emulation with artificial adaptive agents. *Journal of Economic Dynamics & Control*, *22*(2), 179–207. doi:10.1016/S0165-1889(97)00072-9

Chen, S. H., & Yeh, C. H. (1996). Genetic programming learning and the cobweb model. *Advances in genetic programming, 2*, 443-466.

Chen, S. H., & Yeh, C. H. (1997). Using genetic programming to model volatility in financial time series: the cases of Nikkei 225 and S&P 500. In *Genetic programming 1997: Proceedings of the second annual conference.*

Dalkir, M. (2004). A new approach to causality in the frequency domain. *Economic Bulletin*, *3*(44), 1–14.

Damasio, A. (1994). *Descartes' error: emotion, reason and the human mind* (pp. 195–201). New York: Putnam.

Delfin Vidal, R. (2014). The Fractal Nature of Bitcoin: Evidence from Wavelet Power Spectra. *The Fractal Nature of Bitcoin: Evidence from Wavelet Power Spectra (December 4, 2014).*

Diggs, D. H. (2004). *Multiple Step Financial Time Series Prediction with Portfolio Optimization* (Doctoral dissertation). Marquette University.

Econometrica: Journal of the Econometric Society, 263-291.

Faeder, J. R., Blinov, M. L., Goldstein, B., & Hlavacek, W. S. (2005). Rule-based modeling of biochemical networks. *Complexity*, *10*(4), 22–41. doi:10.1002/cplx.20074

Fernandez, V. P. (2005). The international CAPM and a wavelet-based decomposition of value at risk. *Studies in Nonlinear Dynamics & Econometrics, 9*(4).

Gallegati, M. (2008). Wavelet analysis of stock returns and aggregate economic activity. *Computational Statistics & Data Analysis*, *52*(6), 3061–3074. doi:10.1016/j.csda.2007.07.019

Gençay, R., Selçuk, F., & Whitcher, B. (2001). Scaling properties of foreign exchange volatility. *Physica A: Statistical Mechanics and its Applications, 289*(1), 249-266.

Gençay, R., Selçuk, F., & Whitcher, B. J. (2001). *An introduction to wavelets and other filtering methods in finance and economics*. Academic press.

Gladwell, M. (2007). *Blink: The power of thinking without thinking*. Back Bay Books.

Isenberg, D. J. (1987). *Inside the mind of the senior manager. Thinking*. London: Erlbaum.

Kahneman, D., & Tversky, A. (1979). Prospect theory: An analysis of decision under risk.

Kallberg, J., & Pasquariello, P. (2008). Time-series and cross-sectional excess comovement in stock indexes. *Journal of Empirical Finance*, *15*(3), 481–502. doi:10.1016/j.jempfin.2007.06.002

Klein, G. A. (2002). *Intuition at work: Why developing your gut instincts will make you better at what you do*. Currency/Doubleday.

Loschi, R. H., Iglesias, P. L., Arellano-Valle, R. B., & Cruz, F. R. (2007). Full predictivistic modeling of stock market data: Application to change point problems. *European Journal of Operational Research*, *180*(1), 282–291. doi:10.1016/j.ejor.2006.04.016

Manchanda, P., Kumar, J., & Siddiqi, A. H. (2007). Mathematical methods for modelling price fluctuations of financial time series. *Journal of the Franklin Institute*, *344*(5), 613–636. doi:10.1016/j.jfranklin.2006.03.013

Neely, C. J. (1997). Technical analysis in the foreign exchange market: a layman's guide. *Federal Reserve Bank of St. Louis Review*, (Sep), 23-38.

Nekhili, R., Altay-Salih, A., & Gençay, R. (2002). Exploring exchange rate returns at different time horizons. *Physica A: Statistical Mechanics and its Applications, 313*(3), 671-682.

Raiffa, H. (1968). Decision analysis: introductory lectures on choices under uncertainty.

Ranta, M. (2010). *Wavelet multiresolution analysis of financial time series*. Universitas Wasaensis.

Shik Lee, H. (2004). International transmission of stock market movements: A wavelet analysis. *Applied Economics Letters*, *11*(3), 197–201. doi:10.1080/1350485042000203850

Simon, H. A. (1955). A behavioral model of rational choice. *The Quarterly Journal of Economics*, *69*(1), 99–118. doi:10.2307/1884852

APPENDIX

Building a Decision Tree in Tree Plan

Step 1: Open a new worksheet and press CTRL+SHIFT+T to build a new decision tree diagram.

Figure 8. Build a new decision tree diagram

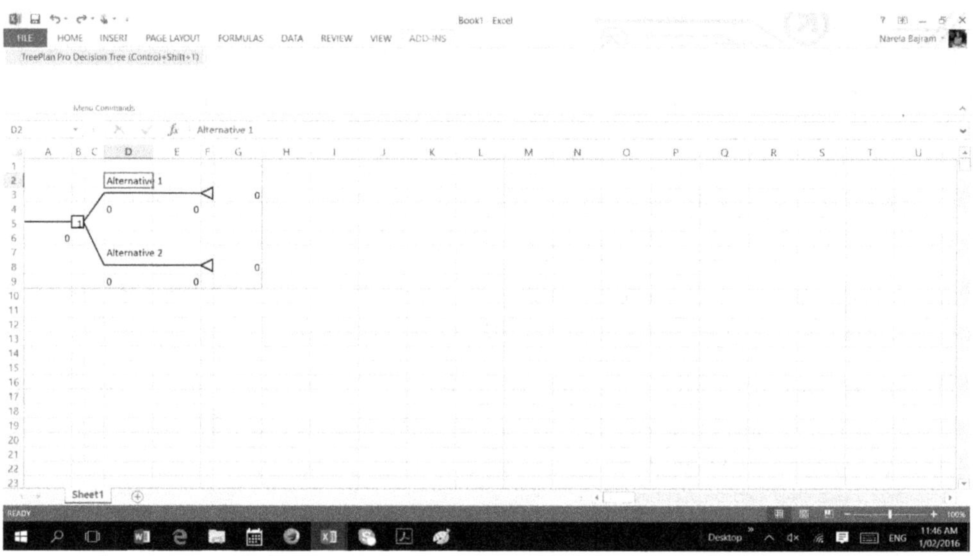

Step 2: Select a node to change the structure of your decision tree and enter branch name, cash flows and probabilities.

Note: we can use expected values or exponential utility function for computing certain equivalents.

Figure 9. Changing the structure of the decision tree

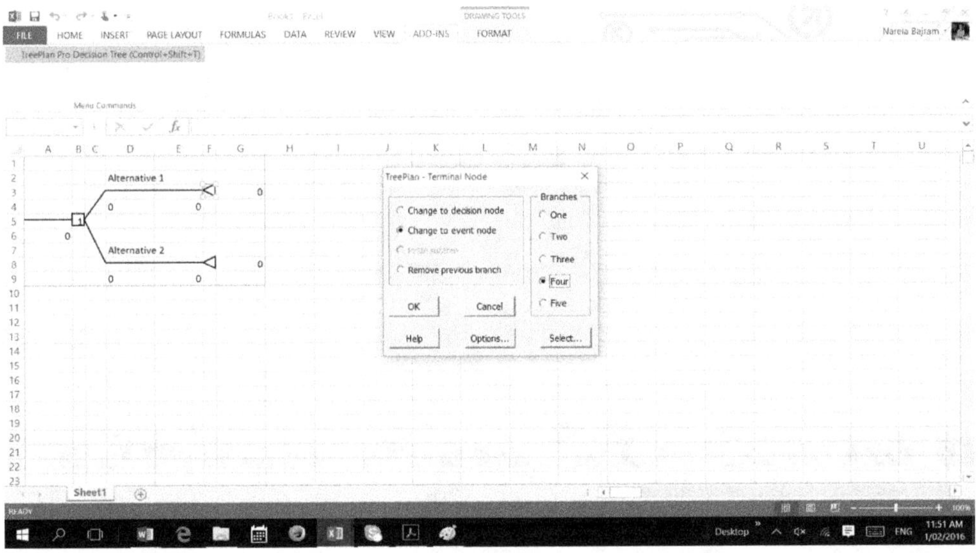

Figure 10. Adding new branch, cash flows and probabilities

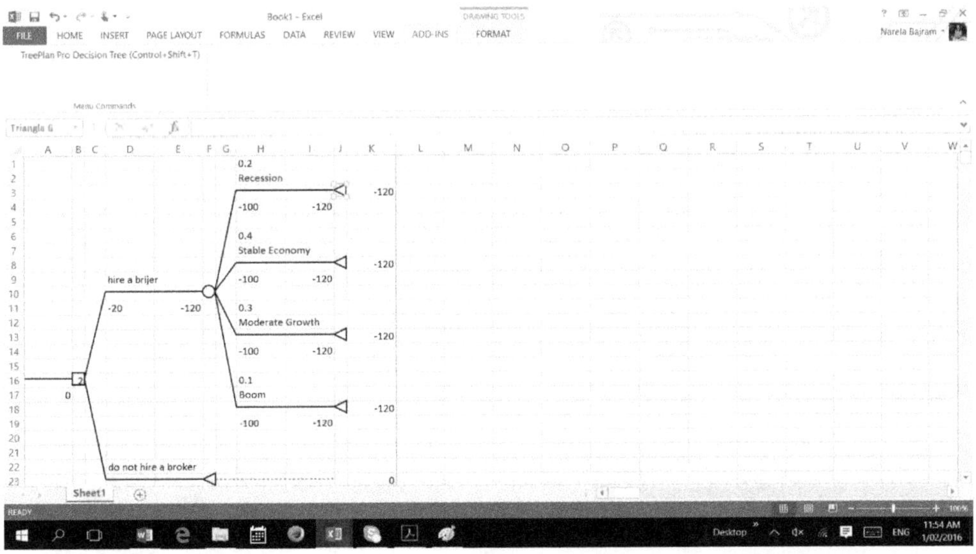

Step 3: Determine the optimal strategy from Tree Plan results

Figure 11. Determining the optimal strategy using the exponential risk utility function

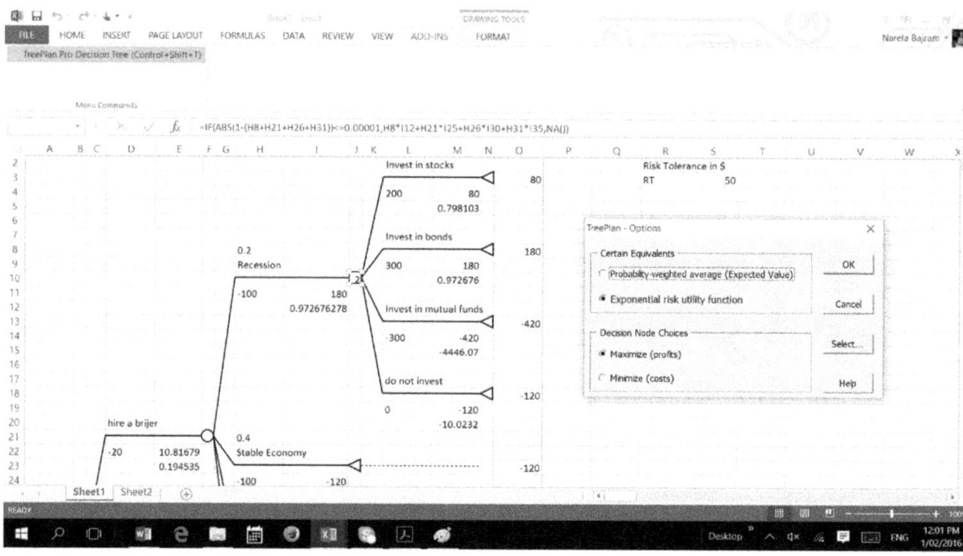

Chapter 3
Portfolio Selection Models:
Single-Period Portfolio Selection

ABSTRACT

The main goal behind the concept of portfolio management is to combine various assets into portfolios and then to manage those portfolios so as to achieve the desired investment objectives. To be more specific, the investors' needs are mostly defined in terms of profit and risk, and the portfolio manager makes a sound decision aimed ether to maximize the return or minimize the risk. The Mean-Variance and Mean-VaR analysis has gained widespread acceptance among practitioners of asset allocation. Although they are the simplest models of investment, sometimes they are sufficiently rich to be directly useful in applied problems and decision theory. Here you will learn how to apply these analyses in practice using computer programs and spreadsheets.

A little over forty years ago, a University of Chicago graduate student in economics, while in search of a dissertation topic, ran into a stockbroker who suggested that he study the stock market. Harry Markowitz took that advice and developed a theory that became a foundation of financial economics and revolutionized investment practice. His work earned him a share of the 1990 Nobel Prize in Economics. (Paul D. Kaplan, 1998, Vice President and Chief Economist).

DOI: 10.4018/978-1-5225-3259-0.ch003

MEAN-VARIANCE PORTFOLIO THEORY

In the finance textbooks, investment instrument that can be bought and sold is often called an asset. Asset allocation is a term used to describe the set of weights of broad classes of investment within a portfolio. For an individual investor, asset allocation can be represented by the investment in stocks, bonds, mutual funds and money market investments. Furthermore, the investor decisions are based on his utility function- level of welfare or satisfaction. The key reason for the utility function to be considered as a general approach to a decision making under risk is its sound theoretical basis.

Because future wealth is uncertain, investors attempt to maximize their expected value of utility. The relationship between wealth and the utility of consuming is described by a utility function, U (•). In general, each investor will have a different U (•), and we can write this formally as,

$$\max E[U(W) = \max E[U(W_1)] = E\{U[(1+\sum_{i=1}^{N} X_i R_i)X_0 \qquad (1)$$
$$subject\ \text{to}\ \sum\nolimits_i X_i = 1$$

where, E represents the expected value of investors utility function U (•), and W is the wealth. U(•) is also called as von Neumann-Morgenstern utility function, based on the game theory work.

In Markowitz mean-variance portfolio theory (M-V), the rate of return of assets is random variable. The goal is then to choose the portfolio weighting factors optimally. Meaning, the investor's portfolio achieves an acceptable expected rate of return with minimal volatility. The variance of the rate of return is taken as a proxy for the volatility.

Let us now consider constructing a portfolio consisting of *n* assets. We have an initial budget $\boldsymbol{x_0}$that we wish to assign. The amount that we assign to asset *i* is $x_{oi} = w_i x_o$ for $i = 1,2,\ldots.n$, where $\boldsymbol{w_i}$ is weighting factor for asset ***i***. What is also important to note, we allow the weights to take negative values. Here, when a negative value occurs, the asset is being shorted. Therefore, to preserve the budget constraint we require that the weights sum to be 1, $\sum_{i=1}^{n} w_1 = 1$. Thus, the sum of the investment is,

$$\sum_{i=1}^{n} w_1 x_0 = x_0 \quad \sum_{i=1}^{n} w_1 = x_0 \qquad (2)$$

The returns are also dependent on each other in a certain way and the dependence will be described by the covariance between them. The covariance between the i-th and the j-th return is denoted by,

$$\sigma_{ij} = \text{cov}\left(r_i r_j\right) = E\left(r_i - \mu_i\right)\left(r_j - \mu_j\right) \quad (3)$$

Note that in this notation, σ_{ij} stands for the variance of the return of i-th asset, r_i is the return of fund i, μ_i is the expected value or mean of r_i, r_j is the return of fund j, and μ_i is the expected value or mean of r_j.

Equation 3 is further simplified to:

$$\sigma_{ij} = E\left(r_i - \mu_i\right)^2 \quad (4)$$

Meaning, given a universe of assets with random return r_i, $i = 1, \ldots, n$, expected return μ_i, and covariance matrix $\Sigma = [\sigma_{ij}]$, we should select portfolio weights w_i adds up to one. Given a vector of weights representing the portfolio, its expected return and variance are defined in the section below.

Return

The return computation is nothing more than finding the weighted average return of the securities included in the portfolio. In some books μ is used for the return instead of $E\left[r_p\right]$.

Then, the return on portfolio is:

$$r = \sum_{i=1}^{n} w_i r_i \quad (5)$$

and the expected rate of return is:

$$E\left[r_p\right] = \sum_{i=1}^{n} w_i E\left[r_i\right] \quad (6)$$

where,

$$\sum_{i=1}^{n} w_i = 1$$

here,

n = the number of securities

w_i = the proportion of the funds invested in security i

r_i, r_p = the return on i^{th} security and portfolio

$E[\,]$ = the expectation of the variable in the parentheses

INTRODUCTION

The Mean-Variance and Mean-VaR analysis has gained widespread acceptance among practitioners of asset allocation. Although they are the simplest models of investment, sometimes they are sufficiently rich to be directly useful in applied problems and decision theory. The concept of classical portfolio management is to combine various assets into portfolios and then to manage those portfolios so as to achieve the desired investment objectives. To be more specific, the investors' needs are mostly defined in terms of profit and risk, and the portfolio manager makes a sound decision aimed ether to maximize the return or minimize the risk.

One of the best financial investing applications in 2016 is "Wealthfront". "Wealthfront" determines the optimal mix of investors chosen asset classes by solving the Efficient Frontier using Mean-Variance Optimization model developed by Markowitz in 1952. This is the foundation of Modern Portfolio Theory where the efficient frontier represents the portfolios that generate the maximum return for every level of risk. Each portfolio is created by choosing a particular mix of asset classes that maximizes the expected return for a specific level of risk, or equivalently minimizes the risk for a specific expected return. The mean - variance model calculates the best risk-return trade-off when combining the asset classes in portfolios. Here the specific level of risk is measured by variance, which could also be defined as a measure of the volatility. The main problem with volatility, however, is that it does not care about the direction of an investment's movement: a stock can be volatile because it suddenly jumps higher. Of course, investors are not distressed by gains.

I do not know the criteria they used to compile the list of 2016 best investment application. But for sure I know that we need to be cautious when we select the application that we intend to use as a guide for our investments.

So, let us see what history has to say in the legislation of risk measurements in financial markets and institutions.

Back in 1973, the Bretton Woods system was replaced by a regime based on freely floating fiat currencies. Following this change, several crashes appear and the volatility explodes with the creation of derived product

For that reason, in the late 1980s, the Bankers Trust bank used for the first time the notion of Value at Risk. However, it was in the 90's, when JP Morgan created RiskMetrics, that the Value at Risk was really used. Sir Dennis Weatherstone, chairman of JP Morgan, wanted to have some daily reports measuring and explaining the firm's risks. Yet, these indicators are specific to each market and not explicit. The need for a well-defined measure of risk was more than obvious. And then we witnessed the Barings Bank Disaster.

- Nicholas Leeson, an employee of Barings Bank in the Singapore office in 1995, had a mandate to look for arbitrage opportunities between the Nikkei 225 futures prices on the Singapore exchange and the Osaka exchange. Over time Leeson moved from being an arbitrageur to being a speculator without anyone in the Barings London head office fully understanding that he had changed the way he was using derivatives.
- In 1994, Leeson was thought to have made $20 million for Barings, one-fifth of the total firm's profit. He drew a $150,000 salary with a $1 million bonus.
- He began to make losses, which he was able to hide. He then began to take bigger speculative positions in an attempt to recover the losses, but only resulted in making the losses worse.
- In 1995, Leeson's total loss was close to 1 billion dollars. As a result, Barings – a bank that had been in existence for 200 years – was wiped out.
- The lesson to be learnt: Both financial and nonfinancial corporations must set up controls to ensure that derivatives are used for their intended purpose. Risk limits should be set and the activities of traders should be monitored daily to ensure that the risk limits are adhered to.

After this lesson in 1995, the Value at Risk was really defined. For investors risk is about the odds of losing money, and VaR as a measure of risk is based on that common-sense fact. By assuming investors care about the odds of a really big loss, VaR answers the question, "What is my worst-case scenario with a given confidence level?" or "How much could I lose in a really bad month?"

So VaR measure gives us a unique definition and a standard risk indicator and was part of the proposition of the Basel II Committee in 2004. It is one of many recommendations (like the utilization of the McDonough ratio instead of the Cook ratio) but after the Basel II, VaR is one of the most used in the financial institution. In order to calculate VaR, most of the financial institutions chose to base their calculation on historical data, over a year. But the 2007 subprime crisis highlighted the limits and the weaknesses remaining in the regulatory measure taken by the Basel II Committee. It was an obligation to fill those gaps and to regulate financial markets and at the same time give some recommendation about risk measurement.

That is why financial institution in December 2010 moved to the stressed VaR. Here we take the value of a year that is representative of a crisis year (depending on the asset we are looking at, it can be for example be the 2007 subprime crisis) and then use the same method used for the VaR calculation using an historic method. This is known as a stressed VaR.

The new risk indicator was than composed by the regular VaR and the stressed one. You can easily see the problem here: if the last year is the worst one, your risk indicator is based on twice the same data. This is where the Basel III Committee gave a new recommendation that should be used in 2016: The Expected Shortfall (ES). Expected Shortfall brings the investors loss average if an extreme event occurs.

For example: Suppose that the VaR at the 99% confidence level of portfolio A is 5 million and that of portfolio B is 8 million. Given these numbers, one may conclude that portfolio B is riskier than portfolio A. However, the investor does not know how much may be lost outside of the confidence interval. When the maximum loss of portfolio A is 1 trillion and that of B is 12 million, portfolio A should be considered as risky one since it loses much more than portfolio B under the worst case. In this case, VaR has tail risk since VaR fails to summarize the choice between portfolios A and B as a result of its disregard of the tail of profit/loss distributions

The Basel III Committee also had to recalibrate the level of confidence in order to stay consistent. That is why, instead of using the 99% level of confidence like for the VaR, the Basel III Committee recommends to use the 97.5% level of confidence for the ES. It allows you to capture the same risk level. In addition, the Basel Committee on Banking Supervision has been revising its market risk framework since 2012. The result of its 'fundamental review of the trading book' (FRTB, BCBS 219) is expected to be implemented by January 2018, with 2016-17 scheduled for calibration and testing. The consultation phase of the new regulatory framework is still ongoing and has featured several Quantitative Impact Studies, highlighting the framework's complexity.

The point of this chapter is to explain the Mean-Variance and Mean – VaR analysis, as well as the Expected Shortfall and to explain how to implement them in practice using computer programs and spreadsheets. We will conclude with their shortcomings.

RISK

Variance is used to model volatility or risk of the portfolio. For a single security the variance is:

$$\begin{aligned} \operatorname{var}(r) &= E\left[r - E[r]\right]^2 = \\ &= E\left[\left(\sum_{i=1}^{n} w_i \left(r_i - E\left[r_i - E[r_i]\right]\right)\right)\right]^2 = \\ &= E\left[\left(\sum_{i,j=1}^{n} w_i w_j \left(r_i - E[r_i]\right)\left(r_j - E[r_j]\right)\right)\right]^2 = \\ &= \sum_{i,j=1}^{n} \sigma_{ij} w_i w_j = \\ &= w^T \sum w \end{aligned} \tag{7}$$

and for the portfolio:

$$Var\left(r_p\right) = \sum_{i=1}^{n}\sum_{j=1}^{n} w_i w_j \rho_{ij} \sigma_i \sigma_j \text{ Equation} \qquad 8$$

where,

ρ_{ij}	=	correlation coefficient between the rates of return on security r_i and r_j
σ_i and σ_j	=	standard deviations of and respectively
w_i and w_j	=	corresponding weights

INVESTING BASICS: THE EFFICIENT PORTFOLIO

Asset allocation modelling is best learned by applying the M-V framework to concrete examples. Through this application in real data examples, we should understand the power and in the same time the limitations of this model.

This section begins with the development of a two asset-class problem, where the investor seeks to diversify. In the first example, we analyze less risky and highly risky assets, while the second considers only highly risky assets. The Excel Outboxes will illustrate how to build and solve the problem (see Appendix 1). Following the two-asset class example, we will extend the model to more asset classes.

The portfolio whose variance is the minimum for the corresponding mean is known as an efficient portfolio. In other words, it illustrates the trade-off that exists between expected return and risk. In the construction of the efficient portfolio frontier, we will discover the benefit of the diversification.

Two Assets Problem

Amina has a total of $50.000 and she is planning to make an investment in the US market of assets. She chose to invest in American Funds US Government Securities (AMUSX) as a less risky assets or/and in USAA Mutual Fund Trust Precious Metal & Minerals Fund (USAGX) as highly risky asset. She needs to decide how much of the $50.000 to invest in AMUSX and how much to invest in USAGX. This decision will determine Amina's portfolio. Table 1 gives the characteristic of each asset.

Suppose that Amina held only the fund B with expected return of 0.49% and standard deviation of 0.088%. She wants to increase the return and accept higher risk if necessary. Suppose that Amina sells some Fund B and construct a new portfolio, allocating her money 40% in fund A and 60% in fund B. The expected rate of return for this portfolio is:

Table 1. Return and Risk

Parameters	Fund A (USAGX)	Fund B(AMUSX)
E(r) or μ	99.45%	0.49%
σ	-1.45%	0.088%
ρ	-0.68	

Note: The data used for the calculation is obtained on the basis of Independent Investment Research, Morningstar (available online: http://www.morningstar.com/) for the period January 2012-June 2014.

$$E[r_p] = w_{fa}E(r_{fa}) + w_{fb}E(r_{fb}) \tag{8}$$

Here, w_{fa} and w_{fb} are the weights of the assets in the portfolio, and subscripts *fa* and *fb* refer to fund A and fund B respectively. Therefore,

$$E[r_p] = (0.4)(99.45) + (0.6)(0.49) = 40.074\% \tag{9}$$

As we can notice Amina has been able to increase the expected rate of return on portfolio from 0.49% to 40.074%. But the higher expected return is related to higher risk. Therefore, the cost of obtaining the highest expected rate of return is:

$$\sigma_p^2 = \left(w_{fa}\sigma_{fa}\right)^2 + \left(w_{fb}\sigma_{fb}\right) + 2w_{fa}w_{fb}\sigma_{fa}\sigma_{fb}\rho \tag{10}$$

or in our case the variance is:

$$\sigma_p^2 = \left[(0.4)(-1.45)\right]^2 + \left[(0.6)(0.088)\right]^2 + 2(0.4)(0.6)(-1.45)(0.088)(-0.68) = 0.283\%$$

and the standard deviation of the portfolio is the square root of the variance.

$$\sigma_p = \sqrt[2]{\sigma_p^2} = 0.532\% \tag{11}$$

In sum, by adding the fund A with a higher rate of return and risk, Amina has been able to increase the expected return to 40.074%, but the overall risk of the portfolio also increased, from 0.088% to 0.532%. In Table 2 are shown various combinations/ portfolios, which might help Amina to make the decision.

Now we can plot the efficient frontier as a line, defined by the lower level of risk for each level of return. For diversified portfolios, the efficient frontier plot is typically a curved line and Figure 1 shows a straight line through the component assets. In Amina's case, there are no gains to be made from diversification. Thus, no portfolio can be discarded as inefficient, and the choice among portfolios depends only on risk preference. Equation 11 points to the proportions that will reduce the portfolio standard deviation to zero (see Table 2).

Table 2. Amina's portfolio combinations

Weights		Variance σ^2	Risk σ	Return E (r)
Fund A (USAGX)	Fund B (AMUSX)			
100%	0%	0.021%	1.45%	99.45%
90%	10%	0.017%	1.31%	89.55%
80%	20%	0.014%	1.17%	79.66%
70%	30%	0.011%	1.03%	69.76%
60%	40%	0.008%	0.89%	59.87%
50%	50%	0.006%	0.76%	49.97%
40%	60%	0.004%	0.62%	40.07%
30%	70%	0.002%	0.48%	30.18%
20%	80%	0.001%	0.34%	20.28%
10%	90%	0.000%	0.21%	10.39%
0%	100%	0.000%	0.09%	0.49%

Figure 1. The efficient frontier

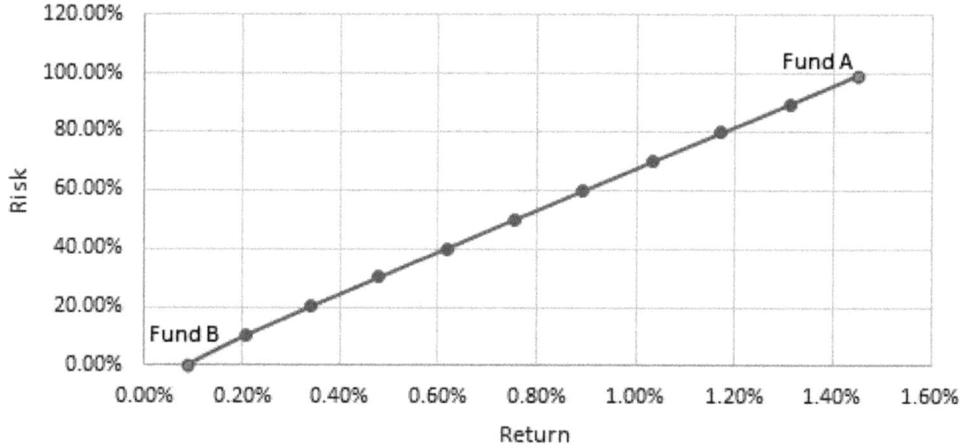

Two-Risky-Assets Problem

Amina has a total of $50.000 and she is planning to make an investment in the US market of assets. She chose to invest in two risky assets:

1. USAA Mutual Fund Trust Precious Metal & Minerals Fund (USAGX), and

2. Fidelity Contra Fund (FCNTX).

She needs to decide how much of the \$50.000 to invest in AMUSX and/ or how much to invest in USAGX. This decision will determine Amina's portfolio. Table 3 gives the characteristic of each asset.

Scenario 1

Suppose that Amina held only the fund B with an expected return of 8.70% and a standard deviation of 1.68%. She wants to increase the return and accept higher risk if necessary. Suppose that Amina sells some Fund B and constructs a new portfolio, allocating her money 40% in fund A and 60% in fund B.

The expected rate of return for this portfolio calculated as in equation 9 is:

$$E\left[r_p\right] = (0.4)(99.45) + (0.6)(8.7) = 45\%$$

As we can notice Amina has been able to increase the expected rate of return on portfolio from 8.7% to 45%. But higher return is related to higher risk. Therefore, the cost of obtaining the highest expected rate of return using equation 10 is:

$$\sigma_p^2 = \left[(0.4)(-1.45)\right]^2 + \left[(0.6)(1.68)\right]^2 + 2(0.4)(0.6)(-1.45)(1.68)(0.11) = 1.22\%$$

and the standard deviation is:

$$\sigma_p = \sqrt[2]{\sigma_p^2} = \sqrt[2]{1.22} = 1.105\%$$

Table 3. Risk and Return

	Fund A (USAGX)	Fund B (FCNTX)
Return E (r)	99.45%	8.70%
Risk σ	-1.45%	1.68%
ρ	0.11	

In sum, by reallocating some of the money to the fund A with a higher rate of return, Amina has increased the expected return to 45%, and reduce the overall risk of the portfolio from 1.68% to 1.105%.

In this example, we can see the power of the diversification.

Scenario 2

Now suppose that Amina liked what she saw happen, and decide to invest more of her money in fund A. So, her portfolio is 70% in fund A and 30% in fund B. What will be the expected rate of return and standard deviation of this portfolio?

Equations 9 and 10 will help us to calculate the $E[r_p]$ and σ_p^2. Thus,

$$E\left[r_p\right] = \left(0.7\right)\left(99.45\right) + \left(0.3\right)\left(8.7\right) = 72.23\%,$$

and,

$$\sigma_p^2 = \left[\left(0.7\right)\left(-1.45\right)\right]^2 + \left[\left(0.3\right)\left(1.68\right)\right]^2 + 2\left(0.7\right)\left(0.3\right)\left(-1.45\right)\left(1.68\right)\left(0.11\right) = 1.93\%$$
$$\sigma_p = \sqrt[2]{\sigma_p^2} = \sqrt[2]{1.22} = 1.39\%$$

We can notice that the expected rate of return has increased also the risk. In Table 4 are shown various combinations/ portfolios, which might help Amina to decide.

Amina now can see that if she chooses to diversify her portfolio then she can increase the expected return and at the same time decrease the risk. For example: *If she chooses to invest only in Fund B then the E [r] =8. 7% and the σ=1. 68%. But if she invests 80% in Fund B and 20% in Fund A than E [r] =26. 85% and the σ=1. 34, meaning the portfolio containing only Fund B is not efficient.*

Now we can plot the efficient frontier as line, defined by the lower level of risk for each level of return. This is illustrated in Figure 2. For diversified portfolios, the efficient frontier plot is typically a curved line.

Portfolios that lie below the efficient frontier are sub-optimal, because they do not provide enough return for the level of risk. The best possible portfolio selection for a given amount of risk lies on the efficient frontier curve, and

Table 4. Various portfolio combinations

	Weights		Variance σ^2	Risk σ	Return E (r)
	Fund A (USAGX)	Fund B (FCNTX)			
	100%	0%	0.02%	1.45%	99.45%
	90%	10%	0.02%	1.30%	90.38%
	80%	20%	0.01%	1.17%	81.30%
	70%	30%	0.01%	1.08%	72.23%
	60%	40%	0.01%	1.04%	63.15%
	50%	50%	0.01%	1.05%	54.08%
	40%	60%	0.01%	1.11%	45.00%
	30%	70%	0.01%	1.21%	35.93%
	20%	80%	0.02%	1.34%	26.85%
	10%	90%	0.02%	1.50%	17.78%
	0%	100%	0.03%	1.68%	8.70%
MVR	50%	50%	0.01%	1.05%	54.08%
Stock A (USAGX)	100%	0%	0.02%	1.45%	99.45%
Stock B (FCNTX)	0%	100%	0.03%	1.68%	8.70%

Figure 2. The efficient frontier

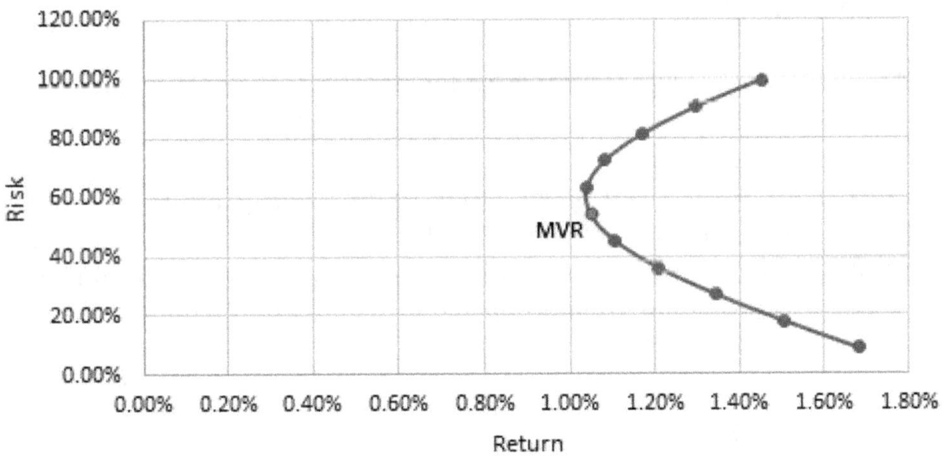

are also called the optimal portfolios. Moreover, the frontier has two regions defined by the portfolios expected return.

$$\begin{array}{ll} Region\ I & \mu_{target} \geq \mu_{MVR} \\ Region\ II & \mu_{target} < \mu_{MVR} \end{array}$$

In the Figure 2, the minimum variance portfolio (MVR) lies at the left most point of the curve. This is a portfolio with the lowest risk across all levels of return. Therefore, the efficient frontier consists only of the portfolios where $\mu_{target} \geq \mu_{MVR}$, and the rational investors will only hold these portfolios.

N Asset Problem and Optimal Portfolio Selection

Amina has a total of $50.000 and she is planning to make an investment in the US market of assets. She chose to invest in the following 5assets:

1. Stock Yards Bancorp, Inc. (SYBT)
2. Amedicn Corporation (AMDA)
3. Trans Enterix (TRXC)
4. Ipath S&P 500 VIX ST Future ETN (VXX)
5. Apple Inc. (AAPL)

She needs to decide how much of the $50.000 to invest in each asset. This decision will determine Amina's optimal portfolio. Table 5 gives the characteristic of each asset.

If there are only two risky assets, we can easily identify the set of portfolios by examining a range of potential weights for one asset, and then create the M-V frontier. However, this technique is not feasible with more than two assets, because there are too many possible asset weight combinations.

Table 5. Risk and Return

	SYBT	AMDA	TRXC	VXX	AAPL
Return E(r) or μ	-0.2051%	16.7074%	-0.7800%	1.3557%	-0.1917%
Risk σ	1.6672%	0.656326	0.075867	0.060351	0.024152

Note: The data used is obtained on the basis of Yahoo Finance (available online: http://finance.yahoo.com/) for the period January 6th – January 27th, 2016.

Therefore, in this section we will explore a more general approach that may be applied to n>2 assets.

We will use Excel Solver to find Amina's Optimal Portfolio (explained in Appendix 2).

The optimal portfolio excels outbox describes how to identify the particular portfolio that Amina would select for a given level of return or for a given level of risk aversion (λ).

Now we are in a position to state the optimization problem. The optimization problem behind the first formulation of mean-variance analysis is,

$$\begin{aligned} \min \quad & w^T \sum w \\ s.t. \quad & w^T \mu = \mu_i \\ & \sum_{i=1}^{n} w_1 = 1 \\ & \mathrm{w}_i \geq 0 \end{aligned} \tag{12}$$

Similarly, the optimization problem behind the second formulation is,

$$\begin{aligned} \max \quad & \mu^T w - \frac{\lambda}{2} w^T \sum w \\ s.t. \quad & \sum_{i=1}^{n} w_1 = 1 \\ & \mathrm{w}_i \geq 0 \end{aligned} \tag{13}$$

Scenario 1. Quadratic Programming Model for Portfolio Optimization: Constraint Approach (Minimize the Risk)

Minimize	→	the portfolio standard deviation
By choosing	→	the weights of the risky assets
Subject to	→	a fully invested portfolio/budget constraint for a given level of return

This can be translated into the program:

$$\begin{aligned} & \min \rightarrow w^T \sum w \\ & s.t. \rightarrow w^T \mu = \mu_i \\ & \qquad \sum_{i=1}^{n} w_1 = 1 \\ & \qquad w_i \geq 0 \end{aligned}$$

The first step is to calculate the individual assets mean (μ), standard deviation (σ) and sharpe ratio (SR). (See Table 6)

Using Excel Solver we generate the following results:

Table 7 shows that the return on the minimum variance portfolio is μ_{mvr} = 0. 1535% and σ_{mvr} = 0. 6512%. This is the portfolio with the lowest risk across all levels of return.

Suppose that Amina wants to construct a portfolio that has a return equal or higher than AMDA's return μ=16. 7074%. As you can notice in Table 6 AMDA has the highest return, compared to other individual assets. We would really want to see the Amina's return after the optimization process. Could she get the AMDA's return and at the same time decrease the overall risk? The solution shown in Table 7 is not all that interesting. It suggests Amina allocates her money only on stock AMDA. Meaning there are no gains to be had from diversification.

Table 6. Mean, standard deviation and sharpe ratio

Individual Assets			
	Return μ	**Risk σ**	**SR= μ/σ**
SYBT	-0.2051%	**1.6672%**	-0.12304
AMDA	**16.7074%**	65.6326%	**0.254559**
TRXC	-0.7800%	7.5867%	-0.10281
VXX	1.3557%	6.0351%	0.224628
AAPL	-0.1917%	2.4152%	-0.07938

Table 7. Portfolio with the lowest risk across all levels of return

Weights	**MVR**	**Target return is 16.7074%**	**Target return is 8%**
SYBT, W_1	39.59%	0%	0%
AMDA, W_2	0.11%	100%	43.28%
TRXC, W_3	0.00%	0%	0%
VXX, W_4	21.42%	0%	56.72%
AAPL, W_5	38.88%	0%	0%
Return μ	0.1535%	16.71%	8%
Risk σ	0.6512%	65.47%	29.28%
Sharpe ratio	0.24	0.26	0.27

Now suppose that Amina's target return (μ) is 8%. Here, in order to optimize the return in the portfolio Amina should invest 43.28% in stock AMDA, and 56.72 in stock VXX.

Scenario 2. Quadratic Programming Models for Portfolio Optimization by Risk Factor 1 (Maximize the Return)

Maximize	→	the investor's utility given his/her level of risk aversion
By choosing	→	the weights of the risky assets
Subject to	→	a fully invested portfolio-budget constraint for a given level of risk

This translates into the equation:

$$\begin{aligned} \max \quad & \mu^T w - \frac{\lambda}{2} w^T \sum w \\ s.t. \quad & \sum\nolimits_{i=1}^{n} w_1 = 1 \\ & \mathrm{w}_i \geq 0 \end{aligned}$$

Suppose that Amina wants to construct a portfolio that has a standard deviation equal or lower than SYBT's standard deviation, σ=1.6672%. In Table 6 you can notice that SYBT has the lowest standard deviation, compared to other individual assets. Amina wants to know if she can construct a portfolio that has equal or lower standard deviation than stock SYBT.

Using Excel Solver we generate the following results:

Table 8 show that Amina should invest 1.73% in AMDA, 2.38% in TRXC, 35.27% in VXX and 60.62% in AAPL, in order to optimize the risk in the portfolio.

Common sense and experience suggest risk aversion coefficients to be in the range between 2 and 4. To specify, from a mathematical perspective coefficient 1 can be interpreted as a risk aversion coefficient. By changing the value of l, we can trace the efficient set. Unfortunately, it is a bit difficult to get a feeling for the parameter l. Anyway, common sense and experience suggest risk aversion coefficients λ in the range between 2 and 4. Therefore, we calculate the weights for two more scenarios where the target risk is 3 and 4. The results are shown in Table 8.

From a mathematical perspective, this is a Quadratic programming model. Coefficient l can be interpreted as a risk aversion coefficient, λ. By changing

Table 8. Portfolio with equal or lower standard deviation than stock SYBT

Weights	Target risk is 1.6672%	Target risk is 3	Target risk is 4
SYBT, W_1	0%	0%	0%
AMDA, W_2	1.73%	3.41%	4.6%
TRXC, W_3	2.38%	0.41%	0%
VXX, W_4	35.27%	43.13%	49.01%
AAPL, W_5	60.62%	53.06%	46.38%
Return μ	0.63%	1.05%	1.34%
Risk σ	1.67%	3%	4%
Sharpe ratio	0.38	0.35	0.34

the value of l, we can trace the efficient set. Unfortunately, it is a bit difficult to get a feeling for the parameter l. Anyway, common sense and experience suggest risk aversion coefficients λ in the range between 2 and 4. Therefore, we calculate the weights for three scenarios where λ is 3 and 4 (See Table 8).

Scenario 3. Maximize the Sharpe Ratio (SR)

The Sharpe ratio describes how much excess return Amina will receive for the extra risk/volatility that she bears for holding a riskier asset. Now suppose that Amina wants to maximize her sharp ratio (SR). Using Excel Solver we generate the following results:

Diversification will allow Amina to achieve a much higher Sharpe ratio than she can get by using any of the individual assets by itself.

Table 9. Maximize the Sharpe Ratio (SR)

Weights	Max SR
SYBT, W_1	13.85%
AMDA, W_2	1.01%
TRXC, W_3	1.52%
VXX, W_4	29.64%
AAPL, W_5	53.98%
Return μ	0.43%
Risk σ	1.09%
Sharpe ratio	0.39

MEAN-VALUE AT RISK

Markowitz in his mean-variance portfolio optimization model used the portfolio variance as a risk measure. It is a measurement of the spread between numbers in a data set. The variance treats both upside and downside payoffs symmetrically. However, while most investors will be disturbed by a drop in prices, most investors will not mind an increase in price. In other word, variance as a risky measure does not sufficiently describe the asset return distribution.

One alternative measure of risk is the Value of Risk (VAR). It measures the worst expected loss over a given time horizon at a given confidence level, 95% or 99% (Best, 1998). Worldwide adoption of the Basel II Accord, beginning in 1999 and approaching its completion in 2009, gives further impetus to the use of VAR. Although the concept of VAR is quite simple and easy to understand, the implementation of value at risk is not an easy job.

The Value at Risk could be calculated in 3 ways:

- Variance-Covariance Method (parametric approach).
- Historical method (non-parametric approach).
- Monte Carlo simulation (non-parametric approach).

In this section, first we will use the variance-covariance method to calculate the portfolio VAR, then apply the historical approach and at the end simulate the shape of the distribution to check if the daily stock returns follow the Gaussian distribution pattern.

Variance-Covariance Method

The variance - covariance method is known also as Liner VaR of Delta normal VaR. It is a parametric approach because when using it, we make the assumption that the returns are normally distributed. This assumption allows volatility to be described in terms of standard deviation, σ.

To calculate the portfolio VaR, we consider the n-asset problem example from the previous section.

Amina has a total of $50.000 and she is planning to make an investment in the US market of assets. She chose to invest in thc following 5 assets:

1. Stock Yards Bancorp, Inc. (SYBT).
2. Amedicn Corporation (AMDA).

3. Trans Enterix (TRXC).
4. Ipath S&P 500 VIX ST Future ETN (VXX).
5. Apple Inc. (AAPL).

She needs to decide how much of the $50.000 to invest in each asset. This decision will determine Amina's optimal portfolio. Table 10 gives the characteristic of each asset.

The mean - VaR model is used to optimize Amina's portfolio (see Appendix 3).

The first step is to calculate the individual asset VaRs by using the following formula:

$$VaR_{asset} = (ZVP) \tag{14}$$

where, Z is the standard value (for 95% confidence level is 1.64), V is the volatility/standard deviation of the asset, and P is the asset value/position. Therefore,

$$VaR_{SYBT} = 1.64 * 1.667 * 42,655.86 = \$1,165.75$$

Excel Solver will generate the Table 11 with the individual stock VaRs.

Then, using a matrix formula given in equation 15 we calculate the portfolio VaR.

$$VaRp = \left(VCV^t\right)^{1/2} \tag{15}$$

where, V is a row vector of VaRs for each individual position, C is a matrix of correlation, and V^t is the transpose of the matrix V.

Table 10. Risk and return

	SYBT	AMDA	TRXC	VXX	AAPL
Return E (r) or μ	-0.2051%	16.7074%	-0.7800%	1.3557%	-0.1917%
Risk σ	1.6672%	0.656326	0.075867	0.060351	0.024152

Note: The data used is obtained on the basis of Yahoo Finance (available online: http://finance.yahoo.com/) for the period January 6th – January 27th,2016.

Table 11. Individual and total asset VaRs

	Volatility/Standard Deviation	Position	Individual VaRs
SYBT	1.667%	$ 19,793.87	$ 646.80
AMDA	65.633%	$ 56.34	$ 72.48
TRXC	7.587%	$ 0	$ -
VXX	6.035%	$ 10,711.64	$ 1,267.07
AAPL	2.415%	$ 19,438.15	$ 920.16
Confidence Level 95%		1.96	
Total		$50,000.00	$ 2,906.50

In Amina's case the portfolio $VaR_{95\%}$ is $2,204.93. Meaning, she is 95% confident that her loss will not exceed $2,204.93 over a one day horizon if she invests $19,793.87 in stock SYBT, $56.34 in stock AMDA, $10,711.64 in stock VXX and $19,438.15 in stock AAPL.

As we can notice from the calculation above, the portfolios VaR is lower than the sum of the individual VARs, 2,204.93 < 2,906.50. This is the positive side of the diversification.

Historical Method

The use of the normal distribution to assess the risk-return trade off will result in an incorrect allocation of assets for investors with low risk tolerance and risk managers wishing to set 99% confidence level. Therefore, instead of trying to specify the distribution of the portfolio return, we can use historical data to simulate the shape of the distribution.

The fundamental assumption of the historical methodology is that we base our results on the past performance of our portfolio and make the assumption that the past is a good indicator of the near-future.

Follow the Appendix 3, for the second part of the historical model. The first step lies in setting the time interval and calculating the daily returns. I choose the *Amedicn Corporation (AMDA)* stock for the period January 6th – January 27th, 2016.For the normal distribution return we need to calculate the mean and the standard deviation of the returns, μ=0. 056 and σ=0. 256.

We want to find the 10% VaR or $VaR_{90\%.}$ We will use the NORMINV formula function in Excel and solve for $VaR_{90\%}$ = -0.27. Meaning, with 90% confidence the loss will not exceed 27% or $13,606.90.

The next step is to analyze the historical data. To calculate the 10% VaR, we need the number of observations. In our case n=14. Now for 10% VaR, we need to look at the bottom 10% cases which is 1.4. The number 1.4 lies between 2nd and 1st return. Using Excel formula functions, we calculate the 2nd and 1st return, -0.132 and -0.142 respectively. Based on this, the 1.4th return or $VaR_{90\%}$ = -0.138. This means that Amina is 90% sure that her maximum loss will be 13,8%.

If we go back and compare this number with the normal distribution VaR, we can notice that is totally different (normal $VaR_{90\%}$=-0.27 and historical $VaR_{90\%}$=-0.138). This tells us that the returns distribution is not strictly normal.

Using the Data Analysis add-in we can easily find the distribution characteristic using the descriptive statistics (see Table 12).

By definition, for normal distribution the kurtosis and skewness should be 0. In our case, as shown in Table 12, the kurtosis is 11.538, meaning that the distribution has heavier tails and sharper peak than the normal distribution. On the other hand, skewness is 3.26, meaning frequent small negative outcomes, and extremely bad scenarios are not as likely. These two measurements show us the deviation from normality. But we should be very careful in using the skewness and kurtosis, because when the sample sizes are small they can give results that are very misleading.

Table 12. Descriptive statistics

Column 1	
Mean	0.0560872
Standard Error	0.0684498
Median	-0.0003137
Mode	#N/A
Standard Deviation	0.2561155
Sample Variance	0.0655952
Kurtosis	11.539878
Skewness	3.2600787
Range	1.0539896
Minimum	-0.1415929
Maximum	0.9123967
Sum	0.7852206
Count	14

Figure 3. Frequency distribution

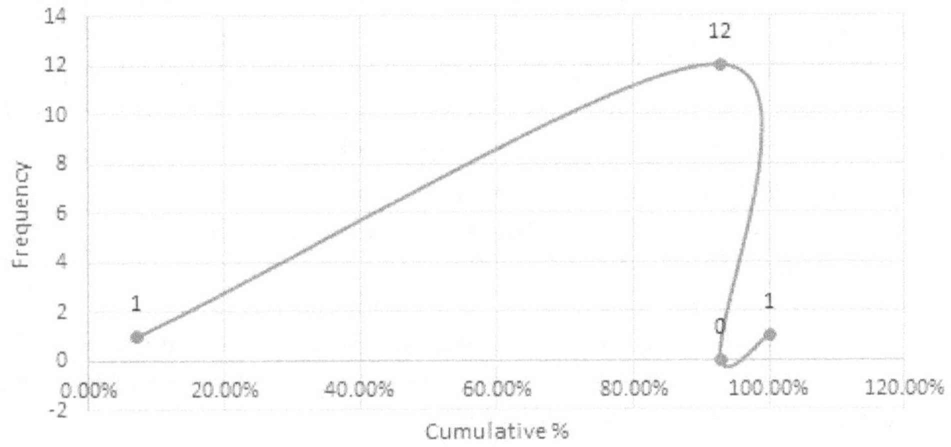

We can also have a look at the shape of the rate distribution by using the histogram in data analysis and scatter plots.

EXPECTED SHORTFALLS

Next, we calculate the expected shortfalls (ES), which represents the expected value of all changes in the portfolio value in the tail. So, the value of the expected shortfall with a probability α is:

$$ES\alpha = E\ \left(X \mid\ X \leq\ \ VaR\alpha\ \left(X\right)\right)$$

The point is to have a metrics close to the VaR, which takes into account the maximal loss; a loss that is worse than the VaR. That also allows one, to take a longer period to trace the history of the crisis and have some indication on some stressed periods.

Why is this so important? We know that events that break banks and other financial institutions do not occur under normal market conditions. This switch from VaR to Expected Shortfall suggested in Basel III Accord reflects a fundamental change in philosophy for market risk calculation and management. In the current Basel II framework, a bank has to survive in normal market conditions with a given confidence level, while the goal of Basel III is to ensure survival in extreme market conditions by capturing tail risks.

We will consider the example given in the previous section. Here the historical 5% VaR told us that we are 95% confident that the loss will not be more than the 9.9% between the January 6th, 2016 and January 26th, 2016 (see Appendix 3). But Amina's concern is what if this is not true? What about the other 5% of which we are not confident? If an extreme event happened, what would be her loss on the average? This is what is known as an expected shortfall or conditional tail expectation.

So in order to calculate the ES, we have to look at the average of the value exceeding 9.9%. In our case if the worst 5% comes true Amin's lose on average will be $ES_{95\%} = 13.7\%$.

It is important to point out that by the Basel III Committee regulations ES should be computed on a duration of ten years, and VaR from the last year data which is not the case in our example.

For easy calculation of both risk measurement, VaR and ES, you can use the following link: http://users.polytech.unice.fr/~dufour/ESCalculator/

Just copy/paste your data in the Date/Price column and choose your confidence level. Then just click on compute to get your results.

It is important to point out that neither VaR nor ES is able to forecast a maximum loss. Both risk measures provide instead a statistical estimation that is valid under normal market conditions – a fact that even senior management sometimes needs to be reminded of.

CONCLUDING REMARKS

If you have a pilot flying a plane who doesn't understand there can be storms, what is going to happen?" he asked. "He is not going to have a magnificent flight. Any small error is going to crash a plane. This is why the crisis that happened was predictable. (Nassim Nicolas Taleb, The Black Swan, 2007)

Since Markowitz published his seminal works on mean-variance portfolio selection in 1952 and 1968, his classical model has been serving as a basis of modern finance theory. The mathematical formulation of the Markowitz's portfolio selection problem is the trade-off between risk and return which combines probability theory and optimization theory to model the behavior of the economic agent. This is the first quantitative treatment of the theory and we cannot call it Modern Portfolio Theory (MPT) as some people, and use it as a main workforce on which analytical portfolio management is based. We should be very careful because this classical model is valid if the return is multi-varieties normally distributed and the investor is averse to risk (prefers lower risk), or if for any given return which is multi-varieties distributed the investor has a quadratic objective function.

As Britten-Jones (1999) notes: "Mean-Variance analysis is important for both practitioners and researchers in finance. For practitioners, theory suggests that mean-variance efficient portfolios can play an important role in portfolio management application. For researchers in finance mean-variance analysis is central to many asset pricing theories as well as to empirical tests of those theories; however, practitioners have reported difficulties in implementing mean-variance analysis."

The difficulties in implementing this analysis in practice mainly arise as a result of the following four assumptions:

- Single-period model. Meaning, investors can only make decisions at the beginning and must wait for the results without adjusting the portfolio weights until the end of the horizon.
- Preferences depend only on the mean and variance of payoffs.
    - At a given mean, lower variance is preferred.
    - At a given variance, a higher mean is preferred.
- Price-taking with no taxes or transaction costs (known as the assumption of "perfect capital markets").
- Expected return, standard deviation and correlation are treated as population parameters. However, in practice these parameters are unavailable. Instead, statistical estimates must be used, where estimation errors can change the optimization results. To minimize this errors investors should have enough historical data. But what if new assets are listed on the market, there is no past information for these securities.
- The results can sometimes be unstable. Meaning a small move along the efficient frontier could correspond to a large change in asset allocation. This can happen if the investor includes very similar assets in the analysis.

In recent year, VaR has become a new benchmark for managing and control risk (Jorion, 1997). As we showed above it measures the worst expected loss over a given time interval under normal market conditions at a given confidence level, and provides users a summary measure of market risk. Unfortunately, VaR based risk management has also few shortcomings. First, VaR measures have difficulties aggregating individual risk, and sometimes discourage diversification (Artzner et.al, 1998). Second, the VaR based risk management is only focusing on controlling the probability of loss, rather than its magnitude (Basak and Shapiro, 1999). The expected losses, may be higher, sometimes with catastrophic outcomes. As David Eingorm, who founded Greenlight Capital- a prominent hedge fund, noted: "This is like an air bag that works all the time, except when you have a car accident." Third, it assumes that the distribution of returns in the future is similar to that in the past, which might not necessarily be true. As the risk consultant Marc Groz puts it, "The years 2005-2006," which were the culmination of the housing bubble, "aren't a very good universe for predicting what happened in 2007-2008."

So what now? It seems that the fact that we could lose a certain amount of money 95% or 99% of the time tells us absolutely nothing about what could happen the other 5 or even 1 percent of the time. Therefore, in the last section we presented the Expected Shortfall (ES) which is more representative risk measure than the Value of Risk. ES give us the loss if an extreme event occurs (the tail risk), but it is still far from the real possible loss.

REFERENCES

Artzner, F., Zantl, R., Rapp, G., & Rädler, J. O. (1998). Observation of a rectangular columnar phase in condensed lamellar cationic lipid-DNA complexes. Physical Review Letters, 81(22), 5015–5018. doi:10.1103/PhysRevLett.81.5015 doi:10.1103/PhysRevLett.81.5015

Basak, S., & Shapiro, A. (2001). Value-at-risk-based risk management: Optimal policies and asset prices. Review of Financial Studies, 14(2), 371–405. doi:10.1093/rfs/14.2.371 doi:10.1093/rfs/14.2.371

Bentham, J., Rosen, F., & Burns, J. H. (1983). *The Collected Works of Jeremy Bentham: Constitutional Code* (Vol. 1). The Rosen Publishing Group.

Boldeman, L. (2007). *The cult of the market: economic fundamentalism and its discontents*. ANU Press.

Britten-Jones, M. (1999). The Sampling Error in Estimates of Mean-Variance Efficient Portfolio Weights. The Journal of Finance, 54(2), 655–671. doi:10.1111/0022-1082.00120 doi:10.1111/0022-1082.00120

Britten-Jones, M. (1999). The Sampling Error in Estimates of Mean-Variance Efficient Portfolio Weights. The Journal of Finance, 54(2), 655–671. doi:10.1111/0022-1082.00120 doi:10.1111/0022-1082.00120

Deng, X. T., Li, Z. F., & Wong, S. Y. (2005). A minimax portfolio selection strategy with equilibrium. European Journal of Operational Research, 166(1), 278–292. doi:10.1016/j.ejor.2004.01.040 doi:10.1016/j.ejor.2004.01.040

Esland, G. M. (1971). Teaching and learning as the organization of knowledge. In Knowledge and control (pp. 70-115).

Granovetter, M. (1985). Economic action and social structure: The problem of embeddedness. American Journal of Sociology, 91(3), 481–510. doi:10.1086/228311 doi:10.1086/228311

Jorion, P. (1997). *Value at Risk: The New Benchmark in Controlling Market Risk*.

Markowitz, H. M. (1968). Portfolio selection: efficient diversification of investments (Vol. 16). Yale university press.

Sinclair, U. (1994). I, candidate for governor: and how I got licked. Univ. of California Press.

Taleb, N. N. (2007). The black swan: The impact of the highly improbable. Random House.

APPENDIX 1

Two Assets Problem

Step 1: Create a spreadsheet, including asset returns for the chosen frequency. In our case asset returns were sampled at monthly intervals.

Step 2: Calculate the mean, variance and standard deviation as shown below.

Step 3: Calculate the Variance-Covariance matrix. It is necessary for the portfolio variance. This step involves few sub steps. When we have more than two assets, covariance can be best calculated by using matrix algebra. Excel allows us matrix manipulations with a few functions such as MMULT () and TRANSPOSE ().

In order to calculate the variance-covariance matrix, we will create a new series and we will name it Excess Return (see Figures 4 and 5).

Now we can obtain the variance-covariance matrix. Bring your cursor to cell C75 and enter the formula MMULT () and then press CTRL+SHIFT+ENTER. To calculate the remaining variances and covariance's select the table and bring your curser in the formula bar. At the end press CTRL+SHIFT+ENTER.

Figure 4. Excess return series

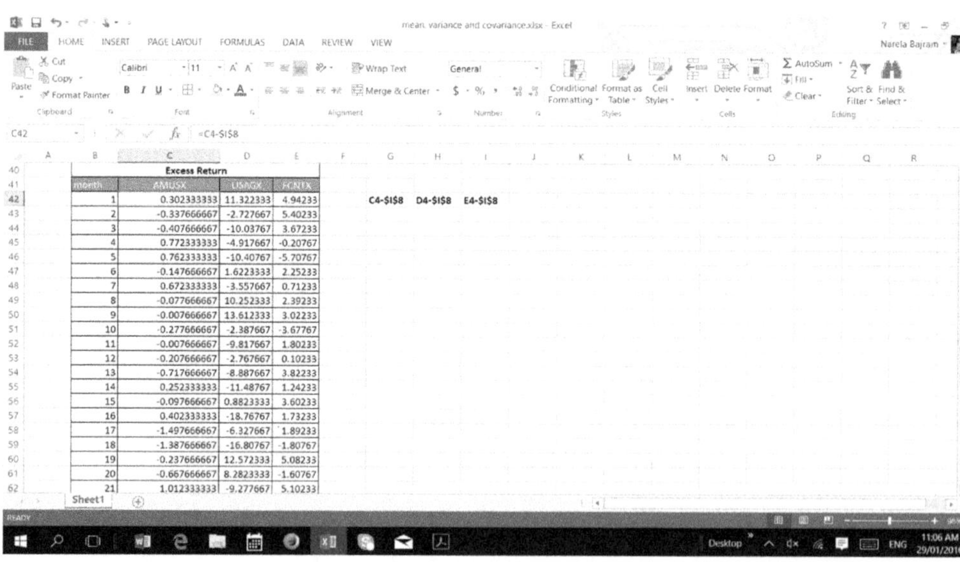

Excess Return			
month	AMUSX	USAGX	FCNTX
1	0.302333333	11.322333	4.94233
2	-0.337666667	-2.727667	5.40233
3	-0.407666667	-10.03767	3.67233
4	0.772333333	-4.917667	-0.20767
5	0.762333333	-10.40767	-5.70767
6	-0.147666667	1.6223333	2.25233
7	0.672333333	-3.557667	0.71233
8	-0.077666667	10.252333	2.39233
9	-0.007666667	13.612333	3.02233
10	-0.277666667	-2.387667	-3.67767
11	-0.007666667	-9.817667	1.80233
12	-0.207666667	-2.767667	0.10233
13	-0.717666667	-8.887667	3.82233
14	0.252333333	-11.48767	1.24233
15	-0.097666667	0.8823333	3.60233
16	0.402333333	-18.76767	1.73233
17	-1.497666667	-6.327667	1.89233
18	-1.387666667	-16.80767	-1.80767
19	-0.237666667	12.572333	5.08233
20	-0.667666667	8.2823333	-1.60767
21	1.012333333	-9.277667	5.10233

Figure 5. Variance-covariance matrix

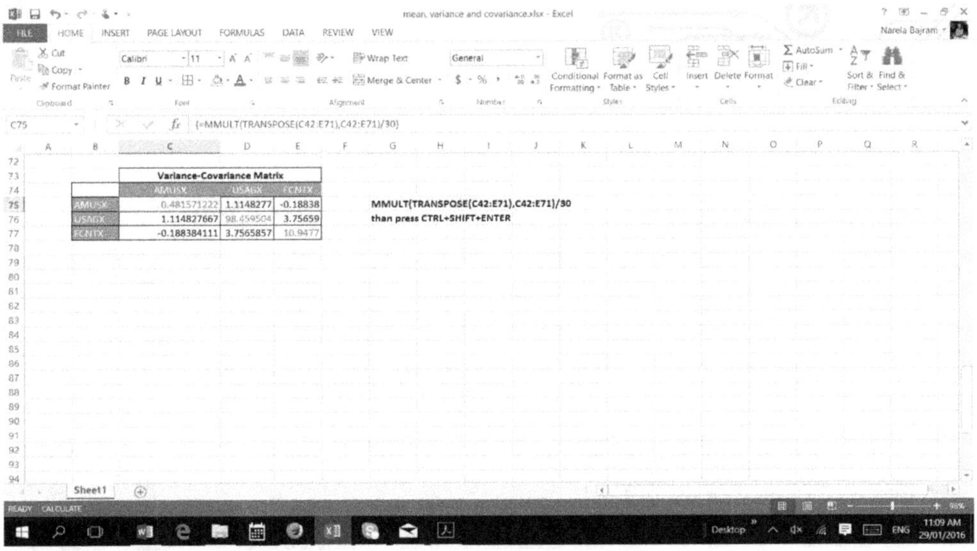

Step 4: We calculate weighted correlation coefficient (Figure 6).

Step 5: Constructing the efficient frontier involves few sub steps. It is necessary to calculate the portfolio variance, standard deviation and return. See Figures 7-10.

Figure 6. Correlation coefficient

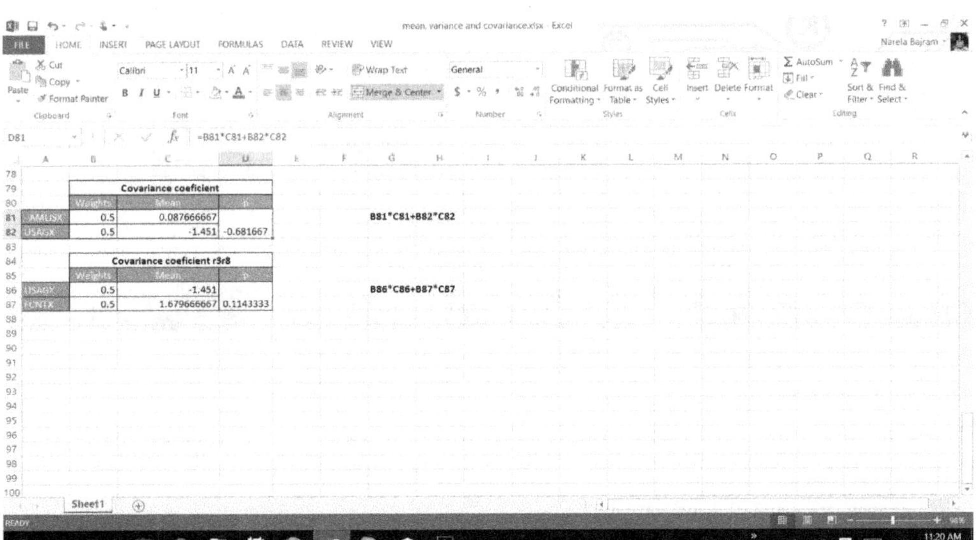

Figure 7. Calculating variance

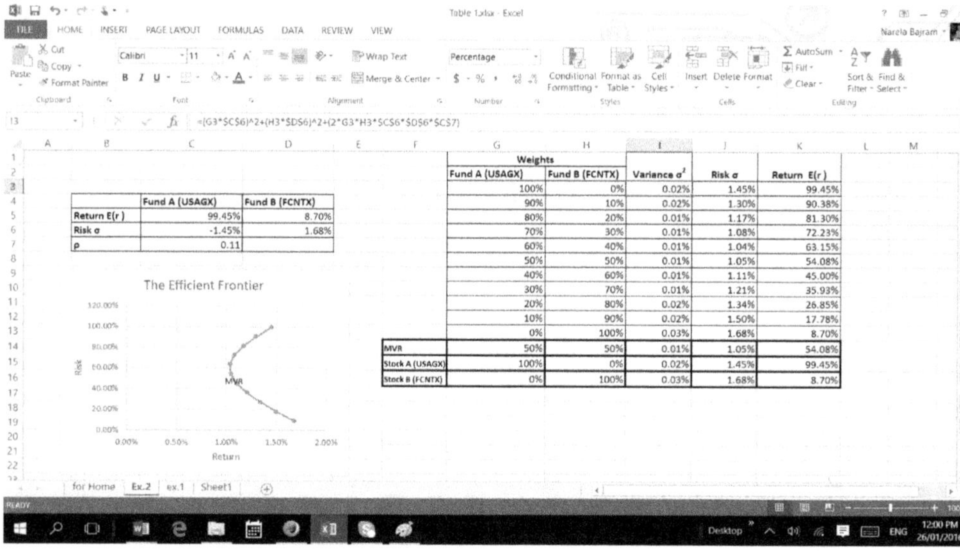

	Fund A (USAGX)	Fund B (FCNTX)
Return E(r)	99.45%	8.70%
Risk σ	-1.45%	1.68%
ρ	0.11	

	Weights				
	Fund A (USAGX)	Fund B (FCNTX)	Variance σ²	Risk σ	Return E(r)
	100%	0%	0.02%	1.45%	99.45%
	90%	10%	0.02%	1.30%	90.38%
	80%	20%	0.01%	1.17%	81.30%
	70%	30%	0.01%	1.08%	72.23%
	60%	40%	0.01%	1.04%	63.15%
	50%	50%	0.01%	1.05%	54.08%
	40%	60%	0.01%	1.11%	45.00%
	30%	70%	0.01%	1.21%	35.93%
	20%	80%	0.02%	1.34%	26.85%
	10%	90%	0.02%	1.50%	17.78%
	0%	100%	0.03%	1.68%	8.70%
MVR	50%	50%	0.01%	1.05%	54.08%
Stock A (USAGX)	100%	0%	0.02%	1.45%	99.45%
Stock B (FCNTX)	0%	100%	0.03%	1.68%	8.70%

Figure 8. Calculating standard deviation

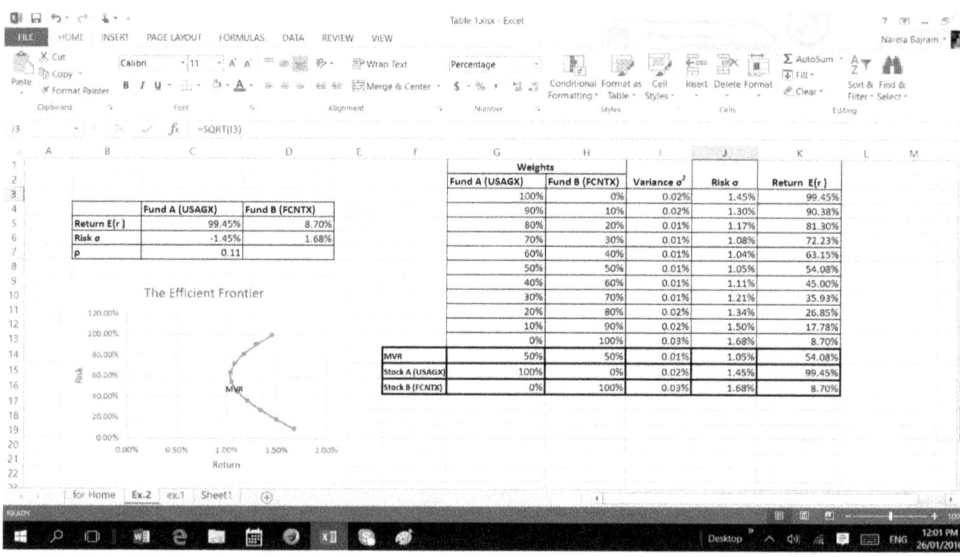

	Fund A (USAGX)	Fund B (FCNTX)
Return E(r)	99.45%	8.70%
Risk σ	-1.45%	1.68%
ρ	0.11	

	Weights				
	Fund A (USAGX)	Fund B (FCNTX)	Variance σ²	Risk σ	Return E(r)
	100%	0%	0.02%	1.45%	99.45%
	90%	10%	0.02%	1.30%	90.38%
	80%	20%	0.01%	1.17%	81.30%
	70%	30%	0.01%	1.08%	72.23%
	60%	40%	0.01%	1.04%	63.15%
	50%	50%	0.01%	1.05%	54.08%
	40%	60%	0.01%	1.11%	45.00%
	30%	70%	0.01%	1.21%	35.93%
	20%	80%	0.02%	1.34%	26.85%
	10%	90%	0.02%	1.50%	17.78%
	0%	100%	0.03%	1.68%	8.70%
MVR	50%	50%	0.01%	1.05%	54.08%
Stock A (USAGX)	100%	0%	0.02%	1.45%	99.45%
Stock B (FCNTX)	0%	100%	0.03%	1.68%	8.70%

Figure 9. Calculating return

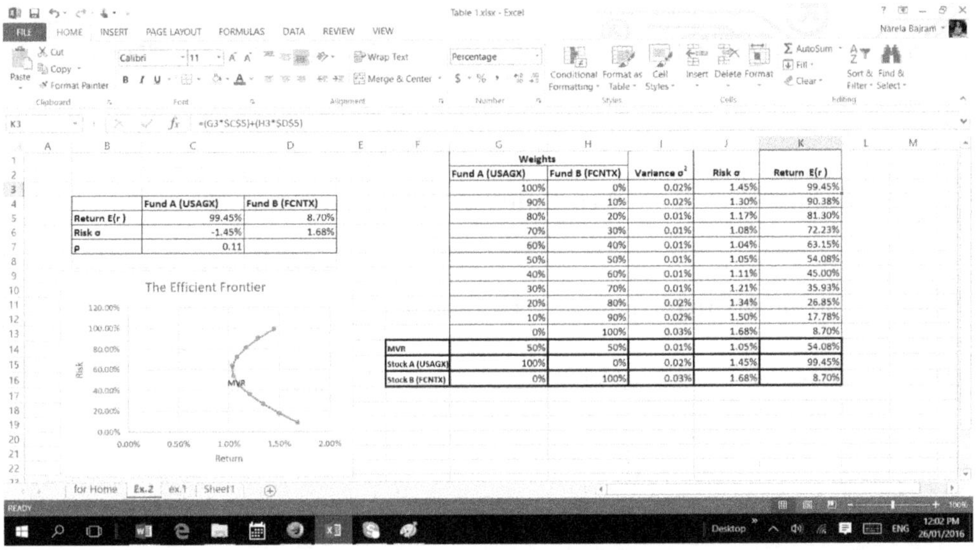

Figure 10. The efficient frontier

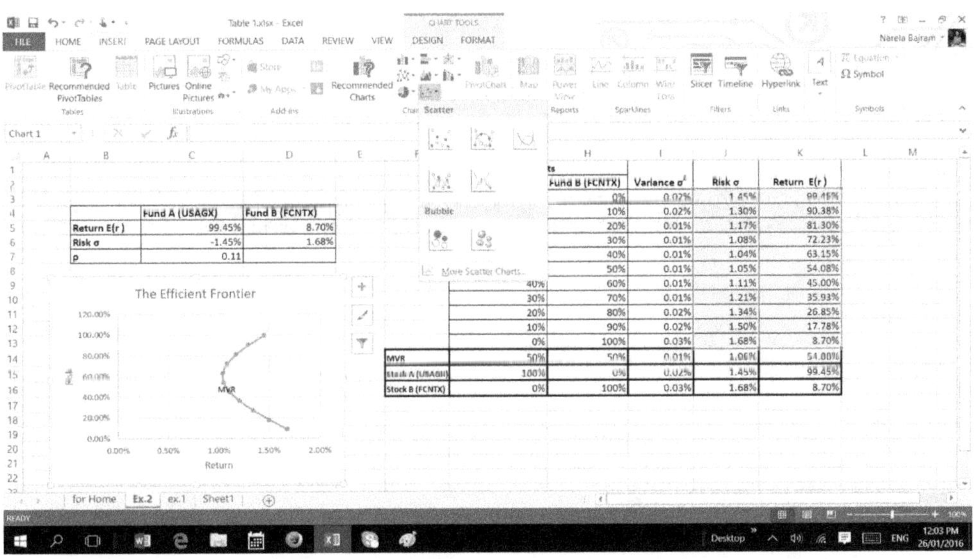

APPENDIX 2

Mean-Variance Optimal Portfolio Model (n Asset Problem)

Step 1: Calculate the individual asset Mean, Standard Deviations and Sharpe Ratio (see Figure 11).

Step 2: Minimum Variance Portfolio (MVR) (see Figure 12).

Figure 11. Individual Mean, Standard Deviation and Sharpe Ratio.

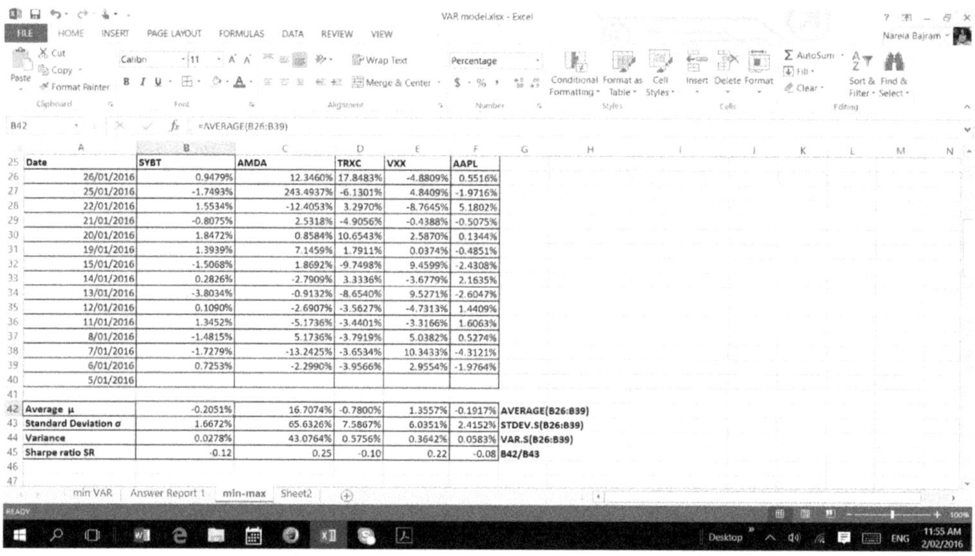

Date	SYBT	AMDA	TRXC	VXX	AAPL	
26/01/2016	0.9479%	12.3460%	17.8483%	-4.8809%	0.5516%	
25/01/2016	-1.7493%	243.4937%	-6.1301%	4.8409%	-1.9716%	
22/01/2016	1.5534%	-12.4053%	3.2970%	-8.7645%	5.1802%	
21/01/2016	-0.8075%	2.5318%	-4.9056%	-0.4388%	-0.5075%	
20/01/2016	1.8472%	0.8584%	10.6543%	2.5870%	0.1344%	
19/01/2016	1.3939%	7.1459%	1.7911%	0.0374%	-0.4851%	
15/01/2016	-1.5068%	1.8692%	-9.7498%	9.4599%	-2.4308%	
14/01/2016	0.2826%	-2.7909%	3.3336%	-3.6779%	2.1635%	
13/01/2016	-3.8034%	-0.9132%	-8.6540%	9.5271%	-2.6047%	
12/01/2016	0.1090%	-2.6907%	-3.5627%	-4.7313%	1.4409%	
11/01/2016	1.3452%	-5.1736%	-3.4401%	-3.3166%	1.6063%	
8/01/2016	-1.4815%	5.1736%	-3.7919%	5.0382%	0.5274%	
7/01/2016	-1.7279%	-13.2425%	-3.6534%	10.3433%	-4.3121%	
6/01/2016	0.7253%	-2.2990%	-3.9566%	2.9554%	-1.9764%	
5/01/2016						
Average μ	-0.2051%	16.7074%	-0.7800%	1.3557%	-0.1917%	AVERAGE(B26:B39)
Standard Deviation σ	1.6672%	65.6326%	7.5867%	6.0351%	2.4152%	STDEV.S(B26:B39)
Variance	0.0278%	43.0764%	0.5756%	0.3642%	0.0583%	VAR.S(B26:B39)
Sharpe ratio SR	-0.12	0.25	-0.10	0.22	-0.08	B42/B43

Figure 12. Minimum Variance Portfolio

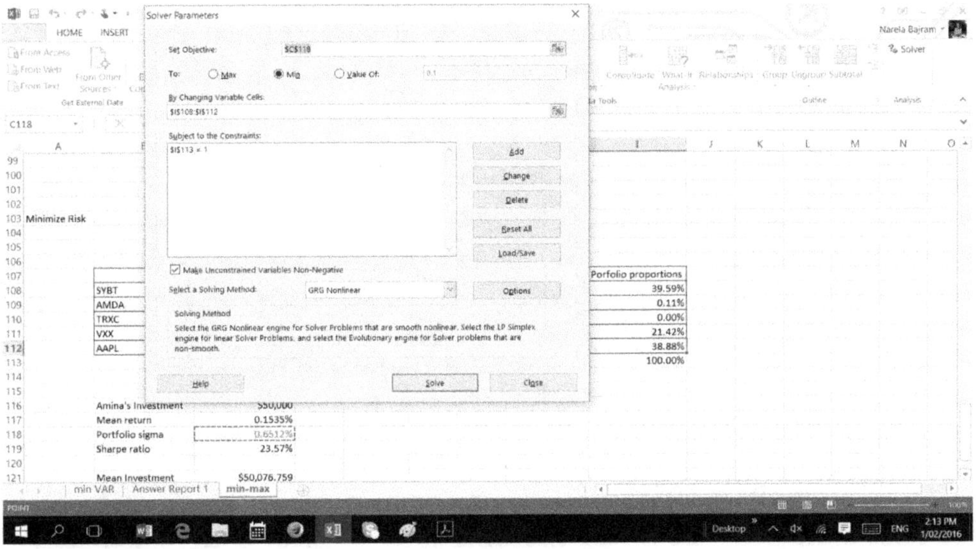

Step 3: Minimize the risk for a given level of return (see Figure 13).

Maximize the return for a given level of risk (see Figure 14).

Figure 13. Minimize the risk for a given level of return

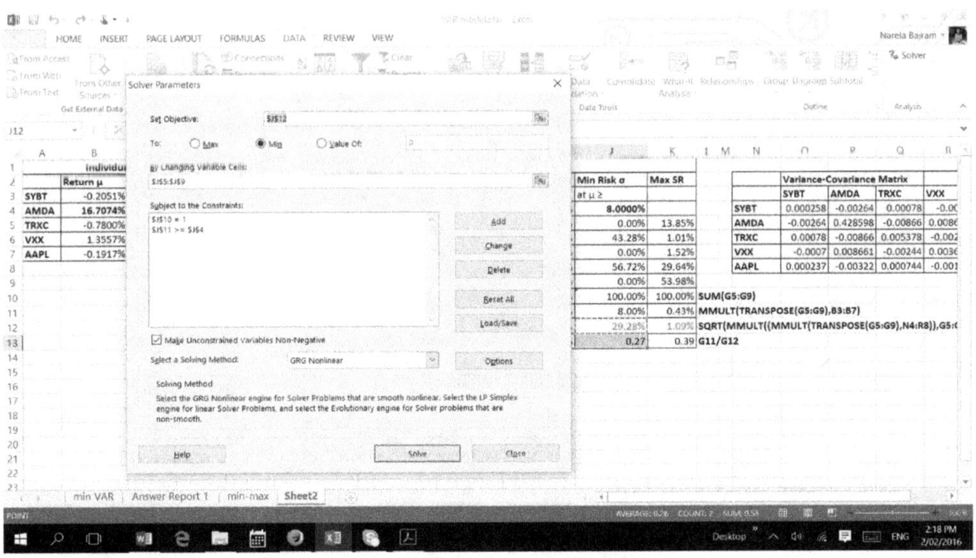

Figure 14. Maximize the return for a given level of risk

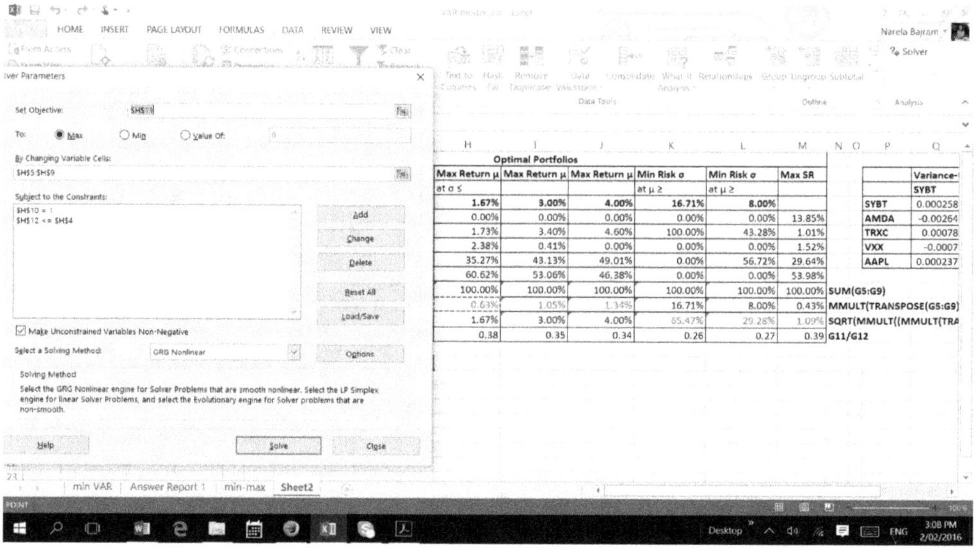

Step 4: Maximize the Sharpe Ratio (SR) (see Figure 15).
Step 5: Excel spreadsheet with the formulas (see Figure 16).

Figure 15. Maximize the Sharpe Ratio

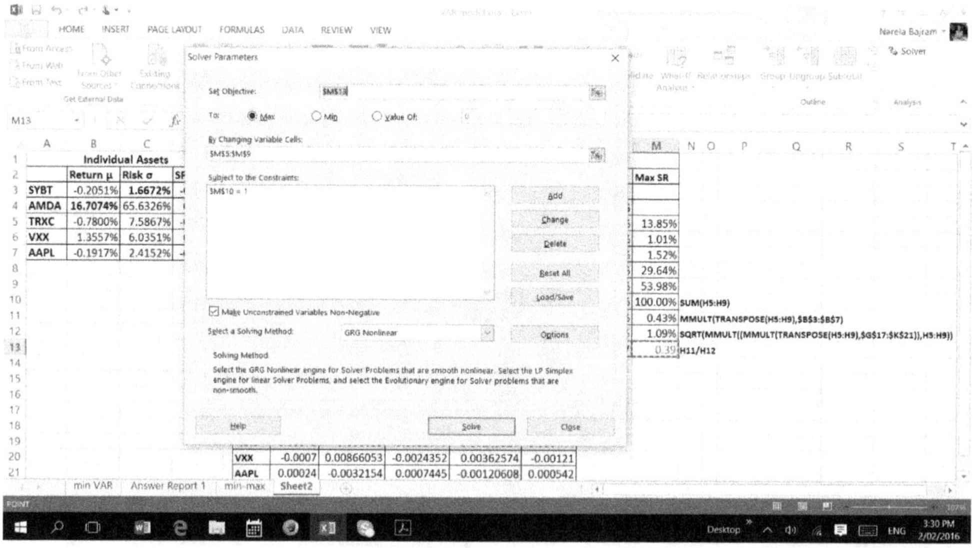

Figure 16. Excel spreadsheet with the formulas

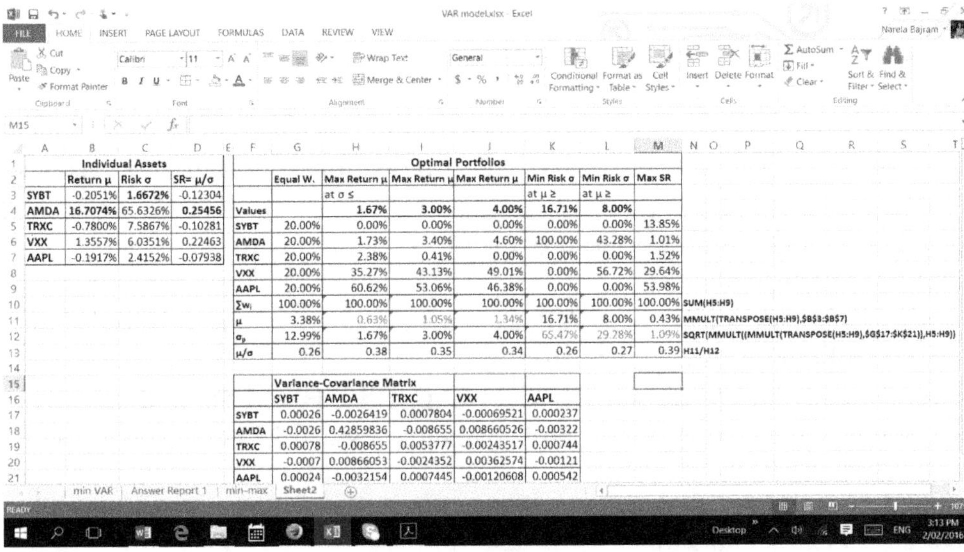

	Individual Assets		
	Return μ	Risk σ	SR= μ/σ
SYBT	-0.2051%	**1.6672%**	-0.12304
AMDA	**16.7074%**	65.6326%	**0.25456**
TRXC	-0.7800%	7.5867%	-0.10281
VXX	1.3557%	6.0351%	0.22463
AAPL	-0.1917%	2.4152%	-0.07938

	Optimal Portfolios							
	Equal W.	Max Return μ	Max Return μ	Max Return μ	Min Risk σ	Min Risk σ	Max SR	
		at σ ≤			at μ ≥	at μ ≥		
Values		**1.67%**	**3.00%**	**4.00%**	**16.71%**	**8.00%**		
SYBT	20.00%	0.00%	0.00%	0.00%	0.00%	0.00%	13.85%	
AMDA	20.00%	1.73%	3.40%	4.60%	100.00%	43.28%	1.01%	
TRXC	20.00%	2.38%	0.41%	0.00%	0.00%	0.00%	1.52%	
VXX	20.00%	35.27%	43.13%	49.01%	0.00%	56.72%	29.64%	
AAPL	20.00%	60.62%	53.06%	46.38%	0.00%	0.00%	53.98%	
$\sum w_i$	100.00%	100.00%	100.00%	100.00%	100.00%	100.00%	100.00%	SUM(H5:H9)
μ	3.38%	0.63%	1.05%	1.34%	16.71%	8.00%	0.43%	MMULT(TRANSPOSE(H5:H9),$B$3:$B$7)
σ_p	12.99%	1.67%	3.00%	4.00%	65.47%	29.28%	1.09%	SQRT(MMULT((MMULT(TRANSPOSE(H5:H9),$G$17:$K$21)),H5:H9))
μ/σ	0.26	0.38	0.35	0.34	0.26	0.27	0.39	H11/H12

	Variance-Covariance Matrix				
	SYBT	AMDA	TRXC	VXX	AAPL
SYBT	0.00026	-0.0026419	0.0007804	-0.00069521	0.000237
AMDA	-0.0026	0.42859836	-0.008655	0.008660526	-0.00322
TRXC	0.00078	-0.008655	0.0053777	-0.00243517	0.000744
VXX	-0.0007	0.00866053	-0.0024352	0.00362574	-0.00121
AAPL	0.00024	-0.0032154	0.0007445	-0.00120608	0.000542

APPENDIX 3: MEAN-VAR OPTIMAL PORTFOLIO MODEL

Variance-Covariance Method

Step 1: Collect the historical stock prices and calculate the returns. Then calculate the asset returns, standard deviation/volatility and variance (see Figure 17).

Step 2: Calculate the portfolio proportions (see Figure 18).

Note: Use the excel solver.

Step 3: Calculate individual VaRs, correlation matrix and at the end the portfolio VaR (see Figure 19).

Note: To calculate VAR step 1, select C56, D56, E56, F56, and G56 then bring your cursor to the formula bar and press CTRL+SHIFT+ENTER

Figure 17. Return, Standard deviation and variance

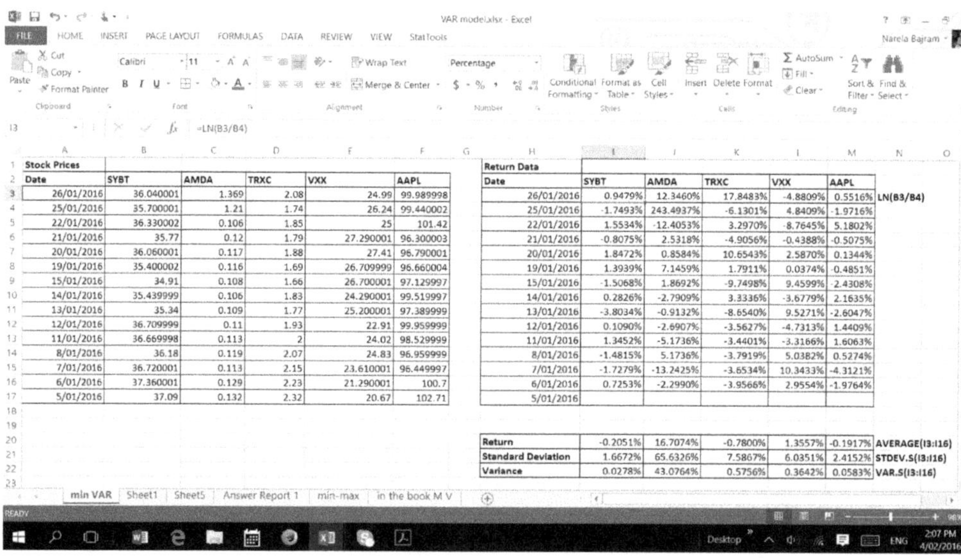

=LN(B3/B4)

Stock Prices					
Date	SYBT	AMDA	TRXC	VXX	AAPL
26/01/2016	36.040001	1.369	2.08	24.99	99.989998
25/01/2016	35.700001	1.21	1.74	26.24	99.440002
22/01/2016	36.330002	0.106	1.85	25	101.42
21/01/2016	35.77	0.12	1.79	27.290001	96.300003
20/01/2016	36.060001	0.117	1.88	27.41	96.790001
19/01/2016	35.400002	0.116	1.69	26.709999	96.660004
15/01/2016	34.91	0.108	1.66	26.700001	97.129997
14/01/2016	35.439999	0.106	1.83	24.290001	99.519997
13/01/2016	35.34	0.109	1.77	25.200001	97.389999
12/01/2016	36.709999	0.11	1.93	22.91	99.959999
11/01/2016	36.669998	0.113	2	24.02	98.529999
8/01/2016	36.18	0.119	2.07	24.83	96.959999
7/01/2016	36.720001	0.113	2.15	23.610001	96.449997
6/01/2016	37.360001	0.129	2.23	21.290001	100.7
5/01/2016	37.09	0.132	2.32	20.67	102.71

Return Data						
Date	SYBT	AMDA	TRXC	VXX	AAPL	
26/01/2016	0.9479%	12.3460%	17.8483%	-4.8809%	0.5516%	LN(B3/B4)
25/01/2016	-1.7493%	243.4937%	-6.1301%	4.8409%	-1.9716%	
22/01/2016	1.5534%	-12.4053%	3.2970%	-8.7645%	5.1802%	
21/01/2016	-0.8075%	2.5318%	-4.9056%	-0.4388%	-0.5075%	
20/01/2016	1.8472%	0.8584%	10.6543%	2.5870%	0.1344%	
19/01/2016	1.3939%	7.1459%	1.7911%	0.0374%	-0.4851%	
15/01/2016	-1.5068%	1.8692%	-9.7498%	9.4599%	-2.4308%	
14/01/2016	0.2826%	-2.7909%	3.3336%	-3.6779%	2.1635%	
13/01/2016	-3.8034%	-0.9132%	-8.6540%	9.5271%	-2.6047%	
12/01/2016	0.1090%	-2.6907%	-3.5627%	-4.7313%	1.4409%	
11/01/2016	1.3452%	-5.1736%	-3.4401%	-3.3166%	1.6063%	
8/01/2016	-1.4815%	5.1736%	-3.7919%	5.0382%	0.5274%	
7/01/2016	-1.7279%	-13.2425%	-3.6534%	10.3433%	-4.3121%	
6/01/2016	0.7253%	-2.2990%	-3.9566%	2.9554%	-1.9764%	
5/01/2016						

Return	-0.2051%	16.7074%	-0.7800%	1.3557%	-0.1917%	AVERAGE(I3:I16)
Standard Deviation	1.6672%	65.6326%	7.5867%	6.0351%	2.4152%	STDEV.S(I3:I16)
Variance	0.0278%	43.0764%	0.5756%	0.3642%	0.0583%	VAR.S(I3:I16)

Figure 18. The portfolio proportions

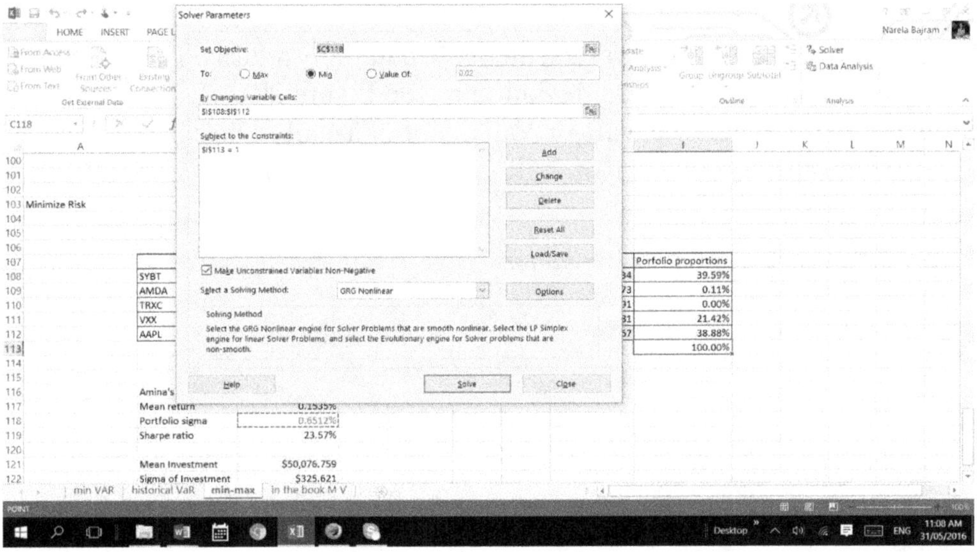

Figure 19. Individual VaRs, correlation matrix and at the end the portfolio VaR.

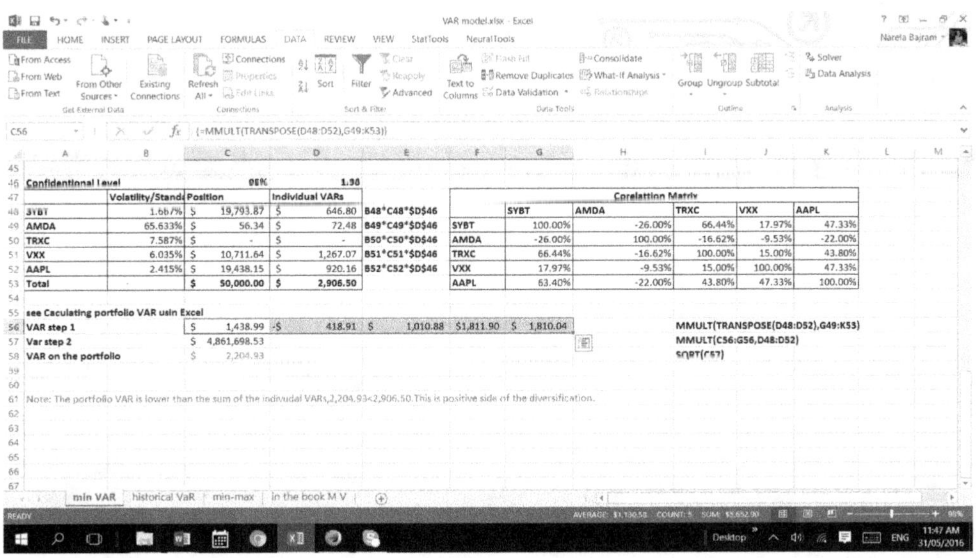

Historical Method

Step 1: Setting the time interval and then calculate daily returns. Then calculate the mean μ and standard deviation σ (see Figure 20).

Step 2: Find out the 10% VaR or VaR $_{90\%}$ of Normally Distributed Data as Well as the Historical 10% VaR (see Figure 21).

Figure 20. Mean and standard deviations

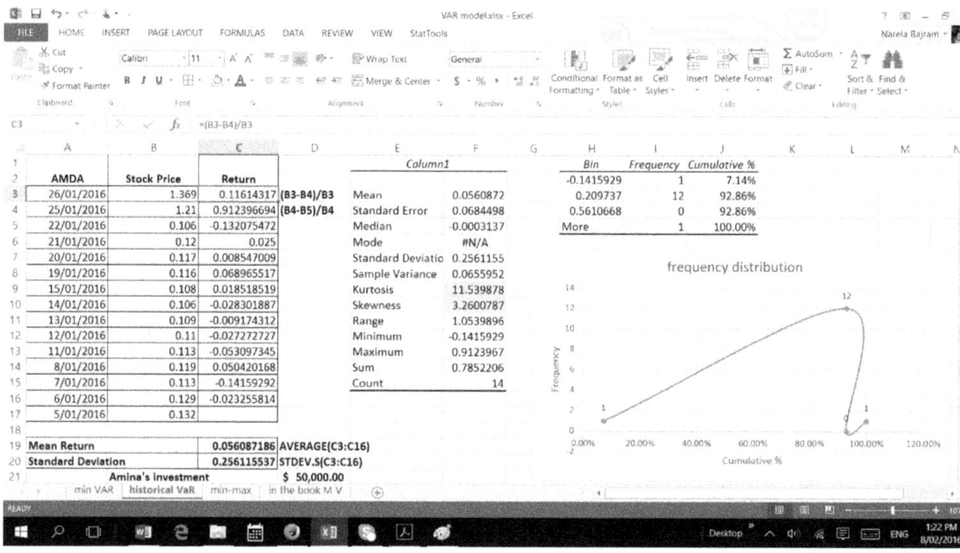

AMDA	Stock Price	Return	
26/01/2016	1.369	0.11614317	(B3-B4)/B3
25/01/2016	1.21	0.912396694	(B4-B5)/B4
22/01/2016	0.106	-0.132075472	
21/01/2016	0.12	0.025	
20/01/2016	0.117	0.008547009	
19/01/2016	0.116	0.068965517	
15/01/2016	0.108	0.018518519	
14/01/2016	0.106	-0.028301887	
13/01/2016	0.109	-0.009174312	
12/01/2016	0.11	-0.027272727	
11/01/2016	0.113	-0.053097345	
8/01/2016	0.119	0.050420168	
7/01/2016	0.113	-0.14159292	
6/01/2016	0.129	-0.023255814	
5/01/2016	0.132		
Mean Return		0.056087186	AVERAGE(C3:C16)
Standard Deviation		0.256115537	STDEV.S(C3:C16)
Amina's investment		$ 50,000.00	

Column1	
Mean	0.0560872
Standard Error	0.0684498
Median	-0.0003137
Mode	#N/A
Standard Deviatio	0.2561155
Sample Variance	0.0655952
Kurtosis	11.539878
Skewness	3.2600787
Range	1.0539896
Minimum	-0.1415929
Maximum	0.9123967
Sum	0.7852206
Count	14

Bin	Frequency	Cumulative %
-0.1415929	1	7.14%
0.209737	12	92.86%
0.5610668	0	92.86%
More	1	100.00%

Figure 21. VaR $_{90\%}$ for normally distributed data and the historical 10% VaR

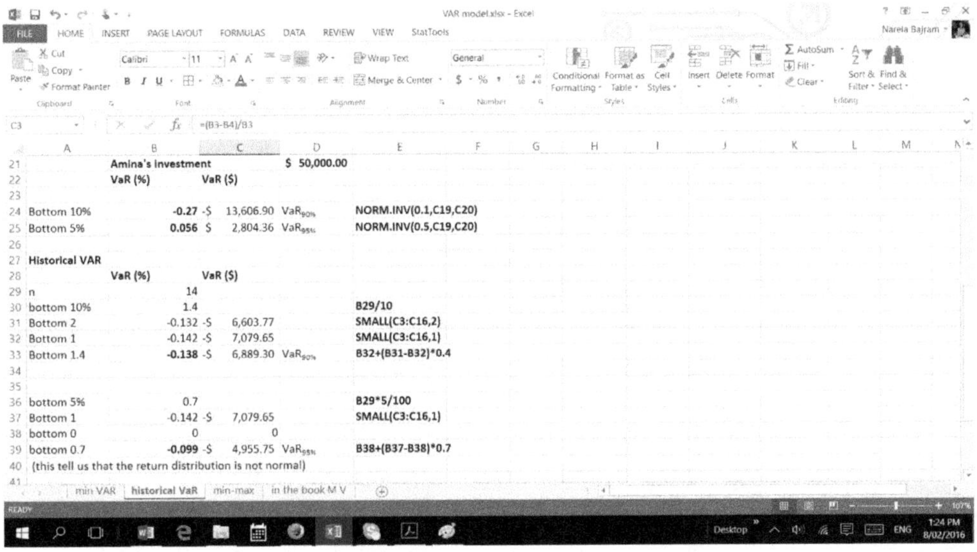

Step 3: Data Analysis- Descriptive statistics and Histogram (see Figure 22).
Step 4: Calculating the Expected Shortfalls (ES) (see Figure 23).

Figure 22. Descriptive statistics and histogram

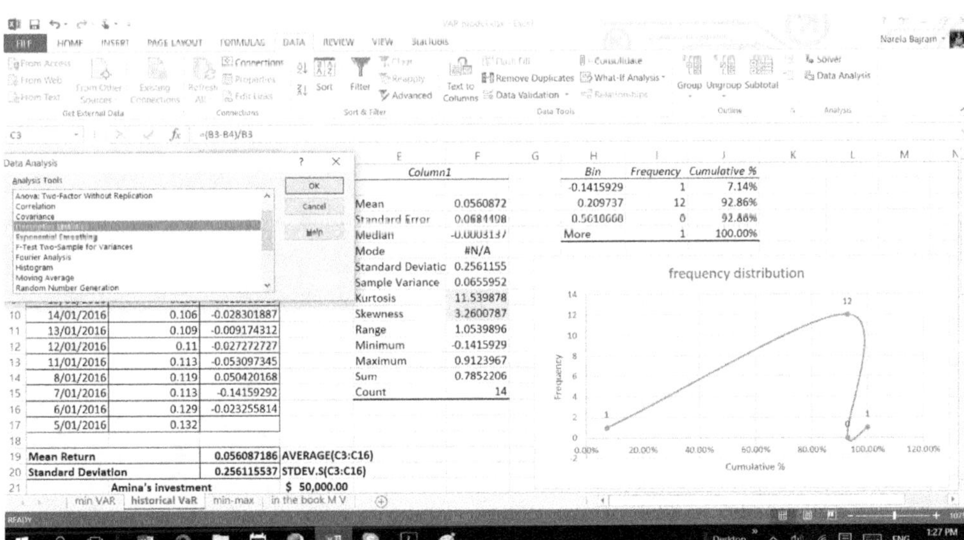

Figure 23. Expected Shortfalls (ES)

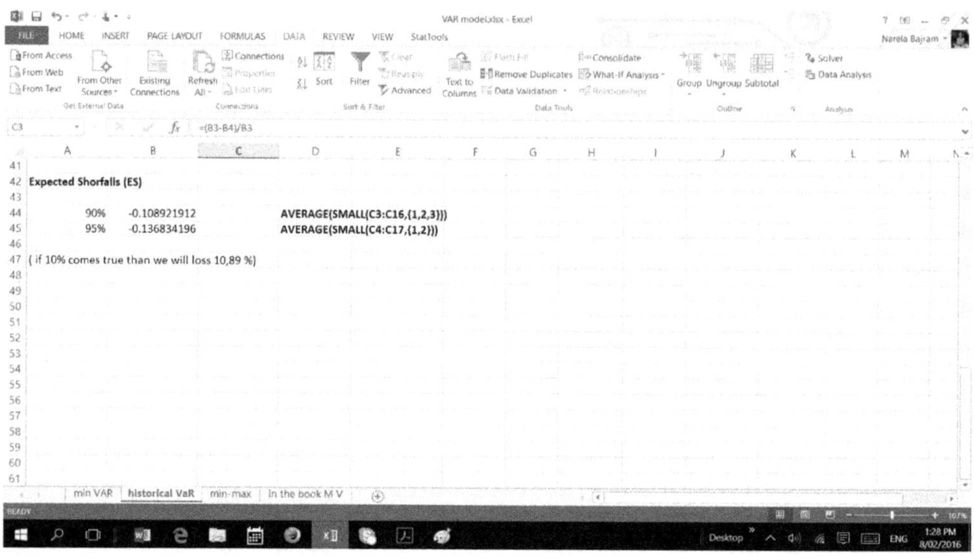

Chapter 4
Extreme Events Theory and Application

ABSTRACT

In standard statistical methodologies, the probability that the extreme event will occur is very small. But the expected losses in real world markets are higher and sometimes with catastrophic outcomes. Here it seems that the fact that we could lose a certain amount of money 95% or 99% of the time tells us absolutely nothing about what could happen the other 5 or even 1 percent of the time. For that reason, instead of estimating the certain loss, as the standard statistical methodologies account, we introduce a technique known as a "tail risk protecting strategy" or "the barbell investment strategy." In this chapter, analyzing the copper market movements I understand that the market has been conditioned to believe that the copper demand will exceed its supply. Therefore, I suggest to protect against a growing price-inflation risk. The analyses are conducted using the statistical software STATA 11 and Excel Spreadsheets.

Our thoughts, our behaviours, our decisions and our emotions are influenced by our physical sensations, by the things we touch, the texture of the things we touch, the temperature of the things we touch, the colours, the smells,' she says. 'All these, without our awareness, influence our behaviours and thoughts and emotions. (Thalma Lobel, Sensation: the New Science of Physical Intelligence, 2014u)

DOI: 10.4018/978-1-5225-3259-0.ch004

THE DESTRUCTION: A SHORT STORY OF THE HUMAN NATURE

It is difficult to get a man to understand something, when his salary depends upon his not understanding it. (Upton Sinclair, 1994)

After decades of inquiry on the issue of pollution, hunting and environment loss, scientists asserted that human action is responsible for pushing life on our shared planet toward mass extinction, and categorize us as a most destructive specie living on the earth. Yes, it is us. Wilson (2002) calculated the Earth would lose half its higher life forms by 2100 if the current rate of human disruption continued. A similar conclusion is a given by a biologist Todd Palmer from the University of Florida. He wrote an e-mail to The Washington Post pointing that: "The smoking gun in these extinctions is very obvious, and it's in our hands."

Now let us go a bit further. Let's talk about the artificial intelligence and its possibilities. Did you watch the movie "Transcendence"? If you have not, then I highly recommended you watch it. In this movie, Dr. Will Caster (Johnny Depp) is a scientist who researches the nature of death and sentience, including artificial intelligence. He and his team work to create a sentient computer; he predicts that such a computer will create a technological singularity, or in his words "Transcendence." His thirst for knowledge evolves to an infinite quest for power, and his loved ones soon realize that it may be impossible to stop him.

While many moviegoers might embrace the power of artificial intelligence displayed in the movie as just science fiction, world famous physicist Stephen Hawking along with computer scientist Stuart Russell, physicists Max Tegmark and Frank Wilczek say it could be an indication of humanity's doom. He also wrote that "one can imagine such technology outsmarting financial markets, out-inventing human researchers, out-manipulating human leaders, and developing weapons we cannot even understand. Where the short-term impact of Artificial Intelligence (AI) depends on who controls it, while the long-term impact depends on whether it can be controlled at all". Meaning this "biggest event in human history" could be humanity's last unless "we learn how to avoid the risks."

Now let us go back to economics. What we know about human behavior, when we talk about economics? Can we really learn how to avoid the risk? I personally don't think so.

For example, the Wall Street crash of 1929, "Black Thursday," was an event that sent the US and indeed the global economy into a tailspin, contributing to the Great Depression of the 1930s. By the time the market had reached bottom at 1932, 90% had been wiped off the value of shares. It took 25 years before the Dow Jones industrial average recovered to its 1929 level.

Let us remember the most recent event, the "Black Friday" in 2008. The shock collapse of the Lehman Brothers Bank, which held assets worth $600 billion, became the symbolic start of the most dramatic financial crisis since the Great Depression. It has destroyed 40% of world wealth and the economies are still recovering.

So what went wrong here? Why did we not see it coming? Can we link this the crashes/destructions with the human nature?

It is interesting how some question turns out to be significant after we hit the bottom, and then when we find our self's again in the boom we simple forget everything that we learned and the process of destruction start all over.

Hancock and Zahawi (2011), explicitly explain how the human behavior is important in the construction of the buble that most of us do not recognize how serious it can be. From their book, is chosen the following three instances that we deal with you.

- In 2004, the deputy governor of the Bank of England, Sir Andrew Large, gave a powerful and eloquent warning about the coming crash at the London School of Economics. The speech was published on the bank's website, but it received no notice. There were no seminars called. No research was commissioned. No newspaper referred to the speech. Sir Andrew in 2005 continued to make similar speeches and argued for another two years that the system was unsustainable. His speeches infuriated the then Chancellor, Gordon Brown, because they warned of the dangers of excessive borrowing. In January 2006, Sir Andrew gave up: he quietly retired before his term was up.
- In 2005, the chief economist of the International Monetary Fund, Raghuram Rajan, made a speech at Jackson Hole, Wyoming in front of the world's most important bankers and financiers, including Alan Greenspan and Larry Summers. He argued that technical change, institutional moves and deregulation had made the financial system unstable. Incentives to make short-term profits were encouraging thc taking of risks, which if they materialized would have catastrophic

consequences. The speech did not go down well. Among the first to speak was Larry Summers, who said the speech was "largely misguided".

- In 2006, Nouriel Roubini issued a similar warning at an IMF gathering of financiers in New York. The audience reaction? Dismissive. Roubini was "non-rigorous" in his arguments. The central bankers "knew what they were doing."

At the end, most of the people, let us say ordinary people, did not see what was coming and therefore were caught totally unprepared. But I cannot say the same for the Political Manipulators and Paid Hacks, as Barry Ritholtz wanted to name the truth deniers on his web blog. I totally agree with his statement that these people are more committed to their ideology and bonuses than the good of the nation. They were paid to hold a certain view. The view of the impeccable efficiency of the capitalist system where the social order and harmony arise naturally in a market economy where each individual makes "rational" choices and takes "rational decisions" in "self-interest". Thus, the system of government was not needed to maintain this social order. But the system in reality occasionally goes wrong, and when this occurs the outcomes are catastrophic. One of the reasons is the emotional element of the financial markets as panic, irrationality and nerves; and if too many people get swept up by these emotions, it can deeper the crisis. Berger and Luckman (1991) stated that the social order exists only as a product of human activity. Equally, if humankind has made society, it has also made the economic system. These insights have considerable significance for the study of human behavior itself. The social and economic systems are not natural types such as a sodium chloride, instead they are social artifacts. From the above, it is also clear that culture is not a once for all influence, it is a continuing process constructed and reconstructed during human interaction. Therefore, the British philosopher and social reformer Benthem (1948) stated that modelling human begins only as self-interested utility maximiser is inherently depressing. In this spirit, Boldmeman (2013) argues that civilization requires the suppression of self-interest through social norms and that in practice, our decisions are deeply affected by socially inculcated values and by our emotions

Finally, all of us: economists, sociologists, psychologists, mathematicians, physicians, computer scientist should work together on developing alternative decision making strategies that will improve the chance of obtaining long run benefits and avoiding the risk. To do this we should know that the risk does not exist "out there," independent of our minds and cultures, waiting to be measured, and the extreme events or black swans, as the philosopher and statistician Nassim Taleb wanted to say, are not events that we can predict because they are usually side-effects of some human research, action or interaction.

Even knowing this, we cannot eliminate the booms and busts which are the result of a cyclical nature of capitalism and the human behavior, but we can protect our self from the catastrophic outcomes. Therefore, the sections that follow are devoted exclusively to protection strategies and their implementation in the financial markets.

THE ROLE OF INFLUENCE

Consider the following scenario: In 2006, everybody took seriously Sir Andrew Large and Raghuram Rajan warnings and follow their recommendations in returning the stability in the financial system.

Possible outcome: Due to the timely human intervention in the financial sector, the year 2008 would not be known as the year of the Great Recession, but as a year where the economy suffered a mild recession.

Economic analyst reaction: "Sir Andrew Large and Raghuram Rajan have failed to predict the bust of the bubble" or "The warning were unfortunately not grounded well."

But unfortunately, we didn't take this warning seriously.

The main reason for disagreement among the economists regarding the importance of the human interaction is the fact that the economics is not an experimental science, as physics is. It would be too easy if we were able to go back in 2008, but instead of ignoring Sir Andrew Large and Raghuram Rajan warnings, accept them and observe the outcome. Only then we would be able to identify the importance of the human interaction without further debate.

Both scenarios, the considered and that occurred in 2008, showed us that others could influence our decisions by setting a frame. Available information is, of course, a critical feature, and actors other than the decision maker may have a strong influence on which information is available.

At this point, there is no mathematical model that can perfectly model human behavior or the external influences toward our decision making, but at least we know in which direction our research should extend.

MANAGING THE RISK: TAIL RISK PROTECTING STRATEGY

When a portfolio of investments is put together, it is assumed that the distribution of returns will follow a normal pattern. Under this assumption, the probability that returns will move between the mean and three standard deviations, either positive or negative, is 99.97%. This means that the probability of returns moving more than three standard deviations beyond the mean is 0.03%, or virtually null. However, the concept of tail risk suggests that the distribution is not normal, but skewed, and has fatter tails. Fatter tails increase the probability that an investment will move beyond three standard deviations. This is known as extreme event. The solid black line in Figure 1 shows a typical bell curve with a normal distribution. But the relatively high number of returns falls outside the normal distribution. In this case, we say that the distribution has fat tails-black dotted lines.

The best explanation for the existence of extreme events is given by Taleb (2007) in his book "The black swan: The impact of the highly improbable." Here we share some information on the back cover of the book.

A BLACK SWAN is a highly improbable event with three principal characteristics: It is unpredictable; it carries a massive impact; and, after the fact, we concoct an explanation that makes it appear less random, and more predictable, than it was. The astonishing success of Google was a black

Figure 1. Fat tail distribution vs normal distribution

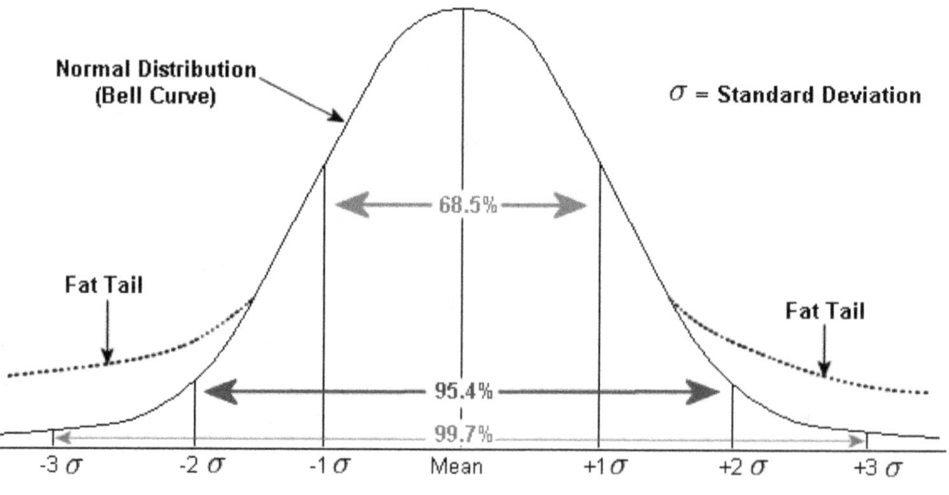

swan; so was 9/11. For Nassim Nicholas Taleb, black swans underlie almost everything about our world, from the rise of religions to events in our own personal lives.

Why do we not acknowledge the phenomenon of black swans until after they occur? Part of the answer, according to Taleb, is that humans are hardwired to learn specifics when they should be focused on generalitites. We concentrate on things we already know and time and time again fail to take into consideration what we don't know. We are, therefore, unable to truly estimate opportunities, too vulnerable to the impulse to simplify, narrate, and categorize, and not open enough to rewarding those who can imagine the 'impossible."

For years, Taleb has studied how we fool ourselves into thinking we know more than we actually do. We restrict our thinking to the irrelevant and inconsequential, while large events continue to surprise us and shape our world. Now, in this revelatory book, Taleb explains everything we know about what we don't know. He offers surprisingly simple tricks for dealing with black swans and benefiting from them.

People tend not to be able to anticipate a future they have never personally experienced (Naseeb Taleb, 2007)

THE BARBELL INVESTMENT STRATEGY

As a general rule in investment management, it is never a good idea to put all your assets and all your risk in a single asset class or investment. You will want to diversify the risk by putting the "eggs" in two baskets, or as Taleb (2007) explained:

If you know that you are vulnerable to prediction errors, and… accept that most "risk measures" are flawed, then your strategy is to be as hyperconservative and hyperaggressive as you can be instead of being mildly aggressive or conservative.

Historically, the barbell is a bond investment strategy. Its focus is on two different segments of the yield curve. Generally, similar amount of money is invested in both short and long term bond maturities with nothing in the middle as shown in Figure 2.

In this section I will show you how to use the sectors performance indicators and equity q ratio in implementing the barbell investment strategy; and construct a portfolio that will be resistant to extreme events, as inflation, deflation or whatever comes.

SECTORS PERFORMANCE

For example, Standard & Poor's 500 index as a winning strategy, consider investing in 10 worst and 10 best performing subsectors. On average this strategy beats the broad market, but here we are not talking about averages. As we saw above, one extreme event can melt down the whole gain from the past years, and push us out of the market. S&P 500 in two years did not beat the index of major stocks, 1997 and 2008. Those years coincided with the Asian and the worldwide financial crises. So, this strategy cannot fight against extreme event, as a rapid increase of the inflation rate.

In this subsection, I will apply the Taleb (2007) barbell investment strategy. Cash investment is $16.463. As shown in Figure 2, on one end, I put my money on extremely safe investments, and these are the US treasury bills, TIPS and Vangurad. Here, I put 80% of my money, or $13.013.

Figure 2. Barbell investing strategy

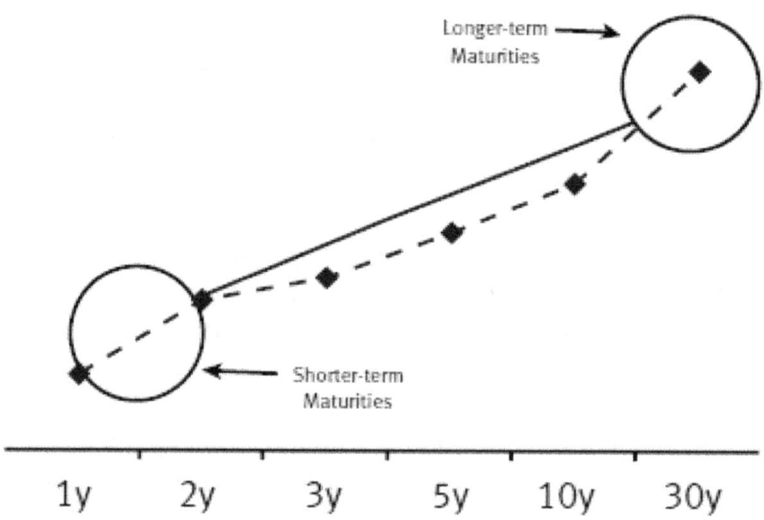

Then, at the other end, I invest 20% or $3.450 in high risk assets that will pay off huge if they work out. The high-risk assets considered in this strategy are the stocks from the worst performed sectors in the last year. The logic is that even a sector has been let down, it tends to catch up eventually. The S&P analysis finds that the worst subsectors were agricultural products, aluminium, casinos/gaming, coal/fuels, department stores, diversified metals/mining, independent power producers, motorcycle makers, oil/gas drilling and oil/gas storage and transport. The source that I am using is the *Sector Watch* analytical reports (S&P Capital IQ, McGraw Hill Financial [NYSE: MHFI]).

In view of that, I choose to invest in the sector of Metal and Mining and Coal, as given in Table 1. The negative side of this strategy is if most of the traders use it, then the outcome will be opposite of the expectation. Furthermore, you have to monitor your portfolio every day and if needed adjust it. Instantaneous reaction is needed.

EQUITY RATIO

Spitznagel (2011) explained the variation of Tobin's Q ratio, and the expected returns to the market from various levels of Equity Q Ratio. Spitznagel is a big believer in Austrian economics, a controversial school of thought that stands opposed to most conventional economic theory. The Austrian approach to the market process is that: "The market is a process." SpitznagelTobin failed to understand the importance of his ratio, for the reason that a high Q ratio suggests stocks have become detached from the underlying economy.

Table 1. Barbell approach in construction portfolio

No	Description	Stock Price	Quantity	Total
1	NYSERACH:XME – SPDR S&P Metals and Mining (ETF)	15.25	100	1.525,00
2	NYSE: YZT- YANZHOU Coal Mining CO LTD (ADR)	3.85	500	1.925,00
3	NYSERCA: BND – VANGUARD Total Bond Market ETF	82	50	4.100,00
4	NYSERCA: STPZ- PIMCO 1-5 Year US TIPS Index Fund	51.47	50	2.573,00
5	NYSEARCA: LTPZ- PIMCO 15+ Year US TIPS Index Fund	63.4	100	6.340,00
6	Extremely safe investments (3+4+5)			13.013,00
7	High risk investment (1+2)			3.450,00
8	Total			16.463,00

Note: The main investment is made on February 15, 2016. I invested in the first 4 assets. On February 25, 2016, I extend my portfolio with one more asset, NYSEARCA: LTPZ- PIMCO 15+ Year US TIPS Index Fund.

Tobin's Q ratio is the ratio between the market value of the stock market against the aggregate net worth of the constituent stocks measured at replacement cost/market value of assets:

$$\text{Equity Q} = \frac{\text{market value of equity}}{mv \text{ of assets - mv of liabilities}} \tag{1}$$

When the ratio is less than one, < 1, then the equity index is considered to be undervalued when the ratio is higher than one, > 1, is considered to be overvalued, and when the ratio is equal to 1, = 1, then the price equals the net worth of the business.. Because this period of over- and under-valuation can last for many years at a time, the Equity Q ratio is not a useful indicator for short-term investment timelines. This metric is more appropriate for formulating expectations for long-term market performance.

Moreover, Spitznagel stated: "Historically, the higher the Q ratio, the fatter the subsequent left tail in the S&P500 (with 99% confidence). While overvaluation is murder on mean returns, as one should expect, it is even worse on risk."

Spitzagel (2011) uses strategy that's worth paying attention to. He profited from corrections in 2000 and 2008, more than doubling his funds. Nonetheless, he maintains that by buying stocks when the *q* ratio is near historic lows and then swapping them for Treasuries when the ratio is near its highs. In this way investors, can outperform the S&P 500.

Now let us return to our portfolio. Figure 3 shows the Equity Q ratio for the coal sector. Notice that it is less than one, q = 0. 72, meaning that the stocks are undervalued.

Figure 3. Coal Equity Q ratio

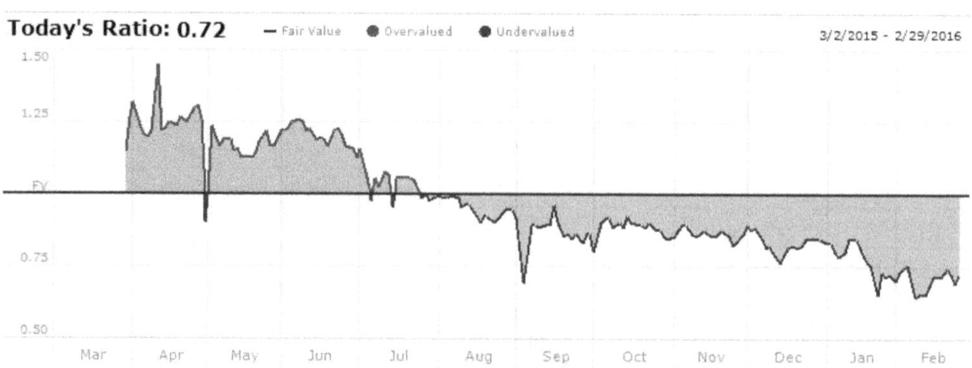

Within 15 days (15.02-29.02) the stock price of our coal stocks increased from 3.85 to 4.36. The expectation is that the price will continue to rise, and the investor will keep them in his or her portfolio until the q ratio reaches its historical highs. Figure 4 shows that the all-time high is 3.32 and the 52 weeks high is q = 1.44.

The more frequently I monitor the *portfolio*, the more likely I will observe a loss. In Table 2, I will keep track of my portfolio gains/losses and the equity q ratio through time.

THE FAULTY APPLICATION OF THE THEORY

I live with my family in a small town, in a country that once was part of Yugoslavia. Yugoslavia was a country characterized as one of the rapidly industrialized countries which has sustained a record of very high rates of economic growth during the 1960 and early 1970. Country with it is own space program today is fractured into 6 separate countries, and all of them are in the group of rising countries, with the exception of Slovenia.

From the early 90s, we were not just staked; we were slowly drowning in a so-called period of transition. It was a period in which our economy, education and most importantly knowledge were completely destroyed. The major transformation is that up to this disintegration we had experts in scientific fields with broad general knowledge. Today we have experts who specialize in some very narrow fields. My father used to say that we have two different

Figure 4. Coal equity Q ratio

Note: *The source is Morningstar. It provides stock market analysis, as well as the sectors q ratios (http://www.morningstar.com/market-valuation/market-fair-value-graph.aspx).*

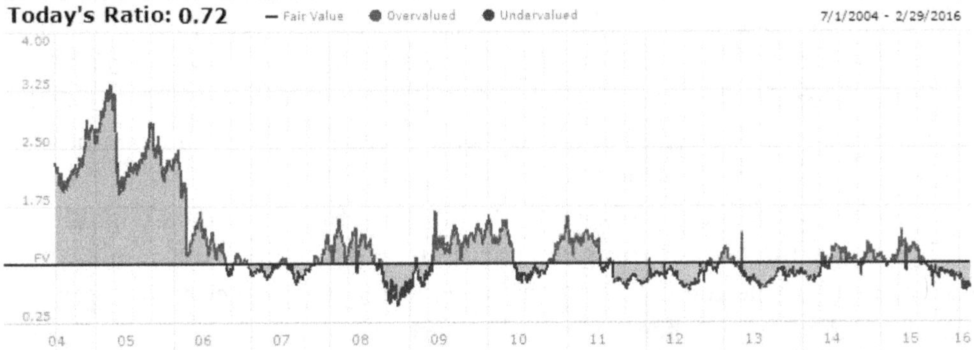

Table 2. Gain/Loss of the portfolio

Data	Gain/Loss of the Portfolio in $	Percentage Change of the Portfolio	Equity Q Ratio for the Coal Subsector
7.03.2016	974,00	5.92%	0.96
8.03.2016	1.161,00	7.06%	0.96
16.03.2016	1.077,50	6.54%	0.93
17.03.2016	1.303,50	7.92%	0.93
21.03.2016	1.500,50	9.11%	0.89
25.03.2016	1.310,50	7.96%	0.88
31.03.2016	1.611,50	9.79%	0.88
04.04.2016	1.708,50	10.38%	0.91
14.04.2016	2.139,00	13%	1.32
15.04.2016	2.176,00	13.22%	1.20
19.04.2016	2.219,50	13.48%	1.18
20.04.2016	2.405,50	14.61%	1.18
23.04.2016	1.991,00	12.09%	1.17
On April 23, 2016, I decided to sell NYSEARCA: XME and NYSE: YTZ coal stocks. The return was $1.707,00. Same day, I reinvested $5.157,00 in the biotechnology sector, to be more specific on the iShares Nadaq Biotechnology ETF. I purchased 18 stock by $288,34. The Q ratio is 0.82, and the expectation is a good investment in the long run.			
Reinvested (23.04.2016)			
Data	**Gain/Loss of the Portfolio in $**	**Percentage Change of the Portfolio**	**Equity Q Ratio for the Biotechnology Subsector**
05.05.2016	-545.58	-10.51%	0.79
31.05.2016	157,30	0.854%	0.85
06.06.2016	372,24	2.04%	0.84
28.06.2016	104.26	0.573%	0.78
08.07.2016	677.50	3.72%	0.84
07.09.2016	948.50	5.21%	0.87

ear specialists; one is for the left and the other for the right ear. At the end, the outcome of this never-ending transition is the lack of scientific mobility.

In the rush for this trend of micro approach we forget the fact that the sciences are interconnected and complement each other. If you cannot find the answer in your scientific field, check another.

So, what happened to my country? The answer is "embodied cognition".

It is a growing research program in cognitive psychology that emphasizes the influential role the environment plays in the development of cognitive processes. The general theory contends that cognitive processes develop when a tightly coupled system emerges from real-time, goal-directed interactions between organisms and their environment; the nature of these interactions influences the formation and further specifies the nature of the developing cognitive capacities.

Or as Eizans (2012), stated:

Embodied cognition implies that if we're truly interested in changing someone's behavior or capacity to learn, we don't need users to consciously change their attitudes. We need only make a change in their environment, via music, imagery, color variation, or even copy tone. This signifies that the work we do, the things we make, and all the options that lead to a system's creation are far from neutral.

Meaning our cognition is shaped by our experiences in the physical world. In support see the study of Williams, Huang and Bargh (2008). The study was set out to establish if the term "a warm person" is more than a figure of speech. Study participants were asked to attend a fourth-floor laboratory.

In the elevator, a research assistant would ask participants if they could hold her cup of coffee while she took their names. Half the participants were handed a hot coffee, while the other half were given an iced coffee. Once their names were recorded, she took back the coffee and they proceeded to the lab, where they were asked to judge an unknown person according to a description of their character.

"The amazing thing was that those who touched a warm cup of coffee in the elevator judged that person as a kinder, friendlier—in other words, warmer—person than those who held a cold cup of coffee," says Lobel. "When they were asked, of course they had no idea that this had any effect on them, but the results showed that just holding something warm or cold before entering the lab influenced their judgments."

Moreover, while I was reviewing the psychological theory, I also understand that humans make sense of economic events with storytelling and interpreting actions of others. No wonder why Taleb's book "The black swan: The impact of the highly improbable" was bestseller. He knew not only what to write, but also how to write. Remember, successful decision making in a social setting depends on your ability to understand the intentions, emotions and beliefs of others.

Now let us take the story a step further, and see why I have chosen to construct a portfolio using the tail risk protection strategy and why I believe that the next extreme event will be high inflation rates.

As a result of the changes in the environment in my country, my husband and I run into a limited number of people with whom we have a more in-depth conversation and talk about our intellectual interests. Therefore, when we met our friends, we share the ideas discussed. One day my husband was visited by a friend, a mid-level executive in the mining industry, and in a short talk he mentions that he conducted a study for copper market movements. His findings were that the copper market will reach its highest peak in 2020. I was surprised, but not in a positive sense, because I already knew that the future was uncertain and not so easily predictable. I also was familiar with the existence of the goal-directed interactions.

But then again this claim, helped me to realize what is actually just about to happen. At the very beginning I noticed that the copper market was highly unstable (see Figure 5), then I noticed the wide application of time domain time series analysis. Models are not universal; rules and limitations exist.

Before we see how the price fluctuation might correspond to stock market crashes, or even more importantly, how the copper market has been influenced, we need to familiarize ourselves with the foundation of the methodology employed. In the course of this investigation, I discovered that agents and copper analysts based their forecast upon time series observation, which is nothing but the Newtonian second law of motion.

Figure 5. Forecast error

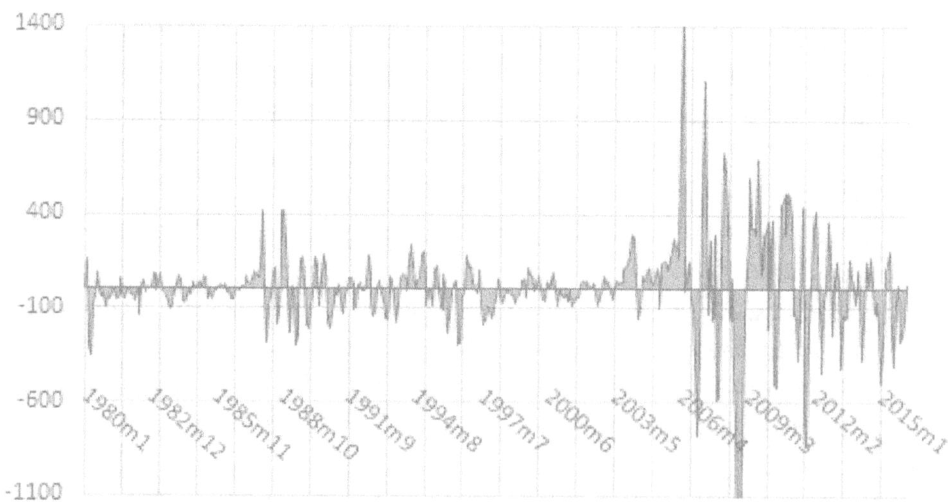

Newtonian Second Law of Motion and Time Series Analysis

In what follows I will try to give a simple explanation of the above mathematical model (time series) whose purpose is to predict the motions of the various objects that we encounter in the world around us.

Newtonian second law of motion states that,

A body continues in its state of rest or of uniform motion in a straight line unless it is compelled to change that state by forces impressed upon it,

$$x = x_0 + \mu t \tag{2}$$

Where x_0 represents the initial position at time t=0, and μ is the uniform velocity.

This means that a particle will move in a straight line if it is undistributed, as shown in Figure 6.

What happens if force is applied in the system? Then,

The change of motion is proportion to the motive force impressed; and is made in the direction of the straight line in which the force is impressed, Figure 7.

This means that the acceleration of particles along a straight line is proportional to the force which is applied in that direction.

$$x = x_0 + \mu_0 t + \frac{at^2}{2} \tag{3}$$

where μ_0 is the velocity at time t=0 and α is the constant acceleration due to motive force.

Figure 6. Moving in a straight line

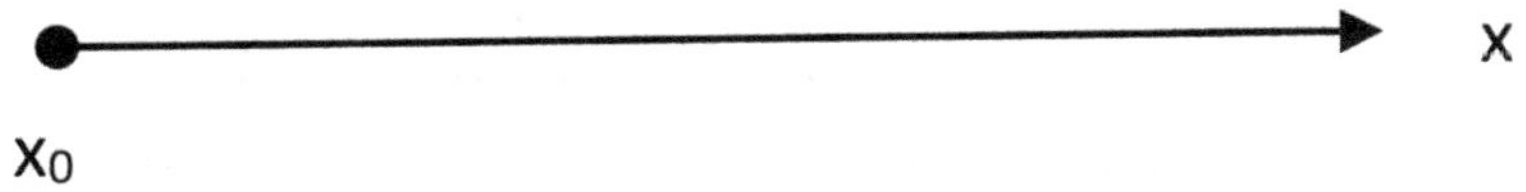

Figure 7. Force applied

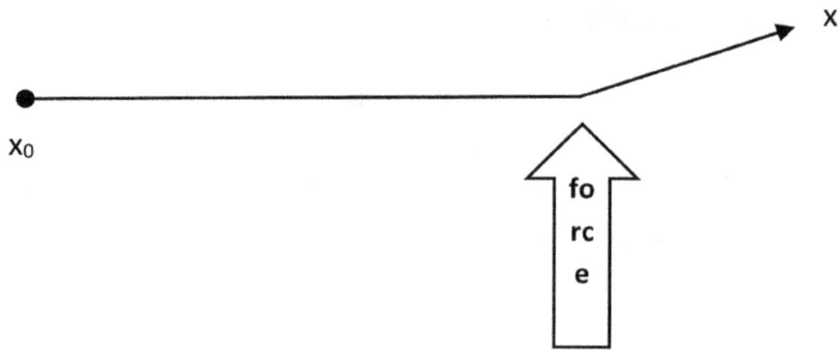

Now let us see how this is applied in the finance theory. The dynamic of the price for a stock is similar to the dynamic of a particle subject to external forces. The following analogies are used, with "shares of a stock" as the "mass of a particle" the "stock price" as the "distance" of the movement of a particle, the "change in excess demand for a stock" as the "external force" exerting on a particle, the "trading values" of a stock as the "kinetic energy". But the acceleration in dynamical systems is not constant and the particle is not moving along a straight line. The movement is parabolic.

Additionally, as we noted the excess demand acts as the external force that causes the stock price to change, therefore the acceleration can be formulated as:

$$a = \frac{1}{m} \Delta ED \tag{4}$$

Where,

ΔED → excess demand

α → is the acceleration of the stock price

m → "mass" of the stock/shares

Here the acceleration is proportional to the change in excess demand and inversely proportional to the "mass" of the stock.

Now let us go back to Equation 3 and replace α with the above formulation. Because all the inputs are known variables we can easily predict the future stock price position, x, and get the stock price movement. An example of graphical presentation of the time series is given in Figure 8.

Figure 8. Trend detection

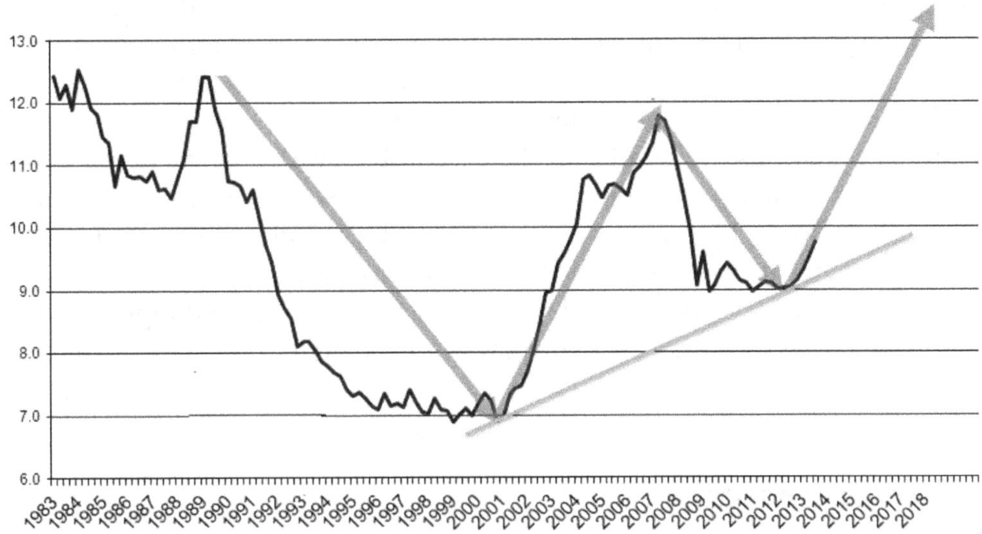

Then Why Richard Fitzpatrick professor of Physics, the University of Texas at Austin states that this is a faulty application of the theory? Up to the beginning of the 20th century scientists generally assumed that they knew everything that there was to be known about Newtonian dynamics. Now they know that this is not the case. The advent of fast electronic computers, in the latter half of the 20th century, allowed scientists to solve nonlinear equations of motion, for the first time, via numerical techniques. In general, such equations are insolvable using standard analytic methods. The numerical investigation of dynamical systems with nonlinear equations of motion revealed the existence of a previously unknown type of motion known as deterministic chaos. The discovery of chaotic motion led to a Renaissance in the study of Newtonian dynamics which started in the late 20th century and is still ongoing. So, the modern view is that Newton's theory is only an approximation which is valid under certain circumstances; i.e. is valid on isolated dynamical systems, in which all of the forces acting on the system originate within the system itself. Or as Fitzpartick (2011) point out: "Newtonian dynamics has been found to give predictions which are in excellent agreement with experimental observations in all situations in which it is expected to be valid."

As a result, "evidence obtained under different experimental conditions cannot be comprehended within a single picture, but must be regarded as complementary in the sense that only the totality of the phenomena exhausts the possible information about the objects." And the principle of complementarity, "implies the impossibility of any sharp separation between the behaviour of atomic objects and the interaction with the measuring instruments which serve to define the conditions under which the phenomena appear."

These are the characteristic features of quantum physics and as you can notice the findings are similar to the recent discoveries in the area of the embodied cognitive psychology. I hope that these discoveries will soon turn conventional wisdom for decision making upside-down and lead to a Renaissance in the economic theory and modelling. We simply cannot extract universal laws of human behavior from time series and represent the socioeconomic behavior, especially not when the system is characterized by large fluctuation.

COPPER MARKET

Copper giants are facing hard times. Copper plants/mining is closing. The demand is low. Industry debt burdens have spiralled out of control as well, Figure 9. Australia is struggling with recession after two decades of growth. China's economy grows at slowest rate in 25 years. Slowdown all around us… According to newsletters and financial analysis copper is the "most attractive long-term fundamental." Why?

Figure 9. Australia commodity leverage

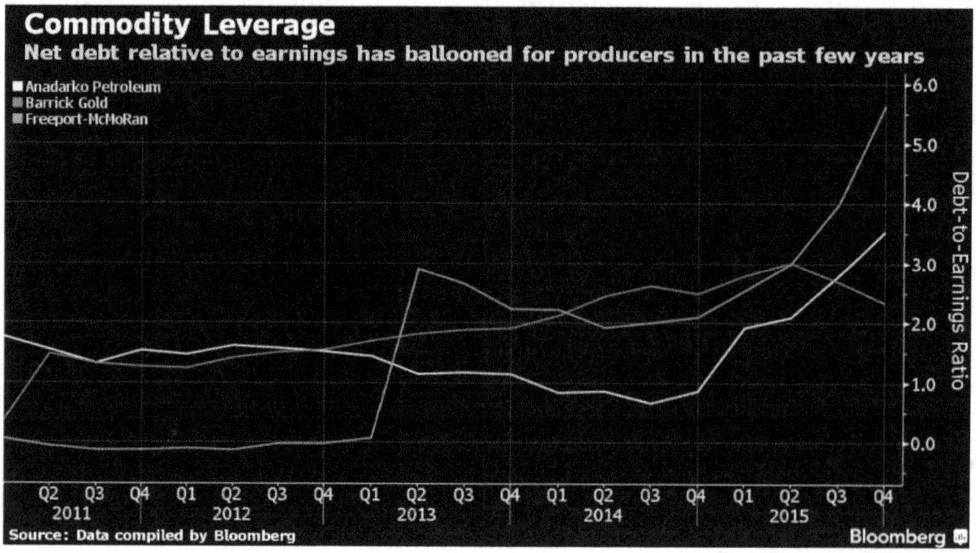

In the previous section, we showed that the copper market is highly unstable; refer to Figure 5. Therefore, in order to increase the market price of copper, the copper giants in collaboration with other countries' governments should reduce these fluctuations and work in parallel with strategies to increase its demand. This is not an easy task, but for sure there is a way.

In what it follows I will try to make it clear how this is done in the real world, and I will leave you to conclude whether this can be explained by the rational agent theory, methodological individualism or effective market hypotheses; theories that characterize the dominant neoclassical theory.

In the recent two decades, the media are utilized as an indispensable instrument in bringing down the price fluctuations. It acts upon human behavior and create positive future expectations that will generate an increase in demand for copper and its price. We will see that same news is found repeating several times, and that the propaganda start in 2014, but the supreme influence has been seen during 2015. Some other interesting fact is that as more people provide comments on this copper forecast titles the more valuable it becomes to other users due to demand-side economics. If you are interested to know how this is possible I recommend you to read "network effects", one of the most important mental models described in psychology?

But this intervention is not enough to enable the desired demand for copper. Additional, larger interference is needed. I had already told the story of my country and the power of the "embodied cognition". As Daniel Eizans, director of Enablement Strategy at Team Detroit, stated: "the findings are both wonderful and scary" (2016). It is not easy to prove the direct involvement of copper giant and governments in changing the human living environment for a particular purpose, but this does not mean that it does not exist.

Some countries such as India, Brazil, Africa and Latin America will be assisted in their fast development and industrialization, and others will be destroyed, as the Middle East. It is all part of the big game.

So let us start first with the media and see what they have to say.

- According to the report *"Metal Deactivator Market: By Metals (Copper, Aluminum, Alloys & Others), By Formulation (Water based & Oil based), By End-User Industry (Industrial, Automotive, Aviation Jet Fuel, Polymers, Food & Agriculture) & By Geography - Forecast (2015 - 2020)*", published by Industry ARC in 2016, the market is estimated to reach $207 Million by 2020 at a high Compound annual growth rate (CAGR).

- In 2015 expectations given by The Goldman Sachs Group- leading American multinational investment banking firm, or that the copper price will rise above the metal's marginal cost until 2020, with price rise back to $5,500.
- In 2016 Simon Lovat, a commodity analyst at fund from Carmignac stated that: "Copper is the most sought after commodity, it is a good time to buy copper assets now, there are some very visible deficits coming up at the end of this decade,".
- Or let me show you the copper forecasts given by Deutsche Bank analysts, responsible for macroeconomic analysis within Deutsche Bank Group and acts as consultant for the bank, its clients and stakeholders: "Small surpluses in 2016 and 2017, a deficit of 280,000 tonnes in 2018, 350,000 in 2019 and 280,000 in 2020."

Isn't it interesting how accurately, they anticipated the future copper trends? Do you think that this is possible? Let us extend our analytical work and see the titles published around the world by prominent global finance market newsletters and information technology investment companies through the years:

- Market Watch, 2014: Global Copper Mining (Mine Production) Market: 3.9% CAGR Forecast to 2020 in New Research Report.
- Market Watch, 2015: Metal Recycling Market (Ferrous, Non-Ferrous) Set to Grow at a CAGR of 7.95% to 2020.
- Bloomberg, 2015: Commodity Markets May Not See a Sustained Rally Until the 2020's.
- CNBC, 2015: Copper faces long bear market: Goldman.
- Market Realist, 2015: Copper's Long-Term Outlook Looks Better.
- Yahoo Finance, 2016: Why Does Freeport Expect a 500,000 Ton Copper Deficit by 2020?
- Yahoo Finance, 2016: Expected shortages boost crowd-pulling power of copper mines.
- Market Realist, 2016: Why Does Freeport Expect a 500,000 Ton Copper Deficit by 2020?
- Market Realist, 2016: Why Is Copper's Long-Term Outlook Better?

The market has been conditioned to believe that copper demand will exceed its supply. This should take the copper price to its highest peak in 2020, which is mathematically well-supported. Please note that world's policy decisions are based on this analysis.

All this study applies the time series modelling, Markov chain models and neural nets as forecasting methodologies. Using copper historical data, I run the same analysis, with the exception of the neural net analysis. The neural nets are believed to perform better on time series data, however, I do not recommend using them in modelling financial market movements. For the Markov chain model refer to chapter 6. And in chapter 7 I will introduce a novel methodology that could help us predict stock price movements, known as the wavelet-based methodology.

Here we will present the two lag time series moving averages. The analyses are conducted using the statistical software STATA 11 and Excel Spreadsheets. I consider a sample of 434 trading months for the period January 1980-February 2016, and the data are obtained on the basis of the International Monetary Fund (available online: https://www.imf.org/external/np/res/commod/External_Data.xls/ external data+copper). Researchers who are interested to repeat these analyses could find the STATA code in appendix I.

Moving Average is a tool commonly used to smooth out short-term fluctuations and identify longer-term economic trends or cycles, see Figure 10

Figure 10. Moving average

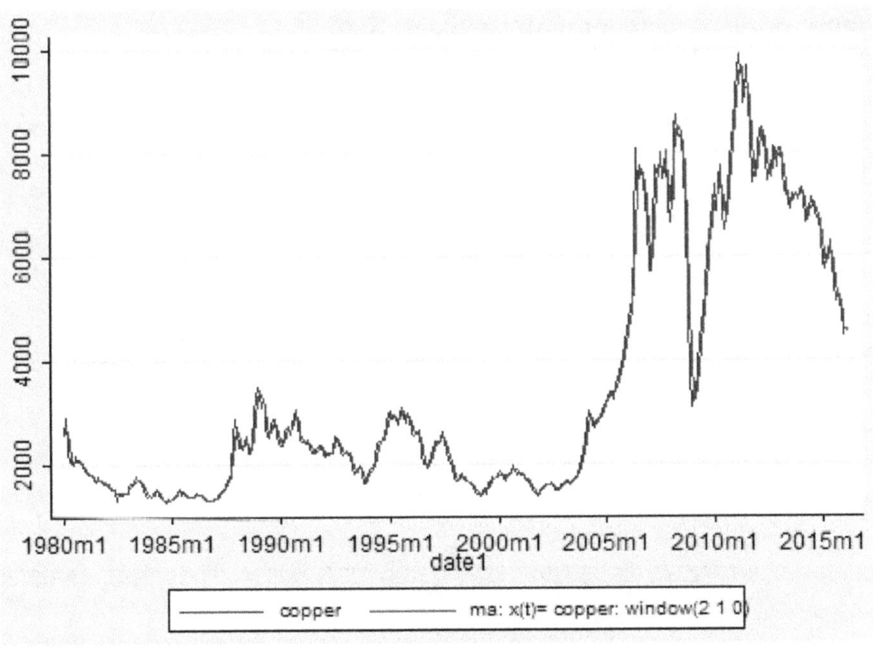

and Figure 11. There are 3 types of trends, namely "Uptrend", "Downtrend" and "Sideway". Each represents a different collective sentiment of the stock market participants, bullishness in an Uptrend, bearishness in a Downtrend and indecision in a sideways market. Knowing the trend, a trader can more easily identify the tops and bottoms of the price movement for buying or selling opportunities.

The common way to interpret the price moving average is to compare its dynamics to the price action. When the instrument's price rises above its moving average, a buy signal appears, if the price falls below its moving average, we have a sell signal.

Figure 10 shows the copper bearish trend. In February 2016, the copper stock price was above its moving average, 4598,62 > 4569,747. If we use trend lines and chart patterns, then we will conclude that a bullish trend is expected, which supports the above reported findings of positive long-run trend.

But this is nothing but falsity application of the theory. Or as Sterman (2000) stated: "When the environment becomes truly complex decision makers fail to respond appropriately by constructing new models. Instead, they seem to revert to older, simpler models." I don't want to give you a wrong impression. I am not saying that we should not make mathematical analysis, we should, but we must be careful not to distinguish economics from sociology and psychology. The future is uncertain and we could not predict the future price movement with such certainty.

Figure 11. Copper price forecast

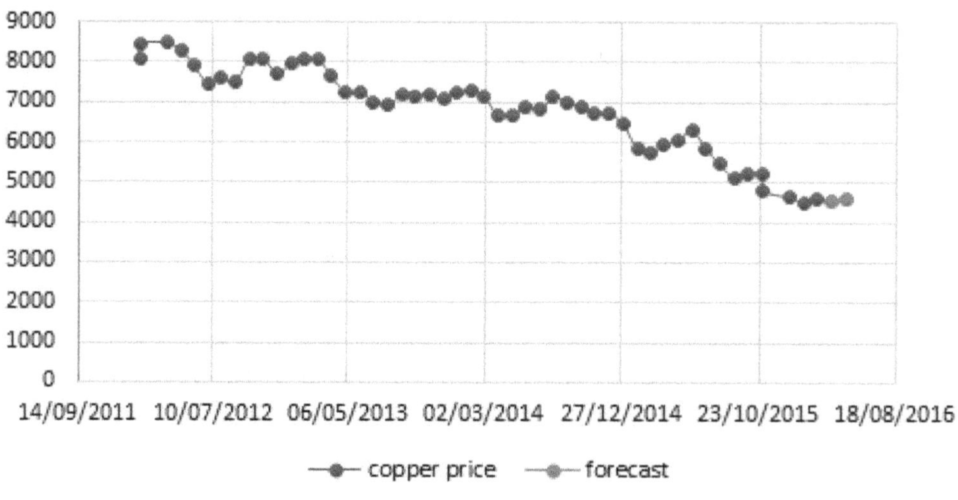

Before I proceed with the analysis, I would like to underline two particular points. As I already mentioned above, proving the involvement of the copper giant and governments in shaping the human environment to its needs is not an easy task; this calls for much more detailed analysis attained in a long run. And the second even more important point is that this is not the target of the book. Maybe that will be in the next book. But I feel an obligation to share with you few goals directed action taken recently with the aim to raise the real demand for copper. I also do not want to exclude the possibility that this may as well end up for a greater good for humanity.

To date, experiments in economics are restricted to situations in which individuals are not influenced by the physical presence of other people. In such contexts, interactions remain at an abstract level, agents guessing what another person is thinking or is about to decide based on money exchange. Physical presence and bodily signals are therefore left out of the picture. Then why would there be salesmen or bank employees working so hard to gain our trust and influence our economic decisions with their smiles, gestures and manners if their actions were useless?

The embodied cognitive psychology teaches us that if we are interested in changing someone's behavior, the implication is that we do not necessarily need to change anything about them; we might instead focus on changing the environment. Allow me apply this definition in the copper demand context.

Because copper is the partner in development, to increase its demand we should modify human environment in order to initiate or support the country's growth. But remember the rapid increase of demand for copper will be initialized with the growth of industrial sector not the service sector, or a simultaneous growth of both.

In 2015 the China's slowdown has been the major factor driving copper prices to levels unseen since the global financial crisis of 2008–2009, settling at $2.287 a pound. In the first quartile of 2016 the copper prices continued to decrease; the downward trend accelerated. But the diverse expectation of the copper price in the last quartile of 2016, captured attention the most.

John Tilton, at Colorado School of Mines, mining economist, said that he was not optimistic about copper prices coming back any time soon. He also stated: "The investment banking firms Goldman Sachs and Citigroup recently issued very pessimistic and very optimistic copper price forecasts, respectively. Analysts for another investment firm, Morgan Stanley Investment Management, are also pessimistic."

What is the rational decision here? Whose predictions are truthful?

Despite my rich knowledge in the application of quantitative methodology in forecasting, I cannot determine with certainty the future of copper price. Both analyses can be considered right or wrong at the same time, because the future price trend is governed by two factors. First by the number of people who will believe in a particular forecast and accordingly make the decisions. And second, whether there will be an emerging country to save us.

After the China's slowdown, all eyes focused on India, as one of the countries that could be the new engine of copper consumption.

The world expectation was a rapid growth followed by a shift from agriculture to industries and then to services. But India shifted directly to services and characterize its self us an outlier in emerging market basket. Is this a new growth recipe? Can India become a developed country without a strong industrial base?

No. The process would be painful and slow.

To clarify, a large services sector in a developing economy or a country with low GDP per capita shows the inability of the government and in India's case, the private sector industries as well to keep up with an accelerated rural-urban migration. Therefore, India's non-agricultural labor force is mostly employed in informal services industry because there is nowhere else to go. As a result, India in 2013/14 has seen a slowdown in the rate of economic growth in 4-5%. Real GDP per capita growth is even lower. This is a reason for worry as India needs a high growth rate to see rising living standards, lower unemployment and encouraging investment. India has fallen behind China, which is a comparable developing economy.

If we desperately need a new engine of copper consumption, then it is time for action. Developments and declines are always accompanied by structural changes. Let us now review the few Indian economy incentives that are followed by the goal directed actions mentioned above.

The year 2014 was a decisive one for Indian politics. The Narendra Modi's campaign was supplemented with "a massively funded and aggressive media campaign". The result is, the biggest election victory, since independence in 1947. Modi became the symbol of a new chapter in India's growth story, stimulating the Indian economy through major reforms in manufacturing and export sector. Additionally, the government not only increased the limits of FDI in Railways, Insurance and Defense but also encouraged privatization of loss-making public sector companies.

Meaning, the path for moving into an Indian world is unlocked. Developed countries will try to modify the Indian natural environment, shaping it to its need, not vice versa. As promised above, I will share with you few recent complex and changing environment events:

- January 20, 2016 India and UK have agreed to open up trade and markets to support growth, carry out structural reforms and address issues related to cross-border tax evasion.

After the talks the India's Finance Minister said:

From the Indian point of view, we were extremely interested in having the British investors look at infrastructure investments in India for which various possibilities were discussed.

The two nations will work together in developing an India-UK partnership fund under the umbrella of National Investment and Infrastructure Fund (NIIF) recently created in India. This fund will seek to increase flows of private sector capital and expertise alongside multilateral support into Indian infrastructure.

The world's fifth largest economy will work on the development of smart cities in India. New Delhi is also looking at London for issuance of rupee-denominated bonds to get UK investors to fund its infrastructure projects.

India, is "extremely keen that large British companies, particularly involved in infrastructure financing, start investing in Indian infrastructure".

- It is well-known that the energy is a key raw material in the metals and mining industry. Energy can form almost 20% of copper's production costs. The copper industry uses a lot of diesel in the production process. Therefore, on February 23, 2016 US President Barack Obama supported India's massive energy needs. In his speech, Obama stressed:

In order to grow the economy, we have got to have energy. In fact, there are countries like India, where it is even more desperate.

"They (Indians) do not have electricity," he said, adding that India needs access to energy in order to develop.

"And if we are not giving them options, if the only message we have for them is, 'Stay poor,' then we are not going to solve the problem... We have got to grow the economy, which means we have got to produce energy and we've got to deal with climate change. The good news is that technology and research and development are accelerating rapidly, and because of the Paris agreement this accelerate progress even more," he said.

- On March 24, 2016 that according the data released by US Treasury shows India makes up 1.8% of US foreign equity holdings as of December 2015 as against 1.6% of China. India has overtaken China in terms of direct equity allocation by US investors.
- TPG Growth founded in 2007 to specialize in growth equity and middle-market buyout opportunities. They assist at all stages of a company's growth, from its inception to its international expansion, by drawing on our geography-specific experience and expert global operational resources from the TPG platforms.

In 2015 in just five months it raised a 3 billion fund and they plan to park the entire sum in India. Then in 2016 has acquired a 26% stake in Mumbai-based broking firm Landmark Insurance. This is the second investment by TPG in the Landmark group in the last one year. Landmark group has auto dealerships in India with 20 showrooms and service center for passenger vehicles, including Mercedes Benz, Honda and Volkswagen. It also has three showrooms and service center for Ashok Leyland, a leading Indian commercial vehicle OEM. Established in the late 90s, Landmark Insurance Broking is among the largest automotive insurance renewal agents in the country with a 1,000-strong workforce, growing at a compounded annual rate of 30-35%.

TPG Growth invests in a broad range of industries including consumer, retail, technology, internet, healthcare, energy, clean tech and renewable, transportation, industrials, and business services.

- March 11, 2016 Asian Development Bank (ABD) supported the government's commitment to build more infrastructure, president Mr. Nakao said ABD will increase its lending to $10 billion to $12 billion for the 3 calendar year 2016 through 2018.

And for the rest of us, there is no other choice except to sit and keep an eye on the game. If we can estimate the time window in which India people will accept these modifications, then we could capture the real copper demand and price trend timely. But each of us has different preferences, beliefs, expectations and needs. All of them together model our behavior.

From what I can see up to now, setting 2020 as a major year for the copper market, is a very ambitious plan; the market boom is set too early. Why?

First, India is not ready to fulfil its economic potential, not yet. Second, similar input does not give always identical output, for example:

The Internet.org application, launched in India in February 2015 in partnership with Reliance Communications, faced a backlash in 2016 with a number of leading technology and Internet firms pulling out of the service after activists claimed it violated the principles of a neutral Internet. To this Daniels (2015) said "I would say India is unique in that respect and very much an outlier. In other markets, Internet.org has been embraced as a pro-connectivity initiative that has garnered a lot of support."

In India the choice could never be between chaos and stability, but between manageable and unmanageable chaos (Sociologist Ashis Nandy, 1980s).

FUTURE COPPER MARKET MOVEMENTS

In what it follows, I will present the two possible scenarios related to the future copper market movements.

Scenario 1: The Copper Demand Will Exceed Its Supply

The media exhibit powerful network effects and model our future expectations. Changes in our expectations or beliefs could have some large effects on future copper price movements. For example, it can influence an agent's decision regarding the choice of a financing source for a certain project. This will move the copper demand curve to right, causing an increase of the copper price.

Additionally, because of the expected positive trend in the copper market, the number of traders/investors will increase. Higher participation of traders on both sides on the market increases expected trading volume, increases the expected utility of risk-averse traders and decreases the variance of the expected market price. In other words, higher liquidity increases trader's utility.

Here it is important to highlight the fact that the price change is followed with a real copper demand -copper consumed by end users, not hoarding. This is the only way to maintain a sustainable growth and avoid market crashes.

Scenario 2: Extreme Events-High Inflation Rates

The traders influenced by the media believe that the copper market will have positive long-term fundamentals and start investing in copper stocks, but this trend is not accompanied with a real increase on the demand side (copper consumed by end users). In this case the future delays and difficulties in bringing new projects on stream, as well as the highly resistant to new spending initiatives, would result in a new market crash.

In sum, this intervention will heat up the inflation and damage the real economy and in the long run the profitability of the companies and the consumption. Or as the economists want to say we will "take a bath".

The probability that an extreme event could occur is higher than the standard statistical methodologies account. Usually they are unpredictable because of side-effects in some human research, intervention or interaction, as the high inflation in this scenario. For that reason, in constructing my portfolio I used the "tail risk, protecting strategy" or in literature know as a "barbell investment strategy". Furthermore, copper stocks are not included in my portfolio. The reason is simple, because of it a high Q ratio, q=1. 98. While overvaluation is murder on mean returns, as you should expect, it is even worse on risk. Meaning, you should buy stocks when they are undervalued and keep them in your portfolio until the q ratio reaches its historical highs.

Figure 12. Copper Q ratio

Note: *The source is Morningstar. It provides stock market analysis, as well as the sectors q ratios (http://www.morningstar.com/market-valuation/market-fair-value-graph.aspx)*

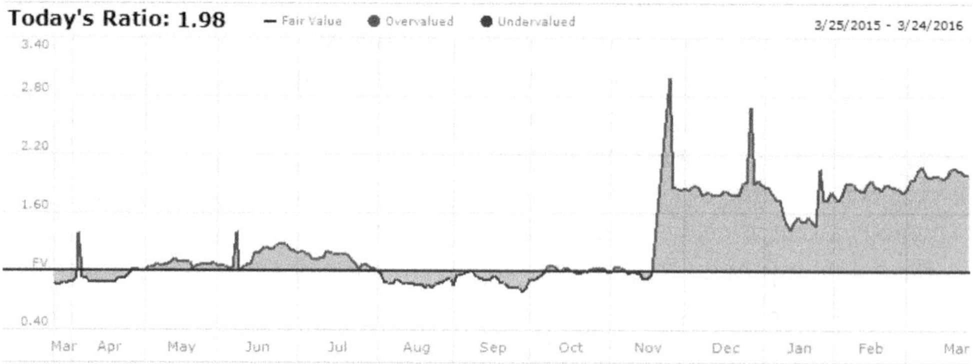

How to Make Decisions

In neoclassical financial economics, the efficient-market hypothesis (EMH) states that asset prices fully reflect all available information. Professor Eugene Fama in 1965 first introduced the concept of EMH. He argued that stocks always trade at their fair value, making it impossible for investors to either purchase undervalued stocks or sell stocks inflated prices. As such, it should be impossible to outperform the overall market through expert stock selection or market timing, and that the only way an investor can possibly obtain higher returns is by chance or by purchasing riskier investments.

Moreover, according the EMH there is no room for fooling investors, and as a result, all investments in efficient markets are fairly priced, i.e. on average investors get exactly what they pay for.

Our findings are contrary to EMH. First, there is a plenty of room for fooling investors.

Second, what the rational decision here is? To invest or not to invest?

At the very begging keep in mind that you should not rely on every information or analysis put out. It is very important to do your homework, because the quality of your decision depends mainly on it. This means that rational decision making is actually a subjective. Therefore: *do not invest in copper stocks due to the stock overvaluation driven primary by investor perception; there is a high possibility of a new market crash as a result of a rapid price increase.*

REFERENCES

Benthem, J. (1948). *An Introduction to the Principles of Morals and Legislation*. New York: Hafner Publishing.

Berger, P. L., & Luckmann, T. (1991). The social construction of reality: A treatise in the sociology of knowledge (No. 10). Penguin UK.

Boldeman, L. (2013). *The cult of the market: economic fundamentalism and its discontents*. ANU Press.

Daniels, C. (2015, May 13). Personal Interview.

Eizans, D. (2016). Creating for the Brain in the Body. Retrieved from http://contentsmagazine.com/articles/creating-for-the-brain-in-the-body/

Eizans (2012, April). Creating for the Brain in the Body. *a Column,* 3. Retrieved from http://contentsmagazine.com/articles/creating-for-the-brain-in-the-body/

Fitzpatrick, R. (2011). *Newtonian dynamics.* Lulu.com.

Hancock, M., & Zahawi, N. (2011). *Masters of Nothing: How the crash will happen again unless we understand human nature.* Biteback Publishing.

Spitznagel, M. (2011). The Dao of Corporate Finance, Q Ratios, and Stock Market Crashes (Working White Paper 13). *Universa.*

Sterman, J. (2000). Business Dynamics: Systems Thinking and Modeling for a Complex World. New York: McGraw Hill.

Taleb, N. N. (2007). *The black swan: The impact of the highly improbable.* Random House.

Williams, L. E., Huang, J. Y., & Bargh, J. A. (2009). The scaffolded mind: Higher mental processes are grounded in early experience of the physical world. *European Journal of Social Psychology, 39*(7), 1257–1267. doi:10.1002/ejsp.665 PMID:20046813

Wilson, E. O. (2002). *The future of life.* Vintage.

APPENDIX

Time Series Analysis

Step 1: Open the Data Editor and Paste the Copper Data Set (see Figure 13)
Step 2: Copy-Paste the Given STATA Code in the "Command Bar" and Then Press "Enter" (see Figure 14).

STATA Code:

```
generate date1 = m(1980m1) + _n - 1
format %tm date1
tset date1
tsset date1, monthly
twoway (tsline copper)
twoway (tsline copper) if tin(2006m1, 2016m2)
pac copper
tssmooth ma copper_ma = copper, window(2 1 0)
twoway (tsline copper copper_ma*), legend(size(small))
```

Figure 13. Data editor in STATA

Figure 14. Command bar

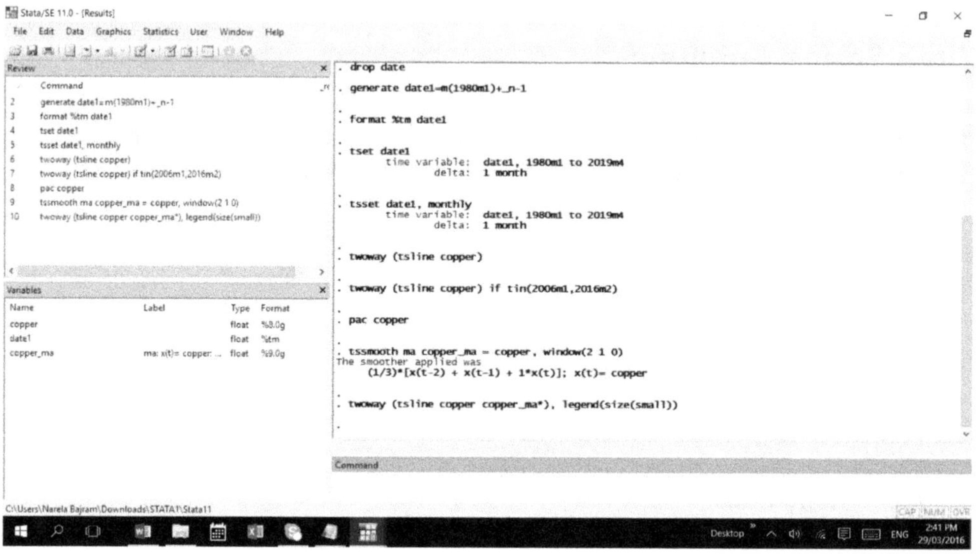

Step 3: Go back to the "Data Editor". You can notice that two new variables are generated. One is the date1 and the second is the copper_ma which represents the models estimates.

Figure 15. Two new variables are generated

Step 4: The forecast error is calculated by the following formula **copper-copper_ma**, or 2926.71,63-2754.67=162,04. Following this procedure we will get Figure 16.

Forecast Errors are graphically represented with scatterplots (see Figure 17).

Figure 16. Forecast Error

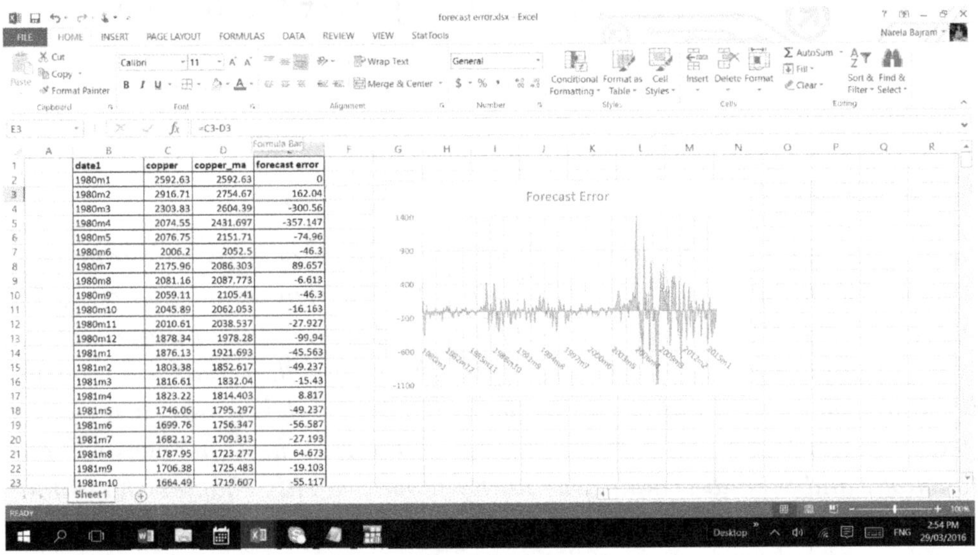

Figure 17. Scatterplots

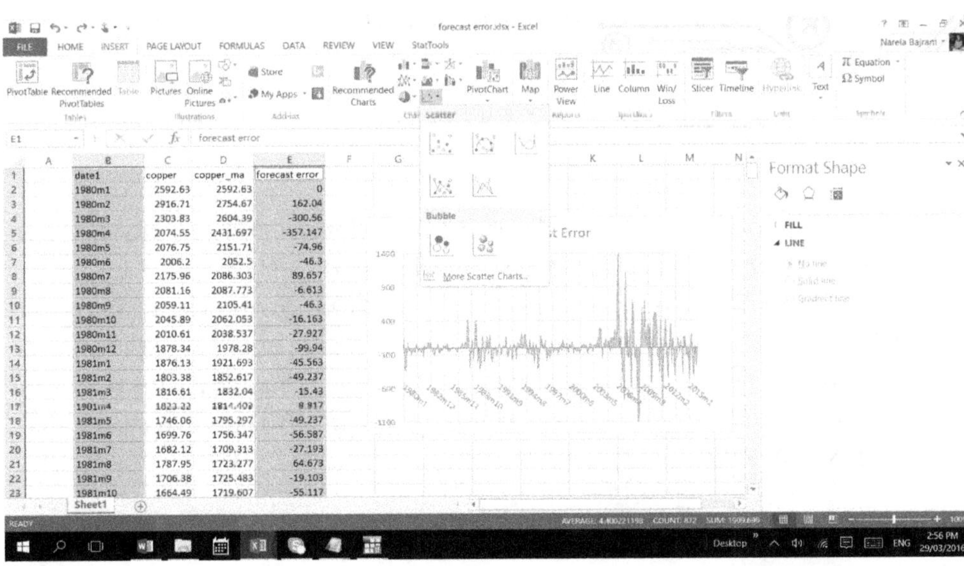

Chapter 5
Dynamic Portfolio Selection:
Asset-Liability Management Model

ABSTRACT

In this chapter I recognize the importance of the stochastic programming as a significant tool in financial planning. The current practice of portfolio optimization is still limited to the simple formulation of linear programming (LR) or quadratic programming (QR) type. For that reason, relevant literature on asset-liability management (ALM) model has been reviewed and two different ALM approaches are compared: first piecewise linear function; and second a nonlinear utility function. This chapter shows that the mathematical programming methodology is ready to challenge the huge problem arising from LP portfolio optimization. A special emphasis was put on the shape of the investors' payoff functions in asset price equilibrium. The results underpin our claim that the nonlinear ALM model generated better asset allocation. An algorithmic construction of ALM model is developed in Wolfram Mathematica 9.

Your child does not seem to have a learning impediment, but he does not seem to want to speak. The schoolmaster pressures you to start considering "other options," namely therapy. You argue with her to no avail (she is supposed to be the "expert"). Then, suddenly, the child starts composing elaborate sentences, perhaps a bit too elaborate for his age group. I will repeat that linear progression, a Platonic idea, is not the norm. (Nassim Nicolas Taleb, The Black Swan, 2007)

DOI: 10.4018/978-1-5225-3259-0.ch005

INTRODUCTION

Due to the development of new branches of financial services and financial products, financial business is becoming more and more complicated, resulting in greater risks. In addition, the financial industry is getting more involved in the economy, both nationally and globally. Nowadays, the financial market could easily drive the global economy in recession and led to more and more loss. But these losses are not due to market risk or credit risk, but instead are due to operational risk. Why?

According the Basel II we recognize three main categories of financial risk: market risk, credit risk and operational risk. Market risk is mainly from the fluctuations of asset prices in the financial market. Credit risk corresponds to the default of counterparties or business institutions involved in the financial market. Operational risk is defined as the risk of loss resulting from inadequate or failed internal processes, people and systems or from external events. This definition includes legal risk, but excludes strategic and reputational risk. According to Yang (2009), "operational risk covers a wide range of events and can result from various sources, where managerial issues normally play significant parts. It can result from human or machines; can be hidden in calculations or documentations; can be external or internal. "

In support let us recall the story of the largest single individual fraud: the Madoff story.

On 11thof December 2008, the former chairman of the NASDAQ stock exchange and business owner of the Wall Street firm Bernard L. Madoff Investment Securities LLC, Bernard Lawrence Madoff was arrested by the FBI on the allegation of a $50 billion fraud, the biggest investor fraud ever attributed to a single individual. This fraud operated as a Ponzi scheme, a rather simple scheme, which pays investors with their own money or the money collected from new investors. For example, assume a client, promised a 15% annual return, and gave Bernie $10 million to invest on January 1. Bernie deposited the client's money in his own bank account. As more clients invested over the course of the year, the amount in Bernie's bank account grew. If the client decided to cash in the entire investment on December 31, Bernie wrote the client a check for $11. 5 million from the company's bank account. Then DiPascali and several loyal investment fund employees fed price data from the previous 12 months for stocks, options, and Treasury Bills into a computer to derive a long list of trades that indicated a $1.500.000 profit.

Then DiPascali mailed these documents and trading tickets to the client as supporting evidence.

Bernie claimed that the Ponzi scheme began in 1991, after which he made no legitimate investments with client money. Statement open for discussion.

In 1987 Bernie was honored from the U.S. Securities and Exchange Commission (SEC) for staying open, for business on "Black Monday", when Dow Jones Industrial Average dropped 508 points or 22.6% in one day of chaotic trading. The only reason why Bernie was able to remain open is his large amount of cash from his illegal investment fund account. The SEC stated that this was unknown activate for them. In short, Madoff promised to its investor's suspicion steady returns and the SEC ignored this tip and other numerous red flags, and instead of opening an investigation they honored him.

But in 2008 as the U.S. economy entered the recession period, investors began to panic and withdraw their money from Madoff's accounts, totalling more than $7 billion. Madoff was unable to cover the redemptions and struggled to obtain the liquidity necessary to meet those obligations, because he only had $487 million in his investment fund bank account.

At the end, we can conclude that Madoff was allowed to carry out his fraud. This is an even bigger crime, which passed without any penalties only with several addressed critics.

However, the worst thing about these scams, is that most of the investors never know until it's too late.

What does the story teach us?

John Allen Pauls, professor of mathematics at Temple University in Philadelphia, gave quite good explanation in one sentence: "Uncertainty is the only certainty there is, and knowing how to live with insecurity is the only security." Meaning, to solve a decision problem, as buying or selling of securities, we should know that the uncertainty, which is everywhere in the financial markets, is unavoidable. As well, we need a dynamical approach which is naturally applicable to problems with uncertainties, and is suited with both market risk and operational risk management.

Therefore, in this chapter I will present the ALM model as one of the major applications for dynamic portfolio optimization problems, and demonstrate how the stochastic programming provides an appropriate framework for mathematical description of them.

In the section that follows I will give a short literature revisit of the Asset and Liability Management (ALM) model with its prime importance in several industries, mainly in energy (Kallrath, Pardalos, Rebennack, & Scheidt, 2009) and finance (Dempster, Pflug, & Mitra, 2008).

Section 3 focuses on the two alternatives of modelling the portfolio decisions for multi-period problems. In particular, it describes the formulation of the objective, the optimization approach and the generation of scenarios. As a first alternative, to develop my investment portfolio, I build an asset allocation plan using a piecewise linear utility function. But in reality, the uncertainty about the parameters is changing over time. Meaning, that the investment opportunity set perceived by the investor, may as well change over time. For that reason, as a second alternative I am applying a nonlinear utility function. And in the last section I present the numerical illustration of the asset allocation problem.

ASSET ALLOCATION MODELS: A LITERATURE REVISIT

As I have said so many times, God doesn't play dice with the world. (Albert Einstein, 1943)

The classical treatments of strategic asset allocation can be traced back to Samuelson (1969) and Merton (1969, 1971). In the light of Markowitz' seminal papers on single-period portfolio selection, the early literature focused on conditions leading to the optimality of myopic policies, i.e., the conditions under which portfolio decisions for multi-period problems coincide with those for single period problems. In addition, the lack of computing power lead to formulate models driven by the quest for closed form solutions. To achieve these objectives, rather restrictive assumptions were made, and many of these models' results turned out to be inconsistent with conventional wisdom as expressed by the so-called Samuelson puzzle: whereas one of the main results from early multi-period portfolio models is that the fractions of risky assets are constant over time, this contradicts the advice obtained from many professionals in practice that investors should hold a share of risky assets which declines steadily as they approach retirement (often called the age effect). Since then, many researchers have tried to resolve this puzzle which is mainly rooted in some of the (simplifying) assumptions used in early models (fixed planning horizon, time-constant investment opportunities, no intermediate consumption, etc.).

Research in the area of life-cycle asset allocation models regained momentum in the early 1990s for two main reasons: first, a number of economic factors increased the number of people with sizeable wealth to invest (the "generation of heirs"), coupled with increased uncertainty about the security of public pension systems. Second, the tremendous growth in computer power enabled the solution of theoretical accounts with more realistic assumptions. A number of additional features have been added to the classical models, in many cases with the goal of resolving the Samuelson puzzle: stochastic labor income, time-varying investment opportunities, parameter uncertainty (with and without learning), special treatment of certain asset classes (real estate), and habit formation, to name just the most important developments.

Ultimately, the objective of a good asset allocation plan is to develop an investment portfolio that will help you reach your financial objectives with the degree of risk you find comfortable. ALM recognizes that static, single-period investment planning models fail to incorporate the multi-period nature of the liabilities faced by the company. A multi-period model aim is to maximize the overall revenue, sometimes as well as revenue at intermediate stages, with restrictions on risk. It refers to the buying and selling of securities to meet current and future liabilities under uncertainty associated usually, but not exclusively with interest-rate movements. Additionally, it permits one to handle several scenarios simultaneously while scenarios present different results of random variables. It provides an adaptive policy that is closer in spirit to the way decision makers have to deal with uncertain futures in real life.

This is a model of prime importance to long-term investors such as insurances, pension funds and banks where the business involves a large amount of liquidity. Indeed, the financial institutions apply the ALM model as a protection of risk which could be present in two aspects: a possible loss of investment and missing the ability to meet liabilities. The returns of assets and the liabilities are both uncertain.

The liabilities may take different forms: pensions paid to the members of the scheme in a pension fund, savers' deposits paid back in a bank, or benefits paid to insurers by the insurance company. A common feature of these problems is the uncertainty of liabilities and the resulting risk of underfunding. The other major uncertainty originates from asset returns. Together they make a nontrivial difficulty in how to manage risk in the model applied by the financial institution. The demand for multi-period planning additionally complicates the problem.

Stochastic programming provides a general purpose-modelling framework, which captures the real-world features such as turnover constraints, transaction costs, risk aversion, limits on groups of assets and other consideration. However, the optimization model turns out to be intractable for the enormous number of decision variables, especially for the multi-stage problems.

One of the first industrially applied models of this type was the stochastic linear program with simple recourse developed by Kusy and Ziemba in 1986. This model captured certain characteristics of ALM problems: it maximized revenues for the bank in the objective under legal, policy, liquidity, cash flow and budget constraints make sure that deposit liability is met as much as possible. Under computational limits at the time when it was developed, this model took the advantage of stochastic linear programming so as to be practical even for the large problems faced in banks.

In this chapter I focus on the asset and liability management (ALM) model which involves the stochastic programming, dynamic property, linear and nonlinear programming model based on the scenario tree. I assume a simple model with tree "assets"; stock A and Stock B and bonds.

Figure1. Event tree

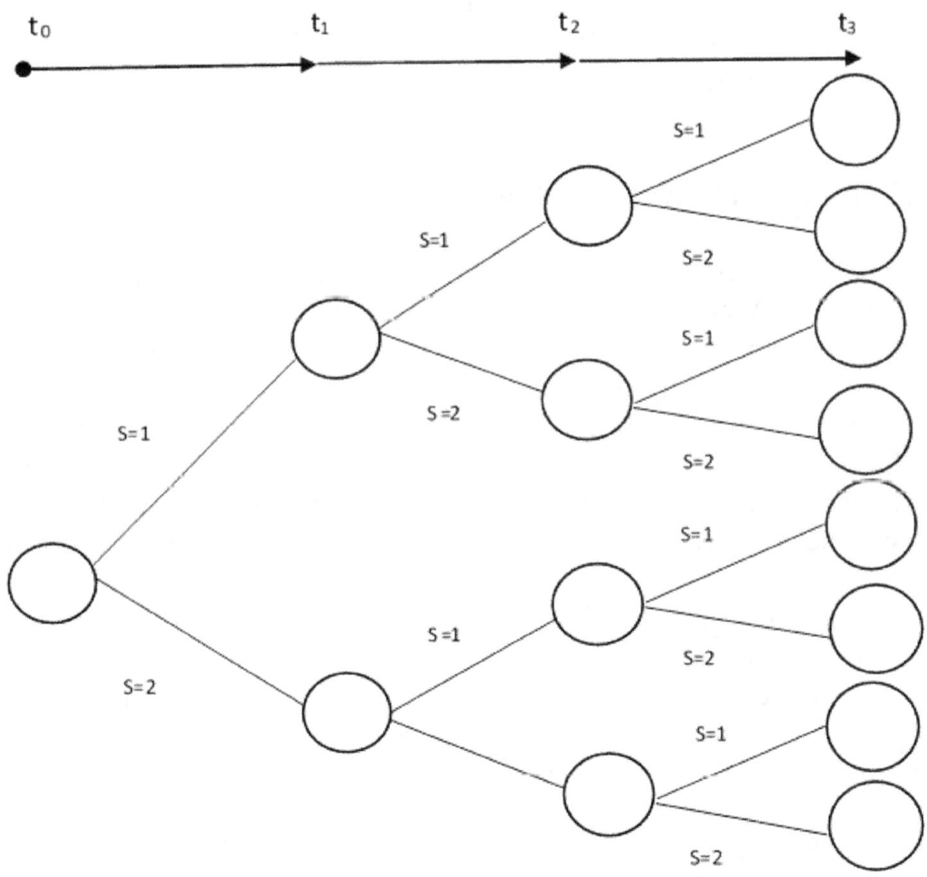

In the application of this model it is important for decision makers to rebalance the portfolio during the investment period as they may wish to adjust the asset allocations according to updated information on the market. The strategy which is currently optimal may not be optimal any more as the situation changes. Thus, it is important to reconsider the strategy and make the necessary change in order to remain in the optimal position. Taking this into account, the problem is multi-period and at the beginning of each period, new decisions are made. Such a multi-stage ALM model allows different decisions through the investing process.

To make it easier to model, we consider the problem stage by stage and with portfolio rebalancing done at the beginning of each stage. Also, the uncertainties of asset returns are implemented with discrete distributions, in which case an event tree is used to capture the uncertainties in multiple stages throughout the whole decision process, as shown in Figure 1. The nodes at each stage represent possible future events. Asset returns, liabilities and cash deposits are subject to uncertain future evolution. Meanwhile, the asset rebalancing is done after knowing which value the asset returns and liabilities take at each node.

THE MULTISTAGE STOCHASTIC MODEL

The best way to introduce multistage stochastic model is a simple asset liability management (ALM) model (Birge and Louveaux, 1967).

We have an initial wealth (W_0), that should be properly invested in such a way to meet a liability (**L**) at the end of the planning horizon H.

If possible, we would like to own a terminal wealth (W_H) larger than the liabilities (L). However, we should account properly for risk aversion, since there could be some chance to end up with a terminal wealth that is not sufficient to pay for the liability, in which case we will have to borrow some money.

Mathematical programming methodology is ready to take on the huge problems going up from LP portfolio optimization. For that reason, a nonlinear, strictly concave utility function of the difference between the terminal wealth (W_H), which is a random variable, and the liability (L) would do the job, and this would lead to a nonlinear programming model.

In what follows, we will present two alternatives how to model the portfolio decisions for multi-period problems. As a first alternative we can build a piecewise linear utility function like the one illustrated in Figure 2.

Figure 2. Piecewise linear utility function

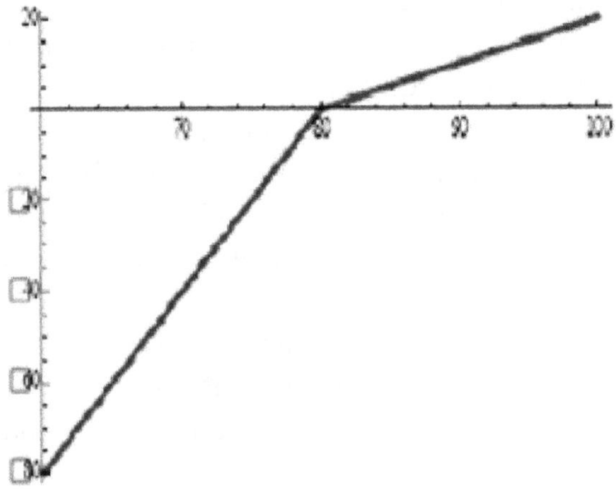

And as a second alternative we can build a nonlinear utility function like the one illustrated in Figure 3.

Model Description

The utility is zero when the terminal wealth (W_H) matches the liability exactly. If the slope r penalizing the shortfall is larger than q, this function is concave (but not strictly).

Figure 3. Nonlinear utility function

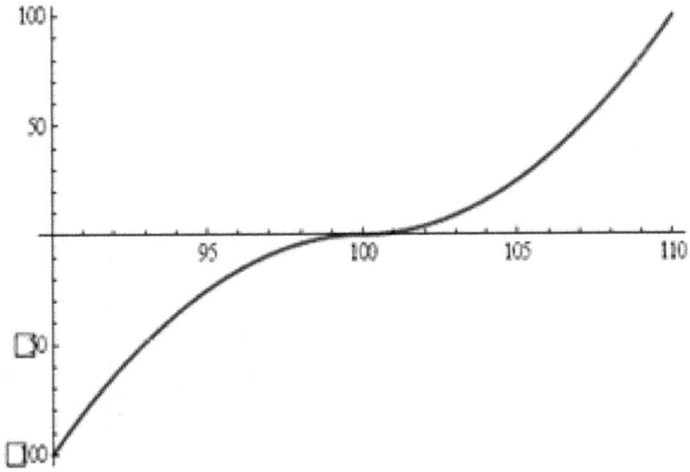

I include 3 assets in my portfolio, two stocks and one bond. For simplicity, I assume that we may rebalance it only at a discrete set of time instants t = 1, ..., H-1, with no transaction cost; the initial portfolio is chosen at time t = 0, and the liability must be paid at time H.

Time period t is the period between time instants t - 1 and t. In order to represent uncertainty, we may build a tree like that in Figure 4, which is a generalization of the two-stage tree. Each node n_k in the tree corresponds to an event, where we should make some decision. We have an initial node n_0 corresponding to time t = 0.

Then, for each event node, we have two branches; each branch is labelled by a conditional probability of occurrence, $P(n_k|n_i)$, where $n_i = a(n_k)$ is the immediate predecessor of node n_k. Here, we have two nodes at time t = 1

Figure 4. Event tree with 8 scenarios

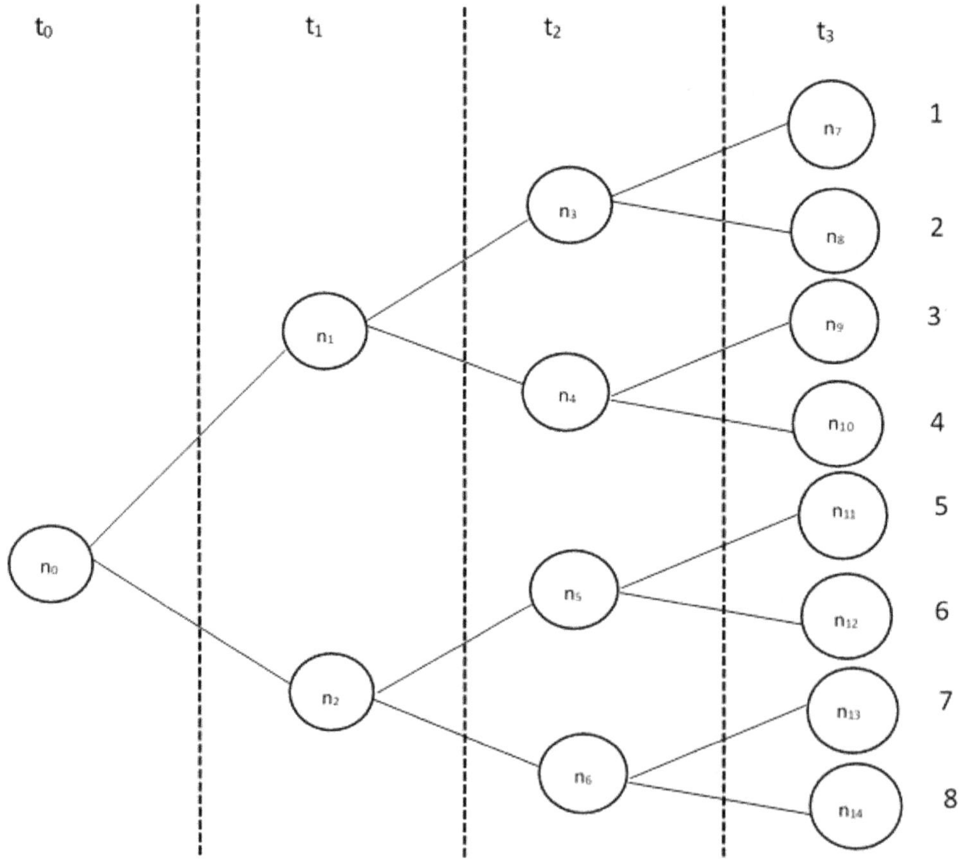

and four at time t = 2, where we may rebalance our portfolio on the basis of the previous asset returns.

Finally, in the eight nodes corresponding to t = 3, the leaves of the tree, we just compare the terminal wealth (W_H) with the liability (L) and evaluate the utility function. Moreover, each node of the tree is associated with the set of asset returns during the corresponding time period. A scenario has been consistent of an event sequence, or in other words, a sequence of nodes in the tree along with the associated asset returns.

In our example, we have 8 scenarios as shown in Figure 4. For instance, scenario 2 consists of the node sequence (n_0, n_1, n_3, n_8).

The probability of each scenario depends on the conditional probability of each node on its path.

If each branch at each node is equally probable, namely the conditional probabilities are always 1/2, then each scenario in the figure has probability $p_s = 1/8$, for s = 1, ..., 8. The branching factor may be arbitrary in principle. Meaning, the more branches we use the better our ability to model uncertainty. Unfortunately, the number of nodes grows exponentially with the number of stages, as well as the computational effort.

At each node in the tree, we must make a set of decisions. In practice, we are interested in the decisions that must be implemented here and now. This suggests that, in order to model the uncertainty as accurately as possible with a limited computational effort, a possible idea is to branch many paths from the initial node, and less from the subsequent nodes. Each decision at each stage may depend on the information gathered so far, but not on the future; this requirement is called a non-anticipatively condition. Essentially, this means that decisions made at time t must be the same for scenarios that cannot be distinguished at time t.

To build a model ensuring that the decision process makes sense, we can associate decision variables with nodes in the scenario trees and write the model in a way that relates each node to its predecessors.

Let us now introduce the following numerical data:

- The initial wealth is W_0=50.
- The target liability is L^s=100.
- There are three assets, say, stocks A and B, and bonds; hence, I = 3.
- In the scenario tree of Figure 4 we have up- and down-branches; in the (lucky) up-branches, total return is 1.28 for stock A, 1.40 for stock B and 1.20 for bonds; in the (bad) down-branches, total return is 1.08 for stock A, 0.99 for stock B and 1.12 for bonds (Barberies NC 2000). We

see that bonds play the role of safer assets, and stocks B are very risky assets here. We also see that returns are a sequence of i.i.d. random variables, but more realistic scenarios can be defined.

- The reward rate q for excess wealth above the target liability is 1.
- The penalty rate r for the shortfall below the target liability is 4.

Also, the model notation:

- N is the set of event nodes; in our case:

$N = \{n_0, n_1, n_2, \ldots, n_{14}\}$

- Each node n ∊ N, apart from the root node n_0, has a unique direct predecessor node, denoted by a(n): for instance, $a(n_3) = n$
- There is a set S ∩N of leaf (terminal) nodes; in our case:

$S = \{n_7, n_8, \ldots, n_{14}\}$

- For each node s ∊ S we have a surplus and shortfall variables w^s_+ and w^s_-, related to the difference between terminal wealth and liability.
- There is a set T ∩ N of intermediate nodes, where portfolio rebalancing may occur after the initial allocation in node n_o; in our case:

$T = \{n_1, n_2, \ldots, n_6\}$

- For each node n ∊$\{n_0\}$ U T there is a decision variable x_{in}, expressing the money invested in asset i at node n.

With this notation, the model may be written as follows:

$$\begin{aligned}
&max \sum\nolimits_{s \in S} \pi^s (q w^s_+ - r w^s_-) \\
&Such \text{ that} \\
&\sum\nolimits_{i=1}^{I} x_i^{n0} = W^0 \\
&\sum\nolimits_{i=1}^{I} R_i^n x_i^{a(n)} = \sum\nolimits_{i=1}^{I} x_i^n, \qquad \forall \text{n} \in \tau \\
&\sum\nolimits_{i=1}^{I} R_i^s x_i^{a(s)} = L^s + w^s_+ - w^s_-, \quad \forall s \in S \\
&x_i^n, w^s_+, w^s_- \geq 0
\end{aligned} \tag{1}$$

where R_i^n is the total return for asset i during the period that leads to node n, and π^s is the probability of reaching the terminal node s ∈ S; this probability is the product of all the conditional probabilities on the path that leads from root node n_0 to leaf node **s**.

PORTFOLIO CHOICE: NUMERICAL ILLUSTRATION

The Wolfram Mathematica programming codes for both linear and nonlinear utility functions, are set out below in the Appendix I and II. For a more detailed description of the functions and the syntax of the language, the reader is referred to the Wolfram Language Guide, https://reference.wolfram.com/language/guide/Syntax.html.

Piecewise Linear Utility Function

This is a linear programming (LP) model that may be easily solved by the simplex algorithm, resulting in the solution of Table 1. We may notice that in the last period the portfolio is not diversified, since the whole wealth is allocated to one asset, and we should wonder if this makes sense. Actually, this can be due the very low branching factor in the scenario tree, and therefore the uncertainty is not accurately represented.

The Nonlinear Utility Functions

When we are approximating a nonlinear utility function by a piecewise linear function, as we notice in the Table 1, the portfolio is not diversified and the

Table 1. Portfolio diversified with piecewise linear function

Node	Stock A	Stock B	Bonds
n_0	16.89	33.12	0
n_1	67.97	0	0
n_2	0	51.02	0
n_3	0	0	87.01
n_4	23.12	50.29	0
n_5	0	71.43	0
n_6	0	50.51	0

wealth in the last time period is allocated to one asset. Actually, this alternative may imply "local" risk neutrality, so that we only care about expected return. Therefore, we should use either a nonlinear programming model or a more accurate representation of utility with more linear pieces.

The second, more realistic alternative presented in this section is the nonlinear utility function (see Figure 3). Here the objective function of the optimization problem becomes:

$$\sum_{s\in S} \pi^s \left(\left(w_+^s\right)^2 - \left(w_-^s\right)^2 \right) \tag{2}$$

where π^s is the probability of reaching the terminal node $s \in S$; this probability is the product of all the conditional probabilities on the path that leads from root node n_0 to leaf node s. And for each node $s \in S$ we have surplus and shortfall variables w^s_+ and w^s_-, related to the difference between terminal wealth and liability.

Results are presented in Table 2.

Comparing the results from Table 1 and Table 2, it is reasonable to state that when using nonlinear programming model, we get a better diversification, since the wealth is allocated in all assets.

CONCLUDING REMARKS

Stochastic programming is recognized as an important tool in financial planning. The current practice of portfolio optimization is still limited to the

Table 2. Portfolio Diversified with Nonlinear Function

Node	Stock A	Stock B	Bonds
n_0	0	50	0
n_1	0	70	0
n_2	21.96	11.70	15.84
n_3	0	98	0
n_4	39.52	0	29.78
n_5	35.37	4.48	23.65
n_6	23.53	21.15	8.36

simple formulation of linear programming (LR) or the quadratic programming (QR) type. For that reason, relevant literature on asset-liability management (ALM) model has been reviewed and two different ALM approaches are compared.

This chapter shows that the mathematical programming methodology is ready to challenge the huge problem arising from LP portfolio optimization. Therefore, a special emphasis was put on the shape of the investors' payoff functions in asset price equilibrium. We note that the assumption of a linear utility function may imply "local" risk neutrality, so that we only care about expected return, resulting allocation of the wealth to one asset, as seen in Table 1. Then again, the results from Table 2 underpin our claim that the nonlinear ALM model generates better asset allocation.

Problems and Issues: Recommendation for Further Work

Despite the widely-accepted benefits of ALM, the associated challenges may prevent an institution from adopting an ALM framework. These difficulties lie primarily in the implementation of ALM. First, each institution has its particular objectives, risk tolerances, and constraints, and it would be difficult to devise an optimization algorithm that would realistically account for these specific characteristics when evaluating portfolio allocation decisions. Second, long-term strategic decisions depend on factors whose forecasts may not be readily available to the institution. Third, risk preferences and their changes over time must be translated into mathematical language, which is far from trivial (Melnikov and Romaniuk, 2006;2008).

In constricting our individual ALM model I have assumed that the liabilities must be met. This may be a very hard constraint; if extreme scenarios are included in the formulation, it may well be the case that the model above is infeasible. Therefore, the formulation should be relaxed in a sensible way; we could consider the possibility of borrowing cash; we could also introduce suitable penalties for not meeting the liabilities. In principle, we could also require that the probability of not meeting the liabilities is small enough; this leads to chance-constrained formulations, for which we refer the reader to the literature (Campbell and Viceira, 2002; Heitsch and Römisch, 2003; Hochreiter and Pflug, 2007; Klaassen, 2002; Wallace & Ziemba, 2005).

REFERENCES

Campbell, J. Y., Chan, Y. L., & Viceira, L. M. (2003). A multivariate model of strategic asset allocation. *Journal of Financial Economics*, *67*(1), 41–80. doi:10.1016/S0304-405X(02)00231-3

Heitsch, H., & Römisch, W. (2003). Scenario reduction algorithms in stochastic programming. *Computational Optimization and Applications*, *24*(2-3), 187–206. doi:10.1023/A:1021805924152

Hochreiter, R., & Pflug, G. C. (2007). Financial scenario generation for stochastic multi-stage decision processes as facility location problems. *Annals of Operations Research*, *152*(1), 257–272. doi:10.1007/s10479-006-0140-6

Klaassen, P. (2002). Comment on Generating scenario trees for multistage decision problems. *Management Science*, *48*(11), 1512–1516. doi:10.1287/mnsc.48.11.1512.261

Melnikov, A., & Romaniuk, Y. (2006). Evaluating the performance of Gompertz, Makeham and Lee–Carter mortality models for risk management with unit-linked contracts. *Insurance, Mathematics & Economics*, *39*(3), 310–329. doi:10.1016/j.insmatheco.2006.02.012

Melnikov, A., & Romanyuk, Y. (2008). Efficient hedging and pricing of equity-linked life insurance contracts on several risky assets. *International Journal of Theoretical and Applied Finance*, *11*(03), 295–323. doi:10.1142/S0219024908004816

Wallace, S. W., & Ziemba, W. T. (Eds.). (2005). *Applications of stochastic programming* (Vol. 5). Siam. doi:10.1137/1.9780898718799

APPENDIX 1

Linear Programming in Wolfram Mathematica 9.0

```
In[1]:=
w0 = 50;
L = 100;
q = 1;
r = 4;
ru = {1.28, 1.40, 1.20};
rd = {1.08, 0.99, 1.12};
pis = Table[1/8, {i, 1, 8}];
x = {{x10, x20, x30}, {x111, x211, x311}, {x112, x212, x312}, {x121,
   x221, x321}, {x122, x222, x322}, {x123, x223, x323}, {x124, x224,
   x324}};
wu = {wu1, wu2, wu3, wu4, wu5, wu6, wu7, wu8};
wd = {wd1, wd2, wd3, wd4, wd5, wd6, wd7, wd8};
wealth = (q wu - r wd).pis;
In[2]:=Total[x[[1]]]
Out[2]:=x10+x20+x30
```

```
In[3]:= Maximize[wealth, {
  Total[x[[1]]] == w0 &&
   x[[1]].ru == Total[x[[2]]] &&
   x[[1]].rd == Total[x[[3]]] &&
   x[[2]].ru == Total[x[[4]]] &&
   x[[2]].rd == Total[x[[5]]] &&
   x[[3]].ru == Total[x[[6]]] &&
   x[[3]].rd == Total[x[[7]]] &&
   x[[4]].ru == L + wu[[1]] - wd[[1]] &&
   x[[4]].rd == L + wu[[2]] - wd[[2]] &&
   x[[5]].ru == L + wu[[3]] - wd[[3]] &&
   x[[5]].rd == L + wu[[4]] - wd[[4]] &&
   x[[6]].ru == L + wu[[5]] - wd[[5]] &&
   x[[6]].rd == L + wu[[6]] - wd[[6]] &&
   x[[7]].ru == L + wu[[7]] - wd[[7]] &&
   x[[7]].rd == L + wu[[8]] - wd[[8]] &&
```

```
x10 >= 0 &&
 x20 >= 0 &&
 x111 >= 0 &&
 x211 >= 0 &&
 x112 >= 0 &&
 x212 >= 0 &&
 x121 >= 0 &&
 x221 >= 0 &&
 x122 >= 0 &&
 x222 >= 0 &&
 x123 >= 0 &&
 x223 >= 0 &&
 x124 >= 0 &&
 x224 >= 0 &&
 x30 >= 0 &&
 x311 >= 0 &&
 x312 >= 0 &&
 x321 >= 0 &&
 x322 >= 0 &&
 x323 >= 0 &&
 x324 >= 0 &&
```

```
wu1 >= 0 &&
wu2 >= 0 &&
wu3 >= 0 &&
wu4 >= 0 &&
wu5 >= 0 &&
wu6 >= 0 &&
wu7 >= 0 &&
wu8 >= 0 &&
wd1 >= 0 &&
wd2 >= 0 &&
wd3 >= 0 &&
wd4 >= 0 &&
wd5 >= 0 &&
wd6 >= 0 &&
wd7 >= 0 &&

wd8 >= 0}, {x10, x20, x111, x211, x112, x212, x121, x221, x122, x222,
  x123, x223, x124, x224, x30, x311, x312, x321, x322, x323, x324,
  wu1, wu2, wu3, wu4, wu5, wu6, wu7, wu8, wd1, wd2, wd3, wd4, wd5,
  wd6, wd7, wd8}]

Out[3]:={-67.6307, {x10 -> 16.8934, x20 -> 33.1066, x111 -> 67.9728,
  x211 -> 0., x112 -> 0., x212 -> 51.0204, x121 -> 0., x221 -> 0.,
  x122 -> 23.1238, x222 -> 50.2868, x123 -> 0., x223 -> 71.4286,
  x124 -> 0., x224 -> 50.5102, x30 -> 0., x311 -> 0., x312 -> 0.,
  x321 -> 87.0052, x322 -> 0., x323 -> 0., x324 -> 0., wu1 -> 4.4062,
  wu2 -> 0., wu3 -> 0., wu4 -> 0., wu5 -> 0., wu6 -> 0., wu7 -> 0.,
  wu8 -> 0., wd1 -> 0., wd2 -> 2.55421, wd3 -> 0., wd4 -> 25.2424,
  wd5 -> 0., wd6 -> 29.2857, wd7 -> 29.2857, wd8 -> 49.9949}}
```

```
In[4]:= x = {{x10, x20, x30}, {x111, x211, x311}, {x112, x212, x312}, {x121,
    x221, x321}, {x122, x222, x322}, {x123, x223, x323}, {x124, x224,
    x324}} /. {x10 -> 16.893424036281242`, x111 -> 67.97278911564622`,
    x112 -> 0.`, x121 -> 0.`, x122 -> 23.123809523809598`,
   x123 -> 0.`, x124 -> 0.`, x20 -> 33.106575963718775`, x211 -> 0.`,
   x212 -> 51.02040816326531`, x221 -> 0.`,
   x222 -> 50.286802721088364`, x223 -> 71.42857142857144`,
   x224 -> 50.51020408163266`, x30 -> 0.`, x311 -> 0.`, x312 -> 0.`,
   x321 -> 87.00517006802718`, x322 -> 0.`, x323 -> 0.`, x324 -> 0.`}
```

```
Out[4]:= {{16.8934, 33.1066, 0.}, {67.9728, 0., 0.}, {0., 51.0204, 0.}, {0.,
  0., 87.0052}, {23.1238, 50.2868, 0.}, {0., 71.4286, 0.}, {0.,
  50.5102, 0.}}
```

```
In[5]:=TableForm[%14]
```

```
Out[5]:=
16.8934,    33.1066,    0.
67.9728,         0.,    0.
0.,         51.0204,    0.
0.,              0.,    87.0052
23.1238,    50.2868,    0.
0.,         71.4286,    0.
0.,         50.5102,    0.
```

APPENDIX 2

Non-Linear Programming in Wolfram Mathematica 9.0

In[1]:=
$w0 = 50;$
$L = 100;$
$q = 1;$
$r = 4;$
$ru = 1.28, 1.40, 1.20;$
$rd = 1.08, 0.99, 1.12;$
$pis = Table[1 / 8, i, 1, 8];$
$x = x10, x20, x30, x111, x211, x311, x112, x212, x312, x121, x221, x321, x122, x222, x322,$
$x123, x223, x323, x124, x224, x324;$
$wu = wu1, wu2, wu3, wu4, wu5, wu6, wu7, wu8;$
$wd = wd1, wd2, wd3, wd4, wd5, wd6, wd7, wd8;$
$wealth = ((wu)^2 - (wd)^2).pis;$
In[2]:= $Total[x[[1]]]$
Out[2]:= $x10 + x20 + x30$

$$
\begin{aligned}
&\text{In}[3]{:=}Maximize[wealth,\{\\
&Total\ [x\ [[1]]] == w0\ \&\&\\
&x\ [[1]].ru == Total[x[[2]]]\ \&\&\\
&x[[1]].rd == Total[x[[3]]]\ \&\&\\
&x[[2]].ru == Total[x[[4]]]\ \&\&\\
&x[[2]].rd == Total[x[[5]]]\ \&\&\\
&x[[3]].ru == Total[x[[6]]]\ \&\&\\
&x[[3]].rd == Total[x[[7]]]\ \&\&\\
&x[[4]].ru == L + wu[[1]] - wd[[1]]\ \&\&\\
&x[[4]].rd == L + wu[[2]] - wd[[2]]\ \&\&\\
&x[[5]].ru == L + wu[[3]] - wd[[3]]\ \&\&\\
&x[[5]].rd == L + wu[[4]] - wd[[4]]\ \&\&\\
&x[[6]].ru == L + wu[[5]] - wd[[5]]\ \&\&\\
&x[[6]].rd == L + wu[[6]] - wd[[6]]\ \&\&\\
&x[[7]].ru == L + wu[[7]] - wd[[7]]\ \&\&\\
&x[[7]].rd == L + wu[[8]] - wd[[8]]\ \&\&
\end{aligned}
$$

$x10 \geq 0$ & &

$x20 \geq 0$ & &

$x111 \geq 0$ & &

$x211 \geq 0$ & &

$x112 \geq 0$ & &

$x212 \geq 0$ & &

$x121 \geq 0$ & &

$x221 \geq 0$ & &

$x122 \geq 0$ & &

$x222 \geq 0$ & &

$x123 \geq 0$ & &

$x223 \geq 0$ & &

$x124 \geq 0$ & &

$x224 \geq 0$ & &

$x30 \geq 0$ & &

$x311 \geq 0$ & &

$x312 \geq 0$ & &

$x321 \geq 0$ & &

$x322 \geq 0$ & &

$x323 \geq 0$ & &

$x324 \geq 0$ & &

$wu1 \geq 0 \,\&\&$
$wu2 \geq 0 \,\&\&$
$wu3 \geq 0 \,\&\&$
$wu4 \geq 0 \,\&\&$
$wu5 \geq 0 \,\&\&$
$wu6 \geq 0 \,\&\&$
$wu7 \geq 0 \,\&\&$
$wu8 \geq 0 \,\&\&$
$wd1 \geq 0 \,\&\&$
$wd2 \geq 0 \,\&\&$
$wd3 \geq 0 \,\&\&$
$wd4 \geq 0 \,\&\&$
$wd5 \geq 0 \,\&\&$
$wd6 \geq 0 \,\&\&$
$wd7 \geq 0 \,\&\&$

wd8 >= 0}, {x10, x20, x111, x211, x112, x212, x121, x221, x122, x222, x123, x223, x124, x224, x30, x311, x312, x321, x322, x323, x324, wu1, wu2, wu3, wu4, wu5, wu6, wu7, wu8, wd1, wd2, wd3, wd4, wd5, wd6, wd7, wd8}]

Out[3]:={8597.34, {$x10$− > 5.86338 * 10^-13, $x20$− > 50., $x111$− > 5.86338 * 10^-13, $x211$− > 70., $x112$− > 26.7924, $x212$− > 10.2567, $x121$− > 5.86338 * 10^-13, $x221$− > 98., $x122$− > 5.86338 * 10^-13, $x222$− > 69.3, $x123$− > 32.9826, $x223$− > 5.61925, $x124$− > 23.451, $x224$− > 20.6492, $x30$− > 5.86338 * 10^-13, $x311$− > 5.86338 * 10^-13, $x312$− > 12.4508, $x321$− > 5.86338 * 10^-13, $x322$− > 5.86338 * 10^-13, $x323$− > 24.9929, $x324$− > 8.93477, $wu1$− > 1024.09, $wu2$− > 10.9158, $wu3$− > 134.998, $wu4$− > 1.08332 * 10^-13, $wu5$− > 5.27578 * 10^-13, $wu6$− > 3.74811 * 10^-13, $wu7$− > 3.73035 * 10^-13, $wu8$− > 5.86338 * 10^-13, $wd1$− > 987.793, $wd2$− > 13.8958, $wd3$− > 137.978, $wd4$− > 31.393, $wd5$− > 19.9239, $wd6$− > 30.8237, $wd7$− > 30.3522, $wd8$− > 44.2233}}

In[4]:= x = {{x10, x20, x30}, {x111, x211, x311}, {x112, x212, x312}, {x121, x221, x321}, {x122, x222, x322}, {x123, x223, x323}, {x124, x224, x324}} /.

{$x10->$ 5.86338 * 10^-13, $x20->$ 50., $x111->$ 5.86338 * 10^-13, $x211->$ 70., $x112->$ 26.7924, $x212->$ 10.2567, $x121->$ 5.86338 * 10^-13, $x221->$ 98., $x122->$ 5.86338 * 10^-13, $x222->$ 69.3, $x123->$ 32.9826, $x223->$ 5.61925, $x124->$ 23.451, $x224->$ 20.6492, $x30->$ 5.86338 * 10^-13, $x311->$ 5.86338 * 10^-13, $x312->$ 12.4508, $x321->$ 5.86338 * 10^-13, $x322->$ 5.86338 * 10^-13, $x323->$ 24.9929, $x324->$ 8.93477, $wu1->$ 1024.99, $wu2->$ 10.9158, $wu3->$ 134.998, $wu4->$ 1.08332 * 10^-13, $wu5->$ 5.27578 * 10^-13, $wu6->$ 3.74811 * 10^-13, $wu7->$ 3.73035 * 10^-13, $wu8->$ 5.86338 * 10^-13, $wd1->$ 987.793, $wd2->$ 13.8958, $wd3->$ 137.978, $wd4->$ 31.393, $wd5->$ 19.9239, $wd6->$ 30.8237, $wd7->$ 30.3522, $wd8->$ 44.2233}}

Out[4]:=5.86338 * 10^-13, 50., 5.86338 * 10^-13, 5.86338 * 10^-13, 70., 5.86338 * 10^-13, 21.9557, 11.7014, 15.8429, 5.86338 * 10^-13, 98., 5.86338 * 10^-13, 39.5207, 1.39266 * 10^-12, 29.7793, 35.3701, 4.47955, 23.647, 23.5345, 21.1466, 8.35944

In[5]:= *TableForm*[%14]

Out[5]:=

5.86338 * 10^-13	50.	5.86338 * 10^-13
5.86338 * 10^-13	70.	5.86338 * 10^-13
21.9557	11.7014	15.8429
5.86338 * 10^-13	98.	5.86338 * 10^-13
39.5207	1.39266 * 10^-12	29.7793
35.3701	4.47955	23.647
23.5345	21.1466	8.35944

Chapter 6
Markov Processes in Finance With Application to Stock Markets

ABSTRACT

Important model that has evolved in the field of finance, is founded on the hypothesis of random walks and most often refers to a special category of Markov chain and Markov process. In these models the human race is presented as nothing more than a system with a large number of individual parts. If every human being acted totally independently of every other human being, then the human race as a whole would behave very much like a thermodynamic system. But people, in general, do not behave independently of each other. They have a tendency to cooperate and compete, which causes the human race to behave less like a thermodynamic system, and more like a complex adaptive system. The performed analysis in this chapter certifies the doubted that the discrete and continuous Markov processes as representations of stationary stochastic processes, cannot accurately anticipate the future trends.

Bad periods in the market are predictably followed by good periods and vice versa (Peter Bernstien, Against The Gods: The Remarkable Story Of Risk, 1998)

DOI: 10.4018/978-1-5225-3259-0.ch006

INTRODUCTION

Important model that has evolved in the field of finance, is the theory of random walks. This theory raised a lot of eyebrows in 1973 when author Burton Malkiel published the book "A Random Walk Down Wall Street", which remains on the top-seller list for finance books.

The question that should be addressed here is: Whether the theory explains the actual stock price fluctuations?

A follower of the random walk theory believes that the markets are efficient and that it is impossible to outperform the market without assuming additional risk; the stock price reflects all available information and the occurrence of new information is seemingly random as well. Under a random walk, historical data on prices and volume have no value in predicting future stock return's; the stock price changes have the same distribution and are independent of each other. In other words, statistical analysis and technical analysis are seen as useless. Buying and selling stocks by just depending only on historical stock prices in an attempt to outperform above the market return will effectively be a game of chance rather than skill. In general, the random walk theory throws serious doubt on many other methods for describing and predicting stock prices and occupy the academic world. Although a number of studies found some statistical evidence against the random walk hypothesis, these were dismissed as economically unimportant and statistically questionable. In support, it is stated that alternative methods could not generate profitable trading rules in the presence of transaction costs, and selection bias can result when the researcher tries to fit a large complex model to a small set of highly correlated time series data.

What is more, The Royal Swedish Academy of Sciences awarded the 2013 Nobel to Eugene Fama at the University of Chicago. The prize was based on the importance of his work, which "laid the foundation for the current understanding of asset prices." Mr. Fama's major contribution, notably with the 1965 paper "Random Walks in Stock Market Prices," has been to show that stock markets are very efficient. The term "efficient" here does not mean what it normally means in economics—namely, that benefits minus costs are maximized. Instead, it means that prices of stocks rapidly incorporate information that is publicly available. That happens because markets are so competitive.

We cannot just say that the theory is in harmony with the actual market situation or not. Our task is to learn how to apply them in practice, and then leave the results to deliver an answer.

But perhaps one of the most interesting examples of the use of Markov chains in practice, is the web search engine, Google.

Do you remember the early search engines? When we were surfing the Web, we were going from page to page by randomly choosing an outgoing link form one page to get to the next. This very often was leading us to dead ends at pages with no outgoing links, or cycles around cliques of interconnected pages, which was a boring and frustrating process. In that time search engine, didn't have a good way of determining which pages were more likely to be relevant. But Larry Page and Sergey Brin, the Google's founders, when they were graduate students at Stanford University made the major change with the development of the Page Rank algorithm. They understand that the motion of the surfer among the web pages can be modelled using Markov chains. The limiting probability that an infinitely dedicated random surfer visits any particular page is its Page Rank. A page has high rank if other pages with high rank link to it. Although Brin and Page did not know it at the time, they were attempting to find the steady-state vector for a particular Markov chain whose transition matrix modelled the hyperlinked structure of the web. After some important modifications to this impressively large matrix, a steady-state vector can be found, and its entries can be interpreted as the amount of time a random surfer will spend at each web page. The calculation of this steady-state vector is the basis for Google's Page Rank algorithm. This is one of the reasons why Google is such an effective search engine.

To illuminate, the idea behind the Page Rank algorithm is similar to the idea of the impact factor used to rank journals. The impact factor of a journal is as the average number of citations per recently published paper in that journal. In general, the higher the impact factor, the more important the journal. By regarding each web page as a journal and each link as a citation, Google attempted to measure the importance of a web page by the number of links leading to it. As with journal citations, having a more credible website (i.e. one affiliated with a major corporation or university or government agency) link to your website increases the likelihood that it is important. As a result, the ranked list of search results that Google returns tend to have the websites with the highest number of credible links listed first.

So, the more in-links a web page has, the more important the page. In-links from respectable pages carry more weight than in-links from less important pages. Also, if a respectable page points to several pages, its weight is distributed proportionally. For example, if an important site like Yahoo points to your website, but also points to 99 others, you only get credit for $1/100^{th}$ of Yahoo's Page Rank.

Today there are many applications of Markov models, some include education, engineering, physics, biology, economics, production, health services, finance and many other fields. But our interested directed toward mathematical finance theory, where the price process of a risky asset is usually modelled as the trajectory of a stochastic process on some underlying probability space. Such a probabilistic approach was first introduced by Bachelier in his PhD thesis "The Theory of Speculation", published in 1900. He introduced the Brownian motion as a model for price fluctuations of the Paris stock exchange. Historically, this is the first paper to use advanced mathematics in the study of finance, therefore, Bachelier is considered a pioneer in the study of financial mathematics and stochastic processes. More fully, as price should stay positive, geometric Brownian motion is used as the basic reference model in the analysis of financial price fluctuations. Additionally, Kreps (1982) showed that such a diffusion model can be justified as the rational expectations equilibrium in a market with rational agents who all believe in this kind of price dynamics, and who instantaneously and rationally discount all available information into the present price. Meaning, the sudden price fluctuations reflect rational changes in the valuation of an asset rather than trader irrational behavior.

Understanding how price behaves is of great importance. We can use the knowledge of price behavior to reduce risk or take better and well informed decisions about the future state of the price. Because the price tomorrow remains uncertain, hence must be described by a probability distribution. Therefore, in this chapter random walk of the stock prices are assumed to be Markov chains and Markov processes accordingly. The main task is to define the probability distribution that best explains the stock market movements. In theory, if the distribution is exponential, then it does not matter how long the stock has been staying in a particular state. In this case, the only thing that the Markov model cares about is the current state of the process. But if the transition from one state to another is described by the Weibull distribution or a Power Law distribution than the time spent in a particular state matter. Here the stock market movement could be better explained applying the Semi-Markov model.

In what follows in this chapter I will introduce the application of the Markov models in stock markets, and provide some examples. For this purpose, I chose 6 market stocks and indexes (S&P500 index, NASDAG Composite index, NYSE Composite index, RUSSEL 2000 index, Alphabet Inc. Google and Apple Inc.).

At the very beginning, we will construct a Markov chain where both time and space are discrete. Such a construction will demonstrate how to use a discrete time Markov chain, which will also be helpful in the continuous time setting of the later section in the chapter. In the extension, we will also present how this analysis is applied to the copper market data, and finally we will try to give the answer to the above stated question.

Numerical calculations and computer implementations have been done by Wolfram Mathematica programming language and spreadsheets which are briefly discussed as well.

Markov decision process is used to model an uncertain dynamic system whose states change with time. A decision maker is required to make a sequence of decisions over time with uncertain outcomes, and an action can either yield a reward or incur a cost. Thus, the goal is to find an optimal sequence of actions that the decision maker must take to maximize the expected reward over a given time interval, which can be finite or infinite. In discrete-time Markov decision processes, actions are taken at discrete intervals. However, in continuous-time Markov decision processes, actions are taken over exponentially distributed time intervals.

DISCRETE MARKOV CHAIN

A Markov chain is a mathematical model that describes a process with probabilities, states and transitions. Each state has its own probability of going into another state, or to remain in the current state. Depending on which state the process is currently being in, there are different probabilities for the process to give different results in the future. These processes are meant to model the evolution over time of real phenomena for which randomness is inherent. The mathematical formulation of the theory of stochastic process was firstly introduced by the Russian mathematician A.A. Markov (1985-1922).

Markovian models are special type stochastic processes for which the future occurrence of any event depends only on the present state. It is said to be memoryless. It does not matter how it got to the current state or for how long it has been staying there. The only thing that the Markov chain cares about is the current state of the process. This is known as a Markov property.

Moreover, the set of values that the Markov process takes is known as its state space. Depending on the values of state space the process may be discrete or continuous. The process with discrete state space is known as Markov chain and with continuous as Markov processes.

Markov chain is one of the most well developed theories of stochastic process. By definition, a stochastic process $\{X_n\}$with discrete state space S is called a Markov chain if for all time $n \geq 0$ and all states $i_0, \ldots, i, j \in S$

$$P\{X_{n+1} + 1 = j \mid X_n = i, X_n - 1 = i_n - 1 \ldots, X_0 = i_0 = P(X_{n+1} = j \mid X_n = i) = P_{ij} \quad (1)$$

where P_{ij} denotes the probability that the chain, whenever in the state i moves into state j, and is referred to as a one-step transition probability. The square matrix $P=(P_{ij})$, where $i, j \in S$, is called the one-step transition matrix, and since when leaving state i the chain must move to one of the states $j \in S$, each row sums to one (e.g., forms a probability distribution): For each $j \in S$:

$$\sum_{j \in S} P_{ij} \quad (2)$$

We are assuming that the transition probabilities do not depend on the time n, and so, in particular, using n=0 in (Equation 1) yields:

$$P_{ij} = P(X_1 = j \mid X_0 = i) \quad (3)$$

The defining Markov property (Equation 1)) can be described in words as the future is independent of the past given the present state. For example, suppose that the daily price of a stock share, such as S&P 500, can be described by a Markov chain. What does that tell us? Simply that the probability distribution of tomorrow's price for one share of a S&P 500 stock depends only on today's price of S&P 500 stock, not on the past prices of S&P 500 stock. Then to predict tomorrow's price of a share of a S&P 500 stock, it does not matter whether the price has increased or decreased during each of the last 365 days. Meaning, a prediction of tomorrow's stock price should be based only on the fact that today's price of S&P 500 stock is \$2,068,75 (18.04.2016). This idea is often referred to as the efficient market hypothesis (EMH).

TRANSITION PROBABILITIES

The conditional probability of any future event $\{X_{n+1}, X_{n+2}, \ldots\}$, given the past event $\{X_{0,} \ldots, X_{n-1}\}$, and the present state $X_t = i$, is independent of the past event and depends only upon the present state. These conditional probabilities $P = (X_{t+1} = j \mid X_t = i\} = P_{ij}$ are called transition probabilities. Here the transition probability P_{ij} is the probability of moving from state i in n^{th} trial, to the state j in $(n+1)^{th}$ trial. By definition,

- If conditional probabilities are defined as $P\{X_{t+1} = j \mid X_t = i\}$ then, for each i and j, the stationary one-step transition probabilities for a Markov Chain are defined as,

$$P\{X_{t+1} = j \mid X_t = i\} = P\{X_1 = j \mid X_0 = i\} \qquad \text{for all } t = 1,2\ldots \tag{4}$$

Stationary transition probabilities indicate that transition probabilities do not change over time.

- n-step transition probabilities are defined as the conditional probability

$$P\{X_{t+n} = j \mid X_t = i\} = P\{X_n = j \mid X_0 = i\} \qquad \text{for all } t = 0,1\ldots \tag{5}$$

Beside the one-step transition probabilities, Markov chains can also have n-step transition probabilities, which is the conditional probability that the process will be in state j after n-steps provided that it starts in the state i at time t.

Chapman-Kolmogorov Equation

We use Chapman-Kolmogorov Equations to provide a method to compute all the n-step transition probabilities:

$$p_{ij}^{(n)} = \sum_{k=0}^{M} p_{ik}^{(m)} p_{kj}^{(n-m)} \quad \text{For all } i = 0,1,\dots,M, \\ j = 0,1,\dots,M, \\ \text{And any } m = 1,2,\dots,n-1, \\ n = m+1, m+2,\dots \tag{6}$$

These equations are used to point out that when we go from one steady state to another in *n* steps, the process will be in some other state after exactly *m* states. Thus, the summation is just the conditional probability that, given a starting point in one state, the process goes to the other state after *m* steps and then to the next state in *n –m* steps.

Therefore, by summing up these conditional probabilities over all the possible steady states must yield

$$p_{ij}^{(n)} = \sum_{k=0}^{M} p_{ik} p_{kj}^{(n-1)} \tag{7}$$

and

$$p_{ij}^{(n)} = \sum_{k=0}^{M} p_{ik}^{(n-1)} p_{kj} \tag{8}$$

This means that these expressions allow us to obtain the *n-step probabilities* from the one-step transition probabilities recursively.

Transition Probability Matrix

The transition matrix is a matrix that describes the transition probabilities for a Markov chain to move from one state to another.

The transition probabilities can be arranged in the form of an nxn matrix known as Transition Probability Matrix. It is called the n-step transition probability matrix of the process and given by:

$$p_{ij}^{n} = \begin{bmatrix} p_{11} & p_{12} & \cdots \\ p_{21} & p_{22} & \cdots \\ \vdots & \vdots & \vdots \end{bmatrix}$$

The matrix has the following properties:

- Pij>0 for all i and j.
- For all i and j, (i.e.) the sum of the element in each row must be 1. This is true because the sum represents the total probability of transition from state i to itself or any other state.
- The diagonal element represents the transition from one state to the same state.

State Transition Diagram

A convenient and useful method to visualize the state of Markov chains when they have stationary transition probabilities and a finite number of states is using a state transition diagram. In such diagram, each state of a Markov chain is drawn as a numbered node, and the conditional probability of moving from one state to another is drawn by connecting the nodes with an edge and labelling the edge with the numbered probability. For example, if the stock price movement is given by the following stochastic process $\{Xt\}$ for $t = 0$, 1,2, ...where:

$$X_t = \begin{Bmatrix} 1 & \text{if the stock price t increased} \\ 2 & \text{if the stock price t decreased} \end{Bmatrix}$$

and

$$\begin{aligned} P\left\{X_{t+1} = 1 \mid X_t = 1\right\} &= 0.6 \\ P\left\{X_{t+1} = 1 \mid X_t = 2\right\} &= 0.4 \\ P\left\{X_{t+1} = 2 \mid X_t = 1\right\} &= 0.8 \\ P\left\{X_{t+1} = 2 \mid X_t = 2\right\} &= 0.2 \end{aligned} \tag{9}$$

Then the state transition diagram for this example is shown in Figure 1.

Figure 1. State Transition Diagram

MODEL DESCRIPTION

The probability matrix is constructed from the past behavior of the system. This transition probability matrix in conjunction with the probability values of the present state of the system is used to determine the probabilities of the next state. Very often the researchers perform this analysis only on one asset. The conclusion that they make on the basis could mislead us. Usually in practice this result is used in support of certain beliefs or theses. To avoid the possibility of confusion, we have randomly chosen 6 assets (2 stocks and 4 indexes), covering 16 years' period of asset prices from 2000 to 2016. This data was gathered from yahoo finance website, online link: https://finance.yahoo.com/market-overview/ Additionally, daily trading was used as data source. The assets are listed in Table 1.

The models are formulated and solved by using the Wolfram Mathematical Programming System.

Determination of the Initial State Vector

If each closing day is taken as a discrete time unit, then the closing price is divided into three states, namely Unchanged (U), Decreases (D) and Increases (I). To determine the initial state vector, let $x_1 = U$, $x_2 = D$ and $x_3 = I$, where x_i is the number of the observations for the share prices in the named states

Table 1. Daily Observed Stock's

Stock's	Total observation days	Index	Total observation days
Apple Inc.	4073	S&P 500	4073
Alphabet Inc. Google	2911	NASDAQ Composite	4033
		Russel 2000	4073
		NYSE Composite	4073

gathered over the period of study, then the state space is E (x_1, x_2, x_3). State probability is the possibility size of the emergence of a variety of states and the state vector is denoted by an $_{(i)} = (\pi_1, \pi_2, \ldots, \pi_n)$ where I = 1, 2,…, n. π_j is the probability of x_j, j = 1, 2,…, n.

The initial state probability of each state is calculated as follows:

$\pi_1 = x_1$ / total obsevation days
$\pi_2 = x_2$ / total obsevation days
$\pi_3 = x_3$ / total obsevation days
Giving:
$n_{(0)} = (x_1$ / observation days, x_2 / observation days, x_3 / observation days)

Setting Up the Three State Transition Matrix

The transition matrix has three states which are stated as follows:

U= asset price remains the same/unchanged
D= asset price decreases
I= asset price increases

The transition probability matrix provides a precise description of the behavior of a Markov Chain. Each probability in the matrix represents the transition from a particular state to the next state or remains in the same. They are usually determined empirically, based on a historical data or experiment.

In our case the analyses are based on historical daily closing prices. Accordingly, Table 2 has been created which displays the price movement patterns. The symbol p_{ij} will be used for the probability of transition from state i to state j. They are formed by dividing each element in every row by the total of each row.

If P represents the transition matrix for Table 2, then:

$$p = \begin{bmatrix} p_{uu} & p_{ud} & p_{ui} \\ p_{du} & p_{dd} & p_{di} \\ p_{iu} & p_{id} & p_{ii} \end{bmatrix}$$

Table 2. Price Movement Patterns

Current Asset Position	Next Asset Position			
	State	Unchanged	Decrease	Increase
	Unchanged	p_{uu}	p_{ud}	p_{ui}
	Decrease	p_{du}	p_{dd}	p_{di}
	Increase	p_{iu}	p_{id}	p_{ii}

Note: State 1 is Unchanged, State 2 is Decrease and State 3 is Increase

A transition matrix has several features:

- It is square, since all possible states must be used both as rows and as columns.
- All entries are between 0 and 1, and this is because all entries represent probabilities.
- The sum of the entries in any row must be 1, since the numbers in the row give the probability of changes from the state on the left to one of the states indicates across the top.

The N-Step Transition Matrix

The absolute probabilities at any stage where n is greater than unity was determined by the use of n-step transition probabilities. This is a higher order transition probability $P_{ij}^{(n)}$ of the transition probability P_{ij}. The n-step matrix shows the behavior of stock price n-steps later. The elements of this matrix represent the probabilities that an object in a given state will be in the next state n-steps later. These repeated transitions were used to evaluate whether the transition probabilities converge over repeated iterations i.e.,

$$\lim_{t \to \infty} P_{ij}^{(n)} \tag{10}$$

This results in steady state probabilities which show the probabilities of the stock prices remaining unchanged, decreasing or increasing regardless of the stocks most recent changes in daily closing prices. The higher order transition probability $P_{ij}^{(n)}$ of the transition matrix Pij was calculated to observe the behavior of the stock and stock index prices.

Forecasting the State Probabilities

Since the state probabilities in different period are denoted by $n_{(i)}$, then $n_{(i+1)} = n_{(i)} * p_{ij}$. Thus, $n_{(i+n)} = n_{(i)} * p_{ij}^{(n)}$. The initial vector is depending on the state in which the asset price is on the last day of the trading period under study (for example 4076 days?). Let us suppose that is in D (decreases) state, then, $n_0 = (0,1,1)$. By multiplying the initial vector and transition matrix, $n_{(1)} = n_{(0)} * p_{ij}$ we can predict or forecast the next state probabilities; in our case this will be the 4077 day of the S&P 500 index.

DECISION MAKING IN DISCRETE TIME: A NUMERICAL ILLUMINATION

Modelling stock price movements has been a complex task since the distribution of financial time series could change over a period of time. Therefore, there is a never-ending debate as to whether these markets are predictable or not. Economists explain market unpredictably in term of the efficient hypothesis. Here prices are expected to be random and unpredictable, because new information, by its very nature, is unpredictable.

In finance, it is convenient to classify stock states by price movements as it remains the same/unchanged (U), the stock decreases (D) and that it increases (I). For example, if a stock price is unchanged is said to be in state 1, a stock price decreases are in state 2, and a stock price increase is in state 3. Now let us think about the question: If we know the probability that the stock from state 1 transit to state 2 or 3, and we know similar information about the stock of state 2 and state 3, then what is the future stock trend?

Using Markov chains, we will learn the answers to such questions.

The transition from the analyzed stocks and stock indexes are compiled in Tables 3, 4, 5, 6, 7, 8 and 9 as follows.

The symbol p_{ij} will be used for the probability of transition from state i to state j in one generation. For example, p_{32} represents the probability that an increase in price is followed by a decrease, or from the Tables above,

$$p_{32} = 0.47; p_{32} = 0.52; p_{32} = 0.54; p_{32} = 0.51; p_{32} = 0.43; \text{ and } p_{32} = 0.49$$

Table 3. S&P500 Index Transition Probabilities

S&P 500 Index	Unchanged	Decrease	Increase
Unchanged	0.01	0.43	0.56
Decrease	0.03	0.42	0.55
Increase	0.05	0.47	0.48

Table 4. NASDAG Composite Index Transition Probabilities

NASDAG Composite Index	Unchanged	Decrease	Increase
Unchanged	0.02	0.63	0.35
Decrease	0.02	0.52	0.46
Increase	0.02	0.52	0.46

Table 5. NYSE Composite Index Transition Probabilities

NYSE Composite Index	Unchanged	Decrease	Increase
Unchanged	0	0.68	0.32
Decrease	0.01	0.51	0.48
Increase	0.01	0.54	0.45

Table 6. RUSSEL 2000 Index Transition Probabilities

RUSSEL 2000 Index	Unchanged	Decrease	Increase
Unchanged	0.06	0.58	0.36
Decrease	0.04	0.49	0.47
Increase	0.05	0.51	0.44

Table 7. Apple Inc. Index Transition Probabilities

Apple Inc.	Unchanged	Decrease	Increase
Unchanged	0.44	0.31	0.25
Decrease	0.21	0.39	0.4
Increase	0.22	0.43	0.35

Table 8. Alphabet Inc. Google Index Transition probabilities

Alphabet Inc. Google	Unchanged	Decrease	Increase
Unchanged	0.06	0.5	0.44
Decrease	0.06	0.48	0.46
Increase	0.06	0.49	0.45

The information from Tables can be written in other forms. For example, Figure 2 is a transition diagram for S&P 500 index that show the three states and the probability of going from one state to another.

In a transition matrix, the states are indicated at the side and at the top. If P represents the transition matrix for the tables above, then:

$$p_{\text{S\&P500}} = \begin{bmatrix} 0.01 & 0.43 & 0.56 \\ 0.03 & 0.42 & 0.55 \\ 0.05 & 0.47 & 0.48 \end{bmatrix}$$

Figure 2. Transition diagram for S&P 500 index

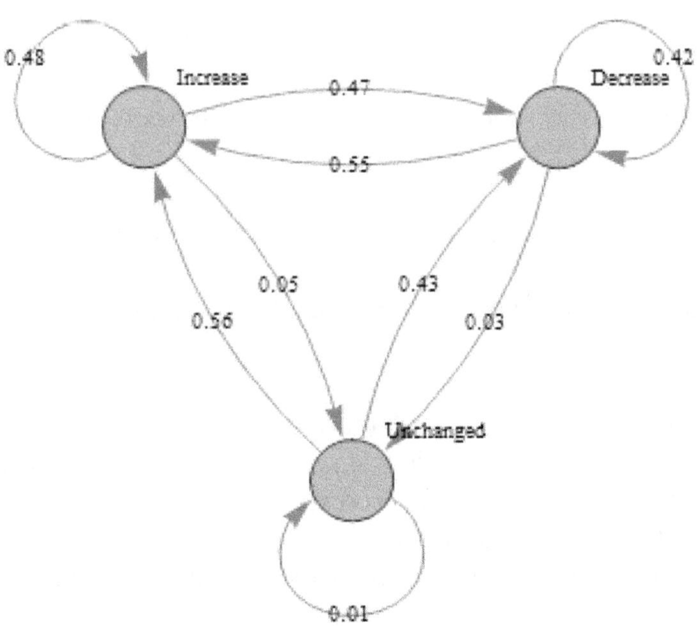

$$p_{\text{NASDAG Com.}} = \begin{bmatrix} 0.02 & 0.63 & 0.35 \\ 0.02 & 0.52 & 0.46 \\ 0.02 & 0.52 & 0.46 \end{bmatrix}$$

$$p_{\text{NYSE Com.}} = \begin{bmatrix} 0 & 0.68 & 0.32 \\ 0.01 & 0.51 & 0.48 \\ 0.01 & 0.54 & 0.45 \end{bmatrix}$$

$$p_{RUSSEL2000} = \begin{bmatrix} 0.06 & 0.58 & 0.36 \\ 0.04 & 0.49 & 0.47 \\ 0.05 & 0.51 & 0.44 \end{bmatrix}$$

$$P_{\text{Apple Inc.}} = \begin{bmatrix} 0.44 & 0.31 & 0.25 \\ 0.21 & 0.39 & 0.4 \\ 0.22 & 0.43 & 0.35 \end{bmatrix}$$

$$P_{\text{Alph.Google}} = \begin{bmatrix} 0.06 & 0.5 & 0.44 \\ 0.06 & 0.48 & 0.46 \\ 0.06 & 0.49 & 0.45 \end{bmatrix}$$

A transition matrix, such as matrix P above, shows two key features of a Markov Chain:

- The outcomes of each experiment are one of a set of discrete states; and
- The outcome of an experiment depends only on the present state, and not on any past states.

Now let us investigate the probabilities for stock movements over two periods. For example, if the stock is in state 3 (increase), what is the probability that a stock will transit to state 2 (decrease)?

To find out we will use a tree diagram to a S&P 500 index, see Figure 3 below. The various probabilities come from transition matrix P. The arrows

Figure 3. Tree Diagram for S&P 500 index

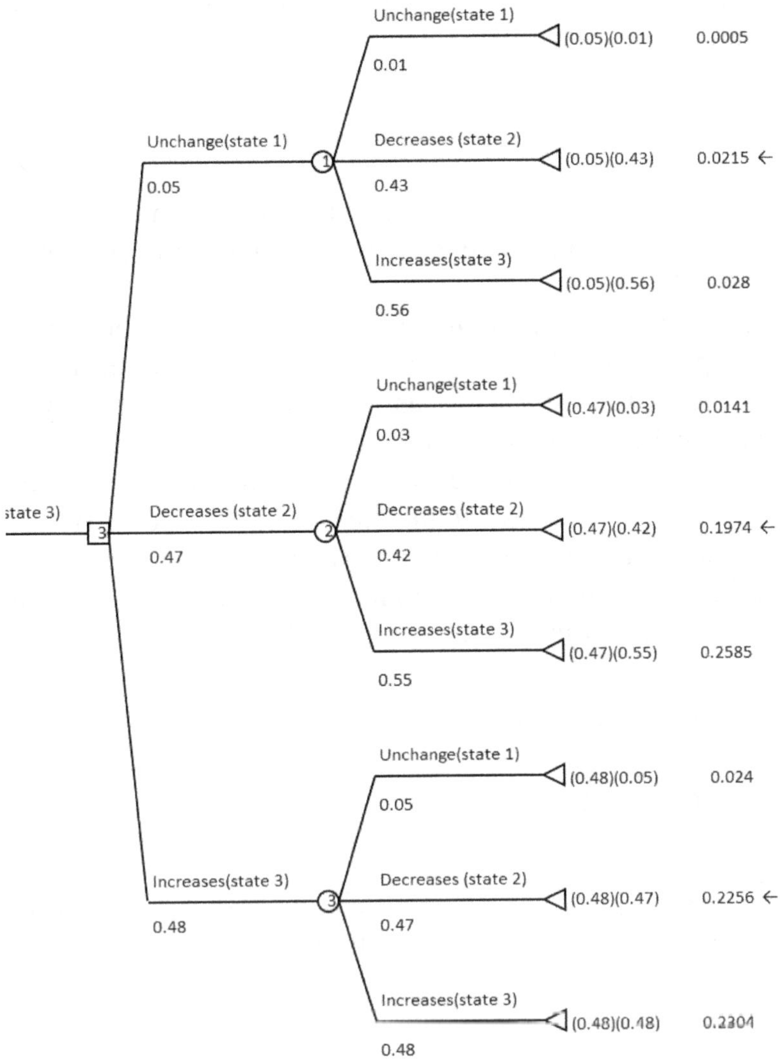

point to the outcomes "stock is in state 2"; the stock can get to state 2 of each previous state, 1,2 or 3. The probability that the stock from state 3 will transit to state 2 is given by the sum of the probabilities indicate with arrows, or:

$$0.0215 + 0.1974 + 0.2256 = 0.4445 \tag{11}$$

Here we use p_{ij} to represent the probability of transiting from state i to state j. This notation can be used to write the probability that a stock in state 3 (I) will transit in state 2 (D):

$$p_{31} * p_{12} + p_{32} * p_{22} + p_{33} * p_{32} \tag{12}$$

This sum of products of probabilities should remind you of matrix multiplication. It is nothing more than one step in the process of multiplying matrix P by itself.

In the next section using the computed transition matrix above, we develop a long-range prediction. Remember, it is not possible to make long-range predictions with all transition matrices. Such predictions are always possible with regular transition matrices. A transition matrix is regular if some power of the matrix contains all positive entries. Also, if a transition matrix P has some zero entries, but P^2 does not, then the matrix is regular. Here, P^2 gives the probabilities of a transition from one state to another in two repetitions of an experiment and represents the matrix product P*P. In our case only NYSE Composite stock index has entry zero, but its P^2 does not.

$$p^2_{\text{NASDAG Com.}} = \begin{bmatrix} 0.02 & 0.63 & 0.35 \\ 0.02 & 0.52 & 0.46 \\ 0.02 & 0.52 & 0.46 \end{bmatrix}$$

$P_{NASDAGCom}$ is a regular transition matrix because it has entries that are greater than 0, i.e. contains all positive entries.

Initial State Vector

Three different states of closing price are considered: remain same/unchanged (U), decrease (D) and increase (I).

The probabilities that the chain is in each of the possible states after n steps are listed in a state vector x_n. If there are m possible states, the state vector would be:

$$x_n = \begin{bmatrix} a_1 \\ \vdots \\ a_j \\ \vdots \\ a_m \end{bmatrix} \leftarrow \text{Probability that the chain is at state j after n steps}$$

State vectors are probability vectors since their entries must sum to 1. The state vector x_0 is called the initial probability vector. The initial probability vector gives the proportion (probability) of the three different states, π_1, π_2 and π_3. Based on the historical daily data the initial state vectors for the 6 stocks and stock indexes can be seen in Tables 9-14.

Table 9. Initial State Vector for S&P 500 Index

S&P 500 Index	State	Proportion π
Unchanged	1	162/4073=0.04
Decreases	2	1830/4073=0.45
Increases	3	2081/4073=0.51

Table 10. Initial State Vector for NASDAG Composite Index

NASDAG Composite Index	State	Proportion π
Unchanged	1	62/4033=0.02
Decreases	2	2113/4033=0.52
Increases	3	1858/4033=0.46

Table 11. Initial State Vector for NYSE Composite Index

NYSE Composite Index	State	Proportion π
Unchanged	1	31/4073=0
Decreases	2	2147/4073=0.53
Increases	3	1895/4073=0.47

Table 12. Initial State Vector for Russel 2000 Index

Russel 2000 Index	State	Proportion π
Unchanged	1	189/4073=0.05
Decreases	2	2044/4073=0.5
Increases	3	1840/4073=0.45

Table 13. Initial State Vector for Apple Inc.

Apple Inc.	State	Proportion π
Unchanged	1	1103/4073=0.27
Decreases	2	1570/4073=0.39
Increases	3	1400/4073=0.34

Table 14. Initial State Vector for Alphabet Google

Alphabet Google	State	Proportion π
Unchanged	1	181/2911=0.06
Decreases	2	1415/2911=0.49
Increases	3	1315/2911=0.45

Finding the Stationary Distribution

The n-step matrix shows the behavior of share price n-steps later. In particular, the elements of this matrix represent the probability that an object in a given state will be in the next state n-steps later. These repeated transitions are used to evaluate whether the transition probabilities converge over repeated iterations. This results in steady state probabilities which show the probabilities of the asset prices remaining same, decreasing or increasing regardless of the share's most recent changes in daily closing price.

From the n-step transition matrixes calculated below, it is noticed that after a period of n trading days, the matrix begins to approach some constant probabilities. After extending matrix multiplication to the 150th power, representing the 150th closing trading day of the market, we see all values converge indicating that an equilibrium is attained. The fact that the transition matrix converges to a steady state system means that the Markov chain is ergodic. Ergodic means that the states are positive recurrent and aperiodic. This is clear as the three states in the matrix each with three nonzero probabilities contained in their row vectors, reflecting the fact that each of the states can be reached any of the states in a finite number of steps.

The results obtained using Wolfram Mathematica Programming Language are as shown below, separated for each stock and stock index.

S&P 500 Index

$$p_{ij_{(S\&P500)}} = \begin{bmatrix} 0.01 & 0.43 & 0.56 \\ 0.03 & 0.42 & 0.55 \\ 0.05 & 0.47 & 0.48 \end{bmatrix}$$

$$p_{ij}^{2} = \begin{bmatrix} 0.041 & 0.448 & 0.511 \\ 0.04 & 0.45 & 0.51 \\ 0.039 & 0.445 & 0.516 \end{bmatrix}$$

$$p_{ij}^{3} = \begin{bmatrix} 0.039398 & 0.445955 & 0.514647 \\ 0.039428 & 0.445994 & 0.514578 \\ 0.039566 & 0.44623 & 0.514203 \end{bmatrix}$$

$$p_{ij}^{6} = \begin{bmatrix} 0.00395 & 0.4461 & 0.5144 \\ 0.0395 & 0.4461 & 0.5144 \\ 0.039 & 0.445 & 0.5144 \end{bmatrix}$$

$$p_{ij}^{30} = \begin{bmatrix} 0.00395 & 0.4461 & 0.5144 \\ 0.0395 & 0.4461 & 0.5144 \\ 0.039 & 0.445 & 0.5144 \end{bmatrix}$$

$$p_{ij}^{150} = \begin{bmatrix} 0.00395 & 0.4461 & 0.5144 \\ 0.0395 & 0.4461 & 0.5144 \\ 0.039 & 0.445 & 0.5144 \end{bmatrix}$$

$$p_{ij}^{200} = \begin{bmatrix} 0.00395 & 0.4461 & 0.5144 \\ 0.0395 & 0.4461 & 0.5144 \\ 0.039 & 0.445 & 0.5144 \end{bmatrix}$$

$$p_{ij}^{1000} = \begin{bmatrix} 0.00395 & 0.4461 & 0.5144 \\ 0.0395 & 0.4461 & 0.5144 \\ 0.039 & 0.445 & 0.5144 \end{bmatrix}$$

The following comments can be made from the above steady state transition matrix:

- After a period of six trading days, the matrix begins to approach some constant probabilities;
- The probability that a stock price will stay unchanged given that it initially either stays unchanged, decreased or increased is 0.039;
- The probability that a stock will decrease given that it initially either stays unchanged, decreased or increased is 0.446; and
- The probability that a stock will increase given that it initially either stays unchanged, decreased or increased is 0.5144.

In sum, this shows that regardless of the stocks most recent changes in closing price, approximately 3.95% of the time they will stay unchanged, 44.61% will drop in value tomorrow and 51.44% will have increased in price. This means that for investors who held an S&P 500 index during the period of study, on the average gained 2095 out of 4073 trading days.

NASDAG Composite Index

$$p_{ij_{(Nasdag)}} = \begin{bmatrix} 0.02 & 0.63 & 0.35 \\ 0.02 & 0.52 & 0.46 \\ 0.02 & 0.52 & 0.46 \end{bmatrix}$$

$$p_{ij}^{2} = \begin{bmatrix} 0.02 & 0.5222 & 0.4578 \\ 0.02 & 0.5222 & 0.4578 \\ 0.02 & 0.5222 & 0.4578 \end{bmatrix}$$

$$p_{ij}^{30} = \begin{bmatrix} 0.02 & 0.5222 & 0.4578 \\ 0.02 & 0.5222 & 0.4578 \\ 0.02 & 0.5222 & 0.4578 \end{bmatrix}$$

$$p_{ij}^{150} = \begin{bmatrix} 0.02 & 0.5222 & 0.4578 \\ 0.02 & 0.5222 & 0.4578 \\ 0.02 & 0.5222 & 0.4578 \end{bmatrix}$$

$$p_{ij}^{200} = \begin{bmatrix} 0.02 & 0.5222 & 0.4578 \\ 0.02 & 0.5222 & 0.4578 \\ 0.02 & 0.5222 & 0.4578 \end{bmatrix}$$

$$p_{ij}^{1000} = \begin{bmatrix} 0.02 & 0.5222 & 0.4578 \\ 0.02 & 0.5222 & 0.4578 \\ 0.02 & 0.5222 & 0.4578 \end{bmatrix}$$

The following comments can be made from the above steady state transition matrix:

- After a period of two trading days, the matrix begins to approach some constant probabilities;
- The probability that a stock price will stay unchanged given that it initially either stays unchanged, decreased or increased is 0.02;
- The probability that a stock will decrease given that it initially either stays unchanged, decreased or increased is 0.5222; and that
- The probability that a stock will increase given that it initially either stays unchanged, decreased or increased is 0.4578.

In sum, this shows that regardless of the stocks most recent changes in closing price, approximately 2% of the time they will stay unchanged, 52.22% will drop in value tomorrow and 45.78% will have increased in price. This means that for investors who held a NASDAG Composite index during the period of study, on the average gained 1846 out of 4033 trading days.

NYSE Composite Index

$$p_{ij_{(Nasdag)}} = \begin{bmatrix} 0 & 0.68 & 0.32 \\ 0.01 & 0.51 & 0.48 \\ 0.01 & 0.54 & 0.45 \end{bmatrix}$$

$$p_{ij}^{2} = \begin{bmatrix} 0.01 & 0.5196 & 0.4704 \\ 0.0099 & 0.5261 & 0.4639 \\ 0.0099 & 0.5252 & 0.4649 \end{bmatrix}$$

$$p_{ij}^{5} = \begin{bmatrix} 0.00990099 & 0.525618 & 0.464481 \\ 0.00990099 & 0.525618 & 0.464481 \\ 0.00990099 & 0.525618 & 0.464481 \end{bmatrix}$$

$$p_{ij}^{30} = \begin{bmatrix} 0.00990099 & 0.525618 & 0.464481 \\ 0.00990099 & 0.525618 & 0.464481 \\ 0.00990099 & 0.525618 & 0.464481 \end{bmatrix}$$

$$p_{ij}^{150} = \begin{bmatrix} 0.00990099 & 0.525618 & 0.464481 \\ 0.00990099 & 0.525618 & 0.464481 \\ 0.00990099 & 0.525618 & 0.464481 \end{bmatrix}$$

$$p_{ij}^{200} = \begin{bmatrix} 0.00990099 & 0.525618 & 0.464481 \\ 0.00990099 & 0.525618 & 0.464481 \\ 0.00990099 & 0.525618 & 0.464481 \end{bmatrix}$$

$$p_{ij}^{1000} = \begin{bmatrix} 0.00990099 & 0.525618 & 0.464481 \\ 0.00990099 & 0.525618 & 0.464481 \\ 0.00990099 & 0.525618 & 0.464481 \end{bmatrix}$$

The following comments can be made from the above steady state transition matrix:

- After a period of five trading days, the matrix begins to approach some constant probabilities;
- The probability that a stock price will stay unchanged given that it initially either stays unchanged, decreased or increased is 0.0099;
- The probability that a stock will decrease given that it initially either stays unchanged, decreased or increased is 0.5256; and that
- The probability that a stock will increase given that it initially either stays unchanged, decreased or increased is 0.4642.

In sum, this shows that regardless of the stocks most recent changes in closing price, approximately 0.99% of the time they will stay unchanged, 52.56% will drop in value tomorrow and 46.42% will have increased in price. This means that for investors who held a NYSE Composite index during the period of study, averaged gains 1891 out of 4073 trading days.

Russel 2000 Index

$$p_{ij(Russel2000)} = \begin{bmatrix} 0.06 & 0.58 & 0.36 \\ 0.04 & 0.49 & 0.47 \\ 0.05 & 0.51 & 0.44 \end{bmatrix}$$

$$p_{ij}^{2} = \begin{bmatrix} 0.04478 & 0.50259 & 0.45259 \\ 0.0455 & 0.503 & 0.45149 \\ 0.0454 & 0.5033 & 0.4513 \end{bmatrix}$$

$$p_{ij}^{5} = \begin{bmatrix} 0.045423 & 0.503117 & 0.45146 \\ 0.045423 & 0.503117 & 0.45146 \\ 0.045423 & 0.503117 & 0.45146 \end{bmatrix}$$

$$p_{ij}^{30} = \begin{bmatrix} 0.045423 & 0.503117 & 0.45146 \\ 0.045423 & 0.503117 & 0.45146 \\ 0.045423 & 0.503117 & 0.45146 \end{bmatrix}$$

$$p_{ij}^{150} = \begin{bmatrix} 0.045423 & 0.503117 & 0.45146 \\ 0.045423 & 0.503117 & 0.45146 \\ 0.045423 & 0.503117 & 0.45146 \end{bmatrix}$$

$$p_{ij}^{200} = \begin{bmatrix} 0.045423 & 0.503117 & 0.45146 \\ 0.045423 & 0.503117 & 0.45146 \\ 0.045423 & 0.503117 & 0.45146 \end{bmatrix}$$

$$p_{ij}^{1000} = \begin{bmatrix} 0.045423 & 0.503117 & 0.45146 \\ 0.045423 & 0.503117 & 0.45146 \\ 0.045423 & 0.503117 & 0.45146 \end{bmatrix}$$

The following comments can be made from the above steady state transition matrix:

- After a period of five trading days, the matrix begins to approach some constant probabilities;
- The probability that a stock price will stay unchanged given that it initially either stays unchanged, decreased or increased is 0.0454;
- The probability that a stock will decrease given that it initially either stays unchanged, decreased or increased is 0.503; and that
- The probability that a stock will increase given that it initially either stays unchanged, decreased or increased is 0.451.

In sum, this shows that regardless of the stocks most recent changes in closing price, approximately 4.54% of the time they will stay unchanged,

50.3% will drop in value tomorrow and 45.1% will have increased in price. This means that for investors who held a Russel 2000 index during the period of study, on the average gained 1837 out of 4073 trading days.

Apple Inc.

$$p_{ij_{(AppleInc)}} = \begin{bmatrix} 0.44 & 0.31 & 0.25 \\ 0.21 & 0.39 & 0.4 \\ 0.22 & 0.43 & 0.35 \end{bmatrix}$$

$$p_{ij}^{2} = \begin{bmatrix} 0.3137 & 0.3648 & 0.3215 \\ 0.3137 & 0.3892 & 0.3485 \\ 0.2641 & 0.3864 & 0.3495 \end{bmatrix}$$

$$p_{ij}^{10} = \begin{bmatrix} 0.277161 & 0.381481 & 0.341358 \\ 0.277161 & 0.381481 & 0.341358 \\ 0.277161 & 0.381481 & 0.341358 \end{bmatrix}$$

$$p_{ij}^{30} = \begin{bmatrix} 0.277161 & 0.381481 & 0.341358 \\ 0.277161 & 0.381481 & 0.341358 \\ 0.277161 & 0.381481 & 0.341358 \end{bmatrix}$$

$$p_{ij}^{150} = \begin{bmatrix} 0.277161 & 0.381481 & 0.341358 \\ 0.277161 & 0.381481 & 0.341358 \\ 0.277161 & 0.381481 & 0.341358 \end{bmatrix}$$

$$p_{ij}^{200} = \begin{bmatrix} 0.277161 & 0.381481 & 0.341358 \\ 0.277161 & 0.381481 & 0.341358 \\ 0.277161 & 0.381481 & 0.341358 \end{bmatrix}$$

The following comments can be made from the above steady state transition matrix:

- After a period of ten trading days, the matrix begins to approach some constant probabilities;
- The probability that a stock price will stay unchanged given that it initially either stays unchanged, decreased or increased is 0.278;
- The probability that a stock will decrease given that it initially either stays unchanged, decreased or increased is 0.381; and that
- The probability that a stock will increase given that it initially either stays unchanged, decreased or increased is 0.341.

In sum, this shows that regardless of the stocks most recent changes in closing price, approximately 2.78% of the time they will stay unchanged, 38.1% will drop in value tomorrow and 34.1% will have increased in price. This means that for investors who held an Apple Inc. during the period of study, on the average gained 1389 out of 4073 trading days.

Alphabet Inc. Google

$$p_{ij_{(AlphabetInc.Google)}} = \begin{bmatrix} 0.06 & 0.5 & 0.44 \\ 0.06 & 0.48 & 0.46 \\ 0.06 & 0.49 & 0.45 \end{bmatrix}$$

$$p_{ij}^{2} = \begin{bmatrix} 0.06 & 0.4856 & 0.4544 \\ 0.06 & 0.4858 & 0.4542 \\ 0.06 & 0.4857 & 0.4543 \end{bmatrix}$$

$$p_{ij}^{4} = \begin{bmatrix} 0.06 & 0.48574 & 0.45425 \\ 0.06 & 0.48574 & 0.45425 \\ 0.06 & 0.48574 & 0.45425 \end{bmatrix}$$

$$p_{ij}^{30} = \begin{bmatrix} 0.06 & 0.48574 & 0.45425 \\ 0.06 & 0.48574 & 0.45425 \\ 0.06 & 0.48574 & 0.45425 \end{bmatrix}$$

$$p_{ij}^{150} = \begin{bmatrix} 0.06 & 0.48574 & 0.45425 \\ 0.06 & 0.48574 & 0.45425 \\ 0.06 & 0.48574 & 0.45425 \end{bmatrix}$$

$$p_{ij}^{200} = \begin{bmatrix} 0.06 & 0.48574 & 0.45425 \\ 0.06 & 0.48574 & 0.45425 \\ 0.06 & 0.48574 & 0.45425 \end{bmatrix}$$

$$p_{ij}^{1000} = \begin{bmatrix} 0.06 & 0.48574 & 0.45425 \\ 0.06 & 0.48574 & 0.45425 \\ 0.06 & 0.48574 & 0.45425 \end{bmatrix}$$

The following comments can be made from the above steady state transition matrix:

- After a period of four trading days, the matrix begins to approach some constant probabilities;
- The probability that a stock price will stay unchanged given that it initially either stays unchanged, decreased or increased is 0.06;
- The probability that a stock will decrease given that it initially either stays unchanged, decreased or increased is 0.486; and that
- The probability that a stock will increase given that it initially either stays unchanged, decreased or increased is 0.454.

In sum, this shows that regardless of the stocks most recent changes in closing price, approximately 6% of the time they will stay unchanged, 48.6% will drop in value tomorrow and 45.4% will have increased in price. This means that for investors who held an Apple Inc. during the period of study, on the average gained 1415 out of 2911 trading days.

Finding the First-Passage Time

First-passage times represent the number of steps taken in going from one given state to another. They are frequently of interest of Markov chains, and here we solve for the expected value E of this random variable.

$$E_{(n_{ij})} = \begin{bmatrix} E_{(UU)} & E_{(UD)} & E_{(UI)} \\ E_{(DU)} & E_{(DD)} & E_{(DI)} \\ E_{(IU)} & E_{(ID)} & E_{(II)} \end{bmatrix}$$

Let E (ud) denote the number of steps before the chain reaches the state decreases (D) for the first time, starting from the state unchanged (U). Thus, the expected first passage time matrix for different states for the following 6 stocks and stock indexes is given below:

S&P 500 Index

$$E_{(S\&P500)} = \begin{bmatrix} 25.32 & 2.22 & 1.79 \\ 24.83 & 2.24 & 1.81 \\ 24.36 & 2.14 & 1.95 \end{bmatrix}$$

If the closing value of share price of S&P500 index is in the unchanged state (U) in day one, then it can be expected to reach the unchanged state (U) for the first time after 25 days. If the closing value of share price either in the state decrease (D) or in the state increased (I) it will take 2 days on average to reach the state increase (I). That is, it does not depend on its initial state. If a price of S&P500 index has either in the state increase (I) or decrease (D) it will take about 25 days on average before it experiences the state of unchanged (U) for the first time. If it is in the state increased (I) then it will take approximately 2 days to reach the state increased (I). And at the end if it is in the state decreased (D) then it will take approximately 2 days to reach the state decreased (D).

NASDAG Composite Index

$$E_{(Nasdag)} = \begin{bmatrix} 50 & 1.7 & 2.4 \\ 50 & 1.9 & 2.2 \\ 50 & 1.9 & 2.2 \end{bmatrix}$$

If the closing value of share price of the NASDAG Composite index is in the state unchanged (U) in day one, then it can be expected to reach the state unchanged (U) for the first time after 50 days. If the closing value of share price either in the state decrease (D) or in the state increased (I) it will take 2 days on average to reach the state increase (I). That is, it does not depend on its initial state. If a price of the NASDAG Composite index is either in the state increase (I) or decrease (D) it will take about 50 days on average before it experience the state of unchanged (U) for the first time. If it is in the state increased (I) then it will take approximately 2 days to reach the state increased (I). And at the end if it is in the state decreased (D) then it will take approximately 2 days to reach the state decreased (D).

NYSE Composite Index

$$E_{(NYSE)} = \begin{bmatrix} 101 & 1.6 & 2.4 \\ 100 & 1.9 & 2.1 \\ 100 & 1.9 & 2.2 \end{bmatrix}$$

If the closing value of share price of the NYSE Composite index is in the state unchanged (U) in day one, then it can be expected to reach the state unchanged (U) for the first time after 101 days. If the closing value of share price is either in the state decrease (D) or in the state increased (I) it will take 2 days on average to reach the state increase (I). That is, it does not depend on its initial state. If a price of the NYSE Composite index is either in the state increase (I) or decrease (D) it will take about 100 days on average before it experiences the state of unchanged (U) for the first time. If it is in the state increased (I) then it will take approximately 2 days to reach the state increased (I). And at the end if it is in the state decreased (D) then it will take approximately 2 days to reach the state decreased (D).

Russel 2000 Index

$$E_{(Russel2000)} = \begin{bmatrix} 22 & 1.8 & 2.3 \\ 22 & 1.9 & 2.1 \\ 22 & 1.9 & 2.2 \end{bmatrix}$$

If the closing value of share price of Russel 2000 index is in the state unchanged (U) in day one, then it can be expected to reach the state unchanged (U) for the first time after 22 days. If the closing value of share price either in the state decrease (D) or in the state increased (I) it will take 2 days on average to reach the state increase (I). That is, it does not depend on its initial state. If a price of Russel 2000 index is either in the state increase (I) or decrease (D) it will take about 22 days on average before it experience the state of unchanged (U) for the first time. If it is in the state increased (I) then it will take approximately 2 days to reach the state increased (I). And at the end if it is in the state decreased (D) then it will take approximately 2 days to reach the state decreased (D).

Apple Inc.

$$E_{(AppleInc)} = \begin{bmatrix} 3.6 & 2.9 & 3.3 \\ 4.7 & 2.6 & 2.8 \\ 4.6 & 2.5 & 2.9 \end{bmatrix}$$

If the closing value of share price of Apple Inc. is in the state unchanged (U) in day one, then it can expect to reach the state unchanged (U) for the first time after 4 days. If the closing value of share price either in the state decrease (D) or in the state increased (I) it will take 3 days on average to reach the state increase (I). That is, it does not depend on its initial state. If a price of Apple Inc. is either in the state increase (I) or decrease (D) it will take about 5 days on average before it experience the state of unchanged (U) for the first time. If it is in the state increased (I) then it will take approximately 3 days to reach the state increased (I). And at the end if it is in the state decreased (D) then it will take approximately 3 days to reach the state decreased (D).

Alphabet Inc. Google

$$E_{(Alphabet)} = \begin{bmatrix} 2.2 & 2.01 & 2.2 \\ 16.7 & 2.06 & 2.2 \\ 16.7 & 2.04 & 2.2 \end{bmatrix}$$

If the closing value of share price of Alphabet Inc. is in the state unchanged (U) in day one, then it can expect to reach the state unchanged (U) for the first time after 2 days. If the closing value of share price either in the state decrease (D) or in the state increased (I) it will take 2 days on average to reach the state increase (I). That is, it does not depend on its initial state. If a price of Alphabet Inc. has either in the state increase (I) or decrease (D) it will take about 17 days on average before it experience the state of unchanged (U) for the first time. If it is in the state increased (I) then it will take approximately 2 days to reach the state increased (I). And at the end if it is in the state decreased (D) then it will take approximately 2 days to reach the state decreased (D).

EXPECTED RETURN TIME

Expected return time to a particular state reflects another aspect of stock price behavior. The expected return time to same state can be directly calculated from visiting rate as well as from the steady state matrix. For a finite irreducible chain the expected return time is the reciprocal of the steady state probabilities. For S&P500 Index the expected return time to the state increases, starting from same state increases is E (n_{ii}) = 1/0.51=1.96. Similarly, the expected return time to the state decreases, starting from the state decreases is E (n_{DD}) =1/0.45=2.22 and remaining same/unchanged is E (n_{uu}) 1/0.039=25.6. Now from the above calculation, it can be concluded that the chain should visit the state increases, on average, in two days, state decreases in two days and the state remaining same/unchanged on average in 25.6 days.

The same calculation can be carried out for the remaining stocks and stock indexes (NASDAG Composite Index, NYSE Composite Index, Russel 2000 Index, Apple Inc. and Alphabet Inc. Google.).

Predicting the Price Movement Trend

It is very fashionable to research on the financial forecasting or stock market prediction. Therefore, in what follows we show how to develop a long-range prediction and determine the stock price movements using the Markov Chain model. The finance theory considers this model as barometer which enables investors to get an idea about the performance of the particular stock or the entire market in general. But the real question is How useful is a Markov Chain for quantitative finance? Before we answer this question, we should look at how to apply Markov Chain technique in practice. In Appendix 1 encloses the Mathematica Programming code which helps to run the analysis.

So, suppose a Markov chain has initial probability vector X_0,

$$X_0 = \left[i_1, i_2, i_3 \ldots . i_n\right]$$

and transition matrix P,

$$p = \begin{bmatrix} p_{uu} & p_{ud} & p_{ui} \\ p_{du} & p_{dd} & p_{di} \\ p_{iu} & p_{id} & p_{ii} \end{bmatrix}$$

The probability vector after n repetitions of the experiment is:

$$X_0 * P^n \tag{13}$$

By virtue of the initial state vector and transition matrix, we can predict state probabilities of various closing dates in future.

Let us start with S&P 500 Index as a subject of the investigation. The initial probability vector which gives the price movements by state for the S&P 500 Index, is [0.04, 0.45, 0.51]. We observed 4073 trading days, therefore the closing price on the 4074th day can be obtained as; $X_0 * P_{(ij)}$ or,

$$\left[0.04, 0.45, 0.51\right] * \begin{bmatrix} 0.01 & 0.43 & 0.56 \\ 0.03 & 0.42 & 0.55 \\ 0.05 & 0.05 & 0.48 \end{bmatrix} = \left[0.039, 0.45, 0.51\right] \tag{14}$$

Accordingly, the state probability vector of the closing price on 4075th day is: $X_1 * P_{(ij)}$ or,

$$\begin{bmatrix}0.039, 0.45, 0.51\end{bmatrix} * \begin{bmatrix}0.01 & 0.43 & 0.56 \\ 0.03 & 0.42 & 0.55 \\ 0.05 & 0.05 & 0.48\end{bmatrix} = \begin{bmatrix}0.039506, 0.446114, 0.514388\end{bmatrix} \tag{15}$$

By using the n-step probability transition matrix and state vectors, we forecast the probabilities of S&P500 Index prices based on the formula: $X_{(i+n)} = n_{(i)} * p_{(ij)}^{(n)}$. The results are posted in Table 15.

From the forecast above, we can notice that irrespective of current price today, the probability of the daily closing index price either increases, decreases or remains the same /unchanged, continues to increase until equilibrium was reached (after 4077 trading days) and then become constant. This is nothing more than observing the financial markets as a diffusion process.

In physics if an object is at equilibrium, then the forces are balanced. *Balanced* is the key word that is used to describe equilibrium situations. Thus, the net force is zero and the acceleration is 0 m/s/s. Objects at equilibrium must have an acceleration of 0 m/s/s. This extends from Newton's first law of motion. But having an acceleration of 0 m/s/s does not mean the object is at rest. An object at equilibrium is either at rest and staying at rest, or in motion and continuing in motion with the same speed and direction. This too extends from Newton's first law of motion.

If the price movements can be successfully explained by the Markov Chain model, then we can conclude that regardless of the S&P500 index price today, the probability that it will increase in the future is 51.4%. Compared

Table 15. Forecast of S&P 500 index daily closing prices

Trading Day	Unchanged	Decreases	Increases
Initial Probability (4073)	0.04	0.45	0.51
4074	0.0394	0.4459	0.5147
4075	0.039506	0.446129	0.514365
4076	0.0394972	0.446113	0.51439
4077	0.0394978	0.446114	0.514388
4078	0.0394978	0.446114	0.514388

to approximate a probability of 44.6% and 3.9% of price decreasing or not gaining value, respectively, investors would be informed that those who bought S&P500 Index shares have more chances of appreciating resulting into capital gains and hence better returns on investment.

Using this information, we compute the price movements of the NASDAG Composite Index, NYSE Composite Index, Russel 2000 Index, Apple Inc. and Alphabet Inc, Google, as illustrated in Tables 16, 17, 18, 19 and 20.

But what will happen if the initial probability vector for the S&P500 index is different from [0.04 0.45 0.51]? If we suppose that [0.01 0.35 0.55] is used, then the results are given in Table 21.

Table 16. Forecast of NASDAG composite index daily closing prices

Trading Day	Unchanged	Decreases	Increases
Initial Probability (4036)	0.015	0.524	0.461
4037	0.02	0.52165	0.45835
4038	0.02	0.5222	0.4578
4039	0.02	0.5222	0.4578

Table 17. Forecast of NYSE Composite index daily closing prices

Trading Day	Unchanged	Decreases	Increases
Initial Probability (4076)	0.008	0.527	0.465
4077	0.00992	0.52531	0.46477
4078	0.0099	0.5256295	0.4644697
4079	0.0099	0.5256295	0.464481781
4080	0.0099	0.5256176	0.46448139
4081	0.0099	0.5256176	0.46448139

Table 18. Forecast Russel 2000 index daily closing prices

Trading Day	Unchanged	Decreases	Increases
Initial Probability (4076)	0.046	0.502	0.452
4077	0.04544	0.50318	0.4514602
4078	0.0454226	0.5031172	0.4514602
4079	0.04542305	0.5031172	0.4514597
4080	0.04542305	0.5031172	0.4514597

Table 19. Forecast Apple Inc. daily closing prices

Trading Day	Unchanged	Decreases	Increases
Initial Probability (4076)	0.04	0.45	0.51
4077	0.2243	0.4072	0.3685
4078	0.265274	0.386796	0.34793
4079	0.27449232	0.38269528	0.3428124
4080	0.27656135	0.38175311	0.341685532
4081	0.277025967	0.3815425126	0.341431519
4082	0.27713	0.381495	0.341375
4083	0.277153	0.381485	0.341362
4084	0.277158	0.381482	0.341359
4085	0.277160	0.381482	0.341358
4086	0.277160	0.381482	0.341358

Table 20. Forecast Alphabet Inc. google daily closing prices

Trading Day	Unchanged	Decreases	Increases
Initial Probability (2915)	0.062	0.486	0.451
2916	0.05994	0.48527	0.45379
2917	0.05994	0.485256	0.453803
2918	0.05994	0.485256	0.453803

Table 21. Transition probabilities, initial probability vector are [0.01 0.35 0.55]

Trading Day	Unchanged	Decreases	Increases
Initial Probability (4073)	0.1	0.35	0.55
4074	0.039	0.4485	0.5125
4075	0.03947	0.446015	0.514515
4076	0.0395	0.44612	0.514379
4077	0.0394875	0.4461139415	0.5143885035
4078	0.0394978	0.446114	0.514388
4079	0.0394978	0.446114	0.514388

The results again are approaching the numbers in the probability vector [0.039, 0.446, 0.514], the same numbers approached with the initial probability vector [0.04 0.45 0.51]. In either case, the long-range trend gives us the probability of 51.4% that the price will increase in future. This example suggests that this long-range trend does not depend on the initial distribution

At the end, we can conclude that the Markov Chain prediction method is purely a probability forecasting method as the predicted results is simply expressed as a probability of a certain state of stock or price in the future rather than be in an absolute state. In this section, we showed how the Markov Chain fits the data and how we can use it to predict trend due to its memoryless property and random walk capability. However, we should be very careful in making investment decisions based only on the Markov Chain model, because the stock market is subject to the influence of various factors of the multiple market forces to psychological factors of investors.

Continues Markov Processes

Brownian motion was the key to deciphering the microscopic world, first in gases and liquids, and later on – surely more difficult I admit – in crystalline solids. We are faced here with an incredible convergence: Brownian motion was actually modelled for the first time by a mathematician, Louis Bachelier, who did not consider physical events, but stock-market quotations! (Jean Philibert, 2005)

In the previous section, we considered stochastic processes that were discrete in both time and space, and that considered the Markov property. Due to the Markov property, the time the system spends in any given state is memoryless. The distribution of the remaining time depends solely on the state but not on the time already spent in the state, the time is exponentially distributed. Or we can say that our predictions of the future should be unaffected by the price one week ago, one month ago, or one year ago, because the only relevant piece of information is the price now.

Remember, predictions are uncertain and must be expressed in terms of probability distributions. So, if the stock price follows a Markov process, then the transition rates follow an exponential distribution (known as a Boltzmann-Gibbs type of transition rates). This is due to the fact that the dynamics between states is fast enough. In this case the stocks have equal changes to transit from one state to another, regardless of the duration in current state.

Therefore, in what follows, we generalize such stochastic models by allowing for time to be continuous and as before, we will take our state space to be either finite or infinite. Solutions of these processes are piecewise constant, right continuous functions from time to states. To specify, we will use the jump Markov process and first-time passage distribution to model the stock price movement and answer the following question:

How fast does the amplitude or the position of a random process reach a given threshold value (target) for the first time?

Jump Markov Process

Jump diffusion processes have experienced renewed interest in the theory of finance. They allow stock prices to change continuously most of the time, but they also take into account the fact that from time to time, larger jumps may occur, which cannot be adequately modelled by pure diffusion type processes. In our case, we can interpret the jump part of the model as the market's response to outside news. Bad and good news arrive according to a Poisson driven process, and the stock price changes in response to the news. In the absence of outside news, the stock prices simply follow a geometric Brownian motion. Here the mean and variance are constant and jumps will only arrive at discrete points in time with intensity λ. The famous Black-Scholes model is based on geometric Brownian motion. Merton (1976), proposed an extension of the Black-Scholes model and provided formula for the price of a European call option on a single stock where the stock price process contains a continuous Poisson jump component, in addition to a continuous log-normally distributed component. He defined the jump diffusion processes as a special type of stochastic process that has large discrete movements, or jumps, rather than small continuous movements.

Today it is widely acknowledged in the academic literature that the traditionally used geometric Brownian motion model for market behavior falls short of explaining empirical observations of market returns and its underlying derivatives' prices (Wang and Chahal, 1997; Zhou, 1997 and Das, 2002).

For that reason, we will start this section by defining the jump Markov processes, and then apply them to real financial market data. The main goal is to determine the transit distribution which is the basis of predictions. The distribution will indicate the model that best describes the stock price movements.

The two basic building blocks of every jump-diffusion model are the Brownian motion (the diffusion part) and the Poisson process (the jump part).

A Markov process jumps from one state to another one at integer times: $t^1, t^2, \ldots, t^n$ at random times $\tau_1, \tau_2, \ldots, \tau_n$. More specifically, if the process is in state x at time t, then it will remain there until sometime t' > t when it instantaneously jumps to a new state x'. The times t^1 and t^2, at which successive jumps occur, and the states x^1 and x^2 reached in these jumps, both form countable sets. This is not the case with continuous Markov process, where the fundamental properties of the continuum prevent us from asking, when the system will leave state x or what will be the next state after x.

Definition of Jumps:

- Jumps are independent of one another and they are defined as a Poisson process with intensity parameter λ
- Jumps are drawn from Poisson probability density or,

$$\frac{(\lambda t)^n}{n!} e^{-\lambda t}$$

The mean waiting time for jumps is $\frac{1}{\lambda}$

- When jumps occur, the underlying value changes to y+ (-) J where J is the magnitude of the jump. Note, this quantity is usually independent from the jump intensity and can be made stochastic; drawn from pre-defined probability distribution.

In general, the underlying asset S_t under jump-diffusion models follows the stochastic differential equation (SDE):

$$\frac{dS_t}{S_{t-}} = (\mu - \lambda k)dt + \sigma dW(t) + (\eta - 1)dN_t \tag{16}$$

where $\{W(t); t > 0\}$ is a standard Brownian motion with $W_0 = 0, \{N_t; t > 0\}$ is a Poisson process, constants μ and σ are drift and volatility of the diffusion part respectively, k is the expected relative jump size, λ is the rate of the Poisson process, and η-1 is a random variable producing a jump from S_t to $S_{t\eta}$.

Since for a jump Markov process, we can ask when the system will leave its current state and what the next state will be, then it makes sense to define for a jump Markov process the following probabilities:

- $q(x,t,\tau) \rightarrow$ probability given $X(t)=x$, then the process will jump away from state x at some instant between t and $t \in \tau$;
- $\omega(E \mid x,t)dE \rightarrow$ probability that the process, upon jumping away from state x at time t will lend in some state lying in the infinitesimal interval $(x+E, x+E+dE)$
- $q*(x,t;\tau) \rightarrow 1-q(x,t,\tau) \rightarrow$ probability given $X(t)=x$, then the process will not jump away from state x in $[t,t+\tau]$.

We now define a process $X_t \in X, t \in R$. We assume X countable and consider transition rates $q(x,y) \geq 0$ for $x, y \in X$ such that x≠ y and want to construct a process with the property that the rate of jumping from state x to state y be q (x, y). In other words, the process must satisfy,

$$P\left(X_{t+h} = y \mid X_t = x\right) = h_q\left(x,y\right) + o\left(h\right) \text{ for all } x \neq y. \tag{17}$$

Let

$$q\left(x\right) = \sum_y q\left(x,y\right) \tag{18}$$

be the exit rate from state x.

To construct the Markov process, we introduce a one- dimensional bi-generalized Poisson process M (.), where for each state x partition the interval $I^x = \left[0, q\left(x\right)\right]$ at intervals I (x, y) of length q (x, y).

Let $x_0 \in X$ and suppose $X_0 = x_0$. Let τ1 be the first time an event of the process M (.) appears in the interval $I^{x0:}$

$$\tau_1 = \inf\left\{t > 0; M\left(I^{x_0} \times \left[0,t\right]\right) > 0\right.$$

Define $x_1 = y$, where y is the unique state satisfying

$$\inf\left\{t > 0 : M\left(I^{x_0} \times \left[0,t\right] > 0\right\} = \inf\left\{t > 0 : M\left(I\left(x_0,y\right)\times\left[0,t\right]\right) > 0\right\} \tag{19}$$

that is, x_1 is determined by the interval I (x_0, x_1) which realizes the Infimum.

Assume now that τ_{n-1} and x_{n-1} are already determined. Driven by the particular facts we define τ_n as:

$$\tau_n = \inf\left\{t > \tau_{n-1} : M\left(I^{x_{n-1}} \times \left(\tau_{n-1,t}\right]\right) > 0\right\} \tag{20}$$

and x_n=y if and only if:

$$\inf\left\{t > \tau_{n-1} : M\left(I^{x_{n-1}} \times \left(\tau_{n-1,t}\right]\right) > 0 = \inf\left\{t > 0 : M\left(I\left(x_{n-1},y\right)\times\left(\tau_{n-1},t\right] > 0\right.\right.\right. \tag{21}$$

Definition: Define $\tau_\infty=\sup_n\tau_n$ and

$$X_t = x_n, \text{if } t \in \left[\tau_n \tau_{n+1}\right) \tag{220}$$

For all t $\in[0,\infty)$

In this way, for each random realization of the one- dimensional bi-generalized Poisson process M (.), we construct a realization of the process X_t for it $\in$ [0, τ_∞). Observe that τ_n is the n-th jump time of the process and x_n is the n-th state visited by the process.

Proposition: The process (Xt: t $\in$ [0, $\tau\infty$)) defined above satisfies the properties from Equation 17.

Proof: By definition,

$$P\left(X_{t+h} = y \mid X_t = x\right) \tag{23}$$

$$= P\left(M\left(I\left(x,y\right)\times\left(t,t+h\right]\right) = 1 + P\left(\text{other things}\right) \tag{24}$$

where the event "other things" is contained in the event:

$$\left\{M\left(\left[0,q_t\left(x\right)\right]\times\left(t,t+h\right]\right) \geq 2\right\}$$

Note: Two or more Poisson event occurs in the rectangle $\left[0,q\left(x\right)\right]\times\left(t,t+h\right])$.
Moreover, it is clear that:

$$P\left(M\left(0,q\left(x\right)\right]\times\left(t,t+h\right]\right)\geq 2\right)=o\left(h\right) \quad (25)$$

$$P\left(M\left(I\left(x,y\right)\times\left(t,t+h\right]\right)=1\right)=hq\left(x,y\right)+o\left(h\right) \quad (26)$$

with this we will finish the proof of the proposition.

FIRST: PASSAGE TIME DISTRIBUTION

First passage time distribution of stochastic processes is key quantities in many fields of sciences, such as mathematical physics, neurology and mathematical finance. Most notable applications in finance are the following. In credit risk modelling a widely used approach, originally proposed by Merton (1974), models the market value of assets as a jump diffusion processes. The jump part is needed here to model significant events or shocks such as a surprise earnings release. When the market value of assets goes below some level, determined in terms of the company's liabilities, then the company needs to default on its obligations. The first passage time density is required in order to obtain the expected discounted cash flows, say for a loan to the considered company. Another application is in market risk analysis. The first passage time density is needed in case we need to evaluate the passage probability of certain loss levels during certain periods. Another application is in derivatives pricing, such as pricing barrier options or look back options, which involve crossing certain levels (Merton, 1976; Metwally and Atiya, 2002), or pricing American options, which entail evaluating the first passage time density for a time varying boundary (Zhang, 1993).

In our case we are interested in the evolution of the passage probability of stock prices in dependence on the particle state at time t, after starting from the initial state at t=0.Being aware of the fact that stock prices may be driven by sudden shifts in the "mood of the market", referring to the human behaviour or extreme event, the main goal in this section is to show if the transit from the initial state to final states for the first time could be represented with the exponential distribution. Remember, the first passage is a generic concept for quantifying when a random quantity such as the position of a diffusing molecule or the value of a stock crosses the starting point for the first time.

The first passage time of the exponential jump diffusion process can be expressed as:

$$\tau_b := \inf\left\{t \geq 0, x_t \geq b\right\}, P > 0 \tag{27}$$

where $X_{\tau b} := \lim \ \sup_{t\to\infty} X_t$ on the set $\{\tau b = \infty\}$. The main problems studied include the distribution of the first passage time

$$P\left(\tau_b \leq t\right) = P\left(\max_{0\leq s\leq t} X_s \geq b\right) \tag{28}$$

For all t>0, the join distribution between the first passage time and the terminal value is

$$P\left(\tau_b \leq t, x_t \geq a\right) \tag{29}$$

KOLMOGOROV FORWARD EQUATION, BACKWARD EQUATION, AND THE GENERATOR MATRIX

When we construct a continuous time Markov chain, we present only the local behavior of the model. This will not give us enough information to understand the long run behavior of a particular system. Therefore, we should learn how these local behaviors determine the global behavior? Or mathematically expressed, how can we find terms of the form:

$$P_{ij}\left(t\right) = P\left\{X\left(t\right) = j \mid X\left(0\right) = i\right\} \tag{29}$$

For i, j ∊ S, the state space, and t ≥ 0?

Forward Equation

First, we should derive the Kolmogorov forward equations. These are ordinary differential equations governing the behavior of the probability P_{ij} (t). We note that the forward equations are valid only if the process in not-explosive. So, a Markov process {X (t), t≥0} is called a pure jump process if there are a finite number of jumps in every time interval. On the other hand, in an explosive jump process, there are infinitely many jumps within a finite interval. Therefore, the Markov process is a pure jump process only if

$$\sum_{n=1}^{\infty} \frac{1}{\lambda_n} = \infty \rightarrow \text{spending only extremely short waiting time at each state} \tag{31}$$

and the explosive Markov jump process is one in which

$$\sum_{n=1}^{\infty} \frac{1}{\lambda_n} < \infty \tag{32}$$

Because of the infinitely many jumps, here we cannot give an answer to the question of what is the last jump before T∞?

In short, the forward equation will be derived by conditioning on the state of the system directly before out time of interest. Thus, in the proceeding, we have:

$$\begin{aligned} P_{ij}^{`}(t) &= \lim_{h \to 0} \frac{P_{ij}\left(t+h\right) - P_{ij}(t)}{h} \\ &= \lim_{h \to 0} \frac{1}{h}\left(P\left\{X\left(t+h\right) = j \mid X\left(t\right) = y, X(0) = i\right\} P\left\{X(t) = y \mid X(0) = i\right\}\right. \\ &= \lim_{h \to 0} \left(\sum_{y \in S} \begin{array}{l} P\left\{X\left(t+h\right) = j \mid X(t) = y, X(0) = i\right\} \\ P\left\{X(t) = y \mid X(0) = i\right\} - P\left\{X(t) = j \mid X(0) = i\right\} \end{array} \right) \end{aligned}$$

however,

$$\sum_{y\in S} P\{X(t+h)=j \mid X(t)=y, X(0)=i\} P\{X(t)=y \mid X(0)=i\}$$
$$= P\{X(t+h)=j \mid X(t)=j, X(0)=i\} P\{X(t)=j \mid X(0)=i\} \tag{32}$$
$$+ \sum_{y\in S} P\{X(t+h)=j \mid X(t)=y, X(0)=i\} P\{P\{X(t)=y \mid X(0)=i\}$$

$$= (1-\lambda(j)h) P_{ij}(t) + \sum_{y\neq j} \lambda(y,j) h P_{iy}(t) + o(h) \tag{33}$$

and so

$$P_{ij}^{`}(t) = \lim_{h\to 0} \frac{1}{h}\left((1-\lambda(j)h-1) P_{ij}(t) + \sum_{y\neq j} \lambda(y,j) P_{iy}(t) h + o(h)\right)$$
$$= -\lambda(j) P_{ij}(t) + \sum_{y\neq j} \lambda(y,j) P_{iy}(t) \tag{34}$$
$$P_{ij}^{`} = -\lambda(j) P_{ij}(t) + \sum_{y\neq j} P_{iy}(t) \lambda(y,j)$$

These are the Kolmogorov forward equation for the process or know as a master equation.

Now if we move from Equation 32 to 33, we had to assume that

$$\sum_{y} P_{iy}(t) o_y(h) = o(h) \tag{35}$$

where we write $o_y(h)$ to show that the size of the error can depend upon the state y. This condition is satisfied for all systems we will consider.

Definition: Let X (t) be a continuous time Markov chain on some state space S with transition matrix $\lambda(i,j) \geq 0$. Recalling that:

$$\lambda(i) = \sum_{j\neq i} \lambda(i,j)$$

The matrix:

$$A_{ij} = \begin{cases} -\lambda(i), & \text{if } i=j \\ \lambda(i,j), & \text{if } i\neq j \end{cases} = \begin{cases} -\lambda(i,j), & \text{if } i=j \\ \lambda(i,j), & \text{if } i\neq j \end{cases} \tag{36}$$

is called the generator, or generator matrix of the Markov chain.

Then the Kolmogorov forward equations 34 can be written as the matrix differential equations:

$$P^{`}(t) = P(t)A,$$

since

$$\begin{aligned}&\left(P(t)A\right)_{ij} = \sum_{y} P_{iy}(t)A_{yj} = P_{ij}A_{jj} + \sum_{y\neq j} P_{iy}A_{yj} \\ &= -\lambda(j)P_{ij}(t) + \sum_{y\neq j} P_{iy}\lambda\left(y,j\right)\end{aligned} \tag{37}$$

kAt least formally, this system can be solved

$$P\left(t\right) = P\left(0\right)e^{tA} = e^{tA} \tag{38}$$

where e^{tA} is the matrix exponential and we used that P(0)=I, the identity matrix. Moreover, the matrix exponential can be defined by:

$$e^{tA} \overset{def}{=} \sum_{k=0}^{\infty} \frac{t^n A^n}{n!} \tag{39}$$

Remember this solution is always valid when the state space is finite. In addition, we can make the following observations refer to the generator A:

- The elements on the main diagonal are all strictly negative.
- The remaining elements in the matrices are non-negative.
- Each row sums to zero.

This generator matrix, given a state space S, completely determines the Markov chain as it contains all the local information, refer to the transition λ (i, j).

Backward Equation

Backward equation is another set of equations, called Kolmogorov's backward equations, which are valid for all continuous time Markov chain. We will begin by finding an integral equation satisfied by Pij (t) and then differentiate it to get the backward equation.

Proposition 1: For all i, j $\in$ S and t $\geq$ 0, we have

$$P_{ij}(t) = \delta_{ij} e^{-\lambda(i)t} + \int_0^t \lambda(i) e^{-\lambda(i)s} \sum_{k \neq i} Q_{ik} P_{kj}\left(t - s\right) ds \tag{40}$$

where, as usual,

$$\delta_{ij} = \begin{Bmatrix} 1, & \text{if } i = j \\ 0, & \text{if } i \neq j \end{Bmatrix}$$

Is the Kronecker delta function, and Q is the transition matrix of the embedded discrete time Markov chain.

Proof: Preparing on the first jump time of the chain T_1, we have:

$$\begin{aligned} &P\left\{X(t) = j \mid X(0) = i\right\} = \\ &= P\left\{X(t) = j, T_1 > t \mid X(0) = i\right\} + P\left\{X(t) = j, T_1 \leq t \mid X(0) = i\right\} \end{aligned} \tag{41}$$

We should handle these terms separately. We will start with the first term on the right side of the equation 41. Here a first transition has not been made, thus $X(t) = j$ if $j = i$ and does so with a probability of 1. That is,

$$\begin{aligned} P\left\{X(t) = j, T_1 > t, X(0) = i\right\} \\ &= P\left\{X(t) = j \mid T_1 > t, X(0) = i\right\} P\left\{T_1 > t \mid X(0) = i\right\} \\ &= \delta_{ij} P_i \left\{T_1 > t\right\} \\ &= \delta_{ij} e^{-\lambda(i)t} \end{aligned} \tag{42}$$

For the second term, we will condition on the time of the first jump happening to (s, s+Δ), for small Δ. As the holding time is exponential with parameter λ (i), this event has a probability

$$\int_{s}^{s+\Delta} \lambda(i)e^{-\lambda(i)r}dr = \lambda(i)e^{-\lambda(i)s}\Delta + 0\left(\Delta^2\right) \tag{43}$$

then we let S_n=nt/N for some large N, denote Δ=t/N, and see:

$$\begin{aligned}
P\left\{X(t) = j, T_1 \le t \mid X(0) = i = \sum_{n=0}^{N-1} P\left\{X(t) = j, T_1 \in \left(s_n, s_{n+1}\right) \mid X\left(0\right) = i\right\}\right. \\
= \sum_{n=0}^{N-1} P\left\{X(t) = j \mid X(0) = i, T_1 \in \left(s_n, s_{n+1}\right) P\left\{T_1 \in \left(s_n, s_{n+1}\right) \mid X\left(0\right) = i\right\}\right. \\
= \sum_{n=0}^{N-1} P\left\{X(t) = j \mid X(0) = i, T_1 \in \left(s_n, s_{n+1}\right)\right\}\left[\lambda(i)e^{\lambda(i)s_n}\Delta + 0\left(\Delta^2\right)\right] \\
= \sum_{n=0}^{N-1} \lambda(i)e^{\lambda(i)s_n} \sum_{k\ne i} P\left\{X(t) = j, X_1 = k \mid X(0) = i, T_1 \in \left(s_n, s_{n+1}\right)\Delta + 0\left(\Delta\right)\right. \\
= \sum_{n=0}^{N-1} \lambda(i)e^{\lambda(i)s_n} \sum_{k\ne i} \left[\begin{matrix} P\left\{X(t) = j \mid X_1 = k, X(0) = i, T_1 \in \left(s_n, s_{n+1}\right)\right\} \\ \times P\left\{X_1 = k \mid X(0) = i, T_1 \in \left(s_{n,} s_{n+1}\right)\right\} \end{matrix}\right] \Delta + 0(\Delta) \\
\approx \sum_{n=0}^{N-1} \lambda(i)e^{\lambda(i)s} \sum_{k\ne i} Q_{ik} P_{kj}\left(t - s_n\right)\Delta + 0(\Delta) \\
\to \int_0^t \lambda(i)e^{\lambda(i)s} \sum_{k\ne i} Q_{ik} P_{kj}\left(t - s\right)ds
\end{aligned} \tag{44}$$

Proposition 2: For all i, j ∈S, we have that Pij(t) is continuously differentiable and:

$$P^{`}(t) = AP(t) \tag{45}$$

which in component form is:

$$e^{`}_{ij}(t) = \sum_{k} A_{ik} P_{kj}\left(t\right) \tag{46}$$

The equation 46 is called the Kolmogorov backwards equations. Here the difference with the forward equation as you can notice is the order of the multiplication of P (t) and A. However, the solution of the backwards equation is:

$$P\left(t\right) = e^{tA,} \tag{47}$$

thus, agreeing with previous results.

Proof: Use the substitution u=t-s in the integral equation to find that:

$$\begin{aligned} P_{ij}(t) &= \delta_{ij}e^{-\lambda(i)t} + \int_0^t \lambda(i)e^{-\lambda(i)s}\sum_{k\neq i} Q_{ik}P_{kj}\left(t-s\right)ds \\ &= \delta_{ij}e^{-\lambda(i)t} + \int_0^t \lambda(i)e^{-\lambda(i)(t-u)}\sum_{k\neq i} Q_{ik}P_{kj}\left(u\right)ds \\ &= e^{-\lambda(i)t}\left[\delta_{ij} + \int_0^t \lambda(i)e^{\lambda(i)u}\sum_{k\neq i} Q_{ik}P_{kj}\left(u\right)ds\right] \end{aligned} \tag{48}$$

and differentiating yields

$$\begin{aligned} P^{`}_{ij}(t) &= -\lambda(i)e^{-\lambda(i)t}\left[\delta_{ij} + \int_0^t \lambda(i)e^{\lambda(i)u}\sum_{k\neq i} Q_{ik}P_{kj}(u)ds\right] + e^{-\lambda(i)t}\times\lambda(i)e^{\lambda(i)t}\sum_{k\neq i} Q_{ik}P_{kj}(t) \\ &= -\lambda(i)P_{ij}(t) + \lambda(i)\sum_{k\neq i} Q_{ik}P_{kj}(t) \\ &= \sum_k\left(-\lambda(i)\delta_{ik}P_{kj}(t)\right) + \sum_k^{k\neq i}\lambda(i)Q_{ik}P_{kj}(t) \\ &= \sum_k\left(-\lambda(i)\delta_{ik} + \lambda(i)Q_{ik}\right)P_{kj}(t) \\ &= \sum_K A_{ik}P_{kj}(t) \end{aligned} \tag{49}$$

Both the Kolmogorov forward and backward equations can be used to solve for the associated probabilities. To make the above computations and find the long run behavior of the stock prices we simply solve the matrix exponentials. This is a more straightforward way, and it is presented in the sections that follow.

MODELLING MARKET PRICE FLUCTUATIONS: A NUMERICAL ILLUMINATION

Finding the "Q" Matrix

The generator matrix is also called as an intensity matrix, rate matrix or "Q" matrix of the Markov chain and is used to describe the process completely. Let the Q matrix of a continuous time Markov chain on a countable set I be defined as $Q = (q_{ij})$ for $i, j \in I$ has the following properties:

$$
\begin{array}{ll}
0 \leq -q_{ii} < \infty & \forall i \\
q_{ij} \geq 0 & \forall i \neq j \\
\sum_{j \in I} q_{ij} = 0 & \forall \mathrm{i}
\end{array} \tag{50}
$$

Thus, in each row of Q the off-diagonal entries are to be any non-negative real numbers subject only to the constraint that the off-diagonal row sum is finite.

$$
q_i = \sum_{j \neq i} q_{ij} < \infty \tag{50}
$$

The diagonal entry q_{ii} is defined as $-q_j$, making the row sum as zero.
The standard form of a generator matrix is:

$$
Q = \left[I_k \mid P \right] \tag{50}
$$

where I_k is the kxk identity matrix and P is a kxr matrix.

According the formulation above, we calculate the S&P500 generator matrix ($Q_{s\&p500}$). The probability matrix $P_{s\&p500}$given below is constructed from the past behavior of the system, covering the 16 years period of daily stock prices from 2000-2016.

$$
P_{S\&P500} = \begin{bmatrix} 0.01 & 0.43 & 0.56 \\ 0.03 & 0.42 & 0.55 \\ 0.05 & 0.47 & 0.48 \end{bmatrix}
$$

and the identity matrix is

$$
ID = \begin{bmatrix} 1 & 0 & 0 \\ 0 & 1 & 0 \\ 0 & 0 & 1 \end{bmatrix}
$$

So the $Q_{s\&p500}$ is:

$$\begin{bmatrix} 0.01 & 0.43 & 0.56 \\ 0.03 & 0.42 & 0.55 \\ 0.05 & 0.47 & 0.48 \end{bmatrix} - \begin{bmatrix} 1 & 0 & 0 \\ 0 & 1 & 0 \\ 0 & 0 & 1 \end{bmatrix} = \begin{bmatrix} -0.99 & 0.43 & 0.56 \\ 0.03 & -0.58 & 0.55 \\ 0.05 & 0.47 & -0.52 \end{bmatrix}$$

From the above $Q_{s\&p500}$ matrix the continuous time Markov chain can be represented by Figure 4.

Thus, each off-diagonal entry q_{ij} assumes the value attached to the (i, j) arrow on the diagram which is the rate of going from i to j. The numbers q_i are called the rate of leaving i which are not shown in the diagram.

Next using this information, we compute the "Q" Matrix for NASDAG Composite Index, NYSE Composite Index, Russel 2000 Index, Apple Inc. and Alphabet Inc, Google, as illustrated below:

$$Q_{NASDAG} = \begin{bmatrix} -0.98 & 0.63 & 0.35 \\ 0.02 & -0.48 & 0.46 \\ 0.02 & 0.52 & -0.54 \end{bmatrix}$$

Figure 4. Markov Graph for a given Q matrix

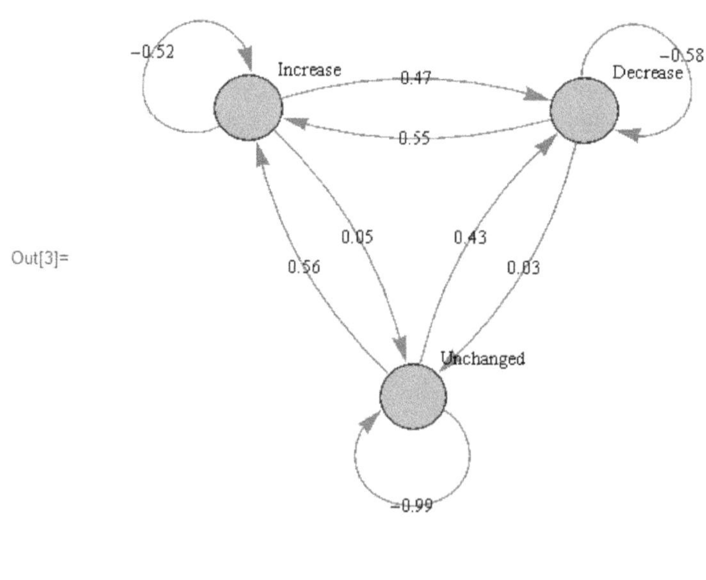

$$Q_{NYSE} = \begin{bmatrix} -1 & 0.68 & 0.32 \\ 0.01 & -0.49 & 0.48 \\ 0.01 & 0.54 & -0.55 \end{bmatrix}$$

$$Q_{Russel2000} = \begin{bmatrix} -0.94 & 0.58 & 0.35 \\ 0.04 & -0.51 & 0.47 \\ 0.05 & 0.51 & -0.56 \end{bmatrix}$$

$$Q_{AlphabetGoogle} = \begin{bmatrix} -0.94 & 0.5 & 0.44 \\ 0.06 & -0.52 & 0.46 \\ 0.06 & 0.49 & -0.55 \end{bmatrix}$$

$$Q_{AppleInc} = \begin{bmatrix} -0.56 & 0.31 & 0.25 \\ 0.21 & -0.61 & 0.4 \\ 0.22 & 0.43 & -0.65 \end{bmatrix}$$

Embedded Markov Chain: The Jump Matrix

If we consider only the transition between the states of a continuous-time Markov chain and not the time spent in the states, we obtain the so-called embedded Markov chain (EMC). The embedded Markov chain has the same state space as the continuous-time Markov chain. Each element of one-step transition probability matrix of the EMC, is denoted by s_{ij}, and represents the conditional probability of transiting form state i into state j. These transition probabilities s_{ij} may be found by:

$$S_{ij} = \begin{cases} \dfrac{-q_{ij}}{q_{ij}} = \dfrac{q_{ij}}{\sum_{k \neq i} q_{ik}} & \text{for } i \neq j \\ 0 & \text{for } i = j \end{cases}$$

Or in matrix form:

$$S = \left(s_{ij}\right) = I - \left(diag\left(Q\right)\right)^{-1} Q \tag{53}$$

where I is the identity matrix and diag(Q) is the diagonal matrix from the matrix Q and setting all the other elements to zero.

This embedded Markov chain has been used in the next section to determine the stationary state probability π_i of the continuous-time Markov chain.

Now let us see how we can determine the jump matrix for the S&P500index using the Equation 53. The diagonal matrix is:

$$diag\left(Q\right) = \begin{bmatrix} -0.99 & 0 & 0 \\ 0 & -0.58 & 0 \\ 0 & 0 & -0.52 \end{bmatrix}$$

and the identity matrix

$$ID = \begin{bmatrix} 1 & 0 & 0 \\ 0 & 1 & 0 \\ 0 & 0 & 1 \end{bmatrix}$$

Placing them in equation 53 we will get the jump matrix for the S&P500 index,

$$P_{S\&P500} = \begin{bmatrix} 0 & 0.434 & 0.566 \\ 0.052 & 0 & 0.948 \\ 0.096 & 0.904 & 0 \end{bmatrix}$$

In the same way we compute the jump matrix for the NASDAG Composite Index, NYSE Composite Index, Russel 2000 Index, Apple Inc. and Alphabet Inc, Google. So we get,

$$P_{NASDAG} = \begin{bmatrix} 0 & 0.64 & 0.36 \\ 0.042 & 0 & 0.958 \\ 0.04 & 0.96 & 0 \end{bmatrix}$$

$$P_{NYSE} = \begin{bmatrix} 0 & 0.68 & 0.32 \\ 0.02 & 0 & 0.98 \\ 0.02 & 0.98 & 0 \end{bmatrix}$$

$$P_{Russel2000} = \begin{bmatrix} 0 & 0.62 & 0.38 \\ 0.08 & 0 & 0.92 \\ 0.09 & 0.91 & 0 \end{bmatrix}$$

$$P_{AlphabetGoogle} = \begin{bmatrix} 0 & 0.53 & 0.47 \\ 0.12 & 0 & 0.88 \\ 0.11 & 0.89 & 0 \end{bmatrix}$$

$$P_{AppleInc.} = \begin{bmatrix} 0 & 0.55 & 0.45 \\ 0.34 & 0 & 0.66 \\ 0.34 & 0.66 & 0 \end{bmatrix}$$

Stationary Distribution

In the previous section, we demonstrated how to compute the jump matrix for continuous-time Markov chain. To find the stationary distribution vector, we must compute a right eigenvector φ of $S_{s\&p500}$ for the eigenvalue 1, that is φ fulfils $\varphi = \varphi S_{s\&P500}$. We will find $\varphi t, S^t - I$ equals:

$$\varphi t = Transpose\left[S_{s\&p500}\right] - I = \begin{bmatrix} -1 & 0.052 & 0.096 \\ 0.434 & -1 & 0.904 \\ 0.566 & 0.948 & -1 \end{bmatrix} \tag{54}$$

where S is the jump matrix and I is the identity matrix.

So the right eigenvector, calculated in Wolfram Mathematica is given by $\varphi = \left(0.209, 1.383, 1.429\right)$ (see Appendix 1 for more details).

From this the stationary distribution π is then given by:

$$\pi = -\frac{\varphi D - 1}{\left\|\varphi D - 1\right\|_1} \tag{55}$$

We have:

$$\varphi D - 1 = \left(-0.211106, -2.38437, -2.74927\right), \text{ so } \left\|\varphi D - 1\right\|_1 = 5.34$$

The stationary distribution or invariant distribution π is the absolute value of (-0.211106, -2.38437, -2.74927) or (0.211106, 2.38437, 2.74927). So:

$$\pi_{s\&p500} = \frac{1}{5.34}\left(0.211106, 2.38437, 2.74927\right)$$

or,

$$\pi_{s\&p500} = \left(0.039, 0.447, 0.515\right) \tag{56}$$

The following comments can be made from the above stationary distribution vector:

- The probability that a stock price will stay unchanged given that it initially either stays unchanged, decreased or increased is 0.039
- The probability that a stock will decrease given that it initially either stays unchanged, decreased or increased is 0.447
- The probability that a stock will increase given that it initially either stays unchanged, decreased or increased is 0.515

In sum, this shows that regardless of the stocks most recent changes in closing price, approximately 3.9% of the time they will stay unchanged, 44.7% will drop in value the next day and 51.5% will have increased in price. This means that for investors who held an S&P 500 index during the period of study, on the average gained 2095 out of 4073 trading days.

In the same way we compute the stationary distribution vector for the NASDAG Composite Index, NYSE Composite Index, Russel 2000 Index, Apple Inc. and Alphabet Inc, Google. So, we get,

$$\pi_{NASDAG} = \frac{1}{5.67}\left(0.1134, 2.962, 2.597\right) \text{ or } \pi_{NASDAG} = \left(0.02, 0.522, 0.458\right)$$

$$\pi_{NYSE} = \frac{1}{5.51}(0.055, 2.896, 2.56) \text{ or } \pi_{NYSE} = (0.0009, 0.53, 0.465)$$

$$\pi_{Russel2000} = \frac{1}{5.51}(0.25, 2.774, 2.49) \text{ or } \pi_{Russel2000} = (0.0455, 0.503, 0.452)$$

$$\pi_{AppleInc.} = \frac{1}{5.6}(1.553, 2.137, 1.912) \text{ or } \pi_{AppleInc.} = (0.277, 0.382, 0.341)$$

$$\pi_{AlphabetGoogle} = \frac{1}{5.56}(0.334, 2.7, 2.526) \text{ or } \pi_{AlhabetGoogle} = (0.06, 0.486, 0.454)$$

Distribution of the First Passage Time

First passage problems can be most simply described as finding the distribution of times according to which a random process first exceeds a prescribed threshold or reaches a specified configuration. The cumulative distribution functions are frequently used to specify this phase distribution.

Therefore, here we will show how to estimate the probability distribution function (PDF) and the cumulative distribution function (CDF) of the first passage time, as well as the mean first passage time.

In contrast to the stationary distribution vector, the mean first passage times give us information about the short-range behavior of the chain. For example, suppose that we want to invest in S&P500 index, but we find that the price has a decreasing trend. Our interest then is not the average number of decreasing days versus increasing days throughout the year, but rather how long we can expect it to increase, given that it is now decreasing.

The mean first passage time from state Si to state Sj is the expected number of time–steps for reaching state Sj for the first time, given that initially the chain was in state Si.

Formally, for $1 \leq i, j \leq n$:

$$m_{i,j} = E\left(F_{i,j}\right) = \sum_{k=1}^{\infty} kP_r\left(F_{i,k} = k\right) \tag{57}$$

Here $F_{i,j}$ is the random variable representing the smallest number of time-steps for reaching state S_j for the first time, given that the system was initially in state S_i.

That is:

$$F_{i,j} = \min\left\{l \geq 1 : X_l = S_j \mid X_0 = S_i\right\} \tag{58}$$

The matrix $M = \left(m_{i,j}\right)$ is called the mean first passage (MFP) matrix of the chain.

Using Wolfram Mathematica Programming Language we compute the mean first passage matrix for S&P500 index, NASDAG Composite Index, NYSE Composite Index, Russel 2000 Index, Apple Inc. and Alphabet Inc, Google, as illustrated in Appendix 1 and generate the following results:

$$FPT_{S\&P500} = \begin{bmatrix} 25.32 & 1.79 & 1.79 \\ 24.83 & 2.24 & 1.82 \\ 24.36 & 2.14 & 1.95 \end{bmatrix}$$

From the matrix above, it is clear that if the S&P 500 index is in the state decreasing we can expect to reach the state increase in 2 days' time. And the others are:

$$FPT_{NASDAG} = \begin{bmatrix} 50 & 1.7 & 2.43 \\ 50 & 1.92 & 2.19 \\ 50 & 1.92 & 2.19 \end{bmatrix}$$

$$FPT_{NYSE} = \begin{bmatrix} 104 & 1.59 & 2.35 \\ 100 & 1.9 & 2.09 \\ 100 & 1.85 & 2.15 \end{bmatrix}$$

$$FPT_{RUSSEL2000} = \begin{bmatrix} 22.02 & 1.81 & 2.39 \\ 22.44 & 1.98 & 2.15 \\ 22.22 & 1.94 & 2.21 \end{bmatrix}$$

$$FPT_{APPLEInc} = \begin{bmatrix} 3.6 & 2.6 & 3.33 \\ 4.6 & 2.6 & 2.78 \\ 4.6 & 2.52 & 2.98 \end{bmatrix}$$

$$FPT_{AlphabetInc.} = \begin{bmatrix} 16.67 & 2.22 & 2.22 \\ 16.67 & 2.06 & 2.18 \\ 16.67 & 2.04 & 2.2 \end{bmatrix}$$

In Figure 5 and 6 PDF and the CDF of the first passage time are plotted. We found that the observed distribution of first-passage times not always follow an exponential distribution at short times.

Using the Random Function in Wolfram Mathematica we also simulate the jumps, given that the S&P500 stock is in state 2-decreases, as shown in Figure 7.

Figure 5. PDF plot for the transit from state 2-decrease unchange. The peak value is 1.92 and the hitting time is 25 days.

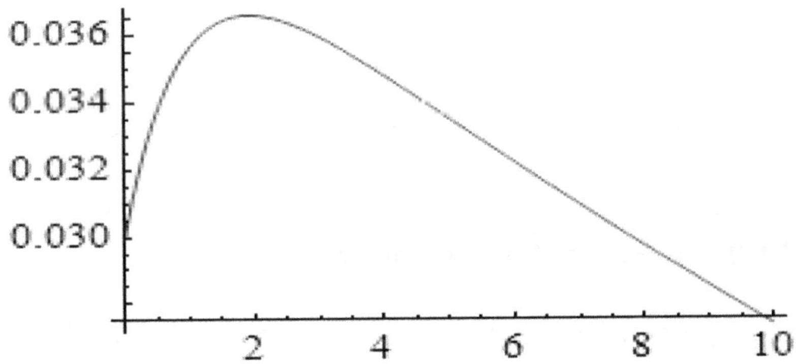

Figure 6. CDF plot. Weibull distribution to state 1- with gamma 1

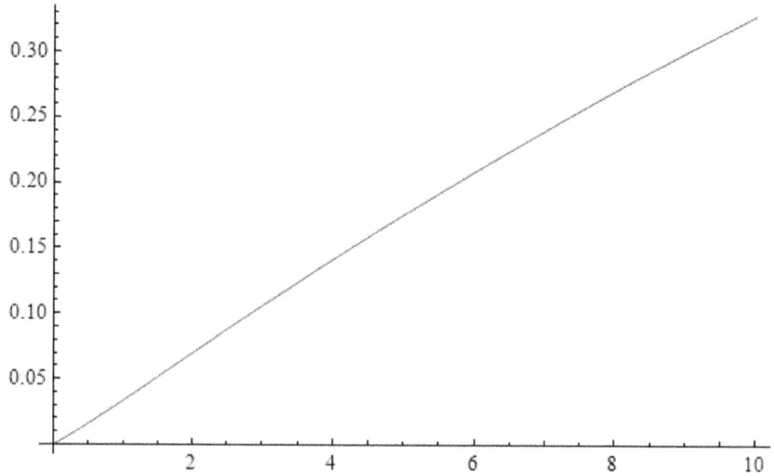

Figure 7. The sample path of Markov jump process with holding times and jump times

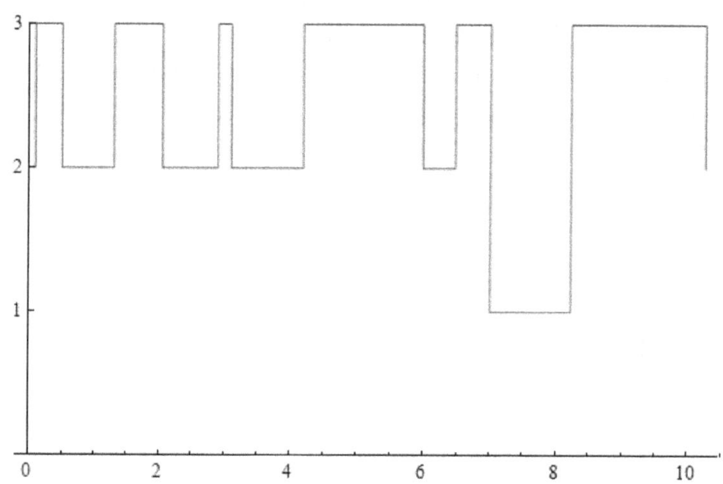

Predicting the Price Movement Trend

Understanding how price behaves is of great importance to the financial analysts and investors. This can reduce the risk or take better and well informed decisions. Or we can state that the success of an investor, especially in a stock market hinges much on the choice of the decision made which in turn depends to a large extent on how well informed one is in stock analysis.

In this chapter, we assume that the markets are efficient, so the price tomorrow remains uncertain; hence must be described by a probability distribution. For that reason, we apply a Markov process prediction method which is also known as probability forecasting method. Meaning, the predicted result is simply expressed the probability of a certain state of stock prices in the future, rather than being in an absolute state. Using the distribution of the first passage time we were able to successfully predict the next day of stock prices using this method. And the forecast matrix for the analyzed stocks and stock indexes are:

$$FPT_{S\&P500} = \begin{bmatrix} 0.22 & 0.36 & 0.42 \\ 0.03 & 0.55 & 0.42 \\ 0.05 & 0.37 & 0.58 \end{bmatrix}$$

The current position of the S & P index in March, 11, 2016 is state 3 increases. Accordingly, in the forecast matrix above, there is a 58% probability that the stock will stay in state 3 and 37% that the price will decrease and move to state 2. In reality the close price on March, 11, 2016 was $ 2,022.19 and on March, 14, 2016 is $ 2,019.64 meaning that the stock price decreases and now the stock is in state 2.

$$FPT_{Russel2000} = \begin{bmatrix} 0.25 & 0.43 & 0.32 \\ 0.04 & 0.59 & 0.37 \\ 0.05 & 0.40 & 0.55 \end{bmatrix}$$

The current position of the Russel 2000 index in March, 15, 2016 is state 2 - decrease. Accordingly, in the forecast matrix above, there is a 59% probability that the stock will stay in state 2 and 37% that the price will be in state 3-increase. In reality the close price on March, 15, 2016 was $1.066,67 and on March, 16, 2016 is $1.074,51 meaning that the stock price increased and now the stock is in state 3.

$$FPT_{NYSE} = \begin{bmatrix} 0.2 & 0.48 & 0.32 \\ 0.01 & 0.61 & 0.38 \\ 0.01 & 0.42 & 0.57 \end{bmatrix}$$

The current position of the NYSE Composite index in March, 15, 2016 is state 2 - decrease. Accordingly, in the forecast matrix above, there is a 61% probability that the stock will stay in state 2 and 38% that the price will be in state 3-increase. In reality the close price on March, 15, 2016 was $10013. 61 and in March, 16, 2016 is $10084, 17 meaning that the stock price increased and now the stock is in state 3.

$$FPT_{NASDAG} = \begin{bmatrix} 0.23 & 0.46 & 0.31 \\ 0.02 & 0.61 & 0.37 \\ 0.02 & 0.41 & 0.57 \end{bmatrix}$$

The current position of the NASDAG Composite index in March, 15, 2016 is state 2 - decrease. Accordingly, in the forecast matrix above, there is a 61% probability that the stock will stay in state 2 and 38% that the price will be in state 3-increase. In reality the close price on March, 15, 2016 was $4.728,67 and on March, 16, 2016 is $4.763,97 meaning that the stock price increased and now the stock is in state 3.

$$FPT_{ALPHABETInc.} = \begin{bmatrix} 0.25 & 0.39 & 0.36 \\ 0.06 & 0.57 & 0.37 \\ 0.06 & 0.39 & 0.55 \end{bmatrix}$$

The current position of the Alphabet Inc. (Google) on March, 15, 2016 is state 3 - increase. According to the forecast matrix above, there is a 55% probability that the stock will stay in state 3-increase and 39% that the price will be in state 2-decrease. In reality the close price on March, 15, 2016 was $751 and in March, 16, 2016 is $757 meaning that the stock stayed in state 3-increase.

$$FPT_{APPLEInc.} = \begin{bmatrix} 0.49 & 0.28 & 0.24 \\ 0.2 & 0.48 & 0.32 \\ 0.2 & 0.34 & 0.46 \end{bmatrix}$$

The current position of the Apple Inc. in March, 15, 2016 is state 3 - increase. According to the forecast matrix above, there is a 46% probability that the stock will stay in state 3-increase and 34% that the price will be in state 2-decrease. In reality the close price on March, 15, 2016 was \$104, 58 and on March, 16, 2016 is \$105.97meaning that the stock stayed in state 3-increase.

From the results above, it can be noticed that the prediction of the stocks are accurate, but this is not the case for the stock indexes. Does this mean that the random walk theory does not explain the stock return/price movements? To answer this question, let us firstly formulate it mathematically by asking whether returns and stock prices are correlated in some ways, so that the current returns/prices will provide some information about future and secondly, analyze the distribution.

In sum, we should determine if the process is in fact a Brownian motion or Winer process. Detailed analysis that will provide the answer to this question will be presented in the next chapter (chapter VIII). As we already mentioned above the success of an investor, especially in a stock market hinges much on the choice of the decision made which in turn depends to a large extent on how well informed one is in stock analysis.

STOCK MARKET RETURN ANALYSIS

In developing a predictive system, our goal is to make as many accurate predictions as possible. Therefore, in this section, we will use the rate of return instead of the price, as one of the most important theoretical indicators for measuring the performance of stocks and mutual funds.

Let P_t be the price of an asset at time index t. The one-period simple net return R_t of a financial time series is calculated with the following formula:

$$R_t = \ln\left(\frac{P_t - P_{t-1}}{P_{t-1}}\right) \tag{59}$$

The probability matrix $P_{S\&P500}$ given below is constructed from the past behavior of the system, covering the 16 years period of daily stock prices from Januray,3th 2000 to March, 8th 2016.

$$P_{s\&P500} = \begin{bmatrix} 0.29 & 0.71 \\ 0.64 & 0.36 \end{bmatrix}$$

and the identity matrix is

$$I = \begin{bmatrix} 1 & 0 \\ 0 & 1 \end{bmatrix}$$

So, the generator matrix, $Q_{S\&P500}$ is:

$$\begin{bmatrix} 0.29 & 0.71 \\ 0.64 & 0.36 \end{bmatrix} - \begin{bmatrix} 1 & 0 \\ 0 & 1 \end{bmatrix} = \begin{bmatrix} -0.71 & 0.71 \\ 0.64 & -0.64 \end{bmatrix}$$

From the above $Q_{S\&P500}$ matrix the continuous time Markov chain can be represented by Figure 8.

Now let us see how we can determine the jump matrix for the S&P500 stock returns using the Equation 53 given in the previous section. The diagonal matrix is:

$$diag\left(Q\right) = \begin{bmatrix} -0.71 & 0 \\ 0 & -0.64 \end{bmatrix}$$

So, if we place the diagonal matrix and identity matrix in equation 53 we will get the jump matrix for the copper price,

$$P_{s\&P500} = \begin{bmatrix} 0 & 1 \\ 1 & 0 \end{bmatrix}$$

Figure 8. State transition diagram

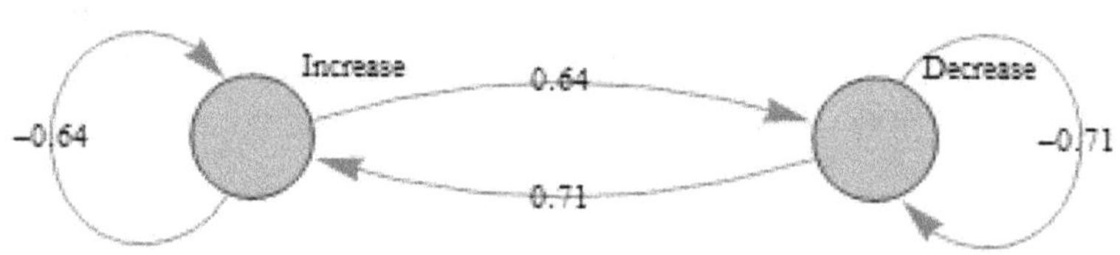

Then, to find the stationary distribution vector, we must next compute a right eigenvector φ of $S_{S\&P500}$ for the eigenvalue 1, that is φ fulfils $\varphi = \varphi S_{s\&p500}$. We will find $\varphi t, S^t - I$ equals:

$$\varphi t = Transpose\left[S_{s\&p500}\right] - I = \begin{bmatrix} -1 & 1 \\ 1 & -1 \end{bmatrix} \tag{60}$$

where $s_{s\&p500}$ is the jump matrix and I is the identity matrix.

The right eigenvector, calculate in Wolfram Mathematica is given by $\varphi = \left(0.707107, 0.707107\right)$. From this the stationary distribution π is then given by

$$\pi = \frac{\varphi D - 1}{\left\|\varphi D - 1\right\|_1}$$

or

$$\pi_{s\&p500=\left(0.47,0.53\right)} \tag{61}$$

The following comments can be made from the above stationary distribution vector:

- The probability that a stock will decrease given that it initially either stays unchanged, decreased or increased is 0.47
- The probability that a stock will increase given that it initially either stays unchanged, decreased or increased is 0.53

In sum, this shows that regardless of the stocks most recent changes in closing price, approximately 47% of the time will drop in value the next day and 53% will have increased in price. This means that for investors who hold a S&P500 index stock during the period of study, on the average gained 2157 out of 4069 trading days.

Next we will calculate the mean first passage time also known as the expected number of time-steps for reaching the state for the first time, given the initial point.

Recall that in contrast to the stationary distribution vector, the mean first passage times give us information about the short range behavior of the chain.

We generate following results:

$$P_{s\&p500} = \begin{bmatrix} 2.11 & 1.41 \\ 1.56 & 1.9 \end{bmatrix}$$

From the matrix above it is clear that if the S&P500 stock is in the state decreasing we can expect to reach the state increase in 2 days. In Figure 9 and 10, PDF and the CDF of the first passage time are plotted. We found that the observed distribution of first-passage times follow an exponential distribution at short times.

Using the Random Function in Wolfram Mathematica we also simulate the jumps, given that the copper stock is in state 2-decreases, as shown in Figure 11.

In the extension of our analysis, using the distribution of the first passage time we were able to successfully predict the next day return using this method. And the forecast matrix for the analyzed S&P500 return is:

Figure 9.PDF plot, return

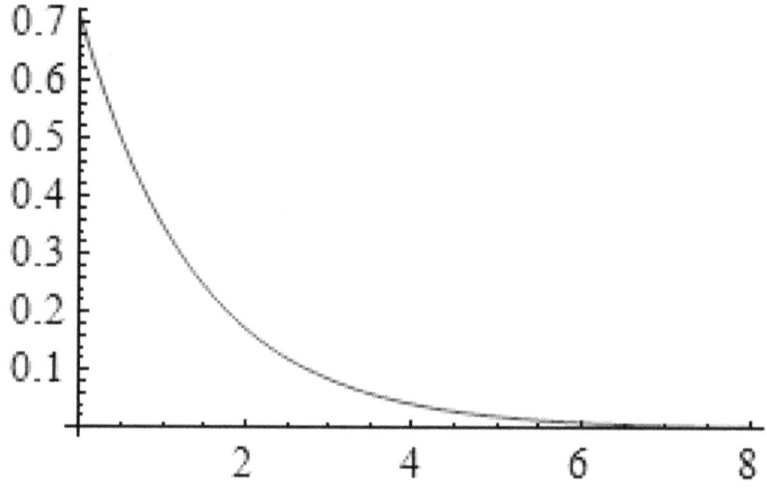

Figure 10.CDF plot, returns

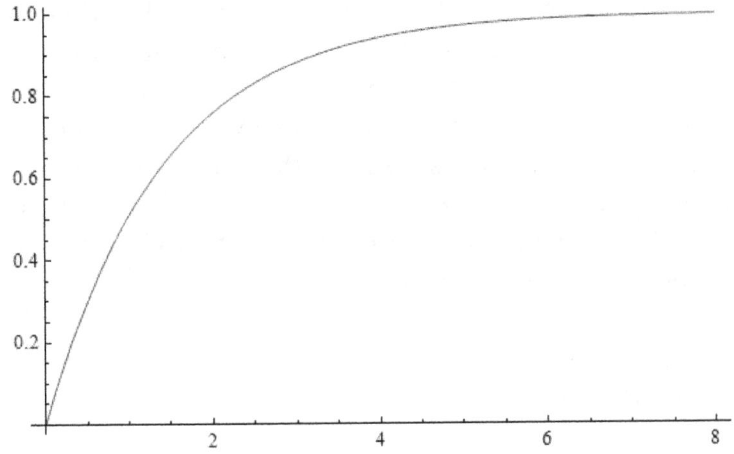

Figure 11. The sample path of Markov jump process with holding times and jump times

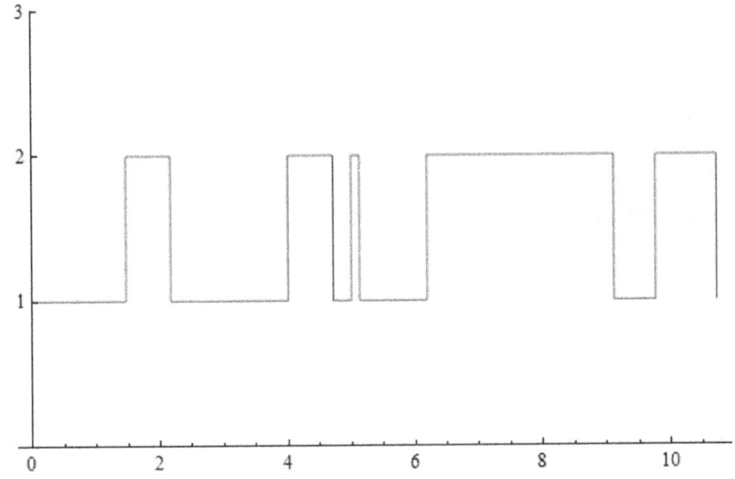

$$FPT_{s\&p500} = \begin{bmatrix} 0.49 & 0.51 \\ 0.47 & 0.53 \end{bmatrix}$$

The current position of the S&P500 index return on March, 8, 2016 is state 1-decreaces. According to the forecast matrix ($FRT_{S\&P500}$) there is a 49% probability that it will stay in state 1 and 51% that will transit to state

2-increases. In March, 9, 2016 the S&P500 index return was -0.01124% and in March, 9, 2016 it was 0.0051%, meaning that the S&P500 return transit to state 2-increased. It can be noticed that the probabilities for up and down movements are almost equal, that is 50%. This is in line with the efficient market theory. Here the return movement is viewed as a random walk, and the distribution of daily returns is assumed that closely resembles a normal distribution, or bell-shaped curve, with an average daily return around zero. The question is: Whether this is the case in all time periods in reality. In-depth analyses are carried out in chapter 7.

COPPER ANALYSIS

In line with the applied Jump Markov model, we have described the changes in copper data in two state states, decrease (D) and increases (I). The probability matrix P_{copper} given below is constructed from the past behavior of the system, covering the 16 year period of monthly stock prices from January 1980 to February 2016.

$$P_{copper} = \begin{bmatrix} 0.58 & 0.42 \\ 0.38 & 0.62 \end{bmatrix}$$

and the identity matrix is

$$I = \begin{bmatrix} 1 & 0 \\ 0 & 1 \end{bmatrix}$$

So, the generator matrix, Q_{copper} is:

$$\begin{bmatrix} 0.58 & 0.42 \\ 0.38 & 0.62 \end{bmatrix} - \begin{bmatrix} 1 & 0 \\ 0 & 1 \end{bmatrix} = \begin{bmatrix} -0.42 & 0.42 \\ 0.38 & -0.38 \end{bmatrix}$$

From the above Q_{copper} matrix the continuous time Markov chain can be represented by Figure 12.

Now let us see how we can determine the jump matrix for the copper stock using the Equation 53 given in the previous section. The diagonal matrix is:

Figure 12. State transition probability diagram

$$diag(Q) = \begin{bmatrix} -0.42 & 0 \\ 0 & -0.38 \end{bmatrix}$$

So, if we place the diagonal matrix and identity matrix in equation 53 we will get the jump matrix for the copper price,

$$P_{copper} = \begin{bmatrix} 0 & 1 \\ 1 & 0 \end{bmatrix}$$

Then, to find the stationary distribution vector, we must next compute a right eigenvectorφ of S_{copper} for the eigenvalue 1, that is φ fulfils $\varphi = \varphi S_{copper}$. We will find $\varphi t, S^t - I$ equals

$$\varphi t = \text{Transpose}\left[\text{S}_{copper}\right] - 1 = \begin{bmatrix} -1 & 1 \\ 1 & -1 \end{bmatrix} \tag{62}$$

where s_{copper} is the jump matrix and I is the identity matrix.

The right eigenvector, calculate in Wolfram Mathematica is given by $\varphi = (1.41, 1.41)$ (see Appendix 2 for more details).

From this the stationary distribution π is then given by

$$\pi = -\frac{\varphi D - 1}{\left\| \varphi D - 1 \right\|_1}$$

or

$$\pi_{s\&p500} = \left(0.47, 0.53\right) \tag{63}$$

The following comments can be made from the above stationary distribution vector:

- The probability that a stock will decrease given that it initially either stays unchanged, decreased or increased is 0.47
- The probability that a stock will increase given that it initially either stays unchanged, decreased or increased is 0.53.

In sum, this shows that regardless of the stocks most recent changes in closing price, approximately 47% of the time will drop in value the next day and 53% will have increased in price. This means that for investors who held a copper stock during the period of study, on the average gained 227 out of 428 trading months.

Next, we will calculate the mean first passage time also known as the expected number of time-steps for reaching the state for the first time, given the initial point.

Recall that in contrast to the stationary distribution vector, the mean first passage times give us information about the short-range behavior of the chain.

We generate following results:

$$P_{copper} = \begin{bmatrix} 2.1 & 2.4 \\ 2.6 & 1.9 \end{bmatrix}$$

From the matrix above it is clear that if the copper stock is in the state decreasing we can expect to reach the state increase in 2 days. In Figure 13 and 14, PDF and the CDF of the first passage time are plotted. We find that the observed distribution of first-passage times follow an exponential distribution at short times.

Using the Random Function in Wolfram Mathematica we also simulate the jumps, given that the copper stock is in state 2-decreases, as shown in Figure 15.

In the extension of our analysis, using the distribution of the first passage time we were able to successfully predict the next day of stock prices using this method. And the forecast matrix for the analyzed copper stock is:

Figure 13. PDF plot

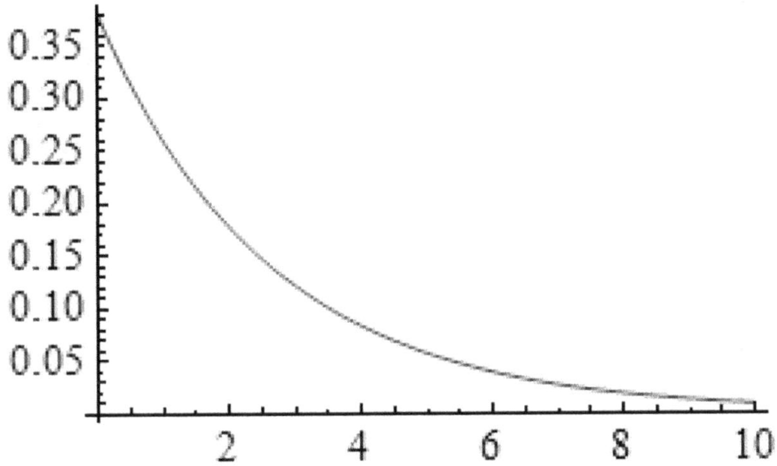

Figure 14. CDF plot

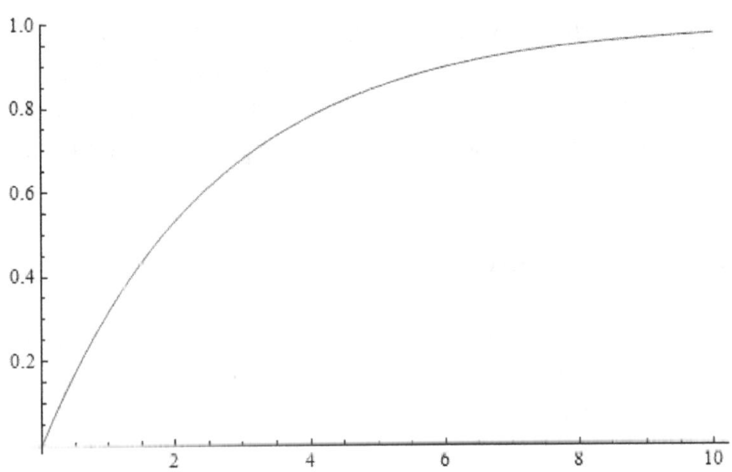

$$FPT_{copper} = \begin{bmatrix} 0.66 & 0.34 \\ 0.32 & 0.68 \end{bmatrix}$$

The current position of the Copper stock on February 2016 (2016m2) is in state 2 - increases. According to the forecast matrix (FRT_{copper}) there is a 68% probability that it will stay in state 2 and 32% that will transit to state

Figure 15. The sample path of Markov jump process with holding times and jump times, copper

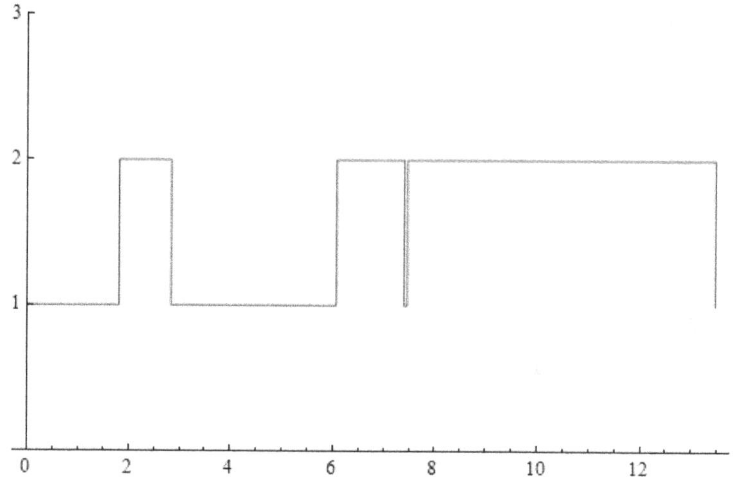

1 - decrease. On February 2016, the copper price was $4.599 and in March 2016 it was $4.947 meaning that the copper stock stayed in state 2 - increases.

According to the results obtained from this model, we can support the expectations of the coppers increasing trend explained in chapter IV.

CONCLUDING REMARKS

Trying to do today's job with yesterday's tools. .... I don't think they are heading in the right direction. (by Patric Dubroy, Doing Today's Job with Yesterday's Tools, 2007)

In the economic textbooks, the human race is presented as nothing more than a system with a large number of individual parts. If every human being (within this system) acted totally independently of every other human being, then the human race as a whole would behave very much like a thermodynamic system. When the economy finds itself in the general equilibrium state it will tend to remain so, and when the economy is near equilibrium (perhaps following a modest shock) the forces of arbitrage—the second law—will drive the economy back to equilibrium in an orderly manner. In addition, when the economy is far from equilibrium, perhaps due to market crash, the energy framework leads to dramatically different predictions. In short, this analysis will direct us to adopt incorrect policy decisions, which will merely deepen the crises.

One of the main reasons why yesterday's model does not fit today's data is because people, in general, do not behave independently of each other. They have a tendency to cooperate and compete, which causes the human race to behave less like a thermodynamic system, and more like a complex adaptive system. So, all real-world systems are indisputably and unconditionally non-stationary. But in this chapter, we want to know: if this non-stationarity is substantial enough to require complex deterministic characterization of the stock price process, or can comparatively simple stationary stochastic models accurately represent the stock price process.

The results showed that the discrete and continuous Markov processes as representations of stationary stochastic processes, cannot accurately anticipate the short-term movement of stock prices and returns. Does this imply that markets are unpredictable because they are random? If this is true, then with a longer time horizon, we can be far more successful. Eventually the market will reach its equilibrium where we can calculate the stationary distribution vector. Stationary states emerge for any share of the waiting-time and jump length distributions. In fact, applying this method we expect the process to reach equilibrium. This is one of the many assumptions we use in our models to explain the dynamics of financial markets.

At the end of this chapter, after all the analyses, it can be understood that the stock's price/returns movements generally cannot be described using normal (or Gaussian) distribution and Markov processes. And then I thought that I should rather use a fat tailed distribution (Semi-Jump Markov Model), presenting a significant percent of events distributed on the extreme ends of the scale. This phenomenon is commonly known as Power Law and recently applied in modelling finance markets. Events placed far from the mean value cause most of the market bubbles and raise the uncertainty significantly, making it difficult for traders to act rationally. Besides, this should emphasize the importance of employing a proper risk management strategy. Recall the copper example given in chapter IV. But something was lacking. I was not fully convinced that this model will capture the real-world price movements. Why? From a mathematical standpoint, it is clear that if we want to declare a "perfect strategy or model" then we should test the investing method against a period of stock quotes that were not used in the finding. This is the opposite approach of what we are doing in economics.

If a random walk theory can be rejected, then predictable components in the stock market exist. But, if there was a way to predict future prices from past data, then it would have immediately been exploited. For example, suppose it was the case that when a stock with very high earnings goes down three days in a row, it has a high chance of rising in the fourth day. The theory maintains that many investors would soon catch on to this pattern and be so eager to buy the stock on the third day, that the price would be driven up by demand, thereby destroying the opportunity. This approach was working in the 60s, 70s and early 80s. Today computer algorithms place orders based on the information received electronically, therefore, we do not know what a stock was worth today. Remember the case with apple AAPL plunge in 2013; 800 000 shares worth nearly $300 million being sold in 17 seconds. It is presumed that a mass self was triggered when AAPL fell to a certain price. As a result of the mass self, Apple has lost its position as the most valuable publicly traded company in the world. This algorithmic trading strategy is widely used by investment banks, pension funds, mutual funds, and other investor-driven institutional traders, to divide large trades into several smaller trades to manage the market impact and risk.

This leads us to the conclusion that the stock price does not fully reflect all available information and they do not evolve according to a random walk theory which is opposed to the efficient market hypothesis (EMH). Now it all make sense. Without doubt we can state that we need new other approaches. This is one of the main reasons why we decided to take this journey and write a book. However, semi- Markovian process where the transit is governed by the power law distribution is not the best solution. We should rather focus on the following: patterns exist, but we do not need the entire history of returns. Systems does not remember where there were 1 year or 2 years ago. The information in complex systems declines exponentially. As Einstein said "God doesn't play dice with the world". Jim Simons and James Weatherall were right, the damage adds up when we apply ideas from physics but we stop thinking like physicists. Too long I was studying great discoveries implemented in a faulty direction. But thanks to my mentor Mehmet Can, a professor of mathematics, who had the patience to work with me closely I learned "How" to think. His lessons completely changed my perception of economics. At the very same moment when I understood, which equations are widely used in analyzing economic phenomena I decided to stop supporting and spreading this mainstream methodology which obviously is harming economics as a science.

We should all together work first to show that new other approaches exist and then reassess the dominant role played by these mainstream methodologies. Second, we should stop leaving out certain important facts and emphasize others. Third, "The History of Economic Thought" books, play an important role in creating student perception of economics, therefore, complete history should deal with modern economics thought also.

REFERENCES

Chahal, M. S., & Jun, W. (1997). Jump diffusion processes and emerging bond and stock markets: An investigation using daily data. *Multinational Finance Journal*, *1*(3), 169–197. doi:10.17578/1-3-1

Das, S. R. (2002). The surprise element: Jumps in interest rates. *Journal of Econometrics*, *106*(1), 27–65. doi:10.1016/S0304-4076(01)00085-9

Merton, R. C. (1974). On the pricing of corporate debt: The risk structure of interest rates. *The Journal of Finance*, *29*(2), 449–470.

Merton, R. C. (1976). Option pricing when underlying stock returns are discontinuous. *Journal of Financial Economics*, *3*(1-2), 125–144. doi:10.1016/0304-405X(76)90022-2

Metwally, S. A., & Atiya, A. F. (2002). Using Brownian bridge for fast simulation of jump-diffusion processes and barrier options. *Journal of Derivatives*, *10*(1), 43–54. doi:10.3905/jod.2002.319189

Zhang, X. L. (1997). Numerical analysis of American option pricing in a jump-diffusion model. *Mathematics of Operations Research*, *22*(3), 668–690. doi:10.1287/moor.22.3.668

Zhou, C. (1997). A jump-diffusion approach to modeling credit risk and valuing defaultable securities.

APPENDIX 1

Discrete Markov Chain in Wolfram Mathematica 9: S&P500 Index

Step 1: Finding the stationary distribution.

```
In[1]:=P={{0.01,0.43,0.56},{0.03,0.42,0.55},{0.05,0.47,0.48}}
Out[1]= {{0.01,0.43,0.56},{0.03,0.42,0.55},{0.05,0.47,0.48}}
In[2]:= MatrixForm[P]
Out[2]//MatrixForm=
(0.01   0.43   0.56
0.03   0.42   0.55
0.05   0.47   0.48)
```

```
In[3]>Graph [{Labeled[1 → 1,"0.01"],Labeled [1 → 2,"0.43"],Labeled[1 → 3,
"0.56"],Labeled  → 1,"0.03"],Labeled[2 → 2,"0.42"], Labeled [2 → 3,"0.55"],
Labeled[3 → 1,"0.05"],Labeled [3 → 2,"0.47"],Labeled[3 → 3,"0.48"]},
VertexSize → Medium, VertexLabels →
{1 → "Unchanged", 2  → "Decrease",3 → "Increase"}]
Out[3] :=
```

```
In[4]:=P2= N[MatrixPower[P, 2]]
Out[4]={{0.041,0.4481,0.5109},{0.0404,0.4478,0.5118},{0.0386,0.4445,0.5169}}
In[5]:=MatrixForm[P2]
Out[5]//MatrixForm=
 (0.041 0.4481 0.5109
0.0404 0.4478 0.5118
0.0386 0.4445 0.5169)
```

Figure 16. State transition diagram

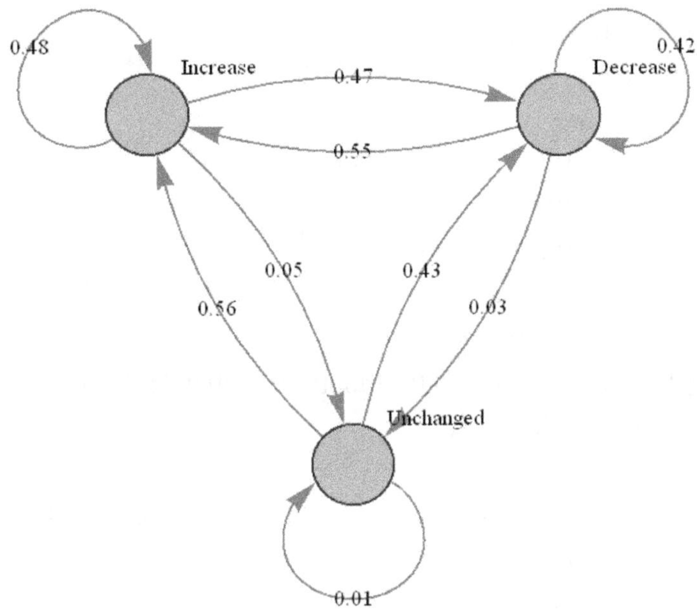

In[6]:= P3 = N[MatrixPower[P, 3]]

Out[6]= {{0.039398,0.445955,0.514647},{0.039428,0.445994,0.514578},
{0.039566,0.446231,0.514203}}

In[7]:= MatrixForm[P3]

Out[7]//MatrixForm=

$$\begin{pmatrix} 0.039398 & 0.445955 & 0.514647 \\ 0.039428 & 0.445994 & 0.514578 \\ 0.039566 & 0.446231 & 0.514203 \end{pmatrix}$$

```
In[8]:= P4 = N[MatrixPower[P, 4]]
Out[8]= {{0.039505,0.446126,0.514369},{0.039503,0.446123,0.514374},
{0.0394927,0.446106,0.514401}}
In[9]:= MatrixForm[P4]
Out[9]//MatrixForm=
(0.039505     0.446126     0.514369
0.039503      0.446123     0.514374
0.0394927     0.446106     0.514401)

In[10]:= P5 = N[MatrixPower[P, 5]]
Out[10]= {{0.0394973,0.446113,0.514389},{0.0394974,0.446114,0.514389},
{0.0394982,0.446115,0.514387}}
In[11]:= MatrixForm[P5]
Out[11]//MatrixForm= (0.0394973   0.446113     0.514389
0.0394974     0.446114     0.514389
0.0394982     0.446115     0.514387)

In[12]:= P6 = N[MatrixPower[P, 6]]
Out[12]= {{0.0394978,0.446114,0.514388},{0.0394978,0.446114,0.514388},
{0.0394978,0.446114,0.514388}}
MatrixForm[P6]
(0.0394978    0.446114     0.514388
0.0394978     0.446114     0.514388
0.0394978     0.446114     0.514388)
In[13]:= P7 = N[MatrixPower[P, 7]]
Out[13]= {{0.0394978,0.446114,0.514388},{0.0394978,0.446114,0.514388},
{0.0394978,0.446114,0.514388}}
MatrixForm[P7]
(0.0394978    0.446114     0.514388
0.0394978     0.446114     0.514388
0.0394978     0.446114     0.514388)
```

In[14]:= P30 = N[MatrixPower[P, 30]]
Out[14]= {{0.0394978,0.446114,0.514388},{0.0394978,0.446114,0.514388},
{0.039In[15]:= MatrixForm[P7]
Out[15]//MatrixForm=
(0.0394978 0.446114 0.514388
0.0394978 0.446114 0.514388
0.0394978 0.446114 0.514388)4978,0.446114,0.514388}}

In[16]:= P30 = N[MatrixPower[P, 30]]
Out[16]= {{0.0394978,0.446114,0.514388},{0.0394978,0.446114,0.514388},
{0.0394978,0.446114,0.514388}}
In[17]:= MatrixForm[P30]
Out[17]//MatrixForm=
(0.0394978 0.446114 0.514388
0.0394978 0.446114 0.514388
0.0394978 0.446114 0.514388)

In[18]:= P150 = N[MatrixPower[P, 150]]
Out[18]= {{0.0394978,0.446114,0.514388},{0.0394978,0.446114,0.514388},
{0.0394978,0.446114,0.514388}}
In[19]:= MatrixForm[P150]
Out[19]//MatrixForm=
(0.0394978 0.446114 0.514388
0.0394978 0.446114 0.514388
0.0394978 0.446114 0.514388)

In[20]:= P200 = N[MatrixPower[P, 200]]
Out[20]= {{0.0394978,0.446114,0.514388},{0.0394978,0.446114,0.514388},
{0.0394978,0.446114,0.514388}}
In[21]:= MatrixForm[P200]
Out[21]//MatrixForm=
(0.0394978 0.446114 0.514388
0.0394978 0.446114 0.514388
0.0394978 0.446114 0.514388)

In[22]:= P1000 = N[MatrixPower[P, 1000]]
Out[22]= {{0.0394978,0.446114,0.514388},{0.0394978,0.446114,0.514388},
{0.0394978,0.446114,0.514388}}
In[23]:= MatrixForm[P1000]
Out[23]//MatrixForm=
(0.0394978 0.446114 0.514388
0.0394978 0.446114 0.514388
0.0394978 0.446114 0.514388

Step 2: Predicting the price movement trend with initial state vector X_0= [0.04, 0.45, 0.51].

In[24]:= Xo=(0.04 0.45 0.51)
Out[24]= {{0.04,0.45,0.51}}
closing price on 4074 th day is
In[25]:= PV = Xo.P
Out[25]= {{0.0394,0.4459,0.5147}}
closing price on 4075 th day is
In[26]:= PV1 = PV.P
Out[26]= {{0.039506,0.446129,0.514365}}
closing price on 4076 th day is

In[27]:= PV2 = PV1.P

Out[27]= {{0.0394972,0.446113,0.51439}}

closing price on 4077 th day is

In[28]:= PV3 = PV2.P

Out[28]= {{0.0394978,0.446114,0.514388}}

closing price on 4078 th day is

In[29]:= PV4 = PV3.P

Out[29]= {{0.0394978,0.446114,0.514388}}

In[30]:= TableForm[{{"0", Xo},{"4074", PV},{"4075", PV1},
{"4076", PV2},{"4077", PV3},{"4078", PV4}}]

Out[30]//TableForm=

0	0.04	0.45	0.51
4074	0.0394	0.4459	0.5147
4075	0.039506	0.446129	0.514365
4076	0.0394972	0.446113	0.51439
4077	0.0394978	0.446114	0.514388
4078	0.0394978	0.446114	0.514388

Step 3: Predicting the price movement trend with different initial state vector X_0=[0.1, 0.35, 0.55].

In[31]:= xo=(0.1 0.35 0.55)

Out[31]= {{0.1,0.35,0.55}}

closing price on 4074 th day is

In[32]:= pv = xo.P

Out[32]= {{0.039,0.4485,0.5125}}

closing price on 4075 th day is

In[33]:= pv1 = pv.P

Out[33]= {{0.03947,0.446015,0.514515}}

closing price on 4076 th day is

```
In[34]:= pv2 = pv1.P
Out[34]= {{0.0395009,0.44612,0.514379}}
```

closing price on 4077 th day is

```
In[35]:= pv3 = pv2.P
Out[35]= {{0.0394976,0.446114,0.514389}}
```

closing price on 4078 th day is

```
In[36]:= pv4 = pv3.P
Out[36]= {{0.0394978,0.446114,0.514388}}
```

closing price on 4079 th day is

```
In[37]:= pv5 = pv4.P
Out[37]= {{0.0394978,0.446114,0.514388}}
In[38]:= TableForm[{{"0", xo}, {"4074", pv}, {"4075", pv1}, {"4076", pv2}, {"4077", pv3},
{"4078", pv4}, {"4079", pv5}}]
```

Out[38]//TableForm=

0	0.1	0.35	0.55
4074	0.039	0.4485	0.5125
4075	0.03947	0.446015	0.514515
4076	0.0395009	0.44612	0.514379
4077	0.0394976	0.446114	0.514389
4078	0.0394978	0.446114	0.514388
4079	0.0394978	0.446114	0.514388

Step 4: Finding the expected first passage time.

If the stock price is in state 1 - Unchanged

In[39]:= spindex=DiscreteMarkovProcess[1,{{0.01, 0.43, 0.56}, {0.03, 0.42, 0.55}, {0.05, 0.47, 0.48}}];

a=Mean[FirstPassageTimeDistribution[spindex,1]]

Out[40]= 25.3179

In[41]:= spindex=DiscreteMarkovProcess[1,{{0.01, 0.43, 0.56}, {0.03, 0.42, 0.55}, {0.05, 0.47, 0.48}}];

b=Mean[FirstPassageTimeDistribution[spindex,2]]

Out[42]= 2.21857

In[43]:= spindex=DiscreteMarkovProcess[1,{{0.01, 0.43, 0.56}, {0.03, 0.42, 0.55}, {0.05, 0.47, 0.48}}];

c=Mean[FirstPassageTimeDistribution[spindex,3]]

Out[44]= 1.79939

If the stock price is in state 2 - Decrease

In[45]:= spindex=DiscreteMarkovProcess[2,{{0.01, 0.43, 0.56}, {0.03, 0.42, 0.55}, {0.05, 0.47, 0.48}}];

a1=Mean[FirstPassageTimeDistribution[spindex,1]]

Out[46]= 24.826

In[47]:= spindex=DiscreteMarkovProcess[2,{{0.01, 0.43, 0.56}, {0.03, 0.42, 0.55}, {0.05, 0.47, 0.48}}];

b1=Mean[FirstPassageTimeDistribution[spindex,2]]

Out[48]= 2.24158

In[49]:= spindex=DiscreteMarkovProcess[2,{{0.01, 0.43, 0.56}, {0.03, 0.42, 0.55}, {0.05, 0.47, 0.48}}];

c1=Mean[FirstPassageTimeDistribution[spindex,3]]

Out[50]= 1.81721

If the stock price is in state 3 - Increase

In[51]:= spindex=DiscreteMarkovProcess[3,{{0.01, 0.43, 0.56}, {0.03, 0.42, 0.55}, {0.05, 0.47, 0.48}}];

a2=Mean[FirstPassageTimeDistribution[spindex,1]]

```
Out[52]= 24.3619
In[53]:= spindex=DiscreteMarkovProcess[3,{{0.01, 0.43, 0.56}, {0.03, 0.42, 0.55},
{0.05, 0.47, 0.48}}];
b2=Mean[FirstPassageTimeDistribution[spindex,2]]
Out[54]= 2.1364
In[55]:= spindex=DiscreteMarkovProcess[3,{{0.01, 0.43, 0.56}, {0.03, 0.42, 0.55},
{0.05, 0.47, 0.48}}];
c2=Mean[FirstPassageTimeDistribution[spindex,3]]
Out[56]= 1.94406
In[57]:= FirstPassage={{a,b,c},{a1,b1,c1},{a2,b2,c2}};
MatrixForm[FirstPassage]


Out[58]//MatrixForm=
(25.3179    2.21857    1.79939
24.826      2.24158    1.81721
24.3619     2.1364     1.94406)
In[59]:= MarkovProcessProperties[spindex,"Absorbing"]
Out[59]= False
In[60]:=MarkovProcessProperties[spindex]
```

APPENDIX 2

Continues Markov Process: The Jump Diffusion Process for S&P 500 Index

$\textbf{In}[1] := P1 = \{\{0.01,\ 0.43,\ 0.56\},\ \{0.03,\ 0.42,\ 0.55\},\ \{0.05,\ 0.47,\ 0.48\}\}$
$\textbf{Out}[1] := \{\{0.01,\ 0.43,\ 0.56\},\ \{0.03,\ 0.42,\ 0.55\},\ \{0.05,\ 0.47,\ 0.48\}\}$

$\textbf{In}[2] := \textit{Matrix Form}\ [P1]$
$(\{0.01,\ 0.43,\ 0.56\},$
$\{0.03,\ 0.42,\ 0.55\},$
$\{0.05,\ 0.47,\ 0.48\})$

The Identical Matrix ID
$\textbf{In}[3] := ID = \{\{1,\ 0,\ 0\},\ \{0,\ 1,\ 0\},\ \{0,\ 0,\ 1\}\}$
$\textbf{Out}[3] := \{\{1,\ 0,\ 0\},\{0,\ 1,\ 0\},\{0,\ 0,\ 1\}\}$

To find the matrix generator Q
$\textbf{In}[4] := Q = P1 - ID$
$\textbf{Out}[4] := \{\{-0.99,\ 0.43,\ 0.56\},\ \{0.03,\ -0.58,\ 0.55\},\ \{0.05,\ 0.47,\ -0.52\}\}$
$\textbf{In}[5] := \textit{Matrix Form}\ [Q]$
$(\{-0.99,\ 0.43,\ 0.56\},$
$\{0.03,\ -0.58,\ 0.55\},$
$\{0.05,\ 0.47,\ -0.52\})$
$In[6] :=$ *Graph*[{*Labeled* [1 → 1," – 0.99"], *Labeled* [1 → 2, "0.43"], *Labeled* [1 → 3, "0.56"], *Labcled* [2 → 1, "0.03"], *Labeled* [2 → 2, "–0.58"], *Labeled* [2 → 3, "0.55"], *Labeled* [3 → 1, "0.05"], *Labeled* [3 → 2, "0.47"], *Labeled* [3 → 3, "–0.52"], *Vertex Size* → *Medium*, *Vertex Labels* →
{1 → "*Unchanged*", 2 → " *Decrease*", 3 → "*Increase*"}]

Step 1: Compute the jump matrix S1 (in the following D1 will denote q's diagonal part). S1=ID-Inverse[D1].Q

Figure 17. Basic properties

Basic Properties	
InitialProbabilities	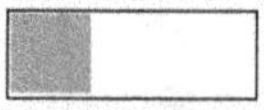
TransitionMatrix	
HoldingTimeMean	{0.010101, 0.724138, 0.923077}
HoldingTimeVariance	{0.010203, 1.24851, 1.77515}
Structural Properties	
CommunicatingClasses	{1, 2, 3}
RecurrentClasses	{1, 2, 3}
TransientClasses	None
AbsorbingClasses	None
PeriodicClasses	None
Periods	{}
Irreducible	True
Primitive	True
Aperiodic	True
Limiting Properties	
LimitTransitionMatrix	
Reversible	False

$\mathbf{In}[6] := D1 = \{\{-0.99,\ 0,\ 0\},\ \{0,\ -0.58,\ 0\},\ \{0,\ 0,\ -0.52\}\}$
$\mathbf{Out}[6] := \{\{-0.99,\ 0,\ 0\},\{0,\ -0.58,\ 0\},\{0,\ 0,\ -0.52\}\}$
$\mathbf{In}[7] := S1 = \ ID - Inverse\ [D1].Q$
$\mathbf{Out}[7] := \{\{0.,\ 0.434343,\ 0.565657\},\ \{0.0517241,\ \text{-}2.22045\times 10^{-16},\ 0.948276\},\ \{0.0961538,\ 0.903846,\ 0.\}\}$
$\mathbf{In}[8] := Matrix\ Form\ [S1]$
$\mathbf{Out}[8] := (\{0.,\ 0.434343,\ 0.565657\},$
$\{0.0517241, -2.22045\times 10^{-16},\ 0.948276\},$
$\{0.0961538,\ 0.903846,\ 0.\})$

Step 2: Compute a right eigenvector φ of S for the eigenvalue 1, that is φ fulfils $\varphi = \varphi S$, we will find $\varphi t, S^t - ID$ equals. right eigenvectors is:

In[9] := $E1 =$ *Transpose* [S1] − ID
Out[9] := {{−1., 0.0517241, 0.0961538}, {0.434343, −1., 0.903846}, {0.565657, 0.948276, −1.}}
In[10] := *Matrix Form* [E1]
Out[10] := ({−1., 0.0517241, 0.0961538},
{0.434343, −1., 0.903846},
{0.565657, 0.948276, −1.})
In[11] := *Eigenvectors* [E1]
Out[11] := {{−0.0367092, −0.688037, 0.724746}, {0.81429, −0.459099, −0.35519}, {0.104497, 0.691467, 0.714811}}
In[12] := N [%]
Out[12] := {{−0.0367092, −0.688037, 0.724746},{0.81429, −0.459099, −0.35519}, {0.104497, 0.691467, 0.714811}}

Step 3: Find the stationary distribution given by $\pi := \varphi D - 1 \parallel \varphi D - 1 \parallel 1$. here the right eigenvector:

In[13] := {0.10449730698280138`, 0.6914665832982282`, 0.714810658157261`} +
{0.10449730698280138`, 0.6914665832982282`, 0.714810658157261`}
Out[13] := {0.208995, 1.38293, 1.42962}

In[14] := *S Distribution* = e1.*Inverse* [D1]
Out[14] := {−0.211106, −2.38437, −2.74927}

We have $\varphi D - 1 = \{-0.211106, -2.38437, -2.74927\}$, *so* $\left\| \varphi D - 1 \right\| 1 = 9.83$, *the stationary distribution or invariant distribution* π *is the absolute value of* {−0.211106, −2.38437, −2.74927} *or* {0.211106, 2.38437, 2.74927}. *So* **♦= 1 / 5.34(0.211106, 2.38437, 2.74927)** *or* :

Figure 18.State Transition Diagram

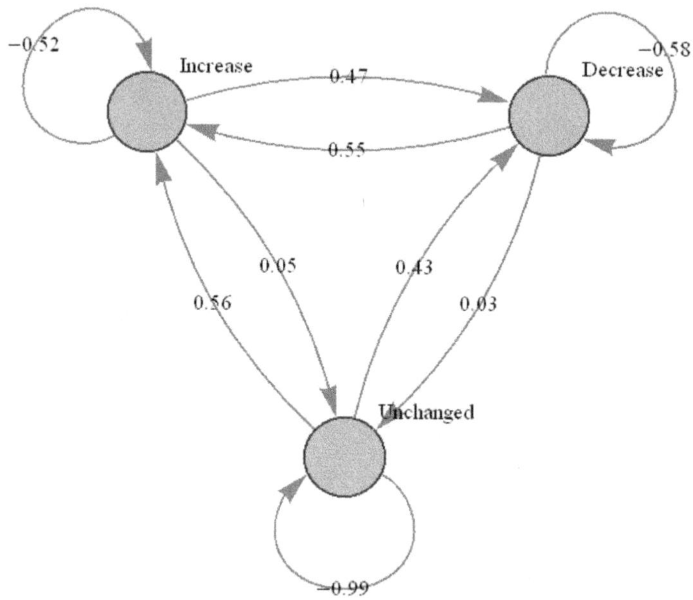

In[15]:= x={0.211106,2.38437,2.74927};
y=1/5.34;
x*y
Out[18]= {0.039533,0.446511,0.514845}
Extended Solution to the Problem

$$\text{In[19]:= ContinuousMarkovProcess[\{1,0,0\},}\begin{bmatrix} -0.99 & 0.43 & 0.56 \\ 0.03 & -0.58 & 0.55 \\ 0.05 & 0.47 & -0.52 \end{bmatrix};$$

$$\text{In[20]:= Graph[ContinuousMarkovProcess[1,}\begin{bmatrix} -0.99 & 0.43 & 0.56 \\ 0.03 & -0.58 & 0.55 \\ 0.05 & 0.47 & -0.52 \end{bmatrix}$$

Out[20]:=

In[21]:=D = FirstPassageTimeDistribution[P], 3];

Find the distribution for the time to transit, from state 1 to state 3

In[22]:=Plot[PDF[D], t], {t, 0, 10}]
Out[22]:=

In[23]:=CDF[D, t];
In[24]:=Plot[CDF[D,t],{t,0,10}] **In[21]:=CDF[D, t];**
Out[24]:=

Mean of the distribution, or the mean time to the first passage

In[25]:=c= Mean [D]
Out[25]:=1.79939
In[26]:=Variance [D]
Out[26]:=3.26512
The hitting time is 1.79 days; or if the stock is in state 1 state 3 in 1.79 days.
In[27]:=D=First Passage Time Distribution [D, 2];
Find the distribution for the time to transit, from state 1 to state 2
In[28]:=pdf= PDF [D, t];
In[29]:=Plot[PDF[D, t], {t, 0, 10}]

In[30]:=CDF[D,t];
In[30]:=Plot[CDF[D,t],{t,0,10}]
Out[30]:=

Mean of the distribution, or the mean time to the first passage

In[31]:=b= Mean [D]

Out[31]:=1.79939

In[32]:=Variance [D]

Out[32]:=3.26512

The hitting time is 2.22 days; or the stock from state 1 will reach state 2 in 2.22 days.

Simulate it:

In[33]:=data=Random Function [P, {0, 10}]

Out[33]:=Temporal Data [1]

In[34]:=List Line Plot[data, Interpolation Order → 0, Plot Range → {0, 3}, Ticks → {Automatic,{1, 2, 3}}]

Out[34]:=

In[35]:=P1=ContinuousMarkovProcess[2, $\begin{bmatrix} -0.99 & 0.43 & 0.56 \\ 0.03 & -0.58 & 0.55 \\ 0.05 & 0.47 & -0.52 \end{bmatrix}$;

In[36]:=D1=FirstPassageTimeDistribution[P1,3];

Find the distribution for the time to transit, from state 2 to state 3

In[37]:=Plot[PDF[D1,t],{t,0,10}]

In[38]:=CDF[D1,t];

In[39]:=Plot[CDF[D1,t],{t,0,10}]

Out[39]:=

Figure 19.State transition diagram

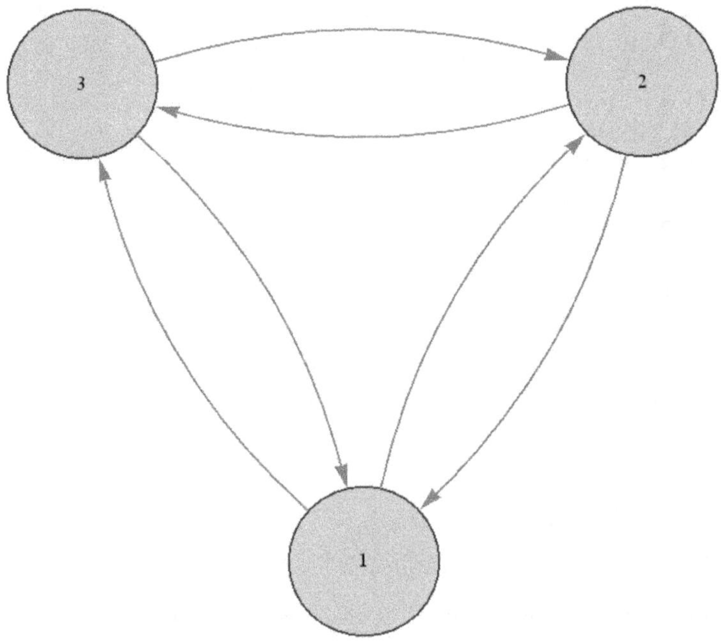

Mean of the distribution, or the mean time to the first passage

In[40]:—c1— Mean[D1]

Out:=1.81721

In[41]:=Variance[D1]

Out:=3.30035

The hitting time is 1.82 days; or if the stock is in state 2 will reach state 3 in 1.82 days.

In[42]:=D1=First Passage Time Distribution [P1, 1];

Find the distribution for the time to transit, from state 2 to state 1

In[43]:=pdf= PDF[D1, t];

In[44]:=Plot[PDF[D1, t],{t, 0, 10}]

Out[44]:=

Figure 20. PDF plot

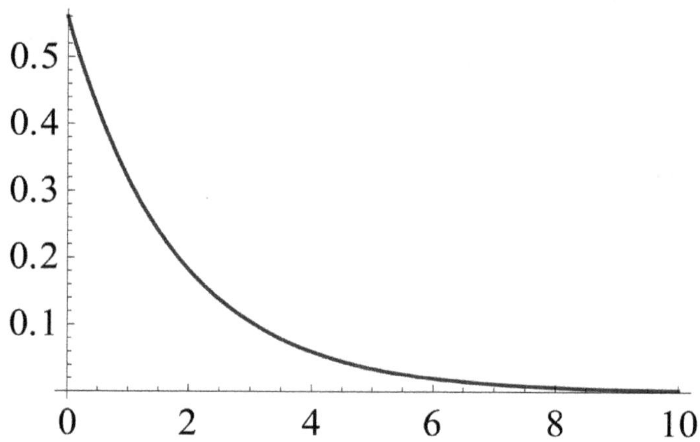

In[45]:=mode= Maximize [pdf, t]

Out[45]:= {0.0365702, {t → 1.91562}}

The mode in Continues Markov Processes is the peak value.

In[46]:=CDF[D1,t];

In[47]:=Plot[CDF[D1,t], {t,0,10}]

Out[47]:=

Figure 21.CDF plot

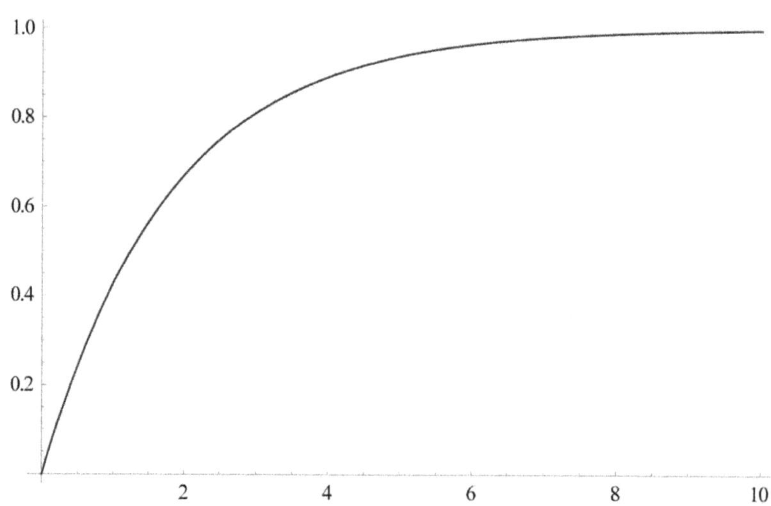

Figure 22.PDF plot

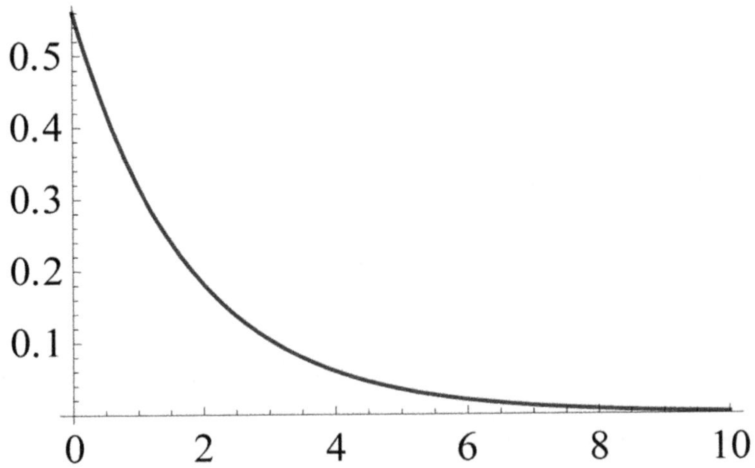

Figure 23.CDF plot

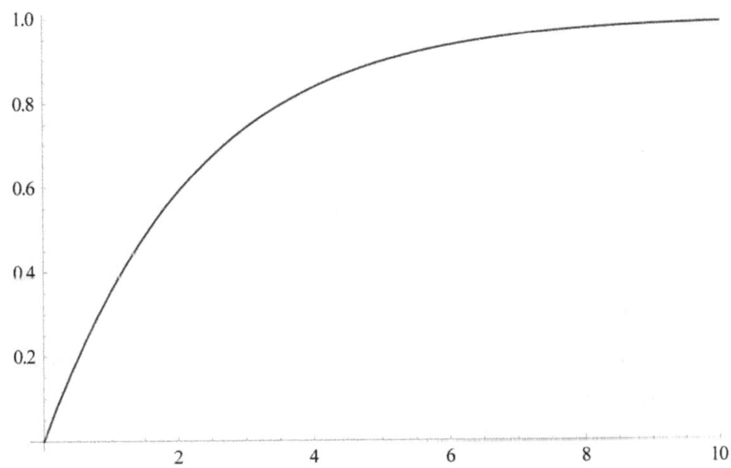

CDF for Weibull distribution with gamma = 1

Mean of the distribution, or the mean time to the first passage

In[48]:=a1=Mean[D1]

Out[48]:=24.826

In[49]:=Variance[D1]

Out[49]:=604.486

The hitting time is 24.83 days; or if the stock is in state 2 will reach state 1-unchange in 24.83 days.

Simulate it:

In[50]:=data=RandomFunction[P1,{0, 10}]

TemporalData[1]

In[51]:= ListLinePlot[data, InterpolationOrder → 0, PlotRange → {0,3}, Ticks → {Automatic,{1,2,3}}]

Out[51]:=

$$\text{In[52]:=P2=ContinuousMarkovProcess[3,} \begin{bmatrix} -0.99 & 0.43 & 0.56 \\ 0.03 & -0.58 & 0.55 \\ 0.05 & 0.47 & -0.52 \end{bmatrix}$$

In[53]:=D2=FirstPassageTimeDistribution[P2,**1**];

Find the distribution for the time to transit, from state 3 to state 1

In[54]:=Plot[PDF[D2,t],{t,0,10}]

Out[54]:=

In[55]:=CDF[D2,t];

In[56]:=Plot[CDF[D2,t],{t,0,10}]

Out[56]:=

Figure 24. The sample path of markov jump process with holding times and jump time

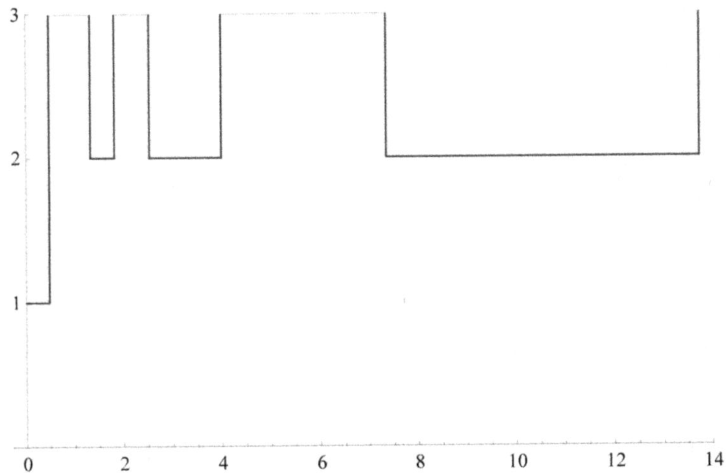

Mean of the distribution, or the mean time to the first passage

In[56]:=a2=Mean[D2]

Out[56]:=24.3619

In[57]:=Variance[D2]

Out[57]:=603.625

The hitting time is 24.36 days; or if the stock is in state 3 will transit to state 1 in 24.36 days.

In[58]:=D2= First Passage Time Distribution[P2,2];

Find the distribution for the time to transit, from state 3 to state 2

In[59]:=Plot[PDF[D2, t], {t, 0, 10}]

Out[59]:=

In[60]:=CDF[D2,t];

In[61]:=Plot[CDF[D2,t], {t,0,10}]

Out[61]:=

Figure 25. PDF plot

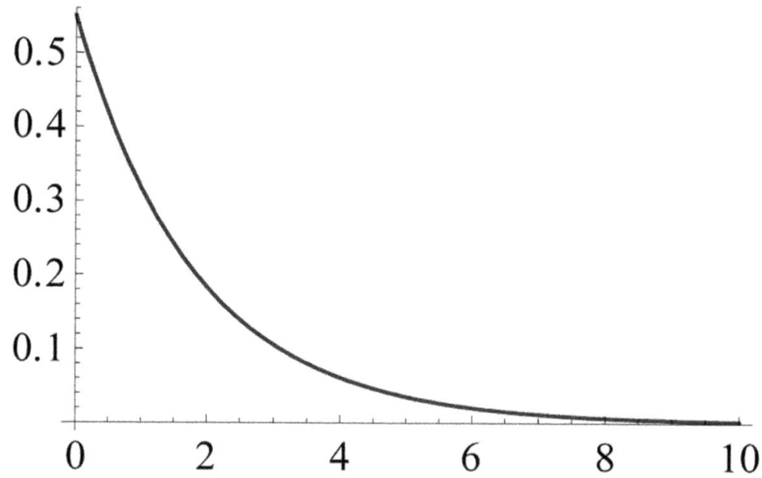

Mean of the distribution, or the mean time to the first passage
In[62]:=b2=Mean[D2]
Out[62]:=2.1364
In[63]:=Variance[D2]
Out[63]:=4.58109

The hitting time is 2.14 days; or if the stock is in state 3 will reach state 2 in 2.14 days.
Simulate it :
In[64]:=data=Random Function[P2,{0, 10}]
Out[64]:=Temporal Data[1]
In[65]:=List Line Plot [data, Interpolation Order → 0 ,Plot Range → {0, 3},Ticks → {Automatic,{1, 2, 3}}]
Out[65]:=

Figure 26.CDF plot

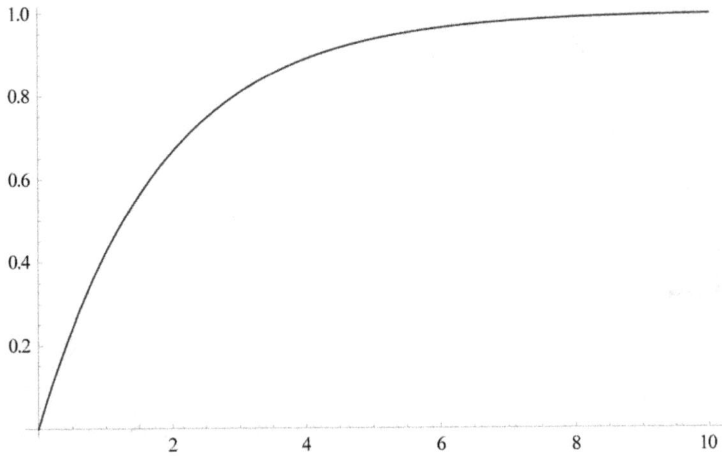

In order to find the hitting times from state 1 to 1, state 2 to 2 and state 3 to 3, first we should find the long-run proportion (the stationary distribution)

Step 1. Find the long - run proportion (À1, À2, À3) of time the process is in state 1, 2 and 3? Note that $\sum \pi=1$.

```
In[66]:=
À1=PDF[P[∞],1]

À2=PDF[P[∞],2]

À3=PDF[P[∞],3]

Out[66]:=0.0394978
Out[67]:=0.446114
Out[68]:=0.514388
```

Figure 27. PDF plot

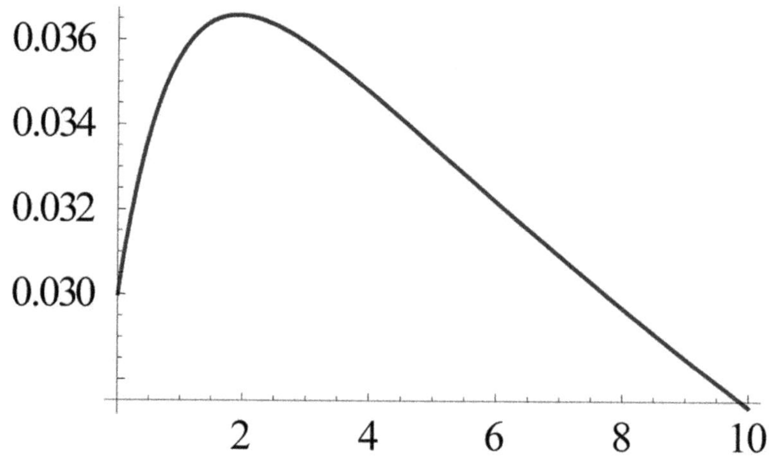

Figure 28. CDF plot

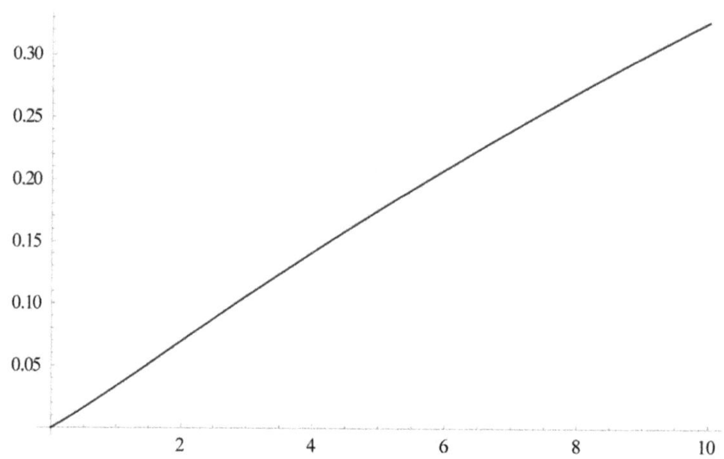

According to the long - run proportions the stock S & P 500 in future will have increasing trend.
Step 2. Find the expected number of steps (time) until the chain revisits state 1,
given that is in state 1 is 1/À or:

In[69]:=a=state1= 1/À1
Out[69]:=25.3179

The stock will revisit state 1 in 25.32 days
Find the expected number of steps (time) until the chain revisits state 2,
given that is in state 2 is 1/À or :
In[70]:=b1=state2=1/À2
Out[70]:=2.24158

The stock will revisit state 2 in 2.24 days
Find the expected number of steps (time) until the chain revisits state 3,
given that is in state 3 is 1/À or :
In[71]:=c2= state3= 1/À3
Out[71]:=1.94406
The stock will revisit state 3 in 1.94 days
The Expected First Passage Times are:

In[72]:=FRT={{a, b, c},{a1, b1, c1},{a2, b2, c2}}
Out[72]:={{25.3179, 1.79939, 1.79939},{24.826, 2.24158, 1.81721},{24.3619, 2.1364, 1.94406}}
In[73]:=Matrix Form[FRT]
Out[73]:=
({25.3179, 1.79939, 1.79939},
{24.826, 2.24158, 1.81721},
{24.3619, 2.1364, 1.94406})

Figure 29. The sample path of markov jump process with holding times and jump times

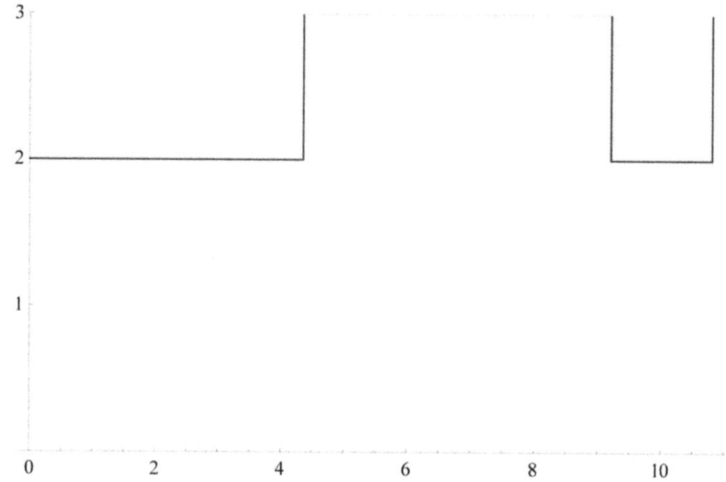

Forecast for March 16, 2016

1. The stock is in state 1.

Figure 30. PDF plot

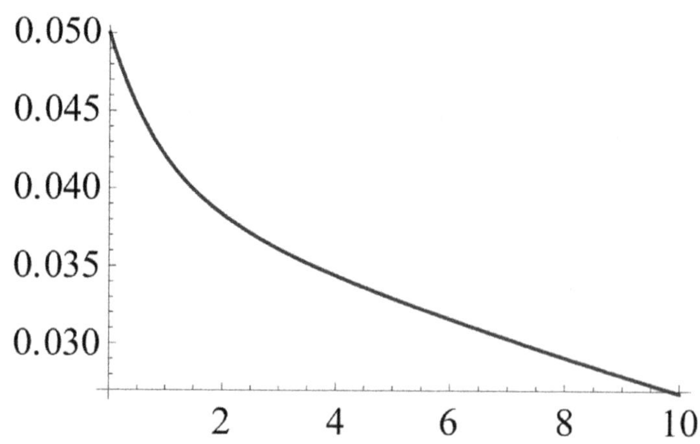

Figure 31. CDF plot

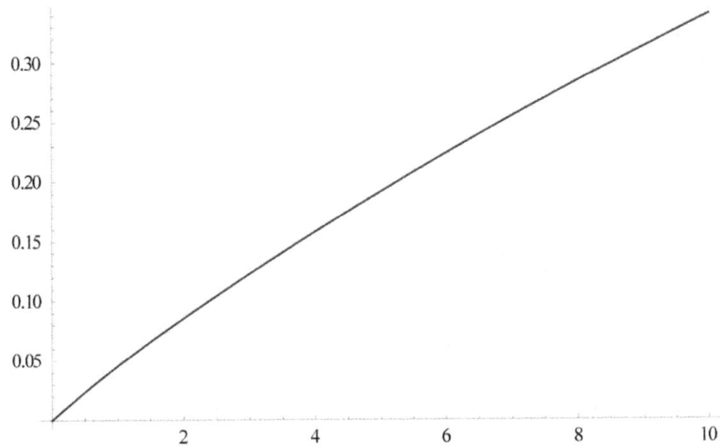

Find the probability that the stock will reach state 3-increase in the next day:
In[74]:=x= CDF[First Passage Time Distribution[P, 3], 1]// N
Out[74]:=0.427728

Find the probability that the stock will reach state 2-decrease in the next day:
In[75]:=y=CDF[First Passage Time Distribution[P, 2], 1]// N
Out[75]:=0.355414

Find the probability that the stock will stay in state 1 in the next day:
In[76]:=xy=1-x-y
Out[76]:=0.216858

2. The stock is in state 2-decrease.

Figure 32. PDF plot

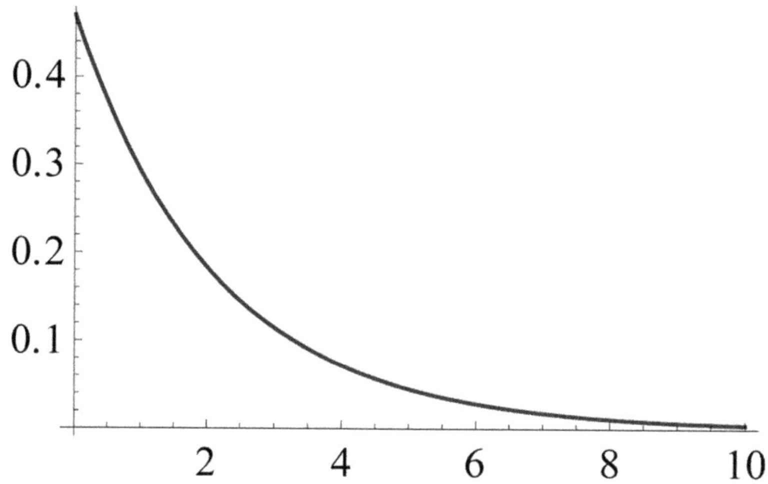

Find the probability that the stock will reach state 1-unchange in the next day :
In[78]:=x1=CDF[First Passage Time Distribution[P1, 1], 1]// N
Out[78]:=0.0334344

Find the probability that the stock will reach state 3-increase in the next day:
In[79]:=y1=CDF[First Passage Time Distribution[P1, 3], 1]//N
Out[79]:=0.423125

Find the probability that the stock will stay in state 1 in the next day:
In[80]:=x1y1=1-x1-y1
Out[80]:=0.543441

3. The stock is in state 3-increase.

Figure 33. CDF plot

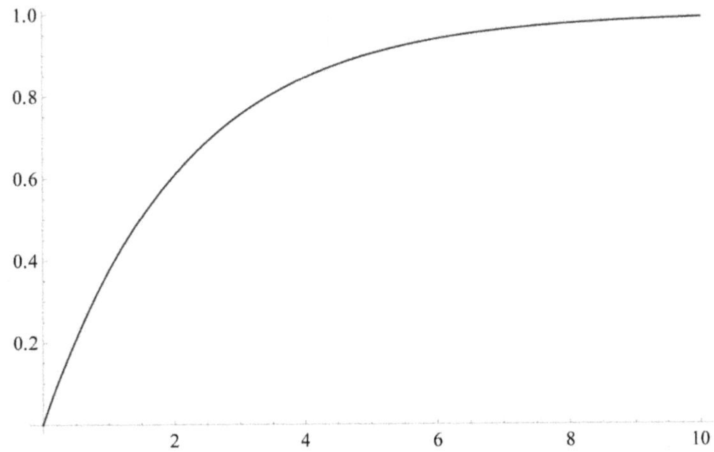

Find the probability that the stock will reach state 1-unchange in the next day:

In[81]:=x2=CDF[First Passage Time Distribution[P2, 1], 1]// N
Out[81]:=0.0454788
In[82]:=y2=CDF[First Passage Time Distribution[P2, 2], 1]// N
Out[82]:=0.374476

Find the probability that the stock will stay in state 1 in the next day:
In[83]:=x2y2=1-x2-y2
Out[83]:=0.580045

Figure 34. The sample path of markov jump process with holding times and jump times

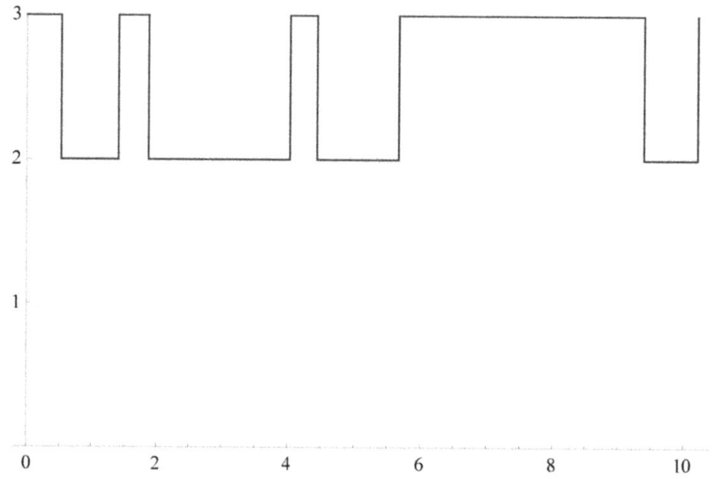

The Forecast Matrix for the Next Day-March 16, 2016.

In[84]:=FM={{xy, y, x},{x1, x1y1, y1},{x2, y2, x2y2}}

Out[84]:={{0.216858, 0.355414, 0.427728},{0.0334344, 0.543441, 0.423125},{0.0454788, 0.374476, 0.580045}}

In[85]:=Matrix Form[FM]

Out[85]:=

{0.216858, 0.355414, 0.427728},

{0.0334344, 0.543441, 0.423125},

{0.0454788, 0.374476, 0.580045})

APPENDIX 3

Copper Analyses: Jump-Markov Process

In[1]:=P1= { {0.58, 0.42}, {0.38,0.62}}
Out [1]:={{0.58,0.42},{0.38,0.62}}
In [2]:=ID={{1,0},{0,1}}
Out [2]:={{1,0},{0,1}}

To find the generator G
In [3]:=Q=P1-ID
Out [3]:={{-0.42,0.42},{0.38,-0.38}}
In[4]:=Matrix Form[Q]
Out [4]:=
{-0.42, 0.42},
{0.38, -0.38}
Step 1.
Compute the jump matrix S1
(in the following D1 will denote Qs diagonal part). S1=ID-Inverse[D1].Q
In [5]:=D1={{-0.42,0},{0,-0.38}}
Out [5]:={{-0.42,0},{0,-0.38}}
In [6]:=S1=ID-Inverse[D1].Q
Out [6]:={{0.,1.},{1.,0.}}
In [7]:=Matrix Form[S1]
Out [7]:=
{0., 1.},
{1., 0.}

Step 2.

Compute a right eigenvector φ of S for the eigenvalue 1, that is φ fulfills $\varphi = \varphi S$, we will find φt, St- Id equals (t means transpose)

Right Eigenvectors is

In [8]:=E1=Transpose[S1]-ID

Out [8]:={{-1.,1.},{1.,-1.}}

In [9]:=Matrix Form[E1]

Out [9]:=

{-1., 1.},

{1., -1.}

In [10]:=Eigenvectors[E1]

Out [10]:={{0.707107,-0.707107},{0.707107,0.707107}}

Step 3. Find the stationary distribution given by À= -φD - 1 ‖ φD - 1 ‖ 1.
Here the right eigenvector:
In [11]:=e1={0.7071067811865475`, 0.7071067811865475`}+
{0.7071067811865475`, 0.7071067811865475`}
Out [11]:={1.41421,1.41421}
In [12]:=S Distribution=e1.Inverse[D1]
Out [12]:={-3.36718,-3.72161}

We have φD - 1 ={-3.36718,-3.72161}, so ‖φD - 1 ‖1 = 9.83, the stationary distribution or invariant distribution À is the absolute value of {-3.36718,-3.72161} or {{3.36718,3.72161}.
So À = 1/7.09 (3.36718,3.72161)
In [13]:=x={3.3671751485073687`,3.7216146378239343`};
y=1/5.34;
x*y
Out [13]:={0.630557,0.696932}

Extended Solution

In[16]:=P=ContinuousMarkovProcess[{1,0}, $\begin{bmatrix} -0.42 & 0.42 \\ 0.38 & -0.38 \end{bmatrix}$;

In[17]:=Graph[ContinuousMarkovProcess[{1,0}, $\begin{bmatrix} -0.42 & 0.42 \\ 0.38 & -0.38 \end{bmatrix}$

Out[17]:

In [18]:=n= First Passage Time Distribution [P, 2];
In [19]:=Plot [PDF [D, t], {t, 0, 10}]
Out [19]:=

In [20]:=CDF[D, t];
In [21]:=Plot [CDF[D, t],{t, 0, 10}]
Out [21]:=

Mean of the distribution, or the mean time to the first passage

In[22]:=b=Mean[D]

Out [22]:=2.38095

In [23]:=labada=1/b

Out [23]:=0.42

In [24]:=Variance[D]

Out [24]:=5.66893

The hitting time is 2.381 days; or if the stock is in state 1 state 2-increase in 2.381 days.

Simulate it:

In [25]:=data=Random Function[P,{0,10}]

Out[25] := Temporal Data[1]

In [26]:=List Line Plot

[data, Interpolation Order → 0, Plot Range → {0, 3}, Ticks → {Automatic,{1, 2, 3}}]

Out[26]:=

In [27]:=P1= Continuous Markov Process [2, $\begin{bmatrix} -0.42 & 0.42 \\ 0.38 & -0.38 \end{bmatrix}$

In [28]:=D1= First Passage Time Distribution[P1, 1];

In [29]:=Plot[PDF[D1, t],{t, 0, 10}]

Out [29]:=

In[30]:=CDF[D1, t];

In [31]:=Plot[CDF[D1, t],{t, 0, 10}]

Out [31]:=

Mean of the distribution, or the mean time to the first passage, variance and »

In [32]:=a=Mean[D1]

Out [32]:=2.63158

In [33]:=Variance[D1]

Out [33]:=5.66893

In [34]:=labada=1/a

Out [34]:=0.38T

he hitting time is 2.63 days; or if the stock is in state 2

will reach state 1-decrease in 2.63 days.

Simulate it:

In [35]:=data=Random Function[P1,{0, 10}]

Out [35]:=Temporal Data[1]

In [36]:=List Line Plot

[data, InterpolationOrder → 0, Plot Range → {0, 3},Ticks → {Automatic,{1, 2, 3}}]

Out [36]:=

In order to find the hitting times from state 1 to 1, state 2 to 2 ,
first we should find the long-run proportion(the stationary distribution)
Step 1. Find the long - run proportion(À1,À2,À3)
of time the process is in state 1, 2 and 3? Note that $\sum \pi=1$.
In [37]:=À1=PDF[P[∞],1]

In [38]:=À2=PDF[P[∞],2]
Out [37]:=0.475
Out [38]:=0.525
According the long - run proportions the Copper stock in future will have increasing trend - 52,5 %.
Step 2. Find the expected number of steps (time)
until the chain revisits state 1, given that is in state 1 is 1/À or:

In [39]:=b1=state1=1/À1
Out [39]:=2.10526

The forecast matrix for the next month
In [47]:=FM={{a1,a},{b,b1}}
Out [47]:={{0.657047,0.342953},{0.316139,0.683861}}
In [48]:=Matrix Form[FM]
Out [48]:=
{0.657047, 0.342953},
{0.316139, 0.683861}

Figure 35. State transition diagram

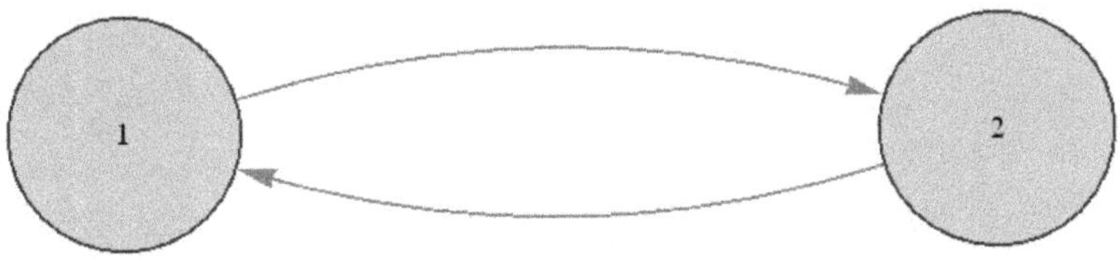

Figure 36. PDF plot

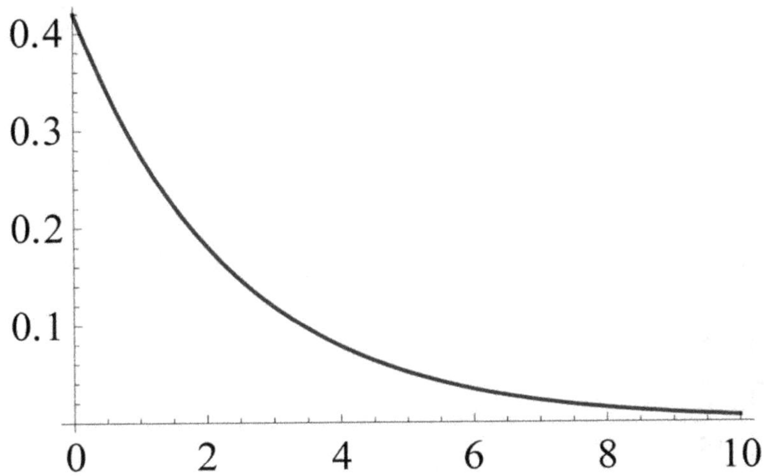

Figure 37. CDF plot

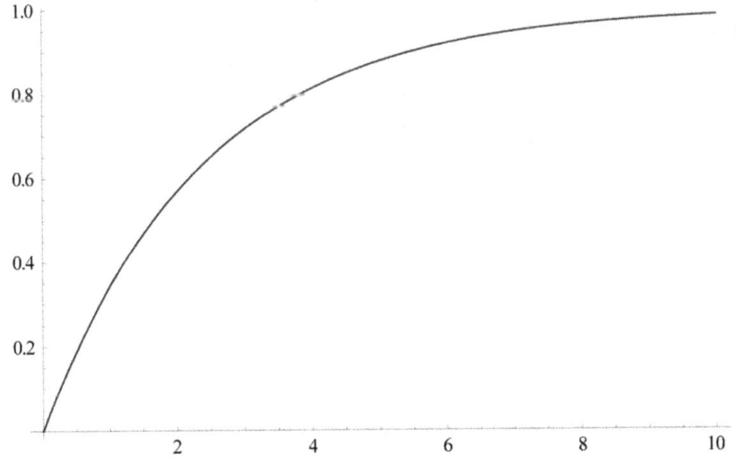

Figure 38. The sample path of markov jump process with holding times and jump times

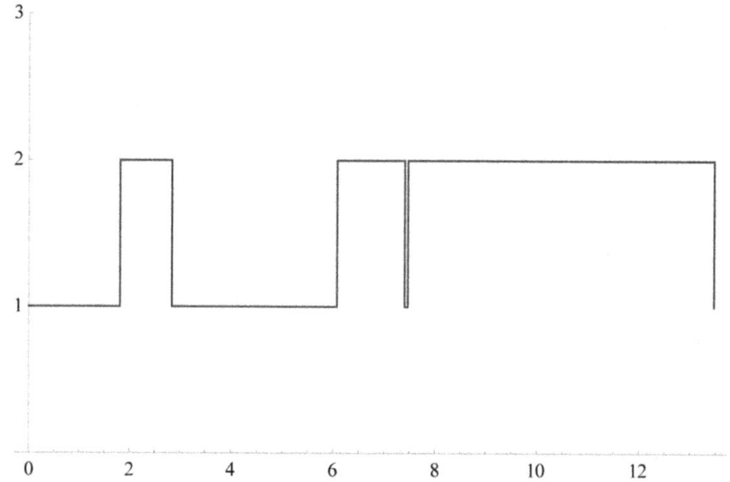

Figure 39. PDF plot

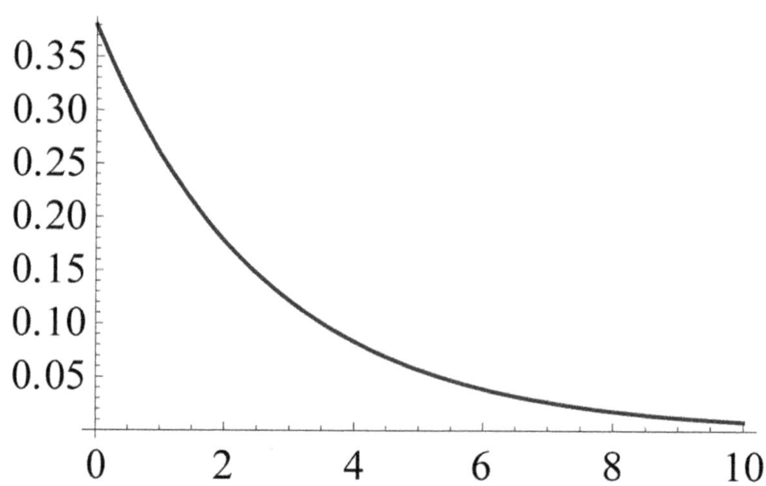

Figure 40. CDF plot

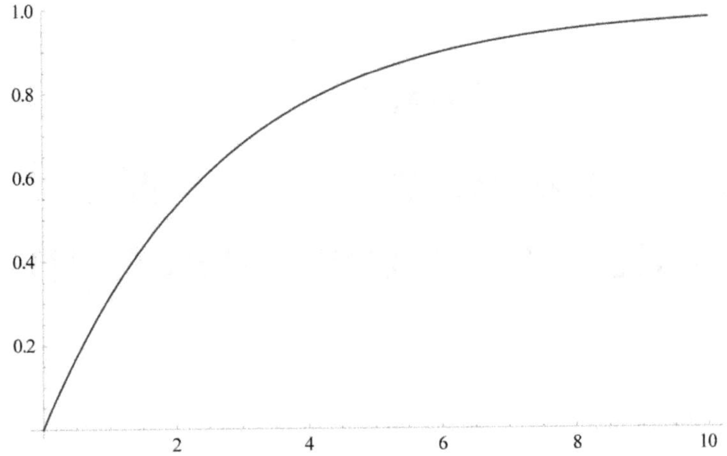

Figure 41. The sample path of markov jump process with holding times and jump times

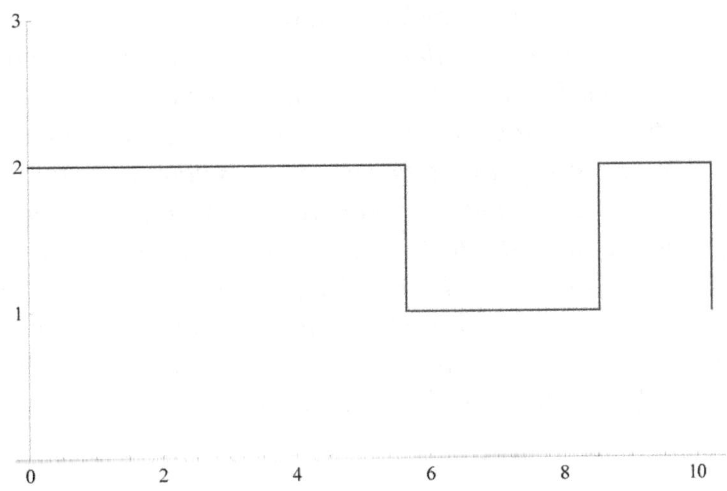

Chapter 7
Fractal and Wavelet Market Analysis in Pattern Recognition

ABSTRACT

Fractal geometry can be seen as a universal language by which nature can be explained or at least described and quantified. Financial markets are one of them. Therefore, in this chapter, I set my focus on complex dynamics, an area that was around for about one hundred year ago and continues to inspire much ongoing research. I show that wavelet-based modelling underlies the process that generates financial market data. It is a method that decomposes a time series into several layers of time series, making it possible to analyze how the local variance, or wavelet power, changes both in the frequency and time domain. Then I calculate the local Holder exponent which is applied to estimate stable and unstable fixed point, or regularity and singularity and based on them, one can adapt its buy-sell strategy timely. The model successfully detects the hoarding effect, noise traders, and the pattern of the short-run price fluctuation. An algorithmic construction of the model is developed in Wolfram Mathematica 9 and MatLab R2016b.

You are looking anomalies; you are looking if the efficient market hypothesis is true. So the random walk theory is true if we do not have enough data. When we are looking anomalies and you have enough data, then the probability that these anomalies are being random is not high. They are there persistent for a sufficiently long time. But these things fade after a while and anomalies could get washed up. (Jim Simons, 2015)

DOI: 10.4018/978-1-5225-3259-0.ch007

INTRODUCTION

In the world, there are two camps of people: those who believe that things happen for a reason and those who believe things happen at random, for no reason. Well, whatever you believe, you should watch the interview held with Jim Simons, co-inverter, mathematician, hedge fund manager and philanthropist. This is one of his rare public appearances.

The link for the interview was sent to me in a very same day I bought the book titled: "The Physics of Wall Street" by Weatheral James Oven. The most interesting part is that Jim Simons is one of the most successful hedge fund managers in the world, and I didn't even know that such a person exists. Renaissance Technologies are funded in 1982 and is still one of the best hedge fund firms. In 2016 the fund returned 21.5%, equal to approximately $2.35 billion in profits.

The interview was very fascinating and informative. Each word bears a deeper meaning, and you simply have to listen carefully. His story confirmed my doubts that have increasingly grown after each chapter. Then I began reading the introduction section of the book "The Physics of Wall Street". The first few sentences are very important:

Warren Buffet isn't the best money manager in the world. Neither is Gorge Soros or Bill Gross. The world's best money manager is a man you've probably never heard of – unless you are a physicist, in which case you'd know his name immediately. Jim Simons is coinventor of brilliant pieces of mathematics called the Chern-Simons 3-form, one of the most important parts of string theory. He's the kind of a scientist whose name is uttered in hashing tones in the physics department of Harvard and Princeton.... And yet, there he is, the founder of the extraordinarily successful firm Renaissance's signature fund in 1988, with another mathematician named James Ax. Renaissance employs about two hundred people. A third of them have PhDs not in finance, but rather, like Simon, in fields like physic, mathematics and statistics. According to MIT mathematician Isadore Singer, Renaissance is the best physics and mathematics department in the world – which, say Simon and others, is why the firm has excelled. Indeed, Renaissance avoids hiring anyone with even the slightest whiff of Wall Street bona fields. PhDs in finance need not apply' nor should trader who got their start at traditional investment bonus or even hedge funds. The secret to Simon's success has been steering clear of the financial expert...

Most of you wonder why Simon avoids hiring people with PhDs in finance or practicians from traditional investment hedge funds. The answer now from this point of view is very simple. Simon has realized a long time ago that the damage comes when we use ideas from physics, but we stop thinking like physicists. And when the year 2008 hammered a lot of banks and hedge funds as the Bear Stearns, Lehman Brothers, insurance giant AIG, Citadel Investment Group, Berkshire Hathaway fund, Jim Simon's Fund earned 80%, even as the financial industry collapsed around him.

Now, after reading this do you still think that things happen at random?

Personally, I don't think so. To confirm my belief lets us go step by step. In the previous chapter I apply Markovian models (also known as random models) and we notice that the current performance does not predict future returns or prices. The answer cannot be found either in the trend following solution (technical analysis as ARIMA, FARIMA, GARCH). One of the reasons is the background noise which makes it difficult to discover the future stock return patterns. Therefore, to improve the prediction and model the stock return behavior, standard neoclassical technique adds white Gause noise in the model.

However, research has shown that the assumptions in traditional models are not valid in some cases. These cases are particularly important for investors. The use of conventional models (e.g., Poisson-type models) results with optimistic performance predictions where returns do not grow with the size of the interval over which it has been measured. Since traditional models have extensively been studied in the past decades, relatively much is known about their properties, although there are still many open problems, as unstable outcomes.

Remember that the stock's price/returns movements generally cannot be described using normal (or Gaussian) distribution and random walk theory models. But attention-grabbing is the fact that they are still unproven in outperforming the markets.

To support this assessment, we will run a few tests of the random walk hypothesis. First, we plot the assets price histogram. Secondly, we test the distribution. Here we want to determine if the data can be identified using the normal distribution. If the result suggests the rejection of the null hypotheses (Ho= the data is normally distributed) then additional distribution tests will be applied. Third, we compute the autocorrelation, also known as a serial correlation or lagged correlation, in asset returns and its volatility. And lastly, we estimate the Hurst exponent. But before we go into all that, let us first go through some finance magazines (as Forbes, Money, Bloomberg Business Week, Kiplinger's and Barron's). In them we find numerous mutual fund performance advertisements. They declare that a particular mutual fund has achieved higher returns than those of similar funds. Why are they using these performance advertisements? Simple: because they are effective; because they know that past returns are a primary factor that investors consider in choosing among funds. For example, Jain and Wu (2000), found that equity funds advertised in *Barron's* or *Money* outperformed non-advertised funds with the same investment objective by an average of approximately 6% over the twelve months prior to the advertisements. However, Mercer, Palmiter and Taha (2010), concluded that investors would be better off ignoring these advertisements, because a large body of studies has found little evidence that high past returns predict high future returns. In fact, advertised mutual funds tend to underperform the market after being advertised.

The limited value of using past returns as an indicator of future performance has not escaped the US Securities and Exchange Commission (SEC). In fact, the financial supervisory body importance is to "help investors understand the limitations of past-performance data" by requiring fund ads publicizing historical returns to include a warning. It states that "past performance does not guarantee future results" and that investors could lose money in the fund being promoted.

The question here is whether the SEC's warning fulfills its intended role. The answer could be found in the study conducted by Mercer, Palmiter and Taha (2010).

This article presents the results of an experiment that tests whether this disclaimer is effective in discouraging investors from relying upon advertised past performance when choosing a mutual fund.

Participants were each shown one version of a performance aid for an equity fund that had outperformed its peers in the past. After reading the ad, participants were asked about their propensity to invest in the fund and about their expectations regarding its future returns. Some participants viewed a version of the ad containing the SEC's warning. Others were shown a version that was identical, except that it had no warning.

They found that the SEC's warning is completely ineffective. Participants who saw the ad with the warning were just as likely to invest in the fund, and had the same expectations regarding its future returns, as participants who saw the ad without the warning. Ironically, the wording of the current disclaimer actually might lead investors to rely more heavily on past performance.

This study confirmed the doubt that the warning's ineffectiveness is not surprising, given its weak language. It only warns that high past returns do not guarantee high future returns and that investors in the fund could lose money. Virtually all investors knew this even before the recent financial crisis battered fund returns.

To see if a stronger warning might be more effective, they showed other participants a version of the ad that contained a warning conveying the lack of a relationship between high past and future returns:

Do not expect the fund's quoted past performance to continue in the future. Studies show that mutual funds that have outperformed their peers in the past generally do not outperform them in the future. Strong past performance is often a matter of chance.

In contrast to the SEC's warning, this stronger one did affect behavior. Participants who viewed the advertising with this stronger warning were considerably less likely to invest in the fund and had lower expectations regarding its future returns.

An important finding from this study is that given that it had no impact on people who focused on the ad, it almost certainly has no impact on the typical investor, who is likely to read it more casually, and who might only skim, or entirely skip, the warning near the bottom of the ad. If the SEC is truly committed to preventing the mutual fund industry from enticing investors into chasing past returns, it should design a warning that better informs investors of the futility of this case.

ARE RETURNS NORMALLY DISTRIBUTED?

Consider the daily closing prices of S&P 500 index (SP500) from Jan 3, 1950to June 27, 2016. We can compute the daily returns of SP500, either using the simple returns or continuously compounded returns. The (one-period) simple return is defined to be $R_t = \{S(t) - S(t-1)\} \,/\, S(t-1)$ at time t, where S (t) is the asset price. For mathematical convenience, the continuously compounded return (also called log return) at time t, $rt = LnS(t)S(t-1)$, is very often also used, especially in theoretical modelling. The financial and economic analysts prefer to say that the logarithm of the price has normalized the data, but the real answer is given by Osborne (1959). He says that we should be interested in the logarithms of prices because logarithms of prices, better reflect how investors feel about their gains and losses, because it has an "equal interval" property.

Then we plot the histogram of the daily returns of SP500, see Figure 1.

As a second step, we perform distribution tests. You can find the results in Table 1.

According to performed tests S&P500 index data does not follow the normal distribution, since $p<0.5$. This can be also shown graphically, see

Figure 1. Histogram of S&P500 daily returns

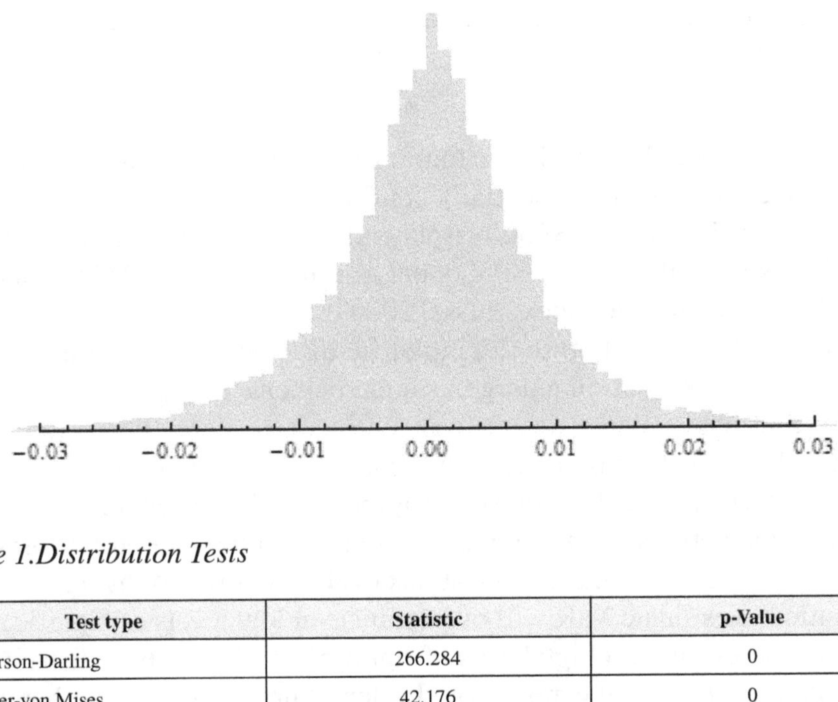

Table 1.Distribution Tests

Test type	Statistic	p-Value
Anderson-Darling	266.284	0
Cramer-von Mises	42.176	0
Jarue- Bera ALM	514945.78	$8.815138897 x 10^{-111820}$
Mardia Combined	514945.78	$8.815138897 x 10^{-111820}$
Mardia Kurtosis	715.283	$9.41833804562346 x 10^{-111103}$
Mardia Skewness	2842.65	$1.314981525575326 x 10^{-619}$
Pearson χ^2	16712	$6.84220235300591 x 10^{-3506}$

Figure 2.Comparison of the histogram of the normalized daily returns of S&P500 Index and the standard normal density

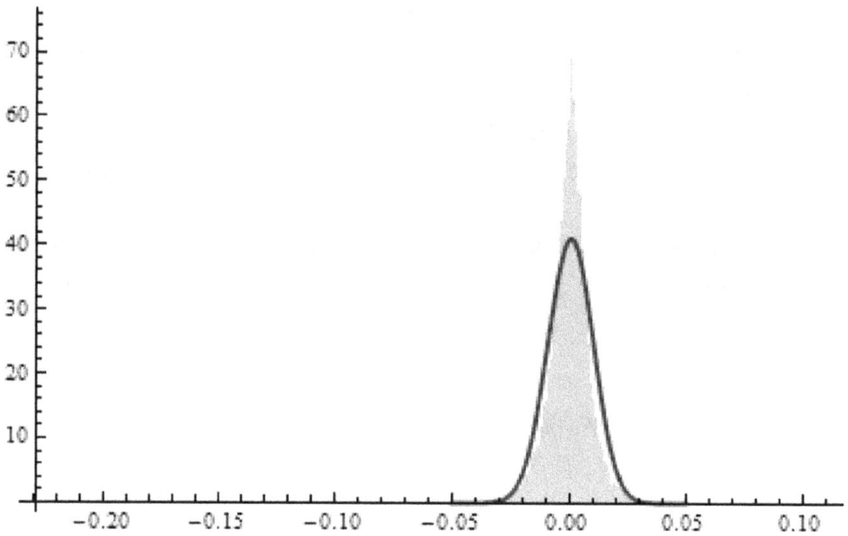

Figure 2. Here we display the histogram along with the standard normal density function, which is essentially confined within (−0. 05, 0.05).

Clearly the histogram of SP500 displays a high peak and asymmetric heavy tails. This is not only true for SP500, but also for the NASDAG Composite Index, NYSE Composite Index, Russel 2000 Index, Apple Inc. and Alphabet Inc, Google. From the Figure 2 leptokurtic distribution, which means the kurtosis of the distribution is large, is quite evident. It helps to measure an asset level of risk.

A leptokurtic distribution means that small changes happen less frequently because historical values have clustered by the mean. However, this also means that large fluctuations are more likely within the fat tails. Leptokurtosis can impact how analysts estimate value at risk (VaR). An investor using a normal distribution to estimate VaR will overestimate at low levels of significance, but will underestimate at high levels of significance if the return distribution is leptokurtic. This is the result of the leptokurtic distribution having a fatter tail. The fat tail means risk is coming from outlier events and extreme observations are much more likely to occur. But which tail is heavier left or right? We will estimate skewness and kurtosis, to answer the above question. We shall use the following equations 1:

$$S = \frac{1}{\left(n-1\right)\sigma^3} \sum_{i=1}^{n} \left(X_i - X\right)^3, \qquad K = \frac{1}{\left(n-1\right)\sigma^4} \sum_{i=1}^{n} \left(X_i - X\right)^4 \tag{1}$$

where, X_i is the sample data set, X is the sample mean, n is the number of data points, σ is the sample standard deviation, S is the sample skewness and K is the sample kurtosis.

For the daily returns of the SP500 data, the sample kurtosis is about 30.0799and the skewness is about -1.01104; the positive skewness means the return has a heavier right tail than the left tail. The right tail is longer; the mass of the distribution is concentrated on the left, as shown in Figure 3.

What is interesting in the leptokurtic future is not something new in economics, contrary, it has been observed since 1950's. However, classical finance models simply ignore this feature. For example, in the Black–Scholes Brownian motion model, the stock price is modelled as a geometric Brownian motion. In this model, the continuous compounded return, Ln (S (t) /S (0)), has a normal distribution, which it is not consistent with leptokurtic feature.

ARE THE STOCK RETURNS PREDICTABLE?

We can formulate this question mathematically by asking whether returns are correlated in some ways, so that the current returns will provide some information about future returns. To test this, we will first compute the

Figure 3. Skewness

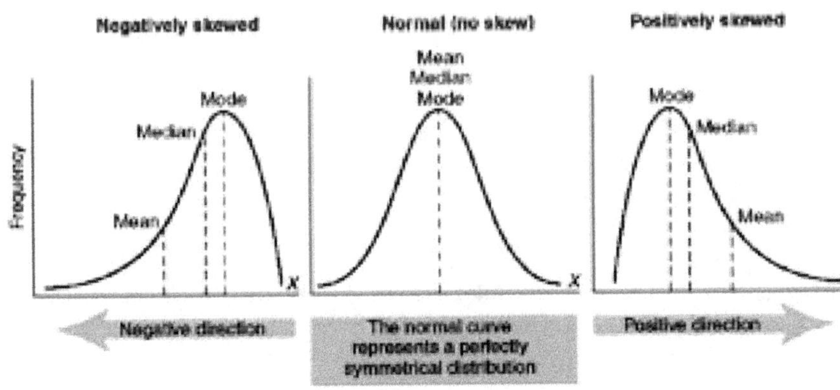

autocorrelation of returns and then the autocorrelation of the volatility of the S&P500 index.

Formula for calculating autocorrelation:

$$\hat{p}_{k} = \frac{\hat{\gamma}_k}{\hat{\gamma}_0} = \frac{\widehat{cov}\,(R_{it}, R_{i,t-k})}{\widehat{var}\,(R_{it})} \qquad (2)$$

where, $\hat{p}_k$ is the sample autocovariance function, $\widehat{cov}\left(R_{it,} R_{i,t-k}\right)$ is the covariance of random variables R_{it} and $R_{i,t-k}$ and $\widehat{var}(R_{it})$ is the variance of random variables R_{it} and $R_{i,t-k.}$

Then we get Figures 4 and 5.

Figure 4 shows no sign of serial correlation between returns, but this is not the case in Figure 5. We can notice a clear positive trend in the autocorrelation of the S&P500 volatility, a clear sign of long memory, or persistent behavior. Meaning while S&P500 returns may be random, its periods of volatility are not. Prediction is possible.

Figure 4. Autocorrelation of returns

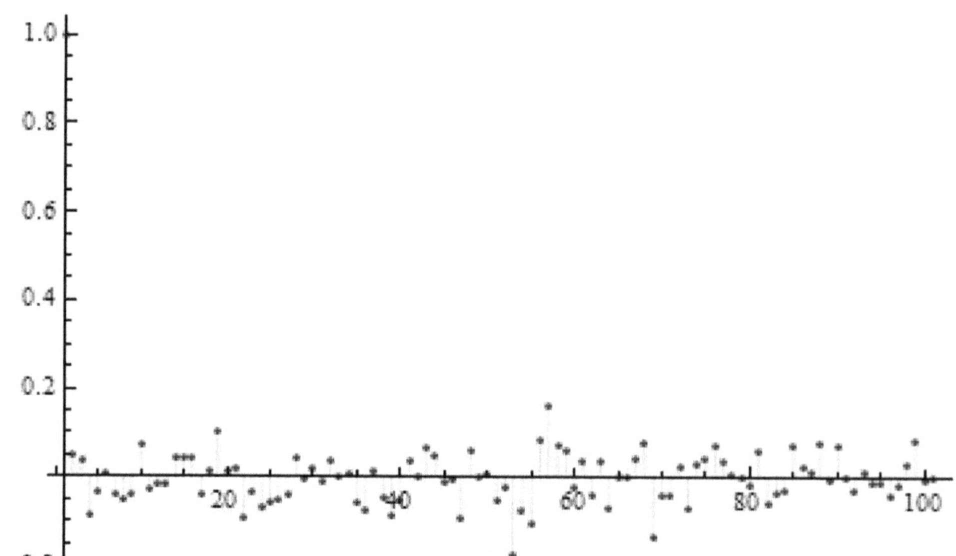

Figure 5. Autocorrelation of volatility

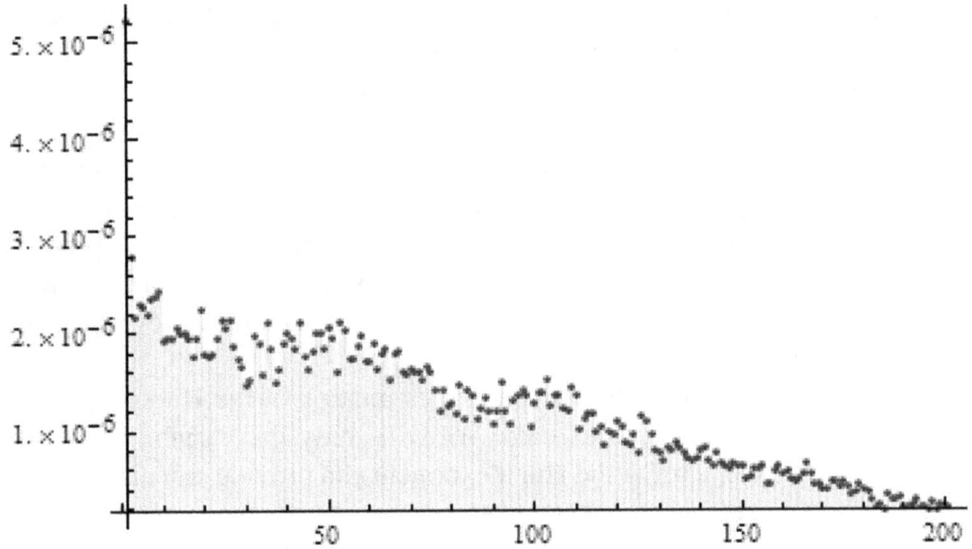

THE HURST EXPONENT

Fractional Gaussian Noise (FGN) is very different from a Markovian process in that it implies a fat-tailed autocorrelation function. (Koutsoyiannia, D. The Hurst Phenomenon and fractional Gaussian noise made easy, Hydrological Sciences Journal)

While investigating the discharge time series of the Nile River in the framework of the design of the Aswan High Dam, Hurst (1951), discovered a special behavior of hydrological and other geophysical time series, which has become known as the "Hurst phenomenon". This behavior is essentially the tendency of wet years to cluster into wet periods, or of dry years to cluster into drought periods. The term "Joseph effect" introduced by Mandelbrot (1977) has been used as an alternative for the same behavior.

For instance, if the Hurst exponent is 0.85, as in the Nile example, then the autocorrelation of lag 100 (years) is as high as 0.15, whereas if the process were Markovian the autocorrelation would be practically zero even for lags 10 times less. Does the explanation of this behavior of natural systems, such as the Nile water level or the Mammoth Creek tree-ring widths, rest of the self-organized criticality principle (e.g. Bak, 1996), i.e. a cooperative behavior, where the different items of large systems act together in some concerted way? Or, does it rest on monotonic deterministic trends (Bhattacharya et al., 1983), which can explain this behavior mathematically? Or, is there any natural mechanism inducing a long memory to the system, which is responsible for the high autocorrelation for a lag of 100 years or more?

Mesa & Poveda's (1993), explanation is much simpler and relies upon an "absence of memory" concept rather than a "long-term memory" concept. That is, not only does the system "disremember" what was the value of the process 100 years (or more) ago, but it further "forgets" what the process meant at that time was. This explanation is consistent with the assertion of the National Research Council (1991), that climate "changes irregularly, for unknown reasons, on all timescales".

In this section, we are interested in the estimation of the Hurst exponent (H) from historical stock index data. We will study the variability of this parameter over time, a see if the Hurst exponent can provide signals that will alert investors to emerging crises and trends.

As I have already mentioned, the assumption that stock returns are normally distributed is widely used in theoretical finance and is accepted as a cornerstone of modern finance. The popularity of this assumption arises from the fact that normally distributed stock returns are an implication of the random walk theory. In understanding the behavior of different security markets, efficiency analysis plays also an important role. EMH requires investor's reaction be random and follow a normal distribution pattern, so that the net effect on market prices cannot be exploited to make abnormal profit.

However, from a theoretical point of view, the normality of stock returns is questionable if the information does not arrive linearly to the market, or, even if it does, if investors do not react linearly to its arrival. What does this mean?

I believe that the answer could be found in the fractal markets hypothesis (FMH). During stable phases of the market, all investment horizons are equally represented so that supply and demand on the market are smoothly cleared. Conversely, unstable periods such as crashes occur when the investment horizons are dominated by only several of them so that supply and demand of different groups of investors are not efficiently cleared-presence of noise traders, when most investors are looking at the same time horizon (the hoarding effect) or both (noise traders and hoarding effect).

What is more, FMH if far less restrictive. Here it is not assumed that all investors are the same, as in the Efficient Market Hypothesis. In the scope of FMH the markets do have a memory, but because the information loss is exponential only short run prediction is possible. The range of techniques used within this framework is extremely wide, but luckily some of the most powerful tools are also the simplest, so we will not get into unnecessary technical details.

ESTIMATING THE HURST EXPONENT

The Hurst parameter H is a measure of the extent of long-range dependence in a time series and takes on values from 0 to 1. Using the Hurst exponent, we can classify time series into types and gain some insight into their dynamics, as given below.

- **A Brownian Time Series if H=0. 5:** In a Brownian time series (also known as a random walk) there is no correlation between the observations and a future observation; being higher or lower than the current observation is equally likely. Series of this kind are hard to predict.
- **An Anti-Persistent Time Series (Also Called Pink Noise or Mean-Reverting Series) if 0<H<0.5:** Anti-persistent ones have strong negative autocorrelations and short memory, or it can be said that such process covers less distance than a random walk. This means that a decreasing process or a time series, then, it is more probable that the process or the time series will show an increasing trend (i.e., values will tend to revert to a mean).

In our case, we analyzed the data of S&P 500 index for the period 1.03.1950-1.06.2016. The Figure 3 provides an example of the correlation function of an anti-persistent, time series and its estimated Hurst exponent. The closer the value is to 0, the more jagged (irregular) will the time series be. Short memory markets have much wider tails than a long-memory market. And the most important characteristic that we should take in consideration when analyzing stock markets is that such series display, seeming trends for some time, but these seeming trends are erratically interrupted by sudden discontinuities.

- **A Persistent Time Series if 0.5<H<1:** A persistent process or a time series have strong positive autocorrelations, or it can be said that such process covers more distance than a random walk. This means that an increase in values will most likely be followed by an increase in the short term and a decrease in values will most likely be followed by another decrease in the short term. A persistent time series has long memory effects and the larger the H value the stronger the trend.

In short, when Markov process scales with Hurst exponent $H \neq 1/2$ then it simply means that the process has non-stationary increments (path dependence). But many financial models simply ignore the dependency structure, and assume that the stock returns have zero autocorrelations. This is, for example, in the case of Black–Scholes option pricing model, and in the capital asset pricing model (CAPM), etc. Indeed, most of the classical models assume that the stock prices satisfy "a random walk hypothesis" with independent asset returns. However, starting in 1980's, researches reveal some fascinating dependent structures among asset returns. Additionally, the Hurst exponent is directly related to the fractal dimension, which measures the smoothness of a surface, or, in our case, the smoothness of a time series. The relationship between the fractal dimension *D*, and the Hurst Exponent *H*, is given by:

$$D = 2 - H \tag{3}$$

where, $0 < H < 1$.

But there are cases when H is higher or smaller than 1. So, when $H > 1$ the surface is no longer asymptotically flat, and when $H < 0$ the roughness distribution of the surface is referred to as fractional noise.

The term fractal was coined by Benot Mandelbrot in 1975, from the Latin fractious or fraction/ broken.

Definition 1: A Fractal is a geometric shape that is self-similar and has fractional dimensions.

Peters (1994), stated that fractal geometry is the geometry of the Demiurge (responsible for the creation of the universe). Unlike Euclidean geometry, it prospers on roughness and symmetry. Objects are infinitely complex. The more closely one examines them, the more detail they reveal. See the example given by Kale and Butar (2011) for a fir tree. They state that a fir tree is a fractal form. It can be visualized as a cone sitting atop a rectangle. Yet, the fir trees are not cones and rectangles. They are a complex network of branches, no branch being the same as any other.

According to Peters (1994), Euclidean geometry cannot replicate a tree. Euclidean geometry recreates the perceived symmetry of the tree, but not the variety that actually builds its structure. Underlying this perceived symmetry is a controlled randomness. This self-similar quality is the defining characteristic of fractals. Euclidean geometry has a primary characteristic that dimensions are integers. For examples, lines are one-dimensional, planes are two-dimensional, and solids are three dimensional. In general, Euclidean shapes are smooth, continuous, and homogeneous. Let us consider a spherical sponge ball. Although it belongs to a three-dimensional space, it has irregularities or holes. It is neither smooth, continuous, or homogeneous. So, it would be fair enough to say that, dimensionally, it is something more than a plane, but less than a solid. Its dimension is somewhere between two and three. It has a non-integer dimension or a fractional dimension.

THE ROLE OF THE HURST EXPONENT IN PREDICTION OF FINANCIAL MARKET ANOMALIES

Singularities are also referred to us as outliers, noise, deviations and exceptions. All of them could affect the investor's behavior. Therefore, the Hurst Exponent (H) for each time series is measured with an intention to access the predictability of a time series and alert investors to emerging crises and trends, if possible. In this section, I will calculate the Hurst Exponent with the intention to discover whether it can be used as an indicator for future price patterns. This is of great importance for the investors to adopt their buy-sell-hold strategy timely.

In our experiment, H was calculated using the returns of the previous 30 trading days. So, beginning January 1th, 2016, a time series of daily Hurst exponents, using data from the previous 30 days, was created. The idea behind this calculation is to discover price patterns.

The first task is to perform the distribution test analysis. The result is in Table 2.

According to the performed tests in the period 6.2016-7.2016 S&P500 index returns do not follow the normal distribution, since $p<0.5$. In all other periods, we can accept the normality hypothesis, since $p>0.5$. This can be also shown graphically, see Figure 6, 7, 8 and 9. Here we display the histogram along with the standard normal density function, of the daily returns of S&P500 stock index by month.

Table 2. Distribution Test by Month

Test type	p-Value, Period 3.2016-4.2016	p-Value, Period 4.2016-5.2016	p-Value, Period 5.2016-6.2016	p-Value, Period 6.2016-7.2016
Anderson-Darling	0.320199	0.747569	0.320199	0.026761*
Cramer-von Mises	0.411668	0.859112	0.411668	0.027024*
Jarue- Bera ALM	0.087513	0.923322	0.087513	0.007068*
Kolmogorov-Smirnov	0.441062	0.868666	0.441062	0.019942*
Kuiper	0.297508	0.789257	0.297508	0.018070*
Mardia Combined	0.087513	0.923322	0.087513	0.007068*
Mardia Kurtosis	0.192000	0.593505	0.192000	0.010615*
Mardia Skewness	0.947549	0.954994	0.947549	0.016702*
Pearson χ^2	0.056712	0.342547	0.056712	0.043604*
Shapiro-Wilk	0.376401	0.637031	0.376401	0.012357*
Watson U^2	0.388794	0.881469	0.388798	0.028115*

Note: if $p < 0.05$ reject the Ho = the data follow the normal distribution.

Figure 6. Norma (distribution fit, p>0.5(3.2106-4.2016)

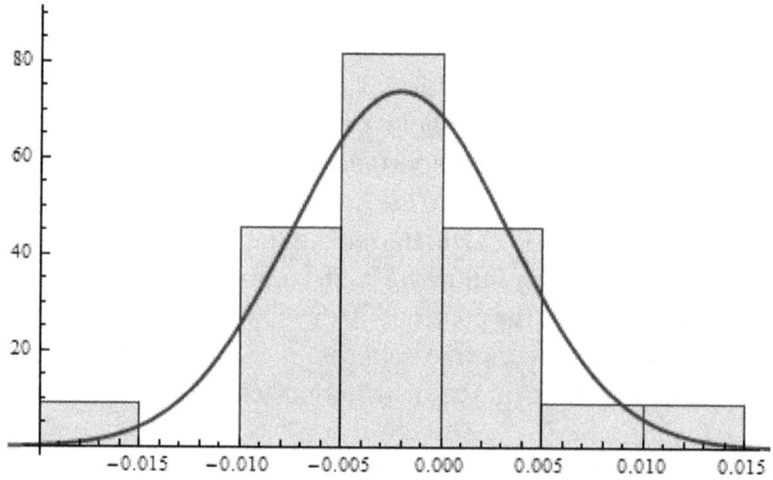

Now we can estimate the Hurst exponent and plot the correlation function. As in previous analysis, we use Wolfram Mathematica Programming Language to perform needed analysis. Full code is given in the Appendix I.

In probability theory, fractional Brownian motion (fBm) is a generalization of Brownian motion. Unlike classical Brownian motion, the increments of fBm need not be independent. Fractional Brownian motion is a continuous-

Figure 7. Normal distribution fit, p>0.5(4.2016-5.2016)

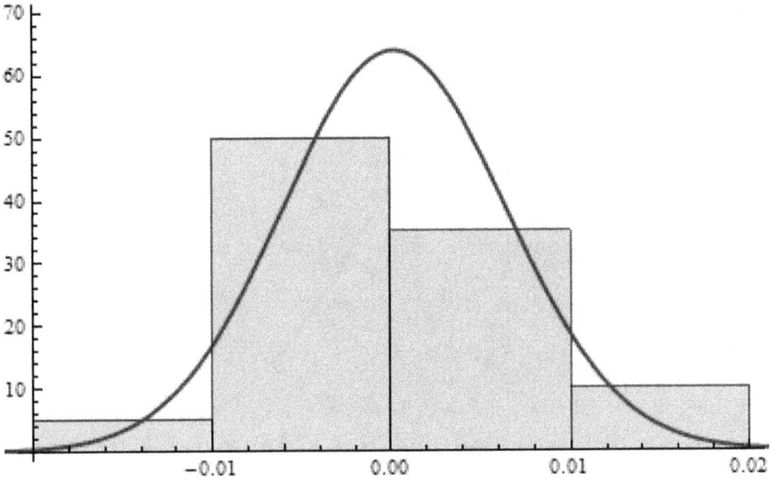

Figure 8. Normal distribution fit, p>0.5 (5.2016-6.2016)

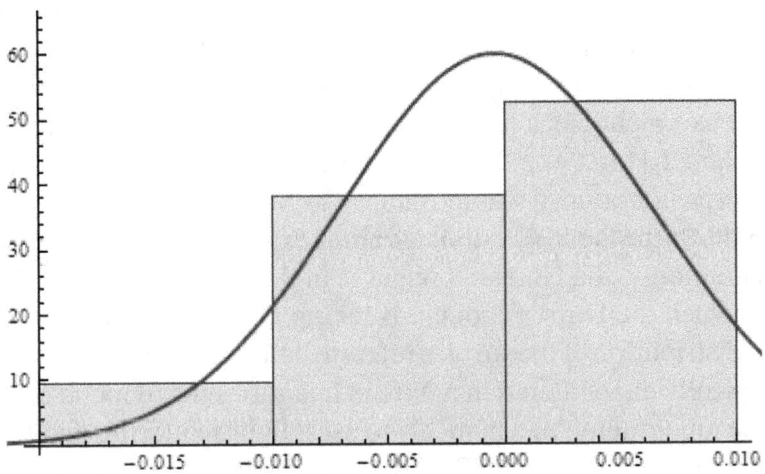

time Gaussian process which starts at zero, has expectation zero for all t in [0, T], and has the following covariance function.

$$E\left[B_H\left(s\right)B_H\left(t\right)\right] = \frac{1}{2}\left(\left|t\right|^{2H} + \left|s\right|^{2H} - \left|t-s\right|^{2H}\right) \tag{4}$$

Figure 9. Fat-tailed distribution, p<0.5 (6.2016-7.2016)

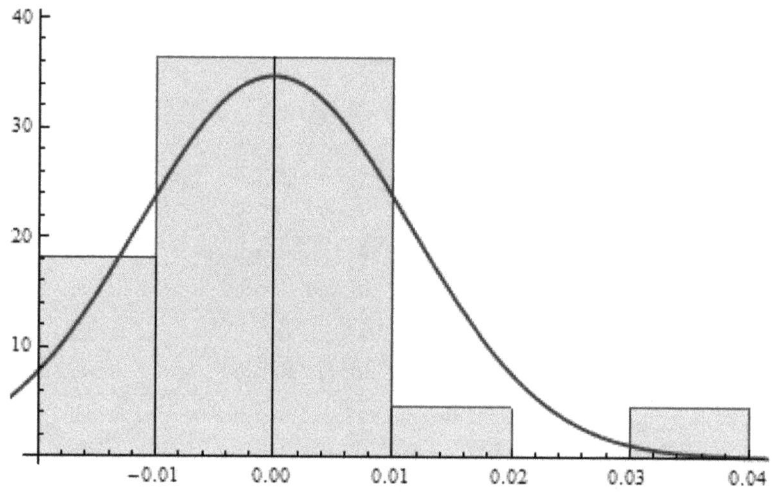

Here *H* is a real number between (0, 1), called the Hurst index or Hurst parameter associated with the fractional Brownian motion for all s, t $\in$ [0, T]. The fractal dimension provides an indication of how rough a surface is and is directly related to the Hurst exponent for a statistically self-similar data set. A small Hurst exponent has a higher fractal dimension and a rougher surface/motion. A larger Hurst exponent has a smaller fractional dimension and a smoother surface/motion. It was introduced by Mandelbrot & van Ness (1968).

Table 3 shows the monthly estimated Hurst exponents for the S&P500 index.

Most commonly, the Hurst exponent is in the interval $0 \leq H \leq 1$. But we have cases when the Hurst exponent is taking a negative value, $H < 0$. This roughness distribution of the surface refers to us as fractional noise. Fractional noise is typically encountered in nature in quantities that depend on the local slope of the topography: mechanical stresses, light scattering and fluid flow (Vandembroucq and Roux, 1997). From the Table 3, we can see that in our

Table 3. Hurst Exponents by Month

Date	Hurst exponent (H)
03.2016-04.2016	0.0034
04.2016-05.2016	-0.32404
05.2016-06.2016	-0.49
06.2016-07.2016	0.289

situation, the H is negative in the period from April through June. Something is roughening the finance market surface, because most investors are looking at the same time horizon. During this period, we can conclude that the markets are not efficient. Hurst exponent H would be decreasing shortly before the turbulent times in the market. After this period the values will tend to revert to a mean and Hurst exponent will start increasing.

Now let us see what was actually happening. On June 26th, 2016 it was announced, that the United Kingdom EU referendum (the "Brexit" vote) will take place. It was expected to create significant market volatility, including significant price gaps and periods of illiquidity.

This example shows us that the Hurst exponent (H) is good at detecting the presence of fractal noise, but not the singularities. Meaning, investors cannot timely adapt their buy-sell-hold strategy, looking only at the Hurst exponent.

In short, Hurst exponent cannot be used to predict the future price patterns, but we can draw another equally important conclusion from this analysis: "as the wind is roughening the surface of the river, something is roughening the stock market surface". It is evident that the stock market surface is not smooth (flat).

THE EFFECT OF SURFACE

Borrowing terms and methodologies from other scientific field is not considered as a crime. Crime is not explaining them well enough, as Albert Einstein said: "If you can't explain it simply, you don't understand it well enough." This was my biggest concern. How to explain the effect of surface, the frequently used terms in econometric analysis as time independent and time dependent variables, and their interconnections. Then I come across a very simple example given in the Whetheral (2013) book. It goes like this:

First, imagine you are standing on a city sidewalk like a grid. Try to picture what would happen if you did a clockwise one direction-north (the direction you are facing, here, is taking the place of an arrow). You might begin by walking forward for a while as you head uptown. When you get to the next corner, you would dead right, east on the crosstown street. But you aren't allowed to turn your body at the corner, since you are trying to walk sideways down the cross street. And when you get to the next corner, where you should start heading south again, you have to walk backward. If you follow these instructions, never once turning your body as you do the lap, you should find yourself back at the original corner looking in just the same direction as before. But now let's imagine a longer journey. Instead of doing a lap around the block, imagine trying to keep yourself pointed in the same direction as you circumnavigate the globe. There are two possible paths around a sphere, see Figure 10. The first path takes the arrow from point A around the equator and back to point A. At the end of the trip, the arrow faces the same direction as when it began. The second trip again starts at point A and travels around the equator, but only halfway. On the other side of the sphere, the path moves up over the North pole and returns to point A that way. At the end of this trip, the arrow is pointing in the opposite direction from when the trip began. The reason you end up facing in a different direction after your second round–the –world trip is that the globe is a curved surface. A city block, meanwhile, is flat, because you do not see the effects of this curvature over short distance.

Let us now go back to our case of study. What we know-or what are our discoveries related to the finance market volatility surface. Looking in the Hurst exponent, which is also a measure of the smoothness of a surface, one can conclude that the market return surface is not flat, and therefore we cannot talk about time independence. Meaning, stock market returns do not evolve according to the random walk theories. But this does not mean that the traditional technical analysis, the time domain models is more accurate.

Remember, financial markets are complex systems continually changing through time, and adapting to the new market situation. So up to now, I understand that:

- The surface is not flat.

Figure 10. Possible Paths Around a Sphere

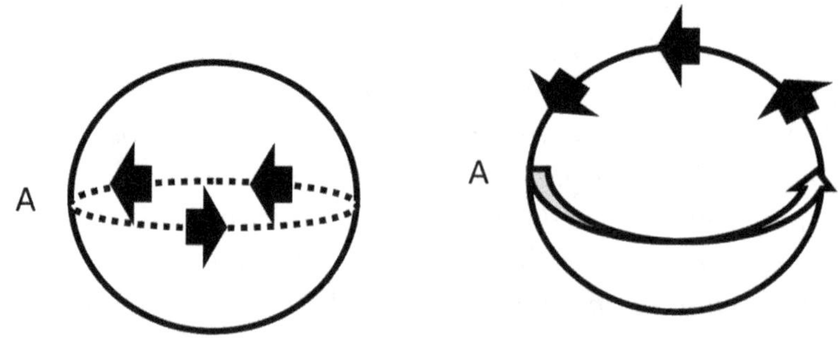

- Time dependent properties exist-history of asset prices plays a significant role.
- Hurst exponent can't detect financial market singularities.
- Anomalies/singularities are not random.
- Future pattern can be predicted.

Isn't this enough to realize that traditional techniques are not modelling the real complex financial dynamics? What are we waiting for more proofs. Why do the economists not want to take up the role of scientists?

We will not go into details, but it is more than obvious that we have a problem.

A NEW METHODOLOGICAL APPROACH

Science is a willingness to accept facts, even when they are opposed to the wishes. Thoughtful men have perhaps always known that we are likely to see things as we want to see them instead of as they are, but thanks to Sigmund Freud we are today much more clearly aware of "wishful thinking." The opposite of wishful thinking is intellectual honesty—an extremely important possession of the successful scientist. Scientists are by nature no more honest than other men, but, as Bridgman has pointed out, the practice of science puts an exceptionally high premium on honesty. It is characteristic of science that any lack of honesty quickly brings disaster (B. F. Skinner, Science and Human Behavior, (New York: Free Press, 1953, p. 12).

When I speak to my colleges for the new methodological approaches, I can feel their pain, anger and ignorance. It is not easy to accept facts which are against your wishes, especially not when you are passionately in love in every branch of economics. But we desperately need the second Renaissance in the economic theory. Instead of spending our time in worshiping and blindly defending mainstream theories we must leave them in the past and start developing and applying new methodologies. We need to make fundamental changes in our empirical analysis. Instead, starting our analysis with the model and then apply the data, we should look into the data first. Let the data, create the model. This is the only valid formula for continued scientific progress, which unfortunately lacks in economic theory in its entirety.

Math really works. For example, the trend following models were great in the 60s, 70s and early 80s. Not today. We are all aware of this fact, the only difference is that some of us admit it and go a step forward and some of us use it as an opportunity to defend the random walk theories which are at the heart of the Efficient Market Hypothesis (EMH).

I always supported and admired the first group of people. The same moment when I understand that the answer for pattern recognition cannot be found neither in the random walk theories, nor in the traditional used technical analysis I decided to go back and start from the beginning. This is the approach that helped me to find my answers. When I finished my novel methodology for pattern detection and put the algorithm on its testing road, I noticed that for data after 80s results were more than impressive. I was able to detect the trend, the magnitude of the price change, hoarding effect and noise traders entering into the market. But for data before 80s the algorithm failed to detect this price pattern. I was really confused. After a few more tests, I understood that there should be some event that made the market to adapt and change its behavior. Something is roughening the surface.

Let me summarize my findings once more to make it more understandable. Standard technical analysis (time domain analysis) was great before the 80s. Suddenly the results that we get are not so accurate. Knowing the fact that nothing is random-everything is happening for a reason, I start searching for an event in the period of 70s and early 80s that can be considered as an initial capsule for this change.

I found my answer in the *algorithmic trading*, today recognized as high frequency trading. They are automated trading platforms that executes buy and sell orders based on an algorithmic computer program. It's a type of trading strategy implemented by large financial firms, such as hedge funds, pension funds and investment banks, that allows them to trade millions of shares every day in transactions that often last less than a second. Investment houses began using these techniques in the 1970s and '80s to guide trades. As the personal computer revolution extended in the '80s and '90s, their proprietary techniques were adopted more broadly.

Remember, these trading algorithms are making the patterns after the 80s. They do not break fractals; they increase market efficiency. So, I applied a methodology which has the mathematical power to analyze these new created patterns and fractals. The algorithm successfully detected:

- The fixed, stable point (the price is fluctuating around its fixed stable point)

- The time when most of the investors settle same investment strategy (group thinking, hoarding effect)
- Detecting the entrance of noise traders/speculators
- Detecting both hoarding effect and noise traders in some time
- Magnitude of price change
- The pattern of the short-run price fluctuation

Now, whether I am the first that discovered this methodology? I really don't think so. I truly believe that large financial institutions in the recent years are using this technique in their in-depth analysis. I also believe that Jim Simons is among the first, who applied them in practice, whit his Renaissance Technologies hedge fund. Just to remind you, his specialty is the study of curved surfaces and spaces.

What about the academic world?

To prevent their extensive use in practice, the published papers related to these methodologies are incomplete (Struzik, 2001; Vidal, 2014; Blackledge, 2010; Kristoufek, 2013). As they are, they cannot be used for pattern detection or even more important as an investment signalling model.

Therefore, the most typical "pattern finding" techniques today are still those of watching the moving averages along with current stock prices to detect trends as they emerge. Most online brokers and trading software come equipped with tools to analyze such trends. From an investors standpoint, this is a bad thing since all this information is essentially public, and so methods using this metric are less likely to yield big profits. Along the same line of thought, the more advanced technique, the less known it is to the average trader. One such advanced technique will be proposed in the section that follows.

A HISTORY OF COMPLEX DYNAMICS

"The world is full of systems which are trying to reach an optimum which does not exist, and consequently they evolve towards structures which are complicated at all scales. This happens in threes, which try to maximize their exposure to light, for the lungs and capillaries, which try to maximize the interface between tissue and blood. The great work of Mandelbrot has been to tell, very loudly and in a very convincing way, that the world is full of complicated phenomena, of complicated objects having structure at all scales." (John Hubbard)

Here I will set my focus on complex dynamics, an area that was around for about one hundred years ago and continues to inspire much ongoing research. Dynamics system theory is an area of mathematics used to describe the behavior of physical systems over time. In particular, the dynamics are mostly related to Newton' law of motion and gravitation, which was introduced in the late 17th century. Let us consider first a particular Newtonian model for the motion of the planets in our solar system. Here the mathematical system is a collection of variables corresponding to the location, and velocity of each of the planets relative to the sun, and this system change over time according to Newton's laws of motion. So, it turns out that, one can describe the dynamics by which the system evolves by ordinary differential equations relating all the system variables to each other and to Newton's laws of motion (Stankewitz and Rolf, 2012). Indeed, Newton very intentionally defined the functions in a Euclidean space, and his model has much in common with a conventional axiomatic system such as Euclidean geometry. Here, knowing the initial state of the system, we often try to analyze the equations which describe how the system variables change over time in order to the answer such questions as: What will the state of the system be tomorrow, next week, month or year? Will small changes or errors in our knowledge of the initial state only lead to small changes or errors in the system at some future time, or will it lead to huge errors in the future? Will the system in the long run settle into equilibrium, known as a stable state of equilibrium? These are exactly how the dynamics of the financial system are understood and described. Moving average models, are broadly used in finance to detect a market trend.

Another important fact that is inevitable to stress is that in physics, up until the beginning of the 20th century, Newton's theory of motion was thought to be telling the story of every particle in the Universe. Today it is known that this is not the case. The modern view is that Newton's theory in only an approximation which is valid under certain circumstances, and non-linear systems are well known to exhibit complex dynamics, ranging from stable to unstable periodic motions and chaotic behavior, under different conditions.

Unfortunately, we cannot witness this awaking in the economics. History doesn't repeat itself, as the followers of technical analysis want to believe. The chaotic systems do not remember what happened, for example 2 years ago. What if the financial system exhibits complex dynamics?

At the beginning of my journey in finding the patterns and equations, I had this impression that we deliberately neglect the facts, and the only logical explanation to me was that the answer to this question for sure has much larger implications. It is true when they say some journeys do not have endings, they lead to new beginnings. These are the journeys that lead to great adventures!

Here, I will share just a part of my great adventure and leave you to decide whether you will believe it or not. We must not forget that sometimes we see what we wish to see.

My personal belief for some time is that that science, art and theology mingle into one, and the occurrence of some shapes, methods in art and theology has for sure some broader meaning. Today I can say that I set my research on the real path and the answer to my question: 'how we can model and predict future paths in financial markets?' was found in the Eastern art and architecture. To be more precise, Islamic, Buddhist, Hindu and Jewish art and architecture.

It is discovered that there is a close relationship between the fractal geometry and some basic concepts in the Eastern architecture. It is also discovered that the occurrence of fractal geometry with its self-similarity property in the Eastern architecture has some goals, and eastern religions in order to express their thoughts, used to show their own faith as iconic image and got closer to nature and its rules.

Let me remind you of the Euclidian geometry and postulates. Euclid believed that the space is homogenous, does not have holes or boundaries (2th postulate) and that the space is flat (5th postulate). The theory fails in regions of space which are sufficiently curved that the propositions of Euclidean geometry do not hold to a good approximation.

What is more, the key concept of many statistical pattern recognition methods is the distance. Because its unrealistically scale dependents, in Euclidian geometry world the apparent texture of the form changes as the scale changes. Regardless of the evident complexity of nature, even with changing the scale, it remains constant. This principle is used in topographic maps to represent large objects in a small sheet of paper, or a screen. But natural forms express behavior, independent of scale. With increased scale, details are increased, so their apparent texture will remain constant. More details of the components are always there to be seen, but we are not able to see them with the naked eye. Distance as one of the two fundamental types of measurement in the Euclidian geometry, is held as constant regardless of the scale, and relatively small changes will occur with the scale change. Contrarily, in fractal geometry, the distance is changing with scale, but its apparent texture remains constant.

Now we can say, that Eastern art is not the art of decoration, as some of us want to say. I share Critchlow (1976) view, that Easter art is created to lead the viewer to an understanding of the underlying reality. But then Why we still use Euclidian geometry in pattern recognition models?

The answer is very simple, Euclidian geometry:

- Build the Western civilization.
- Is considered as a precursor to the Catholic mathematics.
- Is the base of the Renaissance art.

To be more specific, the Catholic Church believed that Euclidian geometry will help us to understand the underlying reality. Look at the Samuel Edgerton explanation written in 1976 in his book titled "The Renaissance Rediscovery of Linear Perspective":

Even before the twelfth century the early church fathers suspected that they might discover in Euclidian geometry God's very thinking process. Geometric line perspective was quickly accepted in western Europe after the fifteenth century because Christians wanted to believe that when they beheld such an image in art, they were perceiving a replica of some essential, underlying structure of reality that God had conceived at the moment of creation.

Renaissance artist used Euclid's Optics in their own work on linear perspective. They used it to create an illusion of depth on a flat surface. The development of linear perspective is one of the most monumental advances in Renaissance art.

A group of Tuscan artists including Filippo Brunelleschi, Leon Battista Alberti, and Leonard DA Vinci are considered as the founders of the Renaissance. They first incorporated linear perspective into their practice and teaching. What is more, in 1435 and 1436, Alberti stimulated painters to learn geometry. He taught them that they must learn geometry if they wanted to be successful. In his book, he even interpreted the basic Euclidean definition of point, line, and plane, and then proposed a simple geometric optical formula for laying out a perspective picture, perhaps a simplified codification of Brunelleschi's method. Another no less important Renaissance painters that used this linear perspective in their art are Michelangelo, Raphael, Titian, Botticelli and Donatello.

Today all the Renaissance pieces are viewed as a great work of art, but at the time they were seen as something much bigger: the replica of reality that God had regarded.

No wonder why Jim Simons named his hedge fund Renaissance. He knew that the space is not flat and therefore, liner perspective is not picturing the reality. By him fractals are real Renaissance.

Now let us go back to science. In historical mathematics, the idea of self-similarity was first introduced in 1967 by Benoit Mandelbrot, when he was analyzing the shape of the British coast. Well, maybe not discovered, but finally put into words. He explained them as being geometric shapes that when divided into parts, each part would be a smaller replica of the whole shape. He came up with the term "fractal" as the new scientific term for this mathematical expression, a Latin word that means "broken" or "fractured". In 1975, he pioneered many researches on Fractal and illustrated the mathematical definition of self-similarity.

Fractal geometry can be seen as a universal language by which nature can be explained or at least described and quantified. Financial markets are one of them. In what follows we show how self-similarity can be detected by the Discrete Wavelet Transform (DWT) and Continuous Wavelet Transform (CWT); as well as how Wavelet Transform Modules Maxima (WTMM) is used to detect fractal dimension of a signal (singularities).

TIME SERIES MODELS

Perhaps the most commonly encountered data types analysis are time series, touching almost every aspect of human life, including finance. One can categorize methods to analyze and model time-series into:

- Time domain.
- Frequency domain.
- Time frequency domain approach.

Time domain refers to the variation of the amplitude of signal to time; how the signal changes over time. As the most widely used models from this group are ARMA, ARIMA, GARCH and ARCH. It is important to remember that ARMA and ARIMA are methods to linear model the data and the forecast remains constant because the model does not reflect recent changes or incorporate new information. In other words, it provides best linear forecasts for the series, and thus plays little role in forecasting model nonlinearity. In practice ARIMA is often used together with ARCH/GARCH model. ARCH/GARCH is method to model the noise term of ARIMA model. It incorporates new information and analyses the series based on conditional variance where users can forecast future values with up to date information. The forecast interval for the mixture model is closer than that of the ARIMA only model.

For example, consider a typical heartbeat analysis with ECG approach. If the doctor maps the heartbeat with time, say the recording is done for 60 minutes, we call it a time domain signal. However, as in ECG a number of peaks or variations in amplitude occur so in frequency domain, over the entire time period of recording, how many times each peak comes is recorded. This is the frequency domain approach, where the frequency is nothing but the number of times each event has occurred. In this group, we have the fast Fourier transform (FFT) analysis.

The FFT converts waveform data in the time domain into the frequency domain, by breaking down the original time-based waveform into a series of sinusoidal terms, each with a unique magnitude, frequency, and phase. This process converts a waveform in the time domain that is difficult to describe mathematically in a more manageable series of sinusoidal functions that when added together, exactly reproduce the original waveform. Such an operation is graphically illustrated in Figure 11.

Plotting the amplitude of each sinusoidal term versus its frequency creates a power spectrum, which is the response of the original waveform in the frequency domain. Here, the height of the peak represents the amplitude of

Figure 11. Illustration of the Fourier Transform of a Continuous Signal. Source: Wavelet Theory and Application for Manufacturing by Gao & Yan, 2011.

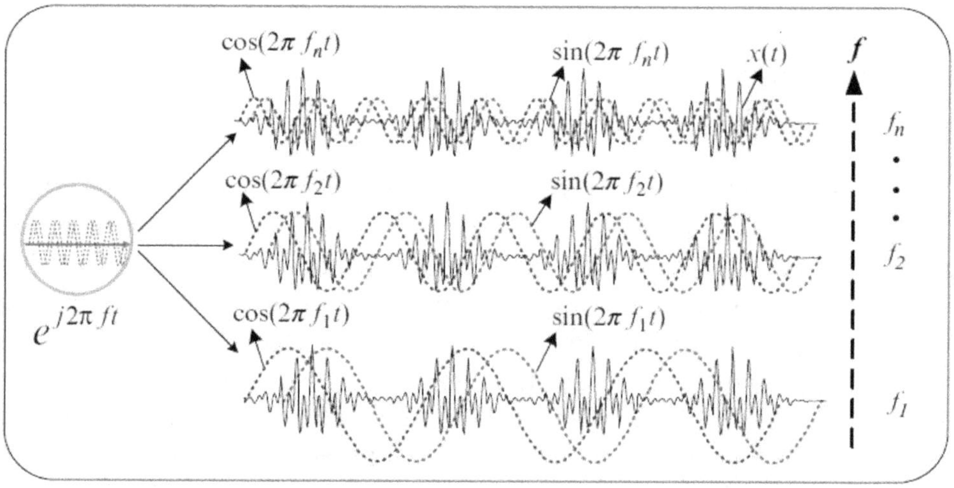

Figure 12. Relationship Between Time, Frequency, and Amplitude. Source: Advanced Spectral Analysis, Pete Bechard. PdMA Corporation

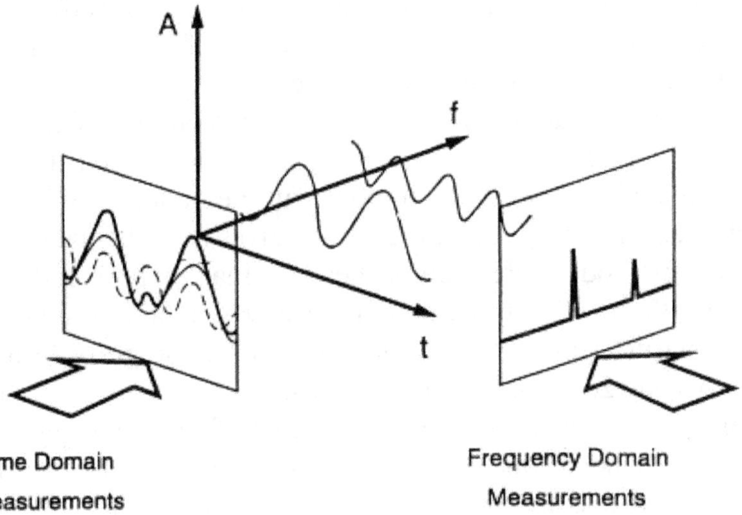

Figure 13. Schematic Overview of the Different Methodological Approaches. Source: "Diagnostic and Experimental Applications of Cortico-Muscular and Intramuscular Frequency Analysis," by Pascal Gross, 2004

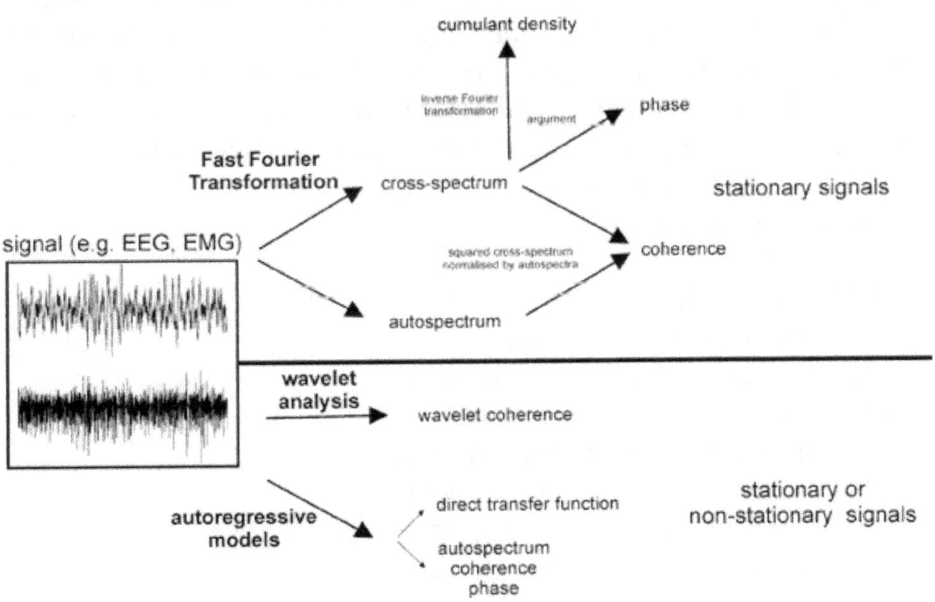

the signal. Figure 12 shows the relationship between the time domain (t), the frequency domain (f), and amplitude (A).

This approach was introduced for the first time back in 1807 by the French mathematician Joseph Fourier. However, because of the rigid objections from some of his colleagues, such as Lagrange, his paper never got published, until some 15 years later in his own book "The Analytical Theory of Heat".

Because the FFT approach carries no time information, frequency and time domain analysis based on the powerful methodology of Wavelets has become increasingly important. Figure 13, gives the schematic overview of the different methodological approaches to signal analysis in the frequency domain. Note that the FFT based model can only be applied to signals assumed to be stationary whereas wavelet analysis and autoregressive models can additionally analyze non-stationary signals.

Therefore, in the upcoming sections, we will focus on the use of Wavelet in analyzing financial time series. I believe that wavelet-based modelling underlies the process that generates financial market data. It is a method that decomposes a time series into several layers of time series, making it possible to analyze how the local variance, or wavelet power, changes both in the frequency and time domain. From a historical point of view, the first reference to the wavelet goes back to the early 20th century, when Alfred Haar wrote his dissertation titled "On the theory of the orthogonal functional systems" in 1909 to obtain his doctoral degree at the University of Gottingen. His research led to the development of a set of rectangular basis functions. Later, an entire wavelet family - the Haar wavelet, was named on the basis of this set of functions, and it is also the simplest wavelet family developed till this date. If we summarize the history of wavelet analysis, we will get the following chronological table:

- 1910, Haar families.
- 1981, Morlet, wavelet concept.
- 1984, Morlet and Grossman, "wavelet".
- 1985, Meyer, "orthogonal wavelet".
- 1987, International conference in France.
- 1988, Mallat and Meyer, multi resolution.
- 1988, Daubechies, compact support orthogonal wavelet.
- 1989, Mallat, fast wavelet transform.

Figure 14. Different Types of Mother Wavelets

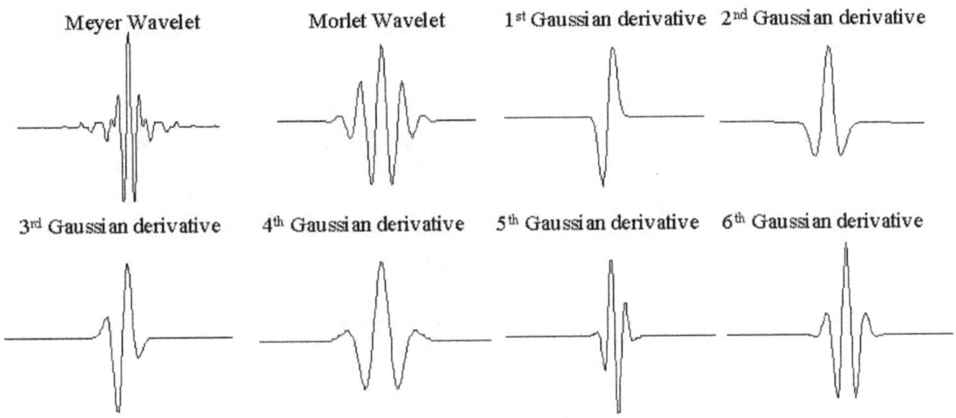

WAVELETS

In comparison to the Fourier transform, the analyzing function of the wavelet transform can be chosen with more freedom, without the need of using sine-forms. A wavelet function ψ (t) is a small wave, also known as mother wavelet, which must be oscillatory in some way to differentiate it between different frequencies. The wavelet contains both the analysis shape and the window. Figure 14 shows some of the most popular mother wavelets.

In this analysis, we apply the Morlet wavelet to detect high and low data frequencies. Unlike sines and cosines, localized in both time and frequency. The process starts with choosing a Morlet wavelet function with a certain weight (s). The frequency domain representation of the Morlet wavelet is

$$\psi_{0(n)} = \pi^{-1/4} e^{i\omega_0 \eta} e^{-\eta^2/2} \tag{5}$$

where *Psi* $\left(\psi_{0(n)}\right)$ is the wavelet value at non-dimensional time *eta*(η), and ω_0 is the wave number that controls the non-dimensional frequency; the number of oscillations within the Gaussian envelope, and is set equal to six to satisfy the admissibility criteria as analytic wavelet (see Lee and Yammamot 1994; and Adisson 2002).

Then slide it over the financial time series and calculate for every point in time (n) the scalar product, as shown in Figure 15.

Figure 15. Morlet wavelet and financial time series

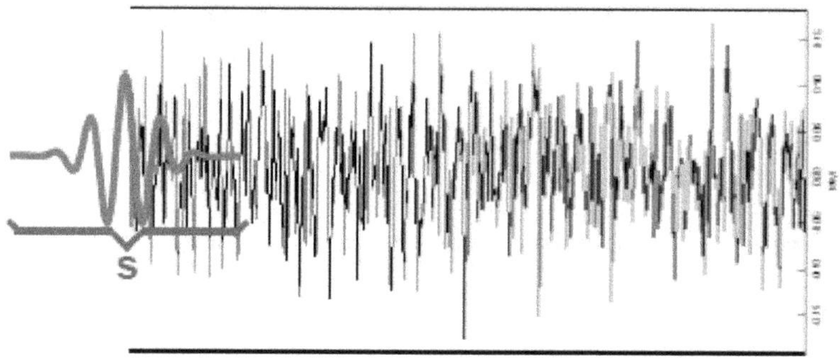

Figure 16. Detecting low and high frequency data

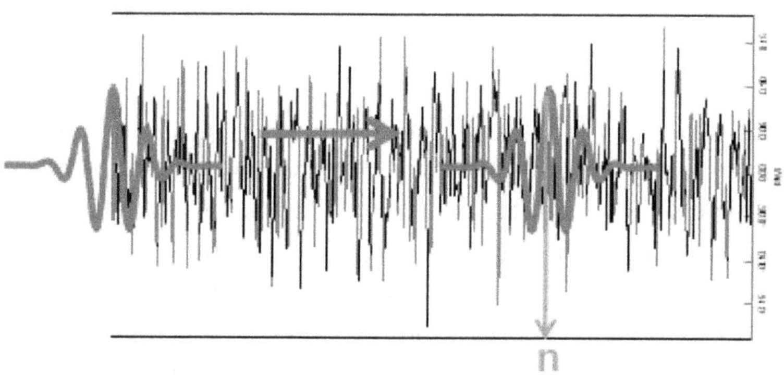

Do this for several different values of the scale(s), see Figure 16. For every point in time (n) we get all considered scales (s). This is an indicator for certain events within the series.

But before we proceed with our analysis, we need to eliminate signal noise. The de-noising process consists of decomposing the original signal, thresholding the detail coefficients, and reconstructing the signal. The decomposition portion of our de-noising example is accomplished via the discrete wavelet transform (DWT). I have picked Biorthogonal Spline Wavelet [3, 3], 4 as analyzing wavelet, with a four-level decomposition. We could have elected to perform more levels of decomposition, as the more levels we chose to decompose our signal, the more detail coefficients we get. But for de-noising our signal in this example, a four-level decomposition provides sufficient noise reduction.

Now we can apply the continuous wavelet transform (CTW) to the de-noised signal, using the Morlet Wavelet, by the equation 6 given below

$$W_n(s) = \sum_{n'=0}^{N-1} x_{n'} * \psi^* \left[\frac{(n' - n)\delta t}{s} \right] \tag{6}$$

where Psi(ψ) is the wavelet kernel function along with the continuous scaling parameter s and time shifting parameter n.

Since the wavelet function is complex, so is the wavelet transform $W_n(s)$. Therefore, we plot the square of the absolute value $|W_n(s)|^2$, power spectrum, see Figure 17.

According to a fractal market hypothesis (FMH) the read marked regions in the power spectrum are associated with the group thinking, or hoarding effect, i.e. most of the investors set some investment strategy. Thus, high power spectrum values should be observed at low time scales associated with high frequencies during periods of high volatility. Moreover, the yellow marked

Figure 17. DJIA Index Power Spectrum
Note: *The red color represents the high frequency data and the blue color low frequency data*

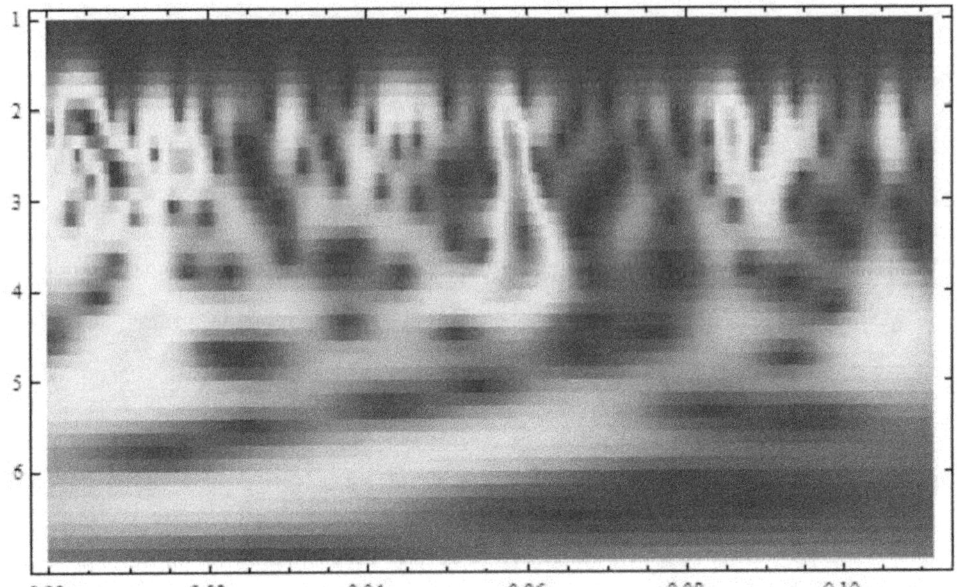

**For a more accurate representation of this figure, please see the electronic version.*

regions observed at high time scales (after scale 5) are associated with the occurrence of noise traders, or speculators. More details will be given in the numerical section.

A NUMERICAL ILLUMINATION: WAVELET ANALYSIS

A time series for the Don Jones Industrial Average (DJIA) index return will be analyzed to find their respective wavelet power spectrum and detected market irregularities (singularities). Financial markets are not always stable. Thus, if we can detect the time when the market is unstable, as well as the type of the singularity we can forecast the expected price paths in the short run.

The data used for this study was obtained from the finance data platform from Yahoo website, a search engine with access to a large collection of financial data sets. Wolfram Mathematica 9 and MatLab R2016b are used for the analysis.

Figure 18. Fractal Pattern

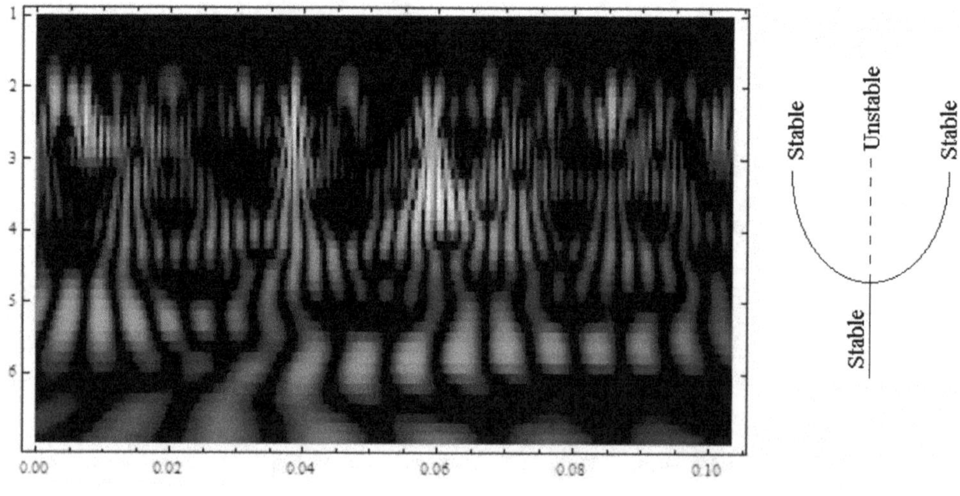

**For a more accurate representation of this figure, please see the electronic version.*

FRACTAL MARKET HYPOTHESIS AND SELF-SIMILARITY

Today we still observe the dynamics of the financial markets with Euclidian axioms. These axioms in finance unfortunately, or fortunately depending, on how you look at it, do not resemble reality. Let me remind you once more, Euclidian geometry is a false representation of the real-life processes, and the financial markets are one of them.

Financial markets are fractal and exhibit self-similar behavior over a finite range of scales. This can be seen in the wavelet scalogram shown in Figure 18. Self-similar curves in the time-frequency plane are visible at first glance. The fractal pattern is present throughout the series, irrespective of scale or wavelet power.

In fact, Figure 18 shows the close connection between chaos and fractals. Fractal mathematics allows us to examine complex, chaotic systems and create more accurate models than those garnered by Random Walk Theory.

DE-TREND FINANCIAL SERIES

The real-world data, known also as time series data, do not exist without noise which can be random, Gaussian white noise, fractal noise, etc. As long as this noise is present in the signal, the analyzed signal may be of very little use. Noise extraction is a difficult task and very often results with incorrect output.

The purpose of the Discrete Transform Wavelet (DTW) de-noising procedure is to extract the noise N (f) from the original received signal with noise SN (f) so that it can be used for further analysis. The signal received SN (f) can be represented as follows,

$$SN(f) = S(f) + N(f) \tag{7}$$

where SN (f) is the original signal with noise, S (f) original signal with no noise, N (f) is the high frequency noise.

Generally, noise is higher in frequency than the original signal. So, if we can remove the high frequency component, we would be able to separate the noise. This can be achieved with DWT method.

DWT can decompose the signal in both time and frequency domain simultaneously. Thus, any frequency y (t) can be decomposed by a sequence of projections into wavelet basis:

$$g_{j,k} = S_{y(t)}\phi_{j,k(t)}dt$$
$$h_{j,k} = S_{y(t)}\psi_{i,k(t)}dt \tag{8}$$

where j represents the number of multi resolution; ϕ is the father wavelet and ψ is the mother wavelet. $gj_{,k}$ and $h_{j,k}$ represent the low frequency and higher frequency coefficient respectively. $\Phi_{j,k}$ and $\psi_{j,k}$ are scaling and translation of ϕ and ψ, defined by

$$\phi_{j,k}(t) = 2^{-\frac{j}{2}}\phi(2^{-j}t - k) = 2^{-\frac{j}{2}}\phi\left(\frac{t - 2^j k}{2^j}\right)$$
$$\psi_{j,k}(t) = 2^{-\frac{j}{2}}\psi(2^{-j}t - k) = 2^{-\frac{j}{2}}\psi\left(\frac{t - 2^j k}{2^j}\right) \tag{9}$$

where $g_{j,k}$ and $h_{j,k}$ are signal representation in the wavelet domain.

The father wavelet and the mother wavelet approximate the low frequency components and the detail high frequency components of the signal, respectively.

The decomposition of a signal using DWT is shown in the Figure 19. Notice that DWT analyses the signal by decomposing the signal into coarse approximation and detail information.

The approximation components are obtained by passing the signal through the low pass filter LPF, or g (n), which removes the high frequency components.

Figure 19. Decomposing the Signal Using DWT

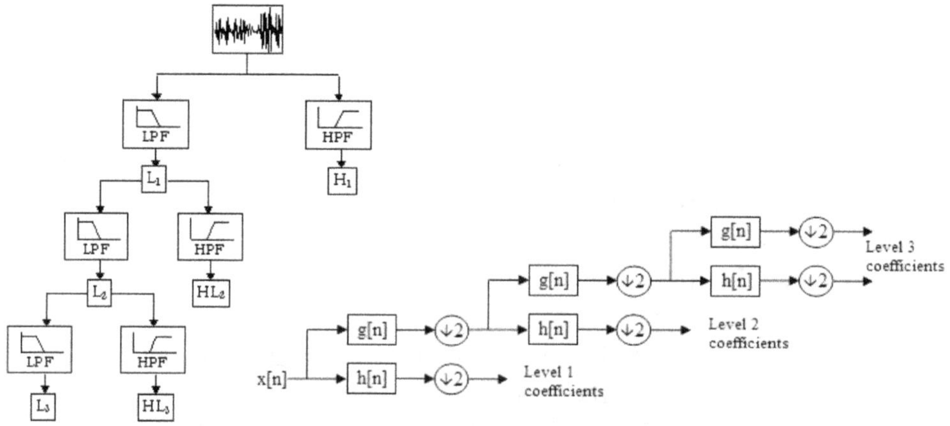

Figure 20. Low- Pass Filter Coefficients

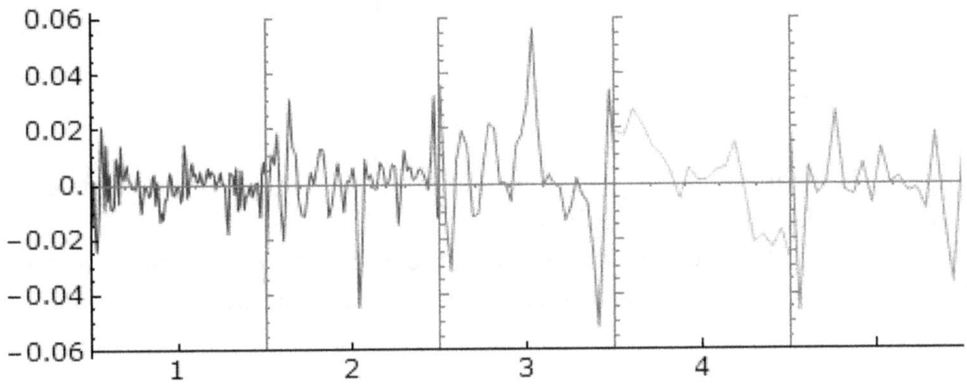

At this stage, the series is split, but the scale remains unchanged. The signal is then sub-sampled, in that way removing half the terminated samples. It should be noted that this process does not affect the series, but affect the scale, which is doubled. Similarly, the detail coefficient is obtained by passing the signal through the high pass filter HPF, or h (n). This constitutes one level of decomposition. The wavelet coefficients accordingly obtained can then be used for the purposes of signal de-noising (see Misiti et al. 2002).

In the DJIA index return analysis, the trend of the series is captured in the low-pass filter coefficients, as shown in Figure 20.

Thresholding all detail coefficients and inverting the series gives the trend, see Figure 21. During the research, it is noticed that both hard and universal thresholding should be used for de-noising.

Figure 21. DJIA Trend

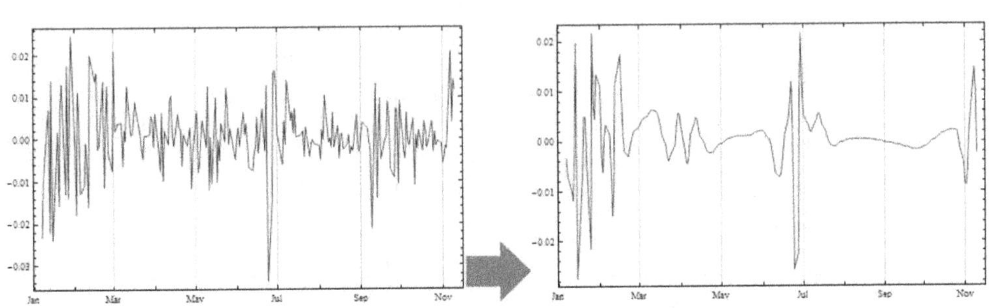

The universal threshold was proposed by Donoho and Johnstone (1995), into their VisuShrink procedure. The universal threshold is:

$$T_{UV} = \sqrt{\left(2logn\right)}\hat{\sigma} \tag{10}$$

where n is the number of data points and $\hat{\sigma}$ is an estimate of the noise level σ and T_{uv} is the universal threshold.

Hard thresholding can be described as the usual process of setting to zero the elements whose absolute values are lower than the threshold or,

$$T_{Hard}\left(x\right) = \begin{Bmatrix} x \left|x\right| & \geq & thr \\ 0 \left|x\right| & < & thr \end{Bmatrix}$$

where "thr" is a threshold value.

From Figure 22, we can notice that hard thresholding can create discontinuities, and thus momentously rate small differences in the transform value whose magnitudes are close the threshold value thr.

In the case of DJIA index the detail coefficients that captured the de-trended series are given in Figure 23.

Now if we want to remove the trend from the original signal, we need to remove the coarse coefficients and inverting, as shown in Figure 24.

Figure 22. Hard threshold signal

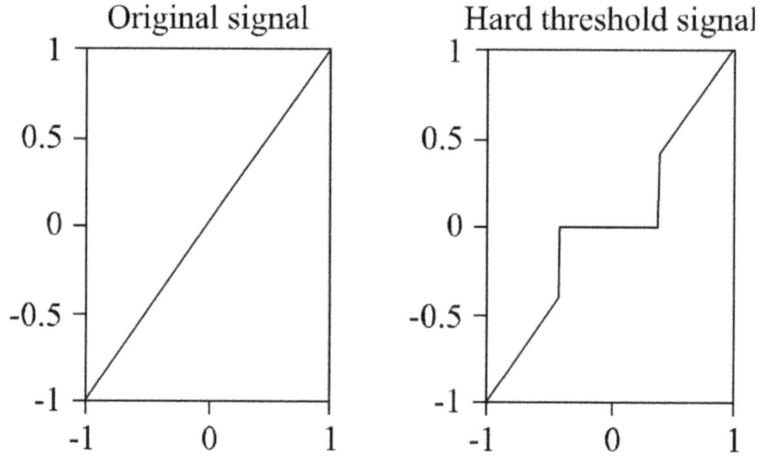

Figure 23. Detail coefficients

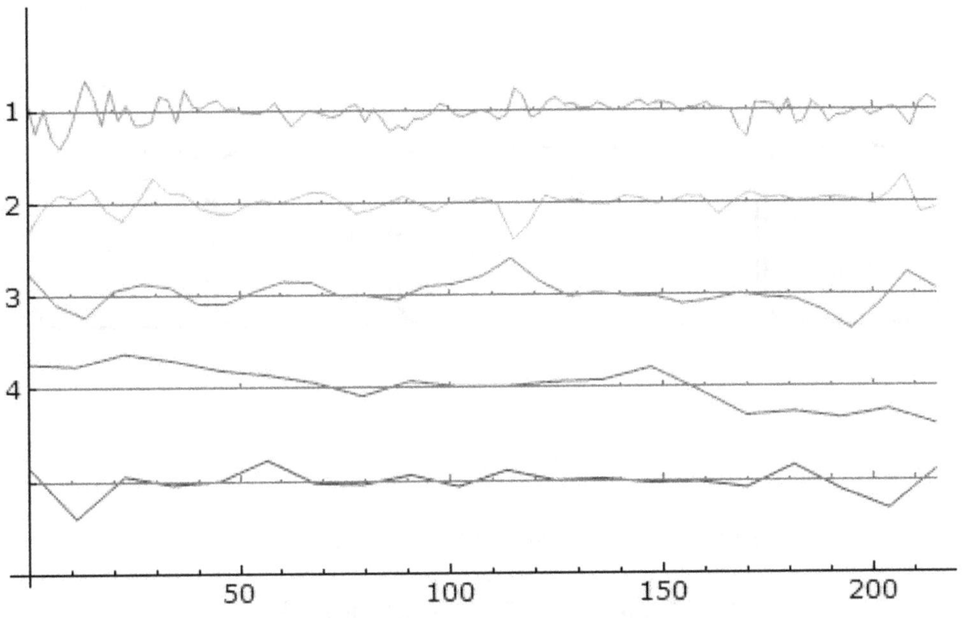

Figure 24. Signal with no trend (noise)

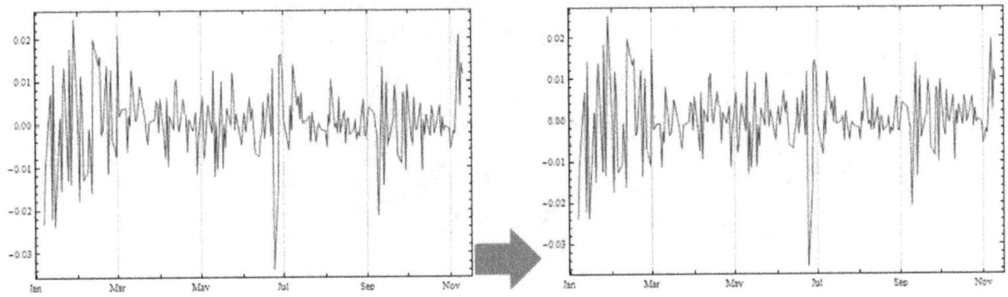

At the end, the graphical representation of de-noising algorithm schema is given (see Figure 25).

CONTINUOUS WAVELET TRANSFORM

The main advantage of using continuous wavelet transform (CWT) in financial time series is its ability to analyze how the wavelet power of the underlying process changes in both the time and frequency domain. Here we will use the

Figure 25. Denosing algorithme schème

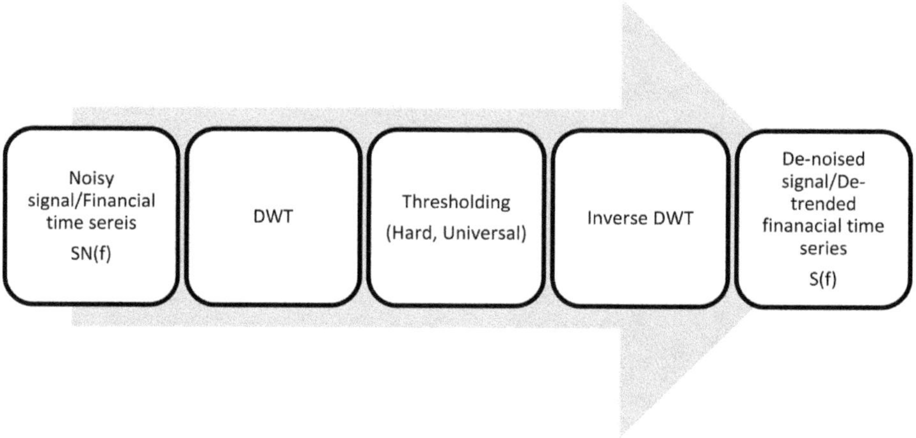

Figure 26. Wavelet Power spectrogram and de-trended signal

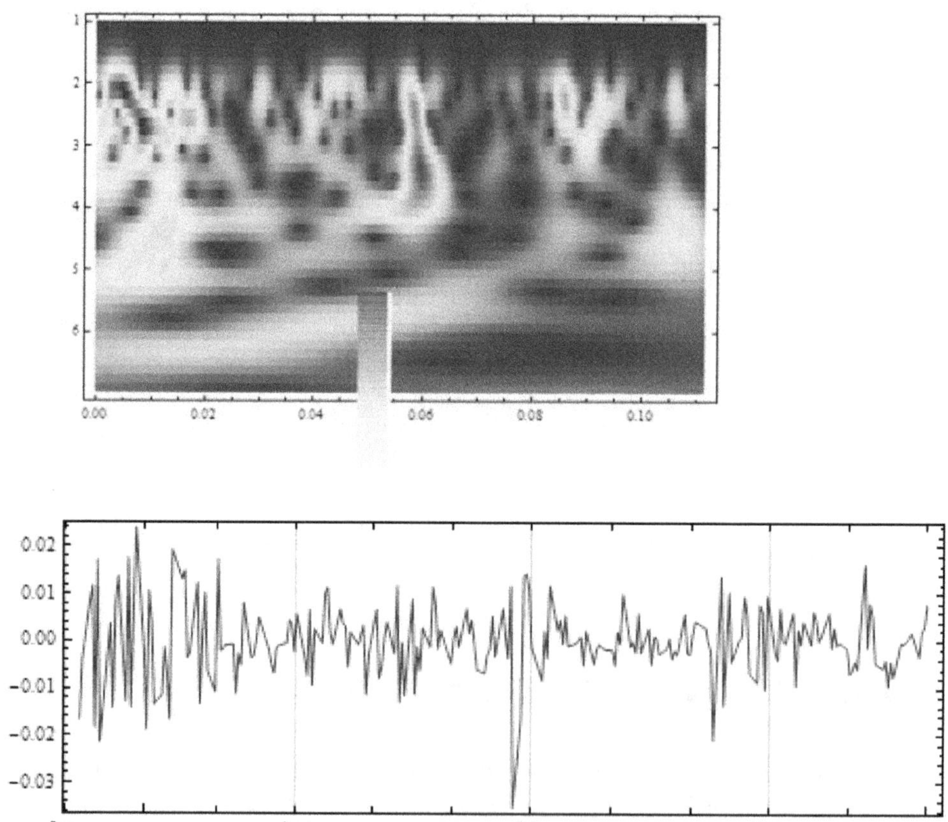

*For a more accurate representation of this figure, please see the electronic version.

Morlet Wavelet, because this wavelet is closely related to human perception, both hearing and vision.

CWT zooms in to display detailed, fine features – known as high frequency data and zooms out to display large, coarse trend- known as low frequency data (Sadowsky 1996). Thus, for signals for which spectral characteristics or statistical properties are likely to change over time, the CWT could be used to identify those signal features that are potentially usable by signal processing for forecasting. In other words, the CWT can be a useful tool for early analysis of signals.

When we apply the Equation 6 to the de-trended data we get Figure 26.

The wavelet spectrogram displays three axes: the horizontal axis represents time, the vertical axis the time scales or frequencies, and the transform's coefficient values. The coefficient values are plotted as rows of colored rectangles whose color corresponds to the magnitude of each coefficient.

Several features can be observed in the Figure 26. First, the highest wavelet power regions, colored in red, orange, and yellow, are associated with periods of high volatility. However, the wavelet power spectrogram correctly captures the biggest price movements in DJIA index: middle January, end of June and begging of September and November. Very often these price movements are explained with dominance of short investment horizons. It is stated that investors with long term horizons stop participating in the market, become short-term investors themselves, or when long-term fundamental information is no longer important or unreliable. I do not support fully this view of fractal markets. I agree that big price movements are result of some market irregularities, but we cannot explain them all with this concept of different investment horizons. What is even more important is that this concept is not mathematically useful. In order to find transition points in the signal, and use them for pattern recognition, we should analyze the local deformations in the signal.

The 3D representation of the wavelet spectrogram is given (see Figure 27). You can notice that the surface is not asymptotically flat. As I already stated: Something is roughening the surface. Therefore, moving average models based on Euclidian geometry, fail to capture accurately the dynamics of the financial markets.

Figure 27. 3D Wavelet Spectrogram

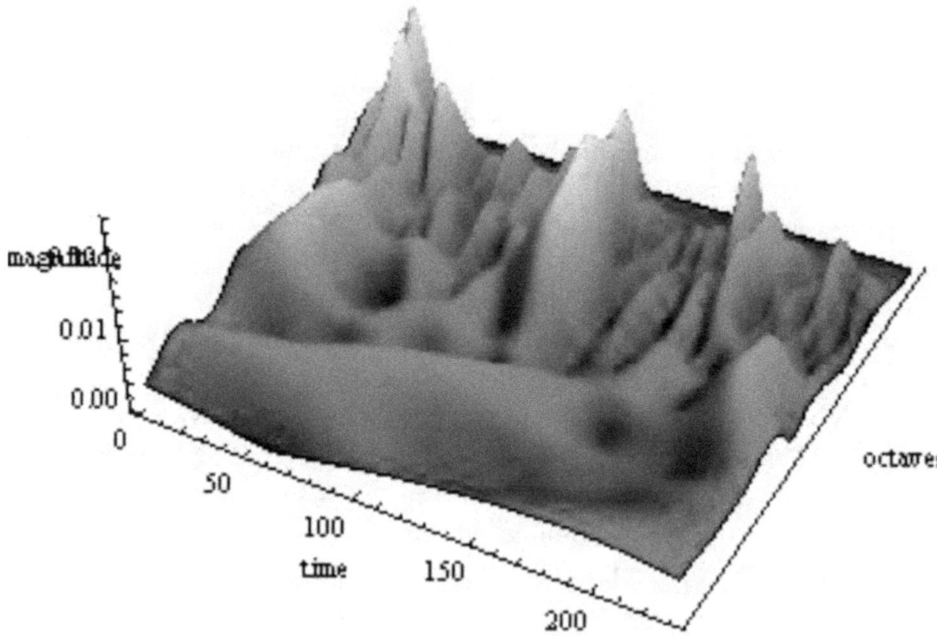

SINGULARITY DETECTION

The first step towards understanding singularity detection is to clearly define what "singularity" means. The following definitions specify *singularities*,

Figure 28. Cusp

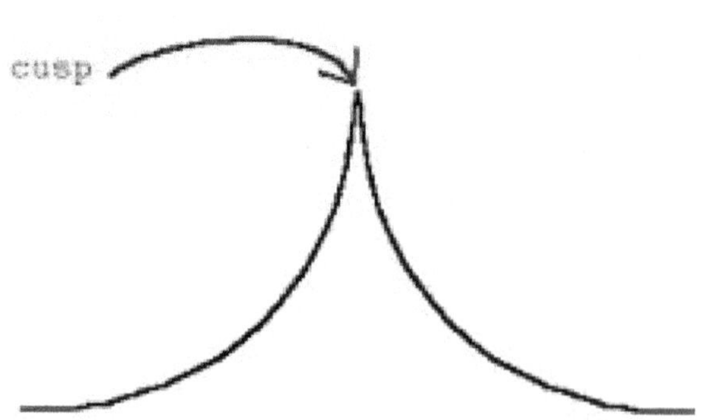

Figure 29. Step edges

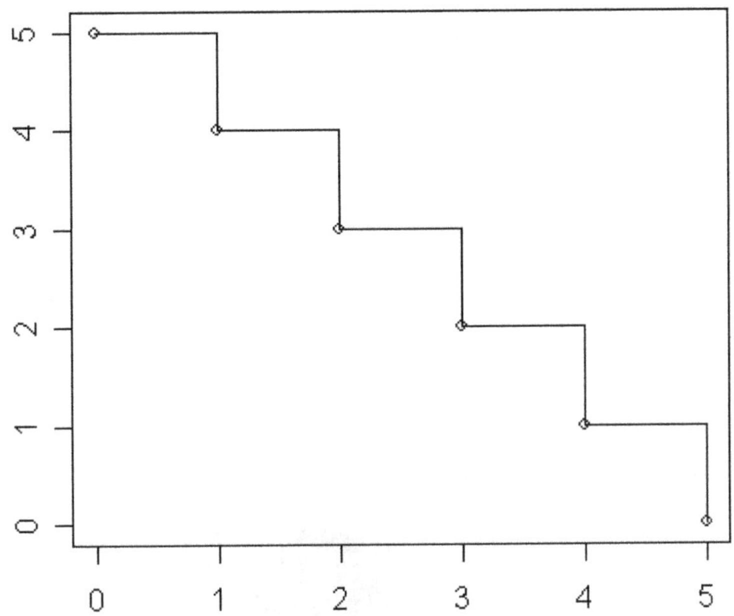

Figure 30. Smooth step edges

as well as two other levels that can be used to detect *singularities*, namely, *edges* and *incidents*.

A singularity in economics is a point where the Efficient Market Hypothesis (EMH), popularly known as a Random Walk Theory, ceases to apply. *Incidents* are defined as "the point of transition between the states of the system observed at a particular resolution", or "as the start and the end point

Figure 31. Dirac impulse

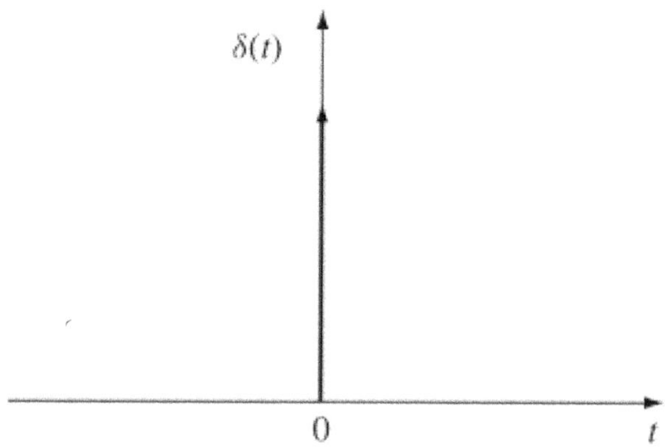

Figure 32. Oscillation singularity

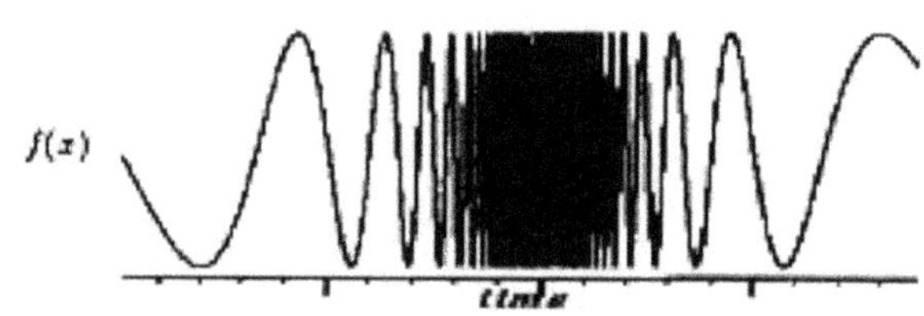

of the singularities" (Varadharajan, 2004). The states need not necessarily be physical, but can be human defined conditions of the data, such as bullish trend and bearish trend. The incidents are considered only as a step on the path of recognizing *singularities*. Meaning, the *singularity* is constructed of *incidents*, and has at least one incident.

Some of the common types of singularities detected in the financial time series are listed below. The figures were taken from Varadharajan (2004) and used for illustration purpose (see Figures 28-32).

In mathematics, a cusp is a type of singular point of a curve, where the tangent vector reverses its sign. In finance, cusps exhibit the bullish and bearish trend of asset prices. But here we will not witness sharp increases or decreases in the price.

Step edges detected in a financial time series represent a sudden jump in the price. This singularity occurs when most of the investors settle same investment strategy (group thinking/ hoarding effect detected).

They represent jumps in the signal that take place over a period of time. This type of singularity occurs when noise traders enter the financial markets.

Figure 33. Possible de-trended asset market signal

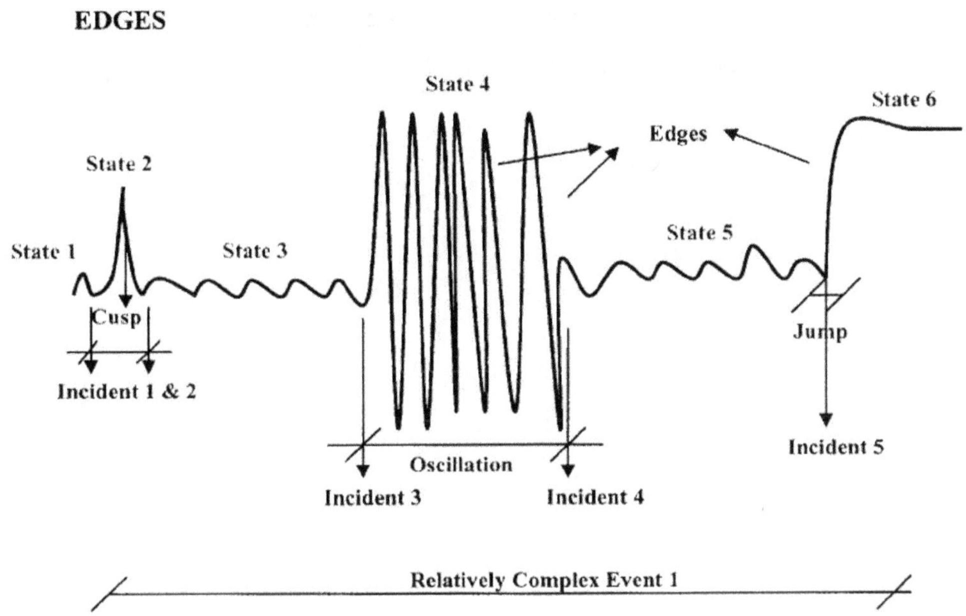

Oscillation singularity occurs when there is a sudden change in the frequency content of the signals, which is a result of the presence of both noise traders and group thinking/hoarding effect. In these cases, the entire period where there is a jump in the frequency of the signal, is considered to be the irregularity.

And at the end, we have the *edges*, which are defined as "the line that marks the local change in the behavior of the signal". *Edges* will help us to detect the incidents, and find the boundaries of the singularities.

In Figure 33, each of the lines represents an edge, and a singularity contains at least one edge. Notice that cusp has two edges, while the oscillation has several. The start and end of these singularities are marked by incidents. The jump, however contains only one edge, which is the singularity and the incident in itself. Thus, in Figure 33 incident 1and 2 are marked as the first singularity, incident 3 and 4 as a second singularity and incident 5 as the third singularity.

Figure 34. Singularity spectrum

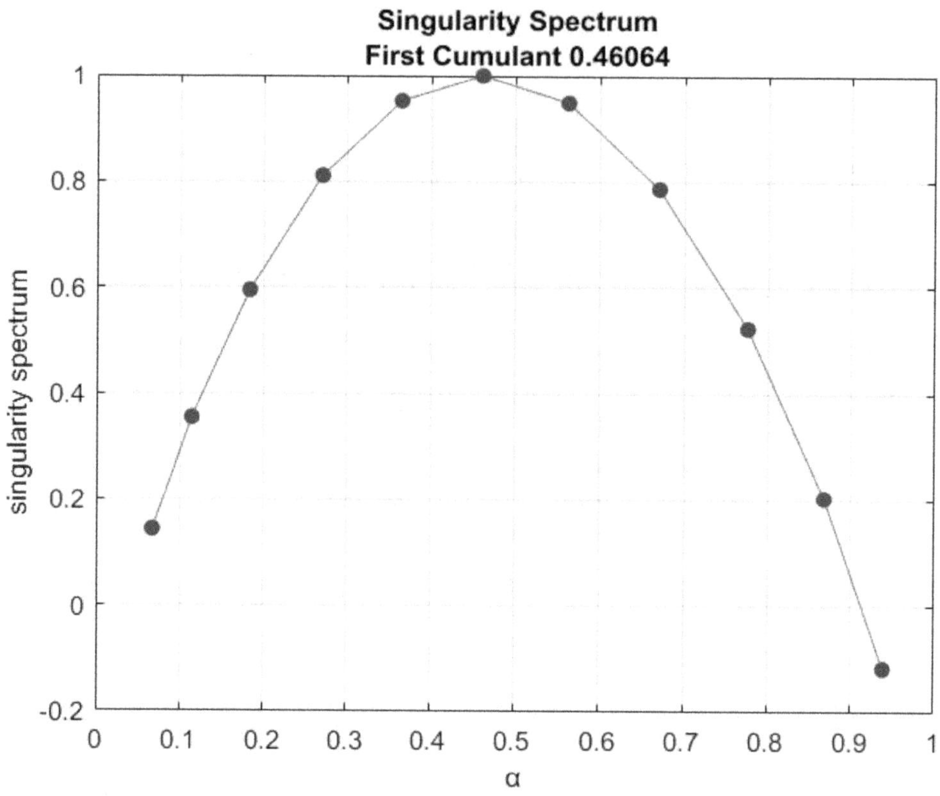

MULTI-FRACTAL ANALYSES

In the previous section, we showed that the Hurst exponent cannot be used as an indicator for upcoming turning point in the stock market. In the literature, it is known that the Hurst exponent as a single scaling parameter (global parameter) is used to describe self-similarity in mono-fractal systems. When I estimate the singularity spectrum and apply a nonlinearity test concerning financial time series, I notice that they are non-linear and multifractal.

Let me explain the procedure in details. In the computation of the singularity spectra the algorithm based on wavelet transform was used. The analyses are done MATLAB using DJIA index return data. First, I estimate the spectrum singularity and the global Holder exponent.

The singularity spectrum quantifies the degree of nonlinearity in the processes generating the output in Figure 34. It is a curve representing the

Hausdorff dimension f (α) as a function of the singularity parameter α presenting a characteristic maximum. It can be interpreted also as "fractal dimension" of the set of points with the scaling index in the range α = α +d α. Here, the maximum value of f (α) corresponds to the box counting dimension of the time series. In our case the fractal dimension is used to analyze the regularity of functions or distributions.

When Lipschitz exponent, also called the Holder exponent, is equal to 1 then we can conclude that there is no singularity present at that location. In our case the Holder exponent is 0.46, meaning the function is singular. For a linear fractal process the output of a system will have the same fractal properties regardless of initial conditions or of driving forces. In contrast, nonlinear fractal processes will generate outputs with different fractal properties that depend on the input conditions or the history of the system. That is, the output of the system over extended periods of time will display different types of singularities. This can be done with the following Matlab code 1.

Matlab Code 1: Singularity Spectrum

Step 1: Import DJIA index return data.

```
c = yahoo;
price = fetch (c,'DJIA','Close','01 / 01 / 15','12 / 09 / 16');
```

Step 2: Create new numerical variable price1 which is the second column (DJIA returns).

Step 3: Run the analysis.

```
[dh, h, cp] = dwtleader(price1);
plot(h, dh,'o -','MarkerFaceColor','b')
grid on
title({'Singularity Spectrum'; ['First Cumulant ' num2str(cp(1))]})
xlabel('α')
ylabel('singularity spectrum')
cp
end
```

Figure 35. Estimated scaling exponents

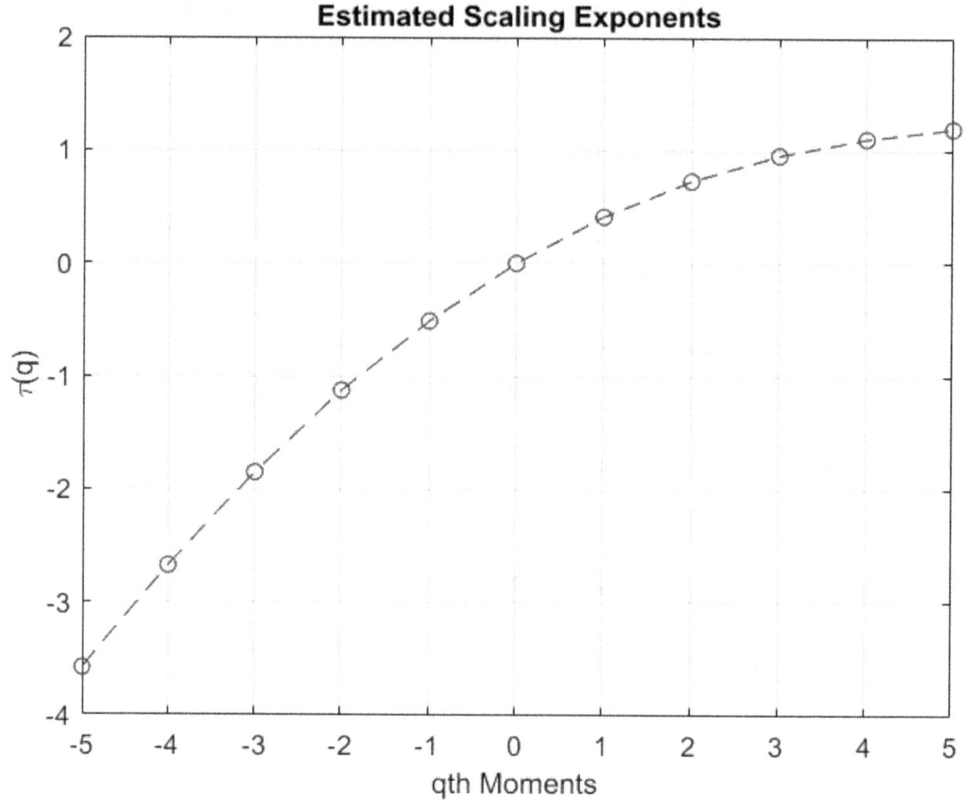

We then calculated the scaling exponent for the qth moment. For mono-fractal processes, the scaling exponents are a linear function of the moments. Linearity is indicated by the second and third cumulates being close to zero. In our case, the nonzero second cumulate (-0.0982) indicates that the process is multifractal. This is also shown in Figure 35, where the scaling exponents are a nonlinear function of the moments.

This can be done by the following Matlab code 2.

Matlab Code 2: Estimated Scaling Exponents

```
[ , ,cp,tauq] = dwtleader(price1);
cp([12])
plot(-5:5,tauq,'bo--');title('EstimatedScalingExponents');
grid on
xlabel('qthMoments')
ylabel('τ(q)')
end
```

EDGE DETECTION WITH WTMM MODEL

Let us recall that edges are "local change in the behavior of the signal", and that they will help us to detect the incidents, and find the boundaries of the singularities. In order to do this, first we need to locate the edges. This can be done by estimating the local Holder exponents, using the Wavelet Transform Modules Maxima (WTMM) model in combination with discrete wavelet transform (DWT). Here, it is important to highlight that you cannot apply the WTMM model to the original signal. First, you need to de-trend the signal using DWT model. In particular, the combinations of methods are

Figure 36. Local holder exponent, 20.11.2016

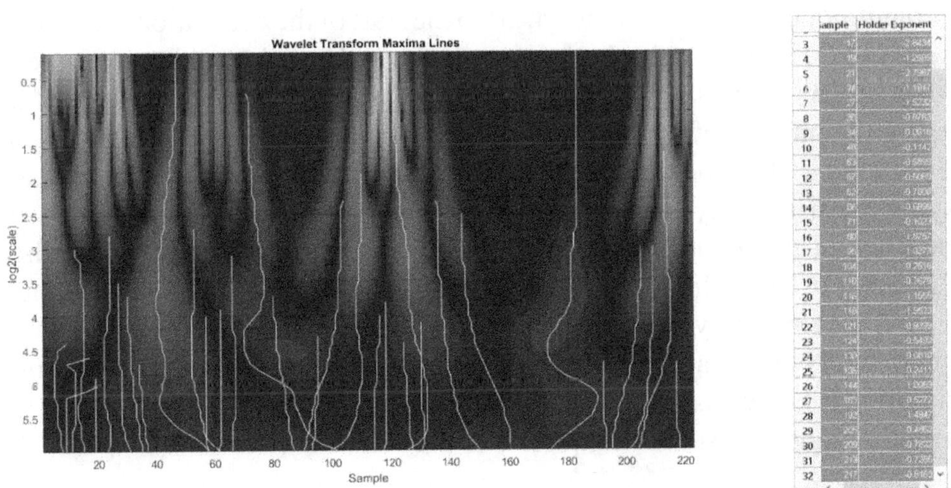

useful when analyzing multifractal signals, that is, signals having multiple fractal dimensions.

Moreover, the WTMM is known as a "mathematical microscope" and it is used by researchers for detecting stable and unstable fixed points, or someone wants to say regularity and singularity in the time series. I use Matlab code 3 given below, to estimate local Holder exponents and draw the Wavelet Transform Maxima Lines, see Figure 36.

Matlab Code 3: Wavelet Transform Modules Maxima (WTMM)

$$wtmm\left(detrended.\ data,'Scaling\ Exponent','local','NumOctaves',\ 6\right);$$

Here, the Holder exponents characterize the behavior of f (x) around a point x_0, and are considered as a smoothness measure of the function. They are linked to the order of differentiability of f (x) at x_0. The sharpness of an edge can be found by measuring its Holder exponent. For example, when a signal has Holder exponent 1 then the market is stable, no singularities detected. Hence, any function that is singular has Holder exponent different from 1. Negative Holder exponent corresponds to sharp irregularities/ oscillation singularity. A dirac impulse has Holder -1 and sharp/step function has Holder exponent 0 (Varadharajan (2004).

Table 4 displays the estimated Holder exponent and they correlate with different types of market irregularities.

Now let us see how we can use the estimates for asset price pattern recognition. In Table 4, on June 14, 2016 the start of the oscillation singularity is detected. This means that both noise traders and hoarding effect are present. What is also interesting, before every oscillation singularity the algorithm detects the entrance of the noise traders. This singularity is detected for example, in May 23, 2016. The noise traders, or popularly known as speculators, are trying to earn money buying low and selling high, therefore, they will push the price of the asset down. This behavior is then captured by the trading algorithm used by the financial institutions and pension fund, and in a few second they will buy a large number of assets. This will push the price up, and we will witness a sharp increase in the asset prices. In the finance theory, this event is known as an extreme/black swan event, which cannot be detected with the standard used techniques.

Table 4. Estimated holder exponent

Data	Sample	Holder Exponent	Note		
1/20/2016	9	-2.5567	Oscillation singularity		
1/25/2016	12	-0.5241	Oscillation singularity		
2/1/2016	17	-2.8434	Oscillation singularity		
2/3/2016	19	-1.2585	Oscillation singularity		
2/5/2016	21	-2.7967	Oscillation singularity		
2/10/2016	24	-1.1947	Oscillation singularity		
2/16/2016	27	-1.5232	Oscillation singularity		
2/19/2016	30	-0.8783	Oscillation singularity		
2/25/2016	34	0.0618	stable fixed point		
3/16/2016	48	-0.1142	Oscillation singularity starts	buy signal	gorup thinking and noise traders are detected
3/23/2016	53	-0.5899	Oscillation singularity		
3/30/2016	57	-0.5089	Oscillation singularity		
4/6/2016	62	-0.7606	Oscillation singularity		
4/12/2016	66	-0.6899	Oscillation singularity		
4/19/2016	71	-0.1023	Oscillation singularity		
5/2/2016	80	1.8757	Oscillation singularity ends	sell signal	
5/23/2016	95	1.0273	the price will start decreasing in a short period of time	wait	noise traders detected
6/6/2016	104	0.2515	stable fixed point		
6/14/2016	110	-0.3579	oscilation singularity starts	buy signal	gorup thinking and noise traders are detected
6/22/2016	116	-1.1555	oscilation singularity		
6/24/2016	118	-1.9523	oscilation singularity		
6/29/2016	121	-0.9399	oscilation singularity		
7/5/2016	124	-0.5492	oscilation singularity		
7/13/2016	130	0.081	Oscilation ends/stable fixed point starts	sell signal	
7/20/2016	135	0.2411	stable fixed point		
8/2/2016	144	1.0053	no singularity		
9/27/2016	183	0.5272	stable fixed point		
10/10/2016	192	1.4947	the price will start decreasing in a short period of time	wait	noise traders detected
10/27/2016	205	-0.4862	Oscilation singularity starts	buy signal	gorup thinking and noise traders are detected
11/2/2016	209	-0.7822	Oscilation singularity starts		
11/8/2016	213	-0.7285	Oscilation singularity starts		
11/14/2016	217	-0.8163	Oscilation singularity starts		

Figure 37. Oscillation Singularity detected in the DJIA index

By observing these singularities over a time, I understand that we can predict the future short-run asset pattern. In particular, when oscillation singularity is detected, we will witness a sharp decrease followed by a sharp increase in prices. This is illustrated in Figure 37.

For example, when the algorithm will estimate the first – (minus) sign, an oscillation singularity starts. At this moment, the algorithm will send the buy signal. The end of the oscillation singularity is the first positive estimate, 0.081. Now the algorithm will send the sell signal, July 13, 2016.

Table 5. Stable fixed points detected

Date	Price
13.07.2016	18.372,12
20.07.2016	18. 595,03
27.09.2016	18.129,96
10.10.2016	18.392,04

If we set our buy-sell strategy, according the wavelet-based algorithm, then the return of one-month period will be 3.95%.

What about the other Holder estimates? Can we use them as an investment tip?

When the Holder exponent is above 1 then noise traders are detected. The price is expected to decrease in a short period of time. Here you should not engage in any investment, you should wait. When the Holder exponent is 0 then group thinking/ hoarding effect is detected. Here a sudden jump in the price is expected, buy signal is sent. And when the Holder exponent is between 0 and 1, a stable fixed point is detected. Notice that when this type of singularity occurs, then the price is not behaving chaotically. On the contrary, it is fluctuating around its average.

For example: On July 13, 2016 the algorithm detected the first stable fixed point where the price was $18.372,12. Table 5, shows that the price in the subsequent singularities is fluctuating around its average and on 27.09.2016 the prices settle at $18.392,04.

CONCLUSION

Explaining chaos to finance and economics students is not an easy task. But the key point is accepting challenges. Most systems in nature are nonlinear, including the financial system. This means that the output is not directly proportional to the input. What is more, all chaotic systems are nonlinear systems. During my research on the subject of chaos, I consulted the book *"Strange Attractors: Creating Patterns in Chaos"* by Julien Sprott. Here, in this conclusion, I would like to share the original Sprott example for Bucks and Bugs. I believe that this example will bring the chaos theory closer to a finance student.

"Suppose you have some money in a bank account that provides interest, compounded yearly, and that you don't make any deposits or withdrawals. Let' X represents the amount of money in your account. When the time comes to the bank to credit your interest, its computer does so by multiplying X by some number. With an interest rate of 10%, the number is 1.1, and your new balance is 1.1 X. If your balance in the nth year is Xn (where n is 1 after the first year, 2 after the second, and so forth), your balance in the year n +1 is

$$X_n + 1 = RX_n \tag{11}$$

where R is equal to 1.0 plus your interest rate. (R is 1.1 in this example.)

You probably know that such compounding leads to exponential growth. In terms of the initial amount X_0, the amount in your account after n years is

$$X_n = X_0 R_n \tag{12}$$

After 50 years at 10% yearly interest, you will have \$117.39 for every dollar you initially invested. The bank can afford to do this only because of inflation and because money is loaned at an even higher interest rate.

Equation 11 is applicable to more than compound interest. It is how many of us have our salaries determined. It also describes population growth. Imagine some species of bug that lives for a season, lays its eggs, and then dies (thus avoiding the confusion of overlapping generations). The next year the eggs hatch, and the number of bugs is some constant R times the number in the previous year. If R is less than 1, the bugs die out over a number of years; and if R is greater than 1, there number grows exponentially.

You also know that exponential growth cannot go on forever, whether it be bucks in the bank, bugs in the back yard or people on the planet. Eventually something happens, such as the depletion of resources, to slow down or even reverse the growth. Mass starvation, disease, crime, and war are some of the mechanisms that limit unbridled human population growth. Thus we need to modify Equation 11 in some way if it is to model growth patterns in nature more closely. Perhaps the simplest modification is to multiply the right-hand side of Equation11 by a term such as (1 - X), whose value approaches 1 as X gets smaller (much less than 1) but is less than 1 as X increases. Since the population dies abruptly as X approaches 1, we must think of X = 1 as representing some large number of dollars or bugs (say a million or a billion); otherwise we would never get very far! So our modified equation, called the logistic equation, is:

$$X_n + 1 = RX_n \left(1 - X_n\right) \tag{13}$$

Now you're going to get your first homework assignment. Take your pocket calculator and start with a small value of X, say 0.1. To reduce the amount of work you have to do, use a fairly large value of R, say 2, corresponding to a doubling every year. Run X through Equation 13 a few times and see what happens. This process is called iteration, and the successive values are called iterates. If you did it right, you should see that X grows rapidly in the first couple of steps, and then it levels off at a value of 0.5. The first few values should be approximately 0.1, 0.18, 0.2952, 0.4161, 0.4859, 0.4996, and 0.5. Compare your results with the unbounded growth of Equation 11.

You might have predicted the above result, if you had thought to set Xn+1 equal to Xn in Equation 13 and solved for Xn. This value is called a fixed-point solution of the equation, because if X ever has that value, it remains fixed there forever. Such a fixed-point solution is sometimes called a point attractor, because every initial value of X between 0 and 1 is attracted to the fixed point upon repeated iteration of Equation 13. Try initial values of X = 0.2 and X = 0.8. A fixed point is also less than 0, such as -0.1, or greater than 1, such as 1.1. You should verify that the iterates are negative and that they get larger and larger, eventually approaching minus infinity. We say that the solution is unbounded and that it attracts to infinity. Thus, the values of X = 0 and X = 1 are like a watershed. Between these values the solution is bounded, and outside these values it is unbounded.

The region between X = 0 and X = 1 is called a basin of attraction because it resembles a bathroom basin in which drops of water find their way to the drain from wherever they start. X = 0 is also a fixed point, but it is unstable because values either slightly above or slightly below zero move away from zero. Such an unstable fixed point is sometimes called a repellor. Chaos can result when two or more repellors are present; the iterates then bounce back and forth like a baseball runner caught in a squeeze play." ("Strange Attractors: Creating Patterns in Chaos" by Julien Sprott, p. 8)

Moreover, the return has a fractal structure and using wavelet based modelling we can estimate its stable and unstable fixed point, or regularity and singularity. As defined by Sprott the stable fixed point is known as attractors and unstable points as a repellers. Chaos can result when two or more repellors are present (for example the detected oscillation singularity). During my research, I also understand that in nature equations that exhibit chaos have solutions that are unstable but bounded. Meaning the solution never settles down to a fixed value or even to a repeating pattern, but neither does it move off to infinity. Such dynamical systems are locally unstable, but the systems are globally stable. In this case, we have an attractor which is not a point, or set of points, or curve it is said that the attractor has a fractal structure. This type of attractor is called strange attractors.

How this can be applied to finance? When we analyze the financial systems in its entirety, we cannot observe the asset return as fixed point, because the asset return has a fractal structure. The asset return should be considered as one of the finance systems strange attractors. In particular, the financial systems are continuous chaotic systems, which are locally unstable and globally stable. Does this mean that the government intervention is more harm than serving financial systems?

Let this be the end of this journey and the begging for another. Maybe yours.

REFERENCES

Delfin Vidal, R. (2014). The Fractal Nature of Bitcoin: Evidence from Wavelet Power Spectra.

Blackledge, J. (2010). The fractal market hypothesis: applications to financial forecasting.

Kristoufek, L. (2013). Fractal markets hypothesis and the global financial crisis: Wavelet power evidence. arXiv:1310.1446

Struzik, Z. R. (2001). Wavelet methods in (financial) time-series processing. *Physica A: Statistical Mechanics and its Applications, 296*(1), 307-319.

Bak, P. (1996). Complexity and Criticality. In *How nature works* (pp. 1–32). Springer New York. doi:10.1007/978-1-4757-5426-1_1

Bhattacharya, R. N., Gupta, V. K., & Waymire, E. (1983). The Hurst effect under trends. *Journal of Applied Probability, 20*(03), 649–662. doi:10.1017/S0021900200023895

Critchlow, K. (1976). *Islamic patterns.* London: Thames & Hudson.

Donoho, D. L., & Johnstone, I. M. (1995). Adapting to unknown smoothness via wavelet shrinkage. *Journal of the American Statistical Association, 90*(432), 1200–1224. doi:10.1080/01621459.1995.10476626

Hurst, H. E. (1951). {Long-term storage capacity of reservoirs}. *Transactions of the American Society of Civil Engineers, 116*, 770–808.

Jain, P. C., & Wu, J. S. (2000). Truth in mutual fund advertising: Evidence on future performance and fund flows. *The Journal of Finance, 55*(2), 937–958. doi:10.1111/0022-1082.00232

Kale, M., & Butar, F. B. (2011). Fractal analysis of time series and distribution properties of Hurst exponent. *Journal of Mathematical Sciences & Mathematics Education*, *5*(1), 8–19.

Misiti, M., Misiti, Y., Oppenheim, G., & Poggi, J.M. (2002). Wavelet Toolbox for Use with MATLAB. the Math works, Inc.

Mandelbrot, B. B. (1977). *Fractals*. John Wiley & Sons, Inc.

Mandelbrot, B. B., & Van Ness, J. W. (1968). Fractional Brownian motions, fractional noises and applications. *SIAM Review*, *10*(4), 422–437. doi:10.1137/1010093

Mercer, M., Palmiter, A. R., & Taha, A. E. (2010). Worthless warnings? Testing the effectiveness of disclaimers in mutual fund advertisements. *Journal of Empirical Legal Studies*, *7*(3), 429–459. doi:10.1111/j.1740-1461.2010.01184.x

Mesa, O. J., & Poveda, G. (1993). The Hurst effect: The scale of fluctuation approach. *Water Resources Research*, *29*(12), 3995–4002. doi:10.1029/93WR01686

Osborne, M. F. (1959). Brownian motion in the stock market. *Operations Research*, *7*(2), 145–173. doi:10.1287/opre.7.2.145

Peters, E. E. (1994). *Fractal market analysis: applying chaos theory to investment and economics* (Vol. 24). John Wiley & Sons.

Peters, E. E. (1996). *Chaos and order in the capital markets: a new view of cycles, prices, and market volatility* (Vol. 1). John Wiley & Sons.

Sadowsky, J. (1996). Investigation of signal characteristics using the continuous wavelet transform. *Johns Hopkins APL technical digest, 17*(3), 258-269.

Stankewitz, R., & Rolf, J. (2012). Complex Dynamics: Chaos, Fractals, the Mandelbrot Set, and More. *Explorations in Complex Analysis*, 1.

Vandembroucq, D., & Roux, S. (1997). Conformal mapping on rough boundaries. mI. Applications to harmonic problems. *Physical Review E: Statistical Physics, Plasmas, Fluids, and Related Interdisciplinary Topics*, *55*(5), 6171–6185. doi:10.1103/PhysRevE.55.6171

Varadharajan, C. (2004). *A wavelet-based system for event detection in online real-time sensor data* [Doctoral dissertation]. Massachusetts Institute of Technology.

Related Readings

To continue IGI Global's long-standing tradition of advancing innovation through emerging research, please find below a compiled list of recommended IGI Global book chapters and journal articles in the areas of risk assessment, project management, and portfolio management. These related readings will provide additional information and guidance to further enrich your knowledge and assist you with your own research.

Aboutalebi, R. (2016). Strategies for Effective Worldwide Supply Chains. In B. Christiansen (Ed.), *Handbook of Research on Global Supply Chain Management* (pp. 1–14). Hershey, PA: IGI Global. doi:10.4018/978-1-4666-9639-6.ch001

Afonso, P., & Jiménez, V. J. (2016). Costing Systems for Decision Making under Uncertainty Using Probabilistic Models. In D. Jakóbczak (Ed.), *Analyzing Risk through Probabilistic Modeling in Operations Research* (pp. 221–245). Hershey, PA: IGI Global. doi:10.4018/978-1-4666-9458-3.ch010

Agarwal, R., & Virine, L. (2017). Integration of Project Risk Management (PRM) into Enterprise Risk Management (ERM). In Y. Raydugin (Ed.), *Handbook of Research on Leveraging Risk and Uncertainties for Effective Project Management* (pp. 294–317). Hershey, PA: IGI Global. doi:10.4018/978-1-5225-1790-0.ch014

Agarwal, R., & Virine, L. (2017). Monte Carlo Project Risk Analysis. In Y. Raydugin (Ed.), *Handbook of Research on Leveraging Risk and Uncertainties for Effective Project Management* (pp. 109–129). Hershey, PA: IGI Global. doi:10.4018/978-1-5225-1790-0.ch005

Agostino, D., Arnaboldi, M., & Azzone, G. (2016). Performance Measurement in Public Networks: Developing a PMS for Network Actors and Network Managers. In A. Ferreira, G. Azevedo, J. Oliveira, & R. Marques (Eds.), *Global Perspectives on Risk Management and Accounting in the Public Sector* (pp. 298–319). Hershey, PA: IGI Global. doi:10.4018/978-1-4666-9803-1.ch015

Aiello, L., & Gatti, M. (2017). Project Portfolio Management and Organization: An Integrated and Circular Model. In L. Romano (Ed.), *Project Portfolio Management Strategies for Effective Organizational Operations* (pp. 288–309). Hershey, PA: IGI Global. doi:10.4018/978-1-5225-2151-8.ch012

Alfirević, N., Šešić, M. D., & Čačija, L. N. (2017). The Fundraising Patterns and the Management Professionalization in Independent Arts Organizations in SEE. In V. Potocan, M. Üngan, & Z. Nedelko (Eds.), *Handbook of Research on Managerial Solutions in Non-Profit Organizations* (pp. 400–420). Hershey, PA: IGI Global. doi:10.4018/978-1-5225-0731-4.ch019

Amaral, A. M., & Araújo, M. (2017). Project Portfolio Selection Using a D.E.A. Approach. In L. Romano (Ed.), *Project Portfolio Management Strategies for Effective Organizational Operations* (pp. 220–244). Hershey, PA: IGI Global. doi:10.4018/978-1-5225-2151-8.ch009

Aparo von Flüe, A. (2017). Are You Pondering What I Am Pondering?: Eccentric Consideration on Strategic Management. In L. Romano (Ed.), *Project Portfolio Management Strategies for Effective Organizational Operations* (pp. 81–118). Hershey, PA: IGI Global. doi:10.4018/978-1-5225-2151-8.ch004

Araya-Leandro, C., Caba-Pérez, M. D., & López-Hernandez, A. M. (2016). Modernization of Governmental Accounting Systems: Situation in the Central American Region. In A. Ferreira, G. Azevedo, J. Oliveira, & R. Marques (Eds.), *Global Perspectives on Risk Management and Accounting in the Public Sector* (pp. 90–107). Hershey, PA: IGI Global. doi:10.4018/978-1-4666-9803-1.ch005

Archibald, R. D. (2017). Inter-Relationships between an Enterprise's Strategic Management Process and Its Program/Project Portfolio Management Process. In L. Romano (Ed.), *Project Portfolio Management Strategies for Effective Organizational Operations* (pp. 39–60). Hershey, PA: IGI Global. doi:10.4018/978-1-5225-2151-8.ch002

Arsenijević, O. M., Orčić, D., & Kastratović, E. (2017). Development of an Optimization Tool for Intangibles in SMEs: A Case Study from Serbia with a Pilot Research in the Prestige by Milka Company. In M. Vemić (Ed.), *Optimal Management Strategies in Small and Medium Enterprises* (pp. 320–347). Hershey, PA: IGI Global. doi:10.4018/978-1-5225-1949-2.ch015

Aydin, E. (2017). "Problems and Suggestions": Non-Governmental Organisations of Sexual Orientation Minorities in the Context of Turkey and United Kingdom. In V. Potocan, M. Üngan, & Z. Nedelko (Eds.), *Handbook of Research on Managerial Solutions in Non-Profit Organizations* (pp. 232–252). Hershey, PA: IGI Global. doi:10.4018/978-1-5225-0731-4.ch011

Ayyıldız, H., Akmermer, B., & Akyüz, A. M. (2017). Marketing Approach for Non-Profit Organizations. In V. Potocan, M. Üngan, & Z. Nedelko (Eds.), *Handbook of Research on Managerial Solutions in Non-Profit Organizations* (pp. 156–181). Hershey, PA: IGI Global. doi:10.4018/978-1-5225-0731-4.ch008

Balakrishna, P., Borener, S. S., Crook, I., Durston, A., & Robinson, M. J. (2016). Applying Probabilistic Risk Assessment to Safety Risk Analysis in Aviation. In D. Jakóbczak (Ed.), *Analyzing Risk through Probabilistic Modeling in Operations Research* (pp. 321–343). Hershey, PA: IGI Global. doi:10.4018/978-1-4666-9458-3.ch013

Bali, S., & Uslu, Y. D. (2017). Enterprise Risk Management in Non-Profit Organization. In V. Potocan, M. Üngan, & Z. Nedelko (Eds.), *Handbook of Research on Managerial Solutions in Non-Profit Organizations* (pp. 75–93). Hershey, PA: IGI Global. doi:10.4018/978-1-5225-0731-4.ch004

Baporikar, N. (2016). Business Process Management. *International Journal of Productivity Management and Assessment Technologies*, *4*(2), 49–62. doi:10.4018/IJPMAT.2016070104

Brzozowski, M., & Ferster, I. (2017). Educational Management Leadership: High School Principal's Management Style and Parental Involvement in School Management in Israel. In V. Potocan, M. Üngan, & Z. Nedelko (Eds.), *Handbook of Research on Managerial Solutions in Non-Profit Organizations* (pp. 55–74). Hershey, PA: IGI Global. doi:10.4018/978-1-5225-0731-4.ch003

Brzozowski, M., & Keydar, E. J. (2017). Approaches towards Measuring Success in Public Elementary Schools. In V. Potocan, M. Üngan, & Z. Nedelko (Eds.), *Handbook of Research on Managerial Solutions in Non-Profit Organizations* (pp. 362–377). Hershey, PA: IGI Global. doi:10.4018/978-1-5225-0731-4.ch017

Bucero, A. (2017). Linking Organization's Strategy and Strategic Planning with Portfolio Management. In L. Romano (Ed.), *Project Portfolio Management Strategies for Effective Organizational Operations* (pp. 61–80). Hershey, PA: IGI Global. doi:10.4018/978-1-5225-2151-8.ch003

Cakar, U., & Kim, H. (2017). Experiences of Non-Profit Organizations in Korea: Development Challenges in an Emerging Economy. In V. Potocan, M. Üngan, & Z. Nedelko (Eds.), *Handbook of Research on Managerial Solutions in Non-Profit Organizations* (pp. 499–528). Hershey, PA: IGI Global. doi:10.4018/978-1-5225-0731-4.ch023

Carini, C., & Teodori, C. (2016). Potential Uses and Usefulness of Italian Local Government Consolidated Financial Reporting: The Case of the Town Council of Brescia. In A. Ferreira, G. Azevedo, J. Oliveira, & R. Marques (Eds.), *Global Perspectives on Risk Management and Accounting in the Public Sector* (pp. 68–89). Hershey, PA: IGI Global. doi:10.4018/978-1-4666-9803-1.ch004

Caron, F. (2016). A Bayesian Approach to Project Control. In D. Jakóbczak (Ed.), *Analyzing Risk through Probabilistic Modeling in Operations Research* (pp. 125–137). Hershey, PA: IGI Global. doi:10.4018/978-1-4666-9458-3.ch005

Castagnoli, E., De Donno, M., Favero, G., & Modesti, P. (2016). A Different Way to Look at Random Variables: Do Decision Makers Look at Functions or at Sets? In D. Jakóbczak (Ed.), *Analyzing Risk through Probabilistic Modeling in Operations Research* (pp. 179–199). Hershey, PA: IGI Global. doi:10.4018/978-1-4666-9458-3.ch008

Castagnoli, E., Favero, G., & Modesti, P. (2016). Price Systems for Random Amounts: A Unified Approach. In D. Jakóbczak (Ed.), *Analyzing Risk through Probabilistic Modeling in Operations Research* (pp. 354–379). Hershey, PA: IGI Global. doi:10.4018/978-1-4666-9458-3.ch015

Chandan, H. C. (2016). Implementation of Green Supply Chain Management in a Globalized Economy. In B. Christiansen (Ed.), *Handbook of Research on Global Supply Chain Management* (pp. 402–418). Hershey, PA: IGI Global. doi:10.4018/978-1-4666-9639-6.ch023

Chapman, R. J. (2017). Complexity Theory and System Dynamics for Project Risk Management. In Y. Raydugin (Ed.), *Handbook of Research on Leveraging Risk and Uncertainties for Effective Project Management* (pp. 152–176). Hershey, PA: IGI Global. doi:10.4018/978-1-5225-1790-0.ch008

Chen, E. J. (2016). Simulation Output Analysis and Risk Management. In D. Jakóbczak (Ed.), *Analyzing Risk through Probabilistic Modeling in Operations Research* (pp. 200–220). Hershey, PA: IGI Global. doi:10.4018/978-1-4666-9458-3.ch009

Chen, Y., Davutyan, N., & Ersoy, İ. (2016). A "Flying High, Landing Soft" Platform for Supplier Diversity. In B. Christiansen (Ed.), *Handbook of Research on Global Supply Chain Management* (pp. 72–84). Hershey, PA: IGI Global. doi:10.4018/978-1-4666-9639-6.ch004

Choptiany, J. M. (2017). A Holistic Multi-Criteria Decision and Risk Analysis Method for CCS and GHG Mitigation Projects. In Y. Raydugin (Ed.), *Handbook of Research on Leveraging Risk and Uncertainties for Effective Project Management* (pp. 384–405). Hershey, PA: IGI Global. doi:10.4018/978-1-5225-1790-0.ch018

Coste, A. I., & Tiron-Tudor, A. (2016). Performance Measurement Perceptions in Romanian Higher Education. In A. Ferreira, G. Azevedo, J. Oliveira, & R. Marques (Eds.), *Global Perspectives on Risk Management and Accounting in the Public Sector* (pp. 346–365). Hershey, PA: IGI Global. doi:10.4018/978-1-4666-9803-1.ch017

Çotur, Ö. K., & Öztürkoğlu, Y. (2016). Partnerships in Supply Chain Management. In B. Christiansen (Ed.), *Handbook of Research on Global Supply Chain Management* (pp. 161–185). Hershey, PA: IGI Global. doi:10.4018/978-1-4666-9639-6.ch010

Couto, M. C., & Ferreira, A. D. (2016). The Importance of Accountability Practices in the Public Sector: Literature Review. In A. Ferreira, G. Azevedo, J. Oliveira, & R. Marques (Eds.), *Global Perspectives on Risk Management and Accounting in the Public Sector* (pp. 188–201). Hershey, PA: IGI Global. doi:10.4018/978-1-4666-9803-1.ch010

Cropley, C. H. (2017). The Case for Truly Integrated Cost and Schedule Risk Analysis. In Y. Raydugin (Ed.), *Handbook of Research on Leveraging Risk and Uncertainties for Effective Project Management* (pp. 76–108). Hershey, PA: IGI Global. doi:10.4018/978-1-5225-1790-0.ch004

Csillag, S., Balázs, E., Kocsis, M., Udvarhelyi, T., & Vago, I. (2017). Eight-Point Project: Action Research, as a Development Tool for Non-Profit Organizations. In V. Potocan, M. Üngan, & Z. Nedelko (Eds.), *Handbook of Research on Managerial Solutions in Non-Profit Organizations* (pp. 483–498). Hershey, PA: IGI Global. doi:10.4018/978-1-5225-0731-4.ch022

Cuadrado-Ballesteros, B., García-Sánchez, I. M., & Martínez-Ferrero, J. (2016). Commercialization of Local Public Services. In A. Ferreira, G. Azevedo, J. Oliveira, & R. Marques (Eds.), *Global Perspectives on Risk Management and Accounting in the Public Sector* (pp. 132–150). Hershey, PA: IGI Global. doi:10.4018/978-1-4666-9803-1.ch007

Cuadrado-Ballesteros, B., Mordán, N., & Frías-Aceituno, J. V. (2016). Transparency as a Determinant of Local Financial Condition. In A. Ferreira, G. Azevedo, J. Oliveira, & R. Marques (Eds.), *Global Perspectives on Risk Management and Accounting in the Public Sector* (pp. 202–225). Hershey, PA: IGI Global. doi:10.4018/978-1-4666-9803-1.ch011

Cunha, A., Ferreira, A. D., & Fernandes, M. J. (2016). The Influence of Accounting Information in the Re-Election of the Mayors in Portugal. In A. Ferreira, G. Azevedo, J. Oliveira, & R. Marques (Eds.), *Global Perspectives on Risk Management and Accounting in the Public Sector* (pp. 108–131). Hershey, PA: IGI Global. doi:10.4018/978-1-4666-9803-1.ch006

Ćwiklicki, M. (2017). Applying Balanced Scorecard in Non-Government Organizations. In V. Potocan, M. Üngan, & Z. Nedelko (Eds.), *Handbook of Research on Managerial Solutions in Non-Profit Organizations* (pp. 134–155). Hershey, PA: IGI Global. doi:10.4018/978-1-5225-0731-4.ch007

Damnjanović, A. M. (2017). Knowledge Management Optimization through IT and E-Business Utilization: A Qualitative Study on Serbian SMEs. In M. Vemić (Ed.), *Optimal Management Strategies in Small and Medium Enterprises* (pp. 249–267). Hershey, PA: IGI Global. doi:10.4018/978-1-5225-1949-2.ch012

Daneshpour, H. (2017). Integrating Sustainable Development into Project Portfolio Management through Application of Open Innovation. In M. Vemić (Ed.), *Optimal Management Strategies in Small and Medium Enterprises* (pp. 370–387). Hershey, PA: IGI Global. doi:10.4018/978-1-5225-1949-2.ch017

del Mar Gálvez-Rodríguez, M., Haro-de-Rosario, A., & Caba-Pérez, M. D. (2017). The Relation between Contingency Factors and the Efficiency of NPOs. In V. Potocan, M. Ünğan, & Z. Nedelko (Eds.), *Handbook of Research on Managerial Solutions in Non-Profit Organizations* (pp. 321–342). Hershey, PA: IGI Global. doi:10.4018/978-1-5225-0731-4.ch015

Dieguez, T., Conceição, O., & Fernandes, Â. (2017). The Challenges of Managing the Private Institutions of Social Solidarity: Experiences from Portugal. In V. Potocan, M. Ünğan, & Z. Nedelko (Eds.), *Handbook of Research on Managerial Solutions in Non-Profit Organizations* (pp. 23–54). Hershey, PA: IGI Global. doi:10.4018/978-1-5225-0731-4.ch002

Duong, L. N., Wood, L. C., & Wang, X. (2016). Review of RFID Applications in Perishable Inventory Management. In B. Christiansen (Ed.), *Handbook of Research on Global Supply Chain Management* (pp. 139–146). Hershey, PA: IGI Global. doi:10.4018/978-1-4666-9639-6.ch008

Emel, G. G., & Petriçli, G. (2016). A Staged Supplier Pre-Evaluation Model: To Determine Risky, Potential and Preferred Suppliers. In B. Christiansen (Ed.), *Handbook of Research on Global Supply Chain Management* (pp. 419–451). Hershey, PA: IGI Global. doi:10.4018/978-1-4666-9639-6.ch024

Ercegovac, I. R., Alfirević, N., & Koludrović, M. (2017). School Principals' Communication and Co-Operation Assessment: The Croatian Experience. In V. Potocan, M. Ünğan, & Z. Nedelko (Eds.), *Handbook of Research on Managerial Solutions in Non-Profit Organizations* (pp. 276–297). Hershey, PA: IGI Global. doi:10.4018/978-1-5225-0731-4.ch013

Fayezi, S., & Zomorrodi, M. (2016). Supply Chain Management: Developments, Theories and Models. In B. Christiansen (Ed.), *Handbook of Research on Global Supply Chain Management* (pp. 313–340). Hershey, PA: IGI Global. doi:10.4018/978-1-4666-9639-6.ch018

Fox, W. P. (2016). Multi-Attribute Decision Making in Risk Analysis. In D. Jakóbczak (Ed.), *Analyzing Risk through Probabilistic Modeling in Operations Research* (pp. 246–290). Hershey, PA: IGI Global. doi:10.4018/978-1-4666-9458-3.ch011

Fox, W. P. (2016). Perfect Partners of Mathematical Modeling with Technology in Risk Assessment. In D. Jakóbczak (Ed.), *Analyzing Risk through Probabilistic Modeling in Operations Research* (pp. 61–90). Hershey, PA: IGI Global. doi:10.4018/978-1-4666-9458-3.ch003

Giacomini, D., Chiaf, E., & Mazzoleni, M. B. (2017). How to Measure Performance in Cooperatives?: A Multiple Case Study. In V. Potocan, M. Üngan, & Z. Nedelko (Eds.), *Handbook of Research on Managerial Solutions in Non-Profit Organizations* (pp. 343–361). Hershey, PA: IGI Global. doi:10.4018/978-1-5225-0731-4.ch016

Giri, B. C. (2016). Risk-Averse Newsboy Problem with Incomplete Demand Information: Risk-Averse Newsboy Problem. In D. Jakóbczak (Ed.), *Analyzing Risk through Probabilistic Modeling in Operations Research* (pp. 344–353). Hershey, PA: IGI Global. doi:10.4018/978-1-4666-9458-3.ch014

Glavee-Geo, R. (2016). The History and Development of Purchasing Management and Its Theoretical Framework: A Review of Transaction Cost Economics. In B. Christiansen (Ed.), *Handbook of Research on Global Supply Chain Management* (pp. 379–401). Hershey, PA: IGI Global. doi:10.4018/978-1-4666-9639-6.ch022

Gökgöz, F., & Atmaca, M. E. (2017). An Optimal Asset Allocation in Electricity Generation Market for the Policy Makers and Stakeholders. In V. Potocan, M. Üngan, & Z. Nedelko (Eds.), *Handbook of Research on Managerial Solutions in Non-Profit Organizations* (pp. 448–482). Hershey, PA: IGI Global. doi:10.4018/978-1-5225-0731-4.ch021

Gökgöz, F., & Atmaca, M. E. (2017). Ranking Turkish Universities Based on Performance Evaluation via DEMATEL-AHP Approach. In V. Potocan, M. Üngan, & Z. Nedelko (Eds.), *Handbook of Research on Managerial Solutions in Non-Profit Organizations* (pp. 421–447). Hershey, PA: IGI Global. doi:10.4018/978-1-5225-0731-4.ch020

Gomes, P., Camões, S. M., & Carvalho, J. (2016). Determinants of the Design and Use of PMS in Portuguese Government Agencies: A Complementary Theoretical Approach. In A. Ferreira, G. Azevedo, J. Oliveira, & R. Marques (Eds.), *Global Perspectives on Risk Management and Accounting in the Public Sector* (pp. 320–345). Hershey, PA: IGI Global. doi:10.4018/978-1-4666-9803-1.ch016

Gul, S., & Williams, T. (2017). Project Complexity for the Uninitiated. In Y. Raydugin (Ed.), *Handbook of Research on Leveraging Risk and Uncertainties for Effective Project Management* (pp. 202–219). Hershey, PA: IGI Global. doi:10.4018/978-1-5225-1790-0.ch010

Gumz, J. (2017). Managing Change: Strategies and Tactics to Review the Portfolio. In L. Romano (Ed.), *Project Portfolio Management Strategies for Effective Organizational Operations* (pp. 334–357). Hershey, PA: IGI Global. doi:10.4018/978-1-5225-2151-8.ch014

Hartlieb, S., & Silvius, G. (2017). Handling Uncertainty in Project Management and Business Development: Similarities and Differences. In Y. Raydugin (Ed.), *Handbook of Research on Leveraging Risk and Uncertainties for Effective Project Management* (pp. 337–362). Hershey, PA: IGI Global. doi:10.4018/978-1-5225-1790-0.ch016

Hass, K. B. (2017). Living on the Edge: Managing Project Complexity. In Y. Raydugin (Ed.), *Handbook of Research on Leveraging Risk and Uncertainties for Effective Project Management* (pp. 177–201). Hershey, PA: IGI Global. doi:10.4018/978-1-5225-1790-0.ch009

Hollmann, J. K. (2017). Complexity Risk and Modeling Disorder. In Y. Raydugin (Ed.), *Handbook of Research on Leveraging Risk and Uncertainties for Effective Project Management* (pp. 139–151). Hershey, PA: IGI Global. doi:10.4018/978-1-5225-1790-0.ch007

Hollmann, J. K. (2017). Systemic Risks and Parametric Modeling. In Y. Raydugin (Ed.), *Handbook of Research on Leveraging Risk and Uncertainties for Effective Project Management* (pp. 61–75). Hershey, PA: IGI Global. doi:10.4018/978-1-5225-1790-0.ch003

Hu, N., & Cheng, H. (2016). Survival Analysis and ROC Analysis in Analyzing Credit Risks: Assessing Default Risks Over Time. In D. Jakóbczak (Ed.), *Analyzing Risk through Probabilistic Modeling in Operations Research* (pp. 380–403). Hershey, PA: IGI Global. doi:10.4018/978-1-4666-9458-3.ch016

Huemann, M., & Ringhofer, C. (2016). Challenge or Potential? Risk Identification in the Context of Sustainable Development: A Case Study. In C. Bodea, A. Purnus, M. Huemann, & M. Hajdu (Eds.), *Managing Project Risks for Competitive Advantage in Changing Business Environments* (pp. 87–105). Hershey, PA: IGI Global. doi:10.4018/978-1-5225-0335-4.ch005

Hulett, D. T. (2017). Monte Carlo Simulation for Integrated Cost-Schedule Risk Analysis: Concepts, Methods, and Tools for Risk Analysis and Mitigation. In Y. Raydugin (Ed.), *Handbook of Research on Leveraging Risk and Uncertainties for Effective Project Management* (pp. 29–60). Hershey, PA: IGI Global. doi:10.4018/978-1-5225-1790-0.ch002

Ivančević, K. (2017). Insurance as an Optimization Tool for Risk Management in Small and Medium-Sized Enterprises. In M. Vemić (Ed.), *Optimal Management Strategies in Small and Medium Enterprises* (pp. 178–197). Hershey, PA: IGI Global. doi:10.4018/978-1-5225-1949-2.ch009

Jakóbczak, D. J. (2016). Data Extrapolation via Curve Modeling in Analyzing Risk: Value Anticipation for Decision Making. In D. Jakóbczak (Ed.), *Analyzing Risk through Probabilistic Modeling in Operations Research* (pp. 1–31). Hershey, PA: IGI Global. doi:10.4018/978-1-4666-9458-3.ch001

Jakóbczak, D. J. (2016). The Method of Probabilistic Nodes Combination in Decision Making and Risk Analysis: Data Extrapolation in Planning. In D. Jakóbczak (Ed.), *Analyzing Risk through Probabilistic Modeling in Operations Research* (pp. 32–60). Hershey, PA: IGI Global. doi:10.4018/978-1-4666-9458-3.ch002

Jarman, M. F., & Dreher, L. G. (2017). Missed Opportunities from Misalignment of Project and Operational Requirements. In Y. Raydugin (Ed.), *Handbook of Research on Leveraging Risk and Uncertainties for Effective Project Management* (pp. 363–383). Hershey, PA: IGI Global. doi:10.4018/978-1-5225-1790-0.ch017

Kač, S. M., Tamše, T., & Gorenak, I. (2017). Intercultural Education and Training of Slovene Police Officers for the Purpose of International Missions. In V. Potocan, M. Üngan, & Z. Nedelko (Eds.), *Handbook of Research on Managerial Solutions in Non-Profit Organizations* (pp. 298–320). Hershey, PA: IGI Global. doi:10.4018/978-1-5225-0731-4.ch014

Kafi, F., & Kafi, M. (2016). Information Quality in Supply Chain Software. In B. Christiansen (Ed.), *Handbook of Research on Global Supply Chain Management* (pp. 105–126). Hershey, PA: IGI Global. doi:10.4018/978-1-4666-9639-6.ch006

Kasemsap, K. (2016). Fostering Supply Chain Management in Global Business. In B. Christiansen (Ed.), *Handbook of Research on Global Supply Chain Management* (pp. 45–71). Hershey, PA: IGI Global. doi:10.4018/978-1-4666-9639-6.ch003

Kittilaksanawong, W. (2016). Value Creation and Appropriation in Buyer-Supplier Relationships: Governance, Competition and Cultures. In B. Christiansen (Ed.), *Handbook of Research on Global Supply Chain Management* (pp. 127–138). Hershey, PA: IGI Global. doi:10.4018/978-1-4666-9639-6.ch007

Klepac, G., Mrsic, L., & Kopal, R. (2016). Efficient Risk Profiling Using Bayesian Networks and Particle Swarm Optimization Algorithm. In D. Jakóbczak (Ed.), *Analyzing Risk through Probabilistic Modeling in Operations Research* (pp. 91–124). Hershey, PA: IGI Global. doi:10.4018/978-1-4666-9458-3.ch004

Kopp, U. (2016). Easier Identification of Risks and Uncertainties with Project Risk Constellations. In C. Bodea, A. Purnus, M. Huemann, & M. Hajdu (Eds.), *Managing Project Risks for Competitive Advantage in Changing Business Environments* (pp. 106–127). Hershey, PA: IGI Global. doi:10.4018/978-1-5225-0335-4.ch006

Kucukbay, F. (2017). Cash Management in Non-Profit Organizations. In V. Potocan, M. Üngan, & Z. Nedelko (Eds.), *Handbook of Research on Managerial Solutions in Non-Profit Organizations* (pp. 94–110). Hershey, PA: IGI Global. doi:10.4018/978-1-5225-0731-4.ch005

Kutsch, E., Hällgren, M., & Turner, N. (2016). The Internalization of Attention at 28,000 Feet: Revisiting the K2 2008 Disaster. In C. Bodea, A. Purnus, M. Huemann, & M. Hajdu (Eds.), *Managing Project Risks for Competitive Advantage in Changing Business Environments* (pp. 196–215). Hershey, PA: IGI Global. doi:10.4018/978-1-5225-0335-4.ch010

Lahmiri, S., & Gagnon, S. (2016). A Sequential Probabilistic System for Bankruptcy Data Classification. In D. Jakóbczak (Ed.), *Analyzing Risk through Probabilistic Modeling in Operations Research* (pp. 138–147). Hershey, PA: IGI Global. doi:10.4018/978-1-4666-9458-3.ch006

Lederer, M., Kurz, M., & Lazarov, P. (2017). Usage and Suitability of Methods for Strategic Business Process Initiatives: A Multi Case Study Research. *International Journal of Productivity Management and Assessment Technologies*, *5*(1), 40–51. doi:10.4018/IJPMAT.2017010103

Lee, I. (2017). A Social Enterprise Business Model and a Case Study of Pacific Community Ventures (PCV). In V. Potocan, M. Üngan, & Z. Nedelko (Eds.), *Handbook of Research on Managerial Solutions in Non-Profit Organizations* (pp. 182–204). Hershey, PA: IGI Global. doi:10.4018/978-1-5225-0731-4.ch009

Levin, G., & Pitotti, N. (2017). Program and Portfolio Management Relationship and Support. In L. Romano (Ed.), *Project Portfolio Management Strategies for Effective Organizational Operations* (pp. 310–333). Hershey, PA: IGI Global. doi:10.4018/978-1-5225-2151-8.ch013

Liu, Z. (2016). Structuring and Managing Supply Network: A Review of Current Literature and Conceptual Framework. In B. Christiansen (Ed.), *Handbook of Research on Global Supply Chain Management* (pp. 341–353). Hershey, PA: IGI Global. doi:10.4018/978-1-4666-9639-6.ch019

Lokuwaduge, C. S. (2016). Exploring the New Public Management (NPM)-Based Reforms in the Public Sector Accounting: A Sri Lankan Study. In A. Ferreira, G. Azevedo, J. Oliveira, & R. Marques (Eds.), *Global Perspectives on Risk Management and Accounting in the Public Sector* (pp. 49–67). Hershey, PA: IGI Global. doi:10.4018/978-1-4666-9803-1.ch003

Lorber, M., Treven, S., & Mumel, D. (2017). Leaders' Behavior in Association with Job Satisfaction and Organizational Commitment. In V. Potocan, M. Üngan, & Z. Nedelko (Eds.), *Handbook of Research on Managerial Solutions in Non-Profit Organizations* (pp. 111–133). Hershey, PA: IGI Global. doi:10.4018/978-1-5225-0731-4.ch006

Maciejczak, M., & Słodki, A. (2017). Initial Price Strategies of Polish Micro and Small Enterprises: An Application of Game Theory for Industrial Organization of the SME Sector. In M. Vemić (Ed.), *Optimal Management Strategies in Small and Medium Enterprises* (pp. 126–143). Hershey, PA: IGI Global. doi:10.4018/978-1-5225-1949-2.ch007

Magalhães, F. R., & Santos, C. (2016). Online Financial Transparency: Local Governments of the MERCOSUR Member Countries. In A. Ferreira, G. Azevedo, J. Oliveira, & R. Marques (Eds.), *Global Perspectives on Risk Management and Accounting in the Public Sector* (pp. 252–273). Hershey, PA: IGI Global. doi:10.4018/978-1-4666-9803-1.ch013

Malega, P. (2017). Small and Medium Enterprises in the Slovak Republic: Status and Competitiveness of SMEs in the Global Markets and Possibilities of Optimization. In M. Vemić (Ed.), *Optimal Management Strategies in Small and Medium Enterprises* (pp. 102–124). Hershey, PA: IGI Global. doi:10.4018/978-1-5225-1949-2.ch006

Malek, N. A., & Takala, J. A. (2017). Regression Analysis for Environmental Practices: Participation among Finnish SMEs. In M. Vemić (Ed.), *Optimal Management Strategies in Small and Medium Enterprises* (pp. 44–59). Hershey, PA: IGI Global. doi:10.4018/978-1-5225-1949-2.ch003

Malewska, K. M. (2017). Intuition in Decision-Making on the Example of a Non-Profit Organization. In V. Potocan, M. Üngan, & Z. Nedelko (Eds.), *Handbook of Research on Managerial Solutions in Non-Profit Organizations* (pp. 378–399). Hershey, PA: IGI Global. doi:10.4018/978-1-5225-0731-4.ch018

Malik, M. S. (2017). Risk Based Contingency in Project Cost Estimates. In Y. Raydugin (Ed.), *Handbook of Research on Leveraging Risk and Uncertainties for Effective Project Management* (pp. 130–138). Hershey, PA: IGI Global. doi:10.4018/978-1-5225-1790-0.ch006

Mendes, H. C., Santos, C., Ferreira, A. D., Marques, R. P., Azevedo, G. M., & Oliveira, J. D. (2016). Local Authorities and the Disclosure of Financial Information via the Internet: The Portuguese Case. In A. Ferreira, G. Azevedo, J. Oliveira, & R. Marques (Eds.), *Global Perspectives on Risk Management and Accounting in the Public Sector* (pp. 274–297). Hershey, PA: IGI Global. doi:10.4018/978-1-4666-9803-1.ch014

Miller, T., de Matta, R., & Xu, M. (2016). High Level Inventory Network Modeling Approaches. In B. Christiansen (Ed.), *Handbook of Research on Global Supply Chain Management* (pp. 15–44). Hershey, PA: IGI Global. doi:10.4018/978-1-4666-9639-6.ch002

Milošević, O. (2017). Critical Review of SME Regulation Optimization in Serbia: A Reflection on Harmonization with the EU Acquis. In M. Vemić (Ed.), *Optimal Management Strategies in Small and Medium Enterprises* (pp. 79–101). Hershey, PA: IGI Global. doi:10.4018/978-1-5225-1949-2.ch005

Mogos, R., Bodea, C., Stancu, S., Purnus, A., & Dascalu, M. (2016). Educating Project Managers to Deal with Project Risks: Improvement of the Educational Programmes Design by Using Curriculum Management Systems. In C. Bodea, A. Purnus, M. Huemann, & M. Hajdu (Eds.), *Managing Project Risks for Competitive Advantage in Changing Business Environments* (pp. 231–257). Hershey, PA: IGI Global. doi:10.4018/978-1-5225-0335-4.ch012

Molnar, R. M. (2017). Structural Change Management for Sustainable SME Development: Applying Classical Management Tools. In M. Vemić (Ed.), *Optimal Management Strategies in Small and Medium Enterprises* (pp. 348–369). Hershey, PA: IGI Global. doi:10.4018/978-1-5225-1949-2.ch016

Nandonde, F. A., & Nguni, W. (2016). Relationship Establishment in SCM in a Market with Enforcement and Regulation Challenges: Case of Tanzania. In B. Christiansen (Ed.), *Handbook of Research on Global Supply Chain Management* (pp. 354–365). Hershey, PA: IGI Global. doi:10.4018/978-1-4666-9639-6.ch020

Nedelko, Z., & Potocan, V. (2017). Management Solutions in Non-Profit Organizations: Case of Slovenia. In V. Potocan, M. Üngan, & Z. Nedelko (Eds.), *Handbook of Research on Managerial Solutions in Non-Profit Organizations* (pp. 1–22). Hershey, PA: IGI Global. doi:10.4018/978-1-5225-0731-4.ch001

Nersesian, R. L. (2017). Incorporating Simulation in Project Scoping. In Y. Raydugin (Ed.), *Handbook of Research on Leveraging Risk and Uncertainties for Effective Project Management* (pp. 406–434). Hershey, PA: IGI Global. doi:10.4018/978-1-5225-1790-0.ch019

Nesbitt, R., & Kotb, A. (2016). Governance in NHS Foundation Trusts: Insights from Company Secretaries. In A. Ferreira, G. Azevedo, J. Oliveira, & R. Marques (Eds.), *Global Perspectives on Risk Management and Accounting in the Public Sector* (pp. 167–187). Hershey, PA: IGI Global. doi:10.4018/978-1-4666-9803-1.ch009

Nonino, F. (2017). Project Selection Frameworks and Methodologies for Reducing Risks in Project Portfolio Management. In L. Romano (Ed.), *Project Portfolio Management Strategies for Effective Organizational Operations* (pp. 245–263). Hershey, PA: IGI Global. doi:10.4018/978-1-5225-2151-8.ch010

Olson, B. (2017). Optimizing Portfolio Value through Comprehensive Project Metrics. In L. Romano (Ed.), *Project Portfolio Management Strategies for Effective Organizational Operations* (pp. 178–201). Hershey, PA: IGI Global. doi:10.4018/978-1-5225-2151-8.ch007

Parth, F. R. (2017). Preparing the Organization for Portfolio Management: Overcoming Resistance and Obstacles. In L. Romano (Ed.), *Project Portfolio Management Strategies for Effective Organizational Operations* (pp. 119–152). Hershey, PA: IGI Global. doi:10.4018/978-1-5225-2151-8.ch005

Parth, F. R. (2017). Project Portfolio Management Growth and Operation: Portfolio Management Structure, Operations, Risk, and Growth. In L. Romano (Ed.), *Project Portfolio Management Strategies for Effective Organizational Operations* (pp. 264–287). Hershey, PA: IGI Global. doi:10.4018/978-1-5225-2151-8.ch011

Pečarič, M. (2016). The Awareness of Mentality in Public Administration as the Key for the Management of Its Complexity. In A. Ferreira, G. Azevedo, J. Oliveira, & R. Marques (Eds.), *Global Perspectives on Risk Management and Accounting in the Public Sector* (pp. 1–24). Hershey, PA: IGI Global. doi:10.4018/978-1-4666-9803-1.ch001

Peng, H. (2016). Condition-Based Maintenance: Capital Goods Industry. In D. Jakóbczak (Ed.), *Analyzing Risk through Probabilistic Modeling in Operations Research* (pp. 292–320). Hershey, PA: IGI Global. doi:10.4018/978-1-4666-9458-3.ch012

Pereira de Campos, C. M., Rodrigues, L. L., & Jorge, S. M. (2016). The Role of Management Accounting Systems in Public Hospitals and the Construction of Budgets: A Literature Review. In A. Ferreira, G. Azevedo, J. Oliveira, & R. Marques (Eds.), *Global Perspectives on Risk Management and Accounting in the Public Sector* (pp. 366–389). Hershey, PA: IGI Global. doi:10.4018/978-1-4666-9803-1.ch018

Pham, T. S., Darabi, F., & Wilmot, N. V. (2016). International Supply Chain Case Study. In B. Christiansen (Ed.), *Handbook of Research on Global Supply Chain Management* (pp. 205–226). Hershey, PA: IGI Global. doi:10.4018/978-1-4666-9639-6.ch012

Pinho, M., & Santos, C. (2016). Plan for Prevention of Risks of Corruption and Related Infractions: The Application of FMEA Methodology. In A. Ferreira, G. Azevedo, J. Oliveira, & R. Marques (Eds.), *Global Perspectives on Risk Management and Accounting in the Public Sector* (pp. 390–412). Hershey, PA: IGI Global. doi:10.4018/978-1-4666-9803-1.ch019

Plumery, R. C. (2017). Risk-Centric Performance Measurement: Deriving Best Value from Performance Management Systems. In Y. Raydugin (Ed.), *Handbook of Research on Leveraging Risk and Uncertainties for Effective Project Management* (pp. 318–336). Hershey, PA: IGI Global. doi:10.4018/978-1-5225-1790-0.ch015

Postăvaru, N., & Leonte, B. (2016). Project Portfolio Risk Management: Managing Risk in Case of Investment Portfolio. In C. Bodea, A. Purnus, M. Huemann, & M. Hajdu (Eds.), *Managing Project Risks for Competitive Advantage in Changing Business Environments* (pp. 279–300). Hershey, PA: IGI Global. doi:10.4018/978-1-5225-0335-4.ch014

Qi, A., & Zheng, L. (2016). Project Risk Management: A Chinese Perspective. In C. Bodea, A. Purnus, M. Huemann, & M. Hajdu (Eds.), *Managing Project Risks for Competitive Advantage in Changing Business Environments* (pp. 45–69). Hershey, PA: IGI Global. doi:10.4018/978-1-5225-0335-4.ch003

Raue, S., & Klein, L. (2016). Systemic Risk Management: A Practice Approach to the Systemic Management of Project Risk. In C. Bodea, A. Purnus, M. Huemann, & M. Hajdu (Eds.), *Managing Project Risks for Competitive Advantage in Changing Business Environments* (pp. 70–85). Hershey, PA: IGI Global. doi:10.4018/978-1-5225-0335-4.ch004

Raydugin, Y. (2017). Integrated Risk-Based and Economic-Based (IRBEB) Methodology for Selection of Project Alternatives. In Y. Raydugin (Ed.), *Handbook of Research on Leveraging Risk and Uncertainties for Effective Project Management* (pp. 459–469). Hershey, PA: IGI Global. doi:10.4018/978-1-5225-1790-0.ch021

Raydugin, Y. (2017). Project Risk Management: Popular Fallacies and Overlooked Best Practices. In Y. Raydugin (Ed.), *Handbook of Research on Leveraging Risk and Uncertainties for Effective Project Management* (pp. 1–28). Hershey, PA: IGI Global. doi:10.4018/978-1-5225-1790-0.ch001

Rinderu, P., Voiculescu, C. I., & Visanescu, D. L. (2016). Risks in Implementing EU-Funded Projects in Romanian Public Higher Education System: Measures for Better Institutional Response. In A. Ferreira, G. Azevedo, J. Oliveira, & R. Marques (Eds.), *Global Perspectives on Risk Management and Accounting in the Public Sector* (pp. 413–441). Hershey, PA: IGI Global. doi:10.4018/978-1-4666-9803-1.ch020

Romano, L. (2017). Adaptive Portfolio Management. In L. Romano (Ed.), *Project Portfolio Management Strategies for Effective Organizational Operations* (pp. 153–177). Hershey, PA: IGI Global. doi:10.4018/978-1-5225-2151-8.ch006

Romano, L. (2017). Portfolio Management as a Step into the Future. In L. Romano (Ed.), *Project Portfolio Management Strategies for Effective Organizational Operations* (pp. 1–38). Hershey, PA: IGI Global. doi:10.4018/978-1-5225-2151-8.ch001

Romano, L., Grimaldi, R., & Colasuonno, F. S. (2017). Demand Management as a Success Factor in Project Portfolio Management. In L. Romano (Ed.), *Project Portfolio Management Strategies for Effective Organizational Operations* (pp. 202–219). Hershey, PA: IGI Global. doi:10.4018/978-1-5225-2151-8.ch008

Rostek, K. B. (2016). Risk Management: Role and Importance in Business Organization. In D. Jakóbczak (Ed.), *Analyzing Risk through Probabilistic Modeling in Operations Research* (pp. 149–178). Hershey, PA: IGI Global. doi:10.4018/978-1-4666-9458-3.ch007

Sá, F., Rocha, Á., & Pérez-Cota, M. (2016). A Literature Review on Quality Models for Online E-Government Services. In A. Ferreira, G. Azevedo, J. Oliveira, & R. Marques (Eds.), *Global Perspectives on Risk Management and Accounting in the Public Sector* (pp. 151–166). Hershey, PA: IGI Global. doi:10.4018/978-1-4666-9803-1.ch008

Sanchez-Ruiz, L., & Blanco, B. (2017). Process Management for SMEs: Barriers, Enablers, and Benefits. In M. Vemić (Ed.), *Optimal Management Strategies in Small and Medium Enterprises* (pp. 293–319). Hershey, PA: IGI Global. doi:10.4018/978-1-5225-1949-2.ch014

Schoper, Y., Böhle, F., & Heidling, E. (2016). Coping Better with the Project's Unknown Unknowns: New Competences for Overcoming Uncertainty in Projects. In C. Bodea, A. Purnus, M. Huemann, & M. Hajdu (Eds.), *Managing Project Risks for Competitive Advantage in Changing Business Environments* (pp. 1–22). Hershey, PA: IGI Global. doi:10.4018/978-1-5225-0335-4.ch001

Serpell, A. F., Ferrada, X., & Rubio, L. (2016). Using a Knowledge-Based Approach to Foster the Use of Risk Management in Construction. In C. Bodea, A. Purnus, M. Huemann, & M. Hajdu (Eds.), *Managing Project Risks for Competitive Advantage in Changing Business Environments* (pp. 258–278). Hershey, PA: IGI Global. doi:10.4018/978-1-5225-0335-4.ch013

Shang, K. (2017). Improving Objectivity in Project Risk Management. In Y. Raydugin (Ed.), *Handbook of Research on Leveraging Risk and Uncertainties for Effective Project Management* (pp. 248–265). Hershey, PA: IGI Global. doi:10.4018/978-1-5225-1790-0.ch012

Sharma, S. K., Bhat, A., Kumar, V., & Agarwal, A. (2017). Path Analysis Model for Supply Chain Risk Management. *International Journal of Information Systems and Supply Chain Management, 10*(2), 21–41. doi:10.4018/IJISSCM.2017040102

Shih, C. P., & Orochena, O. D. (2016). Analyzing the Effect of Transformational Leadership on Innovation and Organizational Performance. *International Journal of Productivity Management and Assessment Technologies, 4*(2), 11–27. doi:10.4018/IJPMAT.2016070102

Silvius, G. (2016). Integrating Sustainability into Project Risk Management. In C. Bodea, A. Purnus, M. Huemann, & M. Hajdu (Eds.), *Managing Project Risks for Competitive Advantage in Changing Business Environments* (pp. 23–44). Hershey, PA: IGI Global. doi:10.4018/978-1-5225-0335-4.ch002

Soniewicki, M. (2017). The Importance of Market Orientation in Creating a Competitive Advantage of Micro, Small, and Medium-Sized Companies in the Internationalization Process. In M. Vemić (Ed.), *Optimal Management Strategies in Small and Medium Enterprises* (pp. 1–21). Hershey, PA: IGI Global. doi:10.4018/978-1-5225-1949-2.ch001

Sönmez, R. (2017). Value Creation through Social Alliances: Theoretical Considerations in Partnership Relationships. In V. Potocan, M. Üngan, & Z. Nedelko (Eds.), *Handbook of Research on Managerial Solutions in Non-Profit Organizations* (pp. 205–231). Hershey, PA: IGI Global. doi:10.4018/978-1-5225-0731-4.ch010

Sowa, F., & Staples, R. (2016). Public Administration in the Era of Late Neo-Liberalism: Placement Professionals and the NPM Regime. In A. Ferreira, G. Azevedo, J. Oliveira, & R. Marques (Eds.), *Global Perspectives on Risk Management and Accounting in the Public Sector* (pp. 25–48). Hershey, PA: IGI Global. doi:10.4018/978-1-4666-9803-1.ch002

Stancu, S. (2016). Managing Risks in the Innovation Projects in the Services Sector: A Case Study for the Mobile Communication. In C. Bodea, A. Purnus, M. Huemann, & M. Hajdu (Eds.), *Managing Project Risks for Competitive Advantage in Changing Business Environments* (pp. 174–195). Hershey, PA: IGI Global. doi:10.4018/978-1-5225-0335-4.ch009

Stefanova, J. S., & Wenner, Z. (2017). Entrepreneurship and Enterprise Value Creation in Support of Smart, Sustainable, and Inclusive Growth in the European Union. In M. Vemić (Ed.), *Optimal Management Strategies in Small and Medium Enterprises* (pp. 268–292). Hershey, PA: IGI Global. doi:10.4018/978-1-5225-1949-2.ch013

Stoian, M., & Stoian, R. (2016). Financial Risk Management: An Introduction. In C. Bodea, A. Purnus, M. Huemann, & M. Hajdu (Eds.), *Managing Project Risks for Competitive Advantage in Changing Business Environments* (pp. 301–311). Hershey, PA: IGI Global. doi:10.4018/978-1-5225-0335-4.ch015

Tavares, M. D., & Rodrigues, L. L. (2016). The Determinants of Sustainability Reporting of the Portuguese Public Sector Entities. In A. Ferreira, G. Azevedo, J. Oliveira, & R. Marques (Eds.), *Global Perspectives on Risk Management and Accounting in the Public Sector* (pp. 226–251). Hershey, PA: IGI Global. doi:10.4018/978-1-4666-9803-1.ch012

Timilsina, B. (2017). Overcoming the Barriers of Strategic Planning, Implementation, and Monitoring in Turbulent Business Environment: A Qualitative Study on Finnish SMEs. In M. Vemić (Ed.), *Optimal Management Strategies in Small and Medium Enterprises* (pp. 226–248). Hershey, PA: IGI Global. doi:10.4018/978-1-5225-1949-2.ch011

Tongiani, M. G., & Zhao, S. (2017). Traditional Italian Food Products on the Chinese Market: Best Practices for Italian Small and Medium Enterprises. In M. Vemić (Ed.), *Optimal Management Strategies in Small and Medium Enterprises* (pp. 22–43). Hershey, PA: IGI Global. doi:10.4018/978-1-5225-1949-2.ch002

Toth, T., & Sebestyen, Z. (2016). Project Risk Management Process for Professionals: A Value-Based Approach. In C. Bodea, A. Purnus, M. Huemann, & M. Hajdu (Eds.), *Managing Project Risks for Competitive Advantage in Changing Business Environments* (pp. 128–149). Hershey, PA: IGI Global. doi:10.4018/978-1-5225-0335-4.ch007

Townley, T. W. (2017). Modeling Risk and Opportunity Reality. In Y. Raydugin (Ed.), *Handbook of Research on Leveraging Risk and Uncertainties for Effective Project Management* (pp. 435–458). Hershey, PA: IGI Global. doi:10.4018/978-1-5225-1790-0.ch020

Trickey, G. (2017). Getting to Grips with Behavioural Bias: How Projects Fail and What To Do About It. In Y. Raydugin (Ed.), *Handbook of Research on Leveraging Risk and Uncertainties for Effective Project Management* (pp. 220–247). Hershey, PA: IGI Global. doi:10.4018/978-1-5225-1790-0.ch011

Tudor, C., & Tudor, M. (2016). On Using Monte Carlo Simulations for Project Risk Management. In C. Bodea, A. Purnus, M. Huemann, & M. Hajdu (Eds.), *Managing Project Risks for Competitive Advantage in Changing Business Environments* (pp. 150–173). Hershey, PA: IGI Global. doi:10.4018/978-1-5225-0335-4.ch008

Turner, R. (2016). Risks in Project Marketing. In C. Bodea, A. Purnus, M. Huemann, & M. Hajdu (Eds.), *Managing Project Risks for Competitive Advantage in Changing Business Environments* (pp. 217–230). Hershey, PA: IGI Global. doi:10.4018/978-1-5225-0335-4.ch011

Vaiappuri, S. K., Kamarulzaman, N. H., Vijayan, G., & Mukherjee, A. (2016). An Empirical View of Knowledge Management. In B. Christiansen (Ed.), *Handbook of Research on Global Supply Chain Management* (pp. 452–465). Hershey, PA: IGI Global. doi:10.4018/978-1-4666-9639-6.ch025

Vecchi, A., & Vallisi, V. (2016). Supply Chain Resilience. In B. Christiansen (Ed.), *Handbook of Research on Global Supply Chain Management* (pp. 147–160). Hershey, PA: IGI Global. doi:10.4018/978-1-4666-9639-6.ch009

Vemić, M. B. (2017). A Further Look at Working Capital Optimization in Medium-Sized Firms: Concepts and Evidence. In M. Vemić (Ed.), *Optimal Management Strategies in Small and Medium Enterprises* (pp. 144–177). Hershey, PA: IGI Global. doi:10.4018/978-1-5225-1949-2.ch008

Vemić, M. B. (2017). Financial Innovation in Medium-Sized Enterprises Optimizes Their Gravitation Towards Capital Markets: Financial Future in Perspective. In M. Vemić (Ed.), *Optimal Management Strategies in Small and Medium Enterprises* (pp. 198–224). Hershey, PA: IGI Global. doi:10.4018/978-1-5225-1949-2.ch010

Vijayan, G., Kamarulzaman, N. H., Mukherjee, A., & Vaiappuri, S. K. (2016). Strategic Value Creation in a Supply Chain. In B. Christiansen (Ed.), *Handbook of Research on Global Supply Chain Management* (pp. 186–204). Hershey, PA: IGI Global. doi:10.4018/978-1-4666-9639-6.ch011

Wodecka-Hyjek, A. (2017). Co-Operation between the Public Administration and Non-Profit Organisations as a Condition of the Development of Public Entrepreneurship: On the Example of the Selected World Solutions. In V. Potocan, M. Üngan, & Z. Nedelko (Eds.), *Handbook of Research on Managerial Solutions in Non-Profit Organizations* (pp. 253–275). Hershey, PA: IGI Global. doi:10.4018/978-1-5225-0731-4.ch012

Yordanova, S. D. (2017). Optimizing Virtual Communities in Tourism to Facilitate Development of Small and Medium-Sized Enterprises. In M. Vemić (Ed.), *Optimal Management Strategies in Small and Medium Enterprises* (pp. 60–78). Hershey, PA: IGI Global. doi:10.4018/978-1-5225-1949-2.ch004

Yumurtacı, I. Ö., & Oflaç, B. S. (2016). Supply Chain Management Practices in Retail-The Trends and Future Perspective. In B. Christiansen (Ed.), *Handbook of Research on Global Supply Chain Management* (pp. 366–378). Hershey, PA: IGI Global. doi:10.4018/978-1-4666-9639-6.ch021

Zhang, Y. (2016). An Empirical Investigation of the Role of E-Communication in International Collaborations. In B. Christiansen (Ed.), *Handbook of Research on Global Supply Chain Management* (pp. 85–104). Hershey, PA: IGI Global. doi:10.4018/978-1-4666-9639-6.ch005

Zomorrodi, M. (2016). Supply Chain Risk Management: A Review of the Literature. In B. Christiansen (Ed.), *Handbook of Research on Global Supply Chain Management* (pp. 516–530). Hershey, PA: IGI Global. doi:10.4018/978-1-4666-9639-6.ch029

Index

M

N

O

P

Q

R

S

V

W

www.ingramcontent.com/pod-product-compliance
Lightning Source LLC
LaVergne TN
LVHW081340300926
849161LV00008B/2030